Voyage of the
Manteño

Voyage of the
Manteño

The Education of a Modern-Day Expeditioner

JOHN HASLETT

St Martin's Press
New York

www.stmartins.com

The illustration on p. vii is by Cameron McPherson Smith.

Design by Kathryn Parise

LIBRARY OF CONGRESS CATALOGING-IN-PUBLICATION DATA

Haslett, John.
    Voyage of the *Manteño* : the education of a modern-day expeditioner / John Haslett.—1st ed.
        p. cm.
    ISBN-13: 978-0-312-32432-2
    ISBN-10: 0-312-32432-4
    1. Haslett, John—Travel—Pacific Ocean. 2. Voyages and travels. 3. Rafts—Pacific Ocean. I. Title.

G530.H35H37 2006
910.9164—dc22   2006018313

First Edition: December 2006

10 9 8 7 6 5 4 3 2 1

This book is dedicated to Annie,
because nobody knows . . .

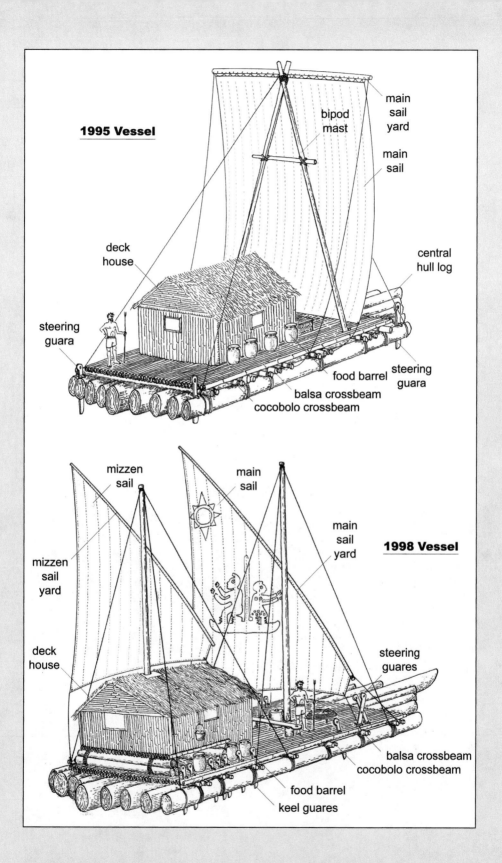

1995 Vessel

main sail yard

bipod mast

main sail

deck house

central hull log

steering guara

steering guara

food barrel

balsa crossbeam

cocobolo crossbeam

mizzen sail

main sail

main sail yard

1998 Vessel

mizzen sail yard

deck house

steering guares

balsa crossbeam

cocobolo crossbeam

food barrel

keel guares

Contents

Author's Note

This book was written over an eleven-year period, from 1995 to 2006. It was drawn from my personal experiences and diaries, from ship's logs and videotapes of events, from tape recordings of Ham radio contacts, and from interviews of participants of the expeditions. If sources conflicted with each other over a detail, I either made my best judgment of which was more likely to be accurate, or I deleted the detail in favor of a generalization. Dialogue was reconstructed from my notes and my memory. Space limited me from including all of the interesting and even compelling aspects of those years. In short, every effort was made to make the manuscript as accurate as possible, but in the end, it is only one person's view—my own.

Some of the characters' names have been changed, and in a few cases, identifying characteristics have been altered. These events occurred long ago. Some of the characters were very young at the time, and they were faced with extraordinary circumstances. It would be folly to attribute the eccentricities a character exhibited *then*, to their lives *now*.

In addition, I'd like to ask the patience of the sailors and the scientists who will read this book. Much of the nautical terminology and the archaeological concepts in this book have been broadly generalized to "humanize the knowledge." This book was written for all those who will never get their chance to sail the sea, or to revel in the details of the history of the seafaring people of ancient Ecuador.

Patrons of the
Illa-Tiki/Manteño Expeditions
1993–1999

AGFA
Alpina Water
American Adventure Productions
American Medical Response
The American Amateur Radio Relay
   League
Baltech Industries
Bryant-Haymes Music
Cemento Nacional de Ecuador
Challenge Air Cargo
Chemtran Services Inc.
CineFilm
Conterra Rescue Products
Cordell Expeditions
Corporacion Naboa de Ecuador
Cruising Equipment
Eastman Kodak
East Penn Manufacturing
The EMF Company
Eye Care Texas
Foreign Trade Export
La Guardacosta de Costa Rica
Hehr Power Systems

Hustler Antennas
Igo Films
Lockhart Industries
Mazda Motores de Ecuador
Museo Salango
The National Geographic Society
Northern California DX Foundation
Peet's Coffee and Tea
Polaroid Corporation
Process Project Inc.
Rescue 3 International
Secosa Corp. de Ecuador
Shade Tree Films
Standard Fruit Corporation
La Television
La Universidad de Costa Rica
Whole Earth Provision Company
Yaesu Radios
Zee Medical Services
Mr. and Mrs. Robert and Sheree
   Anderson
Mr. Roesli Antonis
Mr. and Mrs. William and Patricia Biggs

Ms. Sallie Buntenbah

Mr. Harry Burchardt

Mr. Bruce Butler (W6OSP)

Dr. Peter Capelotti

Mr. Larry Cate

Ing. Jose Chang Lua

Major Desidrio Chavez

Mr. Joaquin Cuellar

Ms. Elizabeth Eckstein

Sr. Freddy Ehlers

Sr. Fabian Espinosa

Ms. Lisa Fitzgerald

Mr. Fabio Gonzales

Mr. John Grant

Capt. Dan Hecker

Mr. Gunthar Hartwig

Ms. Malinda Haslett

Ms. Shirley Haslett

Ms. Theresa Hawley

Mr. Randy Hill

Mr. Dick Hoff (AA5NT)

Mrs. Marian Hoff (N5TVL)

Mr. Marion Jett

Mr. Kevin Karamonous (WD6DIH)

Mr. Steven King, EMT-P

Mr. Bill Kress

The Lewis Family

Mr. Rodney Knelly

Ms. Lori Lonsdale

Mr. Ray Marr

Mr. Radcliff Maumanee

Mr. Tom McDonald

Mr. Robert McKinnie (AL7AW)

Sr. Juan Carlos Mendesaval

Dr. Julia Mooney, M.D.

Dr. Richard Mooney, M.D.

Mr. and Mrs. William and Helen
   Moorer

Colonel Don Claudio Pacheco

Ing. Mario Pescarolo

Mr. Jim Powell

Ms. Tara Russell

Mr. Randy Schmieder

Dr. Robert Schmieder (KK6EK)

Dr. Herb Sigmond, M.D.

Ms. Betty Smith

Ing. Jean-Louie Solari

Mr. Mike Turnbull

La Familia de Vera,
   de Ciruelos

Dr. Don Wilhelmus

The Young Family

Special Thanks for Additional Support

El Armada de Colombia

El Armada de Ecuador

La Comuna de Salango

The Explorer's Club

El Gobierno del Republico de Ecuador

Sra. Lilian Ayallah (HC4I)

Mr. Russell Blair

Mr. Jim Caldwell

Capt. Geoff Carpenter

Ms. Aimee Clatterbuck

Mr. Terry Davidson

Mr. Ray Davis (W5HBI)

Hon. Sra. Jenny Estrada

Fuerza Aérea Ecuatoriana

Dr. Patrick Gay

Ms. Sheryll Harrill (HP1XXS)

Mr. John Hawkins

Mr. Fletcher Henderson (KA4BPR)

Mr. Peter Hess, Esq.

Mr. Chuck Lechner (WB2LMA)

Sr. Francisco Lopez

Mr. Jim Morrisey, EMT-P

El Municipio de Puerto Lopez

Dr. Jorge Palacios Martinez

Capt. Mario Navas

Mr. Alan Peacock (N5NTY)

Mr. Brian Penn
Mr. Mike Pilgrim (K5MP)
Ms. Phyllis J. Santos
The Royal Geographical Society
Mr. Peter Siekierski
The United States Embassy,
    Quito, Ecuador
Dr. Vera de Pedasi, y Chitre
Hon. Sr. Rutilio Vergara de Pedasi
Dr. Earl Weston (W8BXO)
Mr. James Wilmerding (W2EMT)

Ms. Rebecca Winchester
Mr. Dennis Wong, Esq.
C/V *Phoenix*
T/V *Everest*
C/V *Santiago Star*
C/V *Dole California*
F/V *Oyster*
ARC *Sebastian Benalcazar*
S/V *Glory Glory*
GRCR *Punta Burica*
F/V *Luz Estela*

Acknowledgments

This book would not have been possible without the help of my wife, Annie Biggs. Her inspiration, patience, good judgment, and day-to-day cheerleading are irrevocably woven into every word. Thanks also to Cameron MacPherson Smith, who read manuscript after manuscript, and who, because he is traveling on the same road, has made me feel a little less alone. Elizabeth Eckstein, Chrís Buntenbah, and Sandra Haslett deserve credit for being so generous with their photographs. These few, precious shots have done much to illustrate my story. Mimi Eckstein also deserves credit for her editing prowess. Thanks to my friend, Kim Derby, who willingly performed the thankless role of manuscript proofreader. I would also like to recognize Dr. Pete Capelotti, author of *Sea Drift*. Thank heavens he wrote that important book, and put it all in perspective. The two who brought my story to light, my agent, James Vines, and the editor who acquired me, Tim Bent, deserve special thanks for picking me out of obscurity. Heather Florence, who vetted this book, was not only a pleasure to work with, but was reassuring as well. Most of all, a deep heartfelt thanks should go to Marc Resnik, Senior Editor, and to his colleague, Rebecca Heller, who have been refreshingly easy to work with, and whose editorial letter and good advice transformed this book from clumsy to, let us hope, engaging.

Voyage of the
Manteño

A Few Words of
Explanation

I am aware that a minimal raft, adrift in a huge sea, would constitute an ideal laboratory, isolated and inescapable, for the study of human behavior.

Escape is always possible on an island, desert, or mountain. We can always remove ourselves a little or a lot from the others, from what hurts us or bothers us. [But] not on a raft . . .

—Santiago Genovés,
The Acali Experiment: Five Men and Six Women
on a Raft Across the Atlantic for 101 Days

Long before the end, I knew that I would tell a story of struggle in the field. I knew that regardless of whatever I might accomplish in the future, I would be obligated to someday write about the struggle that my colleagues and I had undertaken during two, hellish expeditions in the late 1990s. In those years we fought a series of primitive little wars against the only omnipotent forces still remaining on the earth. These were struggles that seemed antiquated, ones that I think many people felt had already been won by the explorer. That was not the case for us. In a century that saw the world of the explorer become a very safe place to live, we saw madness, mutiny, mud, terror, desperation, failure, disease, death, the surreal, and the sublime. We fought and fought in those years, struggling in our primitive way, until our muscles all but gave out; and ultimately, we were left as survivors on a foreign shore.

In 1995, when I launched my first balsa raft, I believed that I could maneuver around the natural forces of the earth, or at least control my destiny as I endured them. After all, the popular books about voyaging by balsa raft had told of hopeful, optimistic voyages; indeed, they had all been heartwarming stories. But by the time I had built my third balsa raft, in late 1998, my outlook had changed. As I prepared to go to sea once more, I fully expected to wander on the Pacific Ocean for months. By that time I wouldn't have ventured the slightest guess as to what might happen to me, or my vessel, in the end. When someone asked where we might end up, I said, "Panama, Japan, Hawaii, or clinging to the side of a container ship, watching our vessel go down. I honestly have no idea."

What had happened to us was nothing like what the world had come to expect from a balsa raft expedition, and I worried for years that people back home wouldn't understand. The few times I have tried to explain to my friends the bizarre behavior that occurred on my first voyage, or the heroics that saved my life on my second, those same friends have turned ashen, and then silent. I feel very uncomfortable talking openly about some of these things and I knew long before the end—while I was still out in the field—that unless I wrote about it, people would never really understand what had happened to us out there. More than anything, I wanted people to know and perhaps even to *feel* what it would be like to be on an uncertain expedition.

My story gnawed at me for years, but as I began to write I began to see that I must also tell the story of a culture of mariners. Unless I told their story—unless I explained their history—then my own would seem fruitless. The people I speak of are those of the southern coast of Ecuador. They are descended from the ancient Manteño culture. These people were not obscure acquaintances to me; I ate at their tables, watched them raise their children, went to sea with them, and feel closer to them in some ways than to people in my own land.

I went to their country for the first time in the early 1990s. I had been told by many in Ecuador that if I had any interest in building balsa rafts I should go to the fishing village of Salango: This was the seat of the ancient Manteño culture.

One evening at dusk, as the brown countryside turned gray and sharply cooler, I climbed on the back of a truck headed for Salango. Around me stood a group of young fishermen wearing black woolen jackets and caps. Most were in their twenties and were small and lean. They of course asked me why I was going to a little town like Salango, and so I pulled an old book out of my briefcase and showed them pictures of balsa rafts, and then explained my plans to them. One man leaned forward, put his finger on a picture of a balsa raft in the book, and said, "I can do this." His name was Dower Medina, and he would become my friend and voyaging companion throughout those momentous years. The other fishermen around him nodded in agreement with what he had said. They kept pointing at him and repeating the same phrase, over and over again: *"El es marinero. El es marinero."* They seemed so proud to be able to say such a simple thing about him: "He is a mariner."

1

The Worst Day . . . and the Best

There were thousands of people massed around the raft and thousands more spread out on the beach in a mile-wide area. As far as could be seen, even on the hillsides, the Ecuadorans were standing in the hot sun, waiting, focusing all of their attention on the primitive vessel at the center of their own mass. Those who were nearby could reach out and touch it, but for those farther away, the raft was somewhat like an old-fashioned ship-in-a-bottle—wooden and ancient and on display. It sat on top of wooden roller logs that were supposed to work like stone-aged wheels, and I was trying to push it into the ocean and it wouldn't go. For me, and now for the Ecuadorans, a sickening drama was unfolding, a fiasco, a spectacular failure, and spreading through the mass of people in wave after descending wave was a heartbreaking disappointment, a palpable disillusionment. I could see it in their faces, and I could see from where I stood atop the mast, looking out over them, that every single heartbroken Ecuadoran face in that mass of humanity—every single one—was looking at *me*.

Only a few days earlier the national paper had covered its front page with an enormous color photo of the raft and had announced that we would launch it on Sunday, March 19, 1995. Along with all the other attention, it had set off a vast migration to the tiny coastal town of Salango. For three days they had been pouring in from every corner of Ecuador, coming in from towns nobody around here had ever even heard of and sleeping on the beaches and in people's houses. It was incredible. Above all things Salango had always been *disconnected,* a small town at the edge of the Pacific Ocean, a tiny cluster of houses surrounded on three sides by hills and wilderness with but a single desolate road leading to it, and now the entire nation, from the people on the beach to the television audiences behind all of those cameras, had converged on it. But the raft lay there like a farce, worthless; it wouldn't budge.

And there were the Ecuadorans—just standing there in the sun, staring at the debacle, being incinerated. The equator was right down the road and the sun was right overhead, and a purple outline, a malignant ultraviolet gleam of radiation, hung on everything. The sand of the beach blazed so hot with radiation that no one, native or outsider, could cross it barefooted. Standing for hour after hour in the sun was like a moral demonstration for the Ecuadorans because for them staying in the shade was a way of life. It was not uncommon to drive down a road anywhere in the country and see them waiting at midday for a bus, standing against a wall, lined up in a row with their backs against the bricks as though facing a firing squad—hiding under the wall's tiny shadow—flattening their bodies into a thin slice of precious shade. These thousands were now standing out in the open, braving the equatorial sun, the malignant purple intensity, *El Sol*—the most unnatural, detestable thing any Ecuadoran could do—because of the raft, because of a tiny hope for a little good feeling. They were an eight-thousand-year-old culture, but they felt they had nothing great to show for it: no Pyramids, no Colisseum, no Great Wall. They once had the balsa raft, their great maritime achievement, but all of them were gone now, never to be seen again. The once-great Manteño mariners who sailed those rafts had disappeared too, either into the sand or into the Pacific Ocean. They as a people possessed a national feeling of being forgotten, of being an unknown country. But the raft in the center of their own mass had alleviated a little of that unsettling feeling and had replaced it with a little pride. But pride is a small idea. In truth, they had brought with them to the beach nationalism, patriotism, heroism, history, tradition, their cultural dignity, their personal dignity, their legends, stories they had heard when they were children, stories that they had then told to *their* children, and grandchildren—all of it: brotherhood, dreams, sentimentality, hope—*everything*—all concentrated into a singular aching desire to feel good about Ecuador.

And I had broken it all. Their great ship, which I had come from nowhere to build, would not move. It was as though there was something intrinsically wrong with it. This ingenious technology that symbolized them, their mariners, their legendary *marineros*, wasn't good enough; and though many had come together to help build it, I was now the symbol of a faint suggestion that *their* ancient culture wasn't as good as some other nation's. For hour after hour I had been trying to push it heroically into the ocean and it had been a grotesque demonstration of impotence. At the front of the raft, where it pointed out toward the approaching surf, we had tied a long rope to a crossbeam and had then extended it out into the water. This was our first hauling line; and with a little encouragement, volunteers had lined up along the rope, prepared to pull. Then we attached another hauling line to the raft and then another and then people from the crowd seemed to realize the immensity of pulling the giant raft into the sea and began volunteering their own ropes. Soon, approximately one hundred people were lined up in front of the raft, manning six independent lines. People stood on all sides of the vessel, too, pushing against it with all of their might for hours, but the raft hadn't budged an inch. And I had been the center of it all. I had waddled back and forth in the loose sand, obviously wrong in every way, perplexed, peering at the lines and the pushers, wondering what the hell could be the matter, kicking and slinging sand everywhere, sunburned, with sand hanging off me in patches . . . and watching this man flounder, *me,* only made it more sickening for the Ecuadorans. More and more they stared at me, slowly losing confidence. Faces turned blank. The sun glared down on my nose and ears and I was obviously in the wrong place, obviously foreign, and oversized, and dumb, and more and more the Ecuadorans seemed to be looking around aimlessly, as though wanting to turn away, as though wanting some kind of relief from the slow torturous death of so much hope.

Of course it wouldn't move—it was a behemoth! That word—'raft'—must have been the most misleading word I had ever spoken. A raft was something a child played with; this was a vessel that could transport thousands of pounds of cargo across the *open sea.* When the logs for the base of the raft had been delivered to the beach two months before, they had lain in an ungainly mass like an entire pod of beached whales—fifty-five thousand pounds of dead weight. I had seen them felled at the government's experimental forest and I had seen them brought in on flatbed trucks, and all the while I had thought them monsters, impossible to cope with. But for two months afterward we had toiled in the purple radiation to build the giant raft, isolated from the modern world and immersed in the age of woods and timbers, and in that age all things were massive and heavy, blunt and bulky, thick and cumbersome. Simply moving and adjusting the immense building blocks of that era was one of its greatest hazards. Whenever we moved something, anything, we moved it inch by inch. We had never used anything that could be considered a "precision tool"—we had been like cavemen, constantly clubbing or beating or chopping or hacking at something. The blunt instrument was the tool of necessity, and if we were going to move the behemoth across the scalding beach, we would have to do it with the greatest blunt instrument ever developed: the *wanca.*

In the strictest sense, there's no such word—*wanca*. The real word is *palanca,* or simply "lever," but for some reason, Enrique Guillen, our resident genius of primitive technology, had shortened it to just "*wanca.*" When Enrique spoke of a *wanca* he meant a hardwood pole eight inches thick and ten feet long, with one end carved thin and flat so that it looked like a gigantic screwdriver head. This was his lifting machine—the primitive equivalent of a forklift, and a group of seven people could easily lift a medium-sized automobile, or three thousand pounds, with this type of *wanca*. Enrique was now at the back of the raft, directing the townspeople, the Salangueños, to bring in *wanca* after *wanca*. Enrique had curly white hair and skin like brown leather, and I could see from my high vantage point that he was rubbing his left forearm, slowly running his hand up and down, lost in deep thought. Enrique always thought with his forearm: When he was problem solving he'd rub his left forearm very slowly. When he wanted to illustrate a point he was trying to make he'd twist and turn and contort his forearm to represent how he was going to manipulate this log or that log, or rope, or bamboo cane. When something was wrong, he'd shake both forearms in front of his body. He'd hold the palms of his hands out in front of him and wag those meaty forearms of his, saying, "No, that won't work—it'll *break.*" I had come to see that all things in his universe were strong: design, lumber, rigging. Strength was the root of every discussion and strength of construction was the basis for every decision he made. In building the raft he had taught me what breaks on the ocean and what does not. I could see the small, stout man now, wearing as always a paint smeared T-shirt over his massive torso and wedging enormous levers—ten-foot *wancas*—under the stern of the raft.

Up on the coastal road, the only road to Salango, trucks and buses were arriving all the time, coming in from all over the country and disembarking people of all types. I could see them walking and running. They as a people could be best described as clean-cut; their fashion, as it had always been since time immemorial, was well-groomed, with shirttails usually tucked in, and even when in short pants and sandals—which was rare—never disheveled. They could also be described as a highly literate people: though their country was poor, most had been to high school, and all but a very few could read and write well. On the beach were students and teachers, working-class fishermen from every village up and down the coast, groups of teenage girls holding hands, and urbanites in hard-soled shoes from the capital city in the distant Andes. Entire families had come. I could see children in brightly colored clothes running toward the raft in excitement, with their parents and grandparents trotting behind. Audio and video teams from every radio and television station, and journalists from every newspaper in the country, as well as many from other parts of South America, had surrounded the raft at dawn and were now competing for the best shot possible. An Army Reserve unit had arrived, marching, singing patriotic songs, and waving the Ecuadoran flag. These thousands of clean-cut and modest people were simply standing, staring blankly at a gigantic symbol of their history.

For a craft made of round logs and poles, the raft was decidedly straight and flat. Everything had been cut so carefully that the vessel's geometry was one of right angles and flat surfaces. Its massive logs, which had once been crooked and ill fitting, were now a single unit, a forty-four-foot-long rectangle of beige wood that came to a point at the front, just like a conventional ship. Its deck, made up of scores of tan bamboo canes, was a rectangular platform with squared corners. The little bamboo hut at the back of the deck, where we would live while at sea, was essentially a square house, tan and beige, with square windows and a square door.

But it was more, something more than just physical. Several people had talked openly about the fact that upon seeing it for the first time you experienced a very peculiar feeling: There was something about the giant raft that *moved you* for a moment. It caused a strange reaction in you, a transformation: It wiped your mind clean for a moment and immersed you in the fascination of the old days; it sucked you in like a perfect movie when every detail of the wear and the tear and the dirt was exactly as it should be. It didn't look at all like something built by people of the modern era; it looked like something that had been found in a cave. Its little house of bamboo poles, especially, with its perfectly square dimensions and slightly undersized windows and door, gave the raft a dreamlike quality, an otherworldliness. Standing next to it, looking out to sea, you saw nothing of the last five hundred years of civilization—you saw Salango in AD 1500, the day of the ancient Manteño. Even to us, we who had built it, the giant raft sometimes seemed as though it was a foreign object, not a vessel that we ourselves had made but something that a team of archaeologists had discovered in a hermetically sealed tomb, and had brought to the surface, completely intact. But it was *real,* as improbable and as surreal and as frankly weird as that may seem, and big too, and solid. You could touch it and you could slap it. You could walk up to this improbable thing on the sand, this ancient ship from another world, and you could slap the heavy logs with your palms and you could feel a deep thud, and you could grip the raspy ropes in your hands and run them down and feel your skin burning on the hairy fibers. This primitive ship, our creation, this thing that we had built and that was now bigger than us, didn't even show a *sign* of moving—not even the *potential*—to be moved.

We had started at dawn, and for five hours people had pushed and pulled and strained in the purple radiation and the burning sand and the raft had remained completely still . . . not an inch . . . not a millimeter. Worse, we had to get it into the water on that particular day. We had scheduled the launch of the raft so that it occurred on the day of the highest tide of that month. At roughly three o'clock in the afternoon the tide would crest, the ocean would come as close to the raft as possible, and we would have to move the behemoth perhaps as much as seventy-five feet to reach it. If we couldn't push the monster that far before then, the ocean would recede away and not rise to that point again for weeks. Again we tried budging it. Nothing. We tried it over and over again. Nothing! The crowd stood by in the brutal sun, staring at me and the raft, and it was at that sickening moment, after hours of failure, that Enrique worked his way through the crowd, plodding in the sand until he finally reached me, and said, into my ear, "You've got to get up on the mast. Understand? Get everyone perfectly coordinated, and then command them to *push*."

"Yeah—but I'm a gringo, ya know? Will they accept my comman—— ?"

"Yes," he said over his shoulder, walking away, and then disappeared into the crowd to return to the *wancas*.

So I pulled myself up on the bamboo canes of the deck, walked to the rope ladder hanging from the top of the mast, and then climbed up. The mast was made from two long poles, lashed to a point, with a crossbeam lashed in the middle so that it formed a perfect A, thirty feet tall . . . and that's where I stood now, in the center of the A: naked before them, with their soulful stares, and their dignity, and their disillusionment. I wore a T-shirt and shorts, but I was living the universal nightmare of being outdoors and realizing that you are naked, everything is showing, and you just want to cover up—you just want to take it all back. This was an accident! Lord! Nothing had prepared me for this! Yes, I had always been an adventurer, going back to the grassroots days of modern adventure in the 1970s. I had solo canoed white water at the age of twelve, made my first parachute jump at fifteen, dove on shipwrecks at sixteen, and climbed office towers at seventeen. Yes, I had done all of those things, and when I had done them it had been the most natural thing in the world. And because of that it had always seemed natural that someday I would move up to expeditions. Wasn't that where adventurers go *after* all of that other stuff? Wasn't it simply a logical progression? You train your whole life by being an adventurer and then you graduate to "The Big Expedition." Right? Why not? I was frequently nervous and uncomfortable around people or in social situations, but when I rappelled off the wall of a skyscraper in the middle of the night, I felt just fine. So I had come to Salango— come to build a balsa raft—because it was the next sensible step in my life. . . .

But this was different. My God! I had simply read a book! I had read an old book about balsa rafts and had decided to build one and sail it to the Hawaiian

Islands, five thousand nautical miles from Ecuador. I was twenty-nine at the time, unmarried, and had a little money in the bank. I had known fully that if I chose to do the expedition I would be taking a vow of poverty: What money I had would be just enough to get the giant raft into the water. I knew that regardless of wherever I ended up or whatever happened to me, I would emerge penniless. And yet there were no second thoughts or lingering doubts. I had never made a long voyage on the ocean but I knew how to sail and I had experience in lashing timbers, and so the day after turning the last page of that book about rafts I had driven to the hardware store and had bought a small balsawood airplane. What else could I do? It was the only time I had ever seen balsa wood! I had then called the company that made the tiny model, had begun talking to their engineers, and had gotten connected somehow to Henri Kohn, son of "the Balsa King of Ecuador." "I've been waiting for this all my life," he had said. "I've got a model of a balsa raft sitting in my office. Can you meet me in Ecuador in two weeks?" Two weeks later I met Henri and made arrangements to buy balsa logs. I would come to find out that the reason balsawood was so expensive in North America was because it was the product of a long chain of cultivation, processing, transportation, taxation, what have you—*my* wood, on the other hand, would be subjected to none of this. I would be using ordinary logs, which would come from the Ecuadoran forestry service. My twenty-five tons of balsa wood would cost around $130. That was it. One phone call. One tiny airplane. $130. And now I stood three stories above a sea of heads and faces with my bare feet heavy and bony on a hardwood pole and Ecuador looking at me—and it was there that I suddenly realized that I was an obscure man, a nobody, a naive adventurer who eighteen months before had bought a toy airplane in a faraway country. I had known nothing of these people; I had never seen their faces nor heard their voices. I had known nothing of their country, nothing of the Manteño, and nothing of balsa wood. That tiny airplane, sealed in its flimsy plastic bag and costing $1.59, had been all that I knew. And in that moment of freak realization before thousands of Ecuadorans, my mind seemed to blink, as though the scope of what lay before me overloaded my brain, as though the utter improbability of standing where I now stood overwhelmed every feeling that I had ever felt up to that moment. And in the next moment, I drew in the deepest breath I could and I shouted, "ONE! TWO! THREE! PULLLLLLLLL!"

They roared like an attacking army, releasing a ferocious determination— not a *cheer*—this wasn't a happy afternoon at the ball game—it was something pent up, a roar so deep and so massive that it seemed to roll across the beach, wash over the giant raft, and then surge out into the sea. "HAAAAAUUUU-UGGGGHHHHH!" And the raft inched forward!

"READY? ONE! TWO! THREE! PULLLLL!" And it came again—a bawling noise, like a great charging mass of club-wielding medieval soldiers—"HAAAAAUUUUUGGGGHHHHH!" And the raft surged forward an entire foot! "READY?! ONE! TWO! THREE! PULLLLL!" And you could see the muscles in the backs and shoulders of hundreds of human beings suddenly burst up from the skin and flex like the fibers of a gigantic arm and—"HAAAAAUUUGGGHH!"

I was calling out to them and they were answering; they were driving the giant raft into the sea, pushing it with their shoulders and with their arms, driving it toward the exploding surf and getting stronger and stronger with each push.

"ONE! TWO! THREE! PULLLLL!"

"HAAAAAUUUUUUUUGGGHH!"—another surge forward!

"ONE! TWO! THREE! PULLLLL!"

"HAAAAAUUUUUUUUGGGHH!"

Masses of people were surging in on the raft now, cheering and creating a compression of humanity. I saw faces smiling and glowing. I saw women laughing and crying and applauding—all at the same time. I saw an old man, perhaps a grandfather or an uncle, take a small boy by the shoulders and face him toward the raft. The old man pointed proudly at the raft: "This is part of your culture, and you may never see anything like it again." I saw an elderly woman, fragile and skeletal and wearing a faded blue dress, amble out in front of the raft and put her bony hands on one of the hauling lines. She stood out in the surf, with seawater washing up and swirling around her legs—tugging as best as her little body could—smiling and crying long streams of tears.

Waves were coming in all the time and exploding around the pullers in front of the raft. It was one of those afternoons in Salango when the noise and calamity of the breakers couldn't be ignored. Even those who had lived there for fifty years would stop for a moment on a day like this to listen to the long explosions that rolled through the town like distant thunder. Those sounds had been heard in every house in Salango every day for the past eight thousand years. In this region of black volcanic rock and scratchy scrub brush only the Pacific Ocean was fertile; and in this place they were *people of the sea*. Their culture had grown up on this beach, a two-mile-stretch of sand that carved a tan-colored C against the sparkling turquoise water of the bay, and for eighty centuries they had listened to the waves curl over and shatter here. In ancient times they had held religious ceremonies on Isla de Salango, the only island in the bay, a massive monolith of stone and scrub that towered four hundred feet from the surface. And though they didn't leave behind a written history of their own, they had left behind a legacy, recorded mostly by the

Spanish conquistadors, as though they were something to behold—something remarkable, something completely unique in ancient America: a culture of mariners who had built a vast shipping empire using their giant rafts and their unmatched seamanship. The conquistadors had sailed into these waters for the first time in 1526, complete outsiders, like space explorers landing on a new planet, and though they were mariners themselves, they had encountered something that had left them a little dumbfounded: a gigantic raft, sailing on the sea, with ropes and sails "as fine as anything in Spain," and crewed by a people the conquistadors called "great mariners." That raft had come from Salango, and they—those great mariners—were the Manteño. Now on a March afternoon in 1995, amid their sand and their turquoise waters and their towering island, it was as though *they* had come back from the dead.

The scene on the beach now was something that bent the mind. The gigantic raft was clearly walking across the beach, but by tiny bits. Volunteers were coming in to relieve those who could push the raft no longer and runners were being sent to houses for water. More lines were being attached to the front of the raft and more *wancas* were being brought in behind. I could hear passionate calls of encouragement coming from all parts of the enormous crowd. Yelling to them, I asked, "Are you ready?"

"Yes, John," they shouted, "Let's go! Let's GOOOO!"

"PULLLLL!"

"HAAAUUUUUUUGGGHHHHHHHHH!"

"MORE!"

"HAAAGGGHHHHHHHHHHHHHHHHH!"

"MORE!"

"HAAAGGGHHHHHHHHHHHHHHHHH!"

The progress was slow, very slow, but sure, and so we worked like this with the *wancas,* churning and staggering across the burning sand. Half an hour passed, then an hour, and they were still driving. I was enormously relieved that the raft had at last moved, but the sun was beating down and we still had a long way to go.

Though I had been in the field for almost three months, and though I had learned much through the teachings of Enrique, I had awakened that morning wondering if launching the primitive ship into the ocean might be beyond my abilities. As I had walked out on the beach that morning I had noticed that the wear of The Expedition was already showing on my brother, Brock. We had been running our operations out of a hut, a *cabaña* really, a two-roomed bamboo box on short stilts; and for the past eight weeks the remarkable Enrique had led us up the dangerous learning curve of primitive technology and shipbuilding. In that time the radiation had been especially cruel to Brock. He was a slim man, blond, with a bushy yellow beard that the sun had bleached white. At thirty-six, he was five years older than me. He, too, had been raised on the religion of adventure, and I had a lot of faith in his durability. Brock had been the first to join The Expedition, and then afterward I had begun the long process of recruiting people to sail on a balsa raft, and it had been a hair-raising experience. Most people had no idea of what they were up against. One gentleman I interviewed had said, quite sincerely, "I just don't think it will be stimulating enough for me." Another had asked, "My main question is, Will I be able to bring my skateboard?" I later saw these experiences as humorous, but at the time they shocked me. I knew my life was at risk the moment I decided to do the expedition, but over the next seven years I met only a tiny handful of people who really understood the level of danger involved. Dower Medina, the greatest mariner I would ever know, and a Salangueño, joined shortly after Brock, and then a third came along, an Ecuadoran doctor named Eduardo. I met him during one of my many reconnaissance trips leading up to The Expedition. He had an office and a laboratory in a clinic in a remote town in the northern jungle. We needed a physician, and Eduardo seemed perfect; but he disqualified himself in the first week by flatly refusing to carry expeditionary equipment. He said that he was above that type of labor. It was all for the better: I found out several years later that he wasn't really a certified doctor; he had just been pretending to be one.

The fourth to join was a charismatic film director named Annie Biggs. From my vantage point on the mast I could see her now, pushing on the balls of her feet in the loose sand around the raft, moving quickly from one place to another, directing the shooting of various cameras. I had met her while looking for advice on shooting a documentary film. She loved the project, sensed its potential, and had volunteered to organize a film. As always she moved with purpose, and below me I could see her fiery auburn hair weaving through the crowd with her cameraman behind her. She was now standing out in front of the raft, in the surf, shooting the lines of pullers on the ropes. The tide was rising, and some of them were now standing in three feet of water, with sheets of foam climbing up their legs.

At the back of the raft, men staggered and fell after each heave of the *wancas*. They would put five or six shoulders under each giant lever, and, at the signal, would surge forward, driving with the hardened muscles of their legs. When the raft lurched ahead, the *wancas* would come undone and the pushers would fall in all directions. Sweat was pouring down their arms and necks and their shirts and pants were soaked. Sand covered every inch of them, hanging in big patches and shedding off their bodies in clumps. Their stomping, pumping feet had dug a pit in the sand behind the raft and Enrique was down in it on his hands and knees, panting, getting up slower and slower every time, but with more and more determination in his face.

This type of work was dangerous, but we had built the raft in this way. For weeks we had awakened at dawn and had trudged half a mile down the beach, from our *cabaña* to the worksite, pushing on our feet as the loose sand parted under our weight, and then for hour after hour we had pulled on the lines, straining until our forearms ached, pulling as a group, in unison, sometimes as many as five or six of us standing in a column—squeezing one lashing at a time—struggling and grunting against the lonely sounds of an eternal surf and the "*tick tick tick tick*" of the stretching rope—pulling, tightening, retightening, and then retightening again the thousands of feet of rope, until every line, joint, and lashing was snug. Nothing was ever done by one person. When we moved one of the smaller building blocks of the raft, like a mast pole or a crossbeam, we worked like a mule team. We'd tie small poles crosswise to whatever we wanted to move, so that it had handles protruding out at regular intervals, and then ten men would gather, five to a side, and bend down over the handles and count down to a hoist, ". . . one, two, three, heave!" and then the beam or pole, cradled precariously in our arms, would creep up to a height of four feet. Down the line you'd see men's arms and legs quivering under the strain. Now the hard part: To move the crushing timber out to the worksite would require the ten-man team to stagger across the sinking sand. If the men stepped in unison, the timber generated a predictable, controllable motion . . . on the other hand, if one man in the lurching unit got out of sync, it wobbled violently and at twenty different angles—like a nine-hundred-pound fish that was suddenly alive and fighting furiously. When that started you could feel the whole unit, men and timber, collapsing. Men's feet would drag and sweep in the loose sand. They'd stagger. They'd twist in ugly contortions or impulsively throw their hands out in front of them and then the unit would crash on the burning beach, crushing the men in a sandy disaster. Invariably someone would writhe around in the searing sand, clutching a leg or an arm or a rib cage. Someone else, usually me, would then have to ask the dreadful questions: "Did it break? Can you walk?"

But you couldn't lift a balsa log with thirty men or even fifty, and so we had worked with the *wancas*—the big ones—and we knew what they could do. We had put the entire raft, one log at a time, up on blocks—just like putting a back-yard project up on sawhorses—using the *wancas*. Typically we'd set up our standard lifting machine, a *wanca* set up on a stump, and then Enrique would stand to one side of the gigantic lever, his palms up, and signal "wait." Then he'd wave us down slowly: "Gently . . . gently now," and we'd drape our bodies over the *wanca*, committing all of our combined weight, converting seven hundred pounds of downward force into seven thousand pounds of upward force at the other end of the lever. All of that force would concentrate at the tip of the *wanca,* an area the size of a paperback book, and slowly the balsa log would float up. As soon as the whole precarious mass was suspended, one of Enrique's men, a quiet, intelligent man with a weathered face, named Manuco, would shoot under and wedge in a four-inch slice of wood. Hanging motionless on the giant lever, holding the balsa log in the air with the *wanca,* we'd wait breathlessly for Manuco to get out of there, and then relax as soon as he had the slice in place. This was the way things usually went, but occasionally we'd get one of the logs up in the air and the whole thing would crash. The *wanca* would spring out and jerk upward and bounce off its stump, and then there'd be a split second of panic, of men falling and grunting and jumping out of the way and being dragged down. Many days had passed this way, working on the beach with the *wancas,* slowly raising and adjusting twenty-four tons of timber, and then one afternoon Manuco had gone under a suspended log to set a wedge and the massive timber slipped off its block and stomped down like an elephant foot. The split second before it crushed him I saw him bury his face in the beach, and then the fat log thudded on the mushy sand with a "whump!" and he was gone. There was no sign that he had ever existed.

"Hurry! Hurry! Hurry! Hurry! Hurry!"

"Dig! Dig! Dig! Dig! Dig!"

"Huuurrrry!"

We clawed at the sand where his head had been before he disappeared. We dug like frantic dogs, scratching and pulling handfuls of sand until we unearthed his mouth. As soon as he appeared he spit sand and then slowly stretched his mouth open to draw in a shallow breath. He was trapped and couldn't move. Inserting a *wanca* under the log, we draped our bodies over the lever, pried the timber from the ground, and then three men pulled him out, stretching his arm until I thought they might dislocate his shoulder. As soon as they had dragged him out he began to roll around on the sand, groaning.

"What is it? What is it?"

"OHHH . . . my leg. God, my leg hurts."

"Get a truck," Enrique said. "Take him to the pharmacy in Puerto Lopez."

In Puerto Lopez, a town on the other side of the hills, there was a pharmacist who acted as a medic on these occasions. He had given me a tetanus shot once, after I had managed to bury a rusty machete in my shin. How much formal medical training he had I do not know, but he was a gentle man who was gifted with a hypodermic needle. We got a truck, loaded Manuco on the back, and they went speeding down the hill. Afterward we stood there staring blankly at each other, asking with only our eyes—because we didn't want to verbalize the horrible question: "How did he survive that?" Incredibly, unbelievably, nothing in Manuco had broken. I went to his *cabaña* that night and compensated him for his trip to the pharmacist, but still, I felt lowered. What was money? My adventure had almost killed him that day. I was thankful that we had been building the raft over soft, loose sand. Concrete pavement might have killed him. He returned to work the following day, limping, and when I asked about the leg he just waved it away, and we went back to work, toiling on the Salango shore.

The sand had saved us that day, but working in it could be real hell; and by now, under the purple radiation, the Ecuadorans had been dragging the monster across the mushy, grainy beach for three hours. The tide was almost completely in and the surf was pounding the pullers on the ropes out in front. A wave would break on top of them and they'd go down like bowling pins in the foam, then struggle back to their feet with the seawater pouring off their clothes. After the first half hour of shouting across the beach my voice had started to labor and after an hour and a half it was gone. I bawled out the cadence now in a raspy growl and felt my vocal chords tearing like the threadbare cloth of an old bedsheet. Many in the crowd had been with us since dawn and had been frying in the radiation for eight hours, but not a single one had left. The sun scorched them and burned them, sweat poured down their faces and their happy smiles melted to anguish; but they refused to rest, and inch by painful inch, the raft was creeping toward the water's edge.

Some of those who were pulling were from the outside, but most were the Salangueños. Over the previous weeks, we had melded with these people. Living as we had in our *cabaña,* immersed as we had been in our world of primitive shipbuilding, news from the outside world had rarely reached us. Salango sat quietly at the edge of the Pacific Ocean, isolated; and now in the final years of the twentieth century there was some electricity in the town but no running water, and no telephones. Communication still traveled in the same way it always had: Any piece of important news—like the arrival of our gigantic balsa logs or a near-record catch by one of the town's trawlers—could travel across Salango, moving down the long dirt streets, from mouth to mouth and from cinderblock house to chicken coup to bamboo house, passing through a steady succession of best friends, cousins, in-laws, friends of parents, old friends from school days, sisters, uncles, and friends of uncles, in less than ten minutes. A telephone would indeed come to Salango someday, but for now it was a place where the electronic age had not yet been. Indeed, *nothing* had ever penetrated Salango's oldness. In a modern world, it remained ancient.

Whenever you walked through those dirt streets, down the rows of square cinder-block houses in Salango, you saw bundles of forgotten fishing lines snarled around sun-bleached buoys, boats in various states of construction, use, and decay; and you always saw fishermen, going out to sea or returning from it. Sometimes the townspeople would spread their nets in front of their houses and tend to them all day, studiously sewing and mending them in silence. You got the feeling that if somehow the surf noise stopped, then they too would suddenly stop, frozen in midmotion until the surf started up again. In this rugged place "the catch" was still an event, and in Salango, when one of the big wooden trawlers would bring in an unusually large load of fish, the townspeople, from the kids to the old folks, would gather at the beach to revel in the good news. Here, on the sandy curve where we had built our raft, the sight of a bursting net, of thousands of gray and white fish, would inspire just as much hope and just as much celebration in the Salangueños as it had the first time they had brought in such a catch, thousands of years ago. The smaller fishermen, those who didn't work on one of the trawlers, usually went out to sea in flimsy open boats, fifteen to eighteen feet in length, with outboard motors on their sterns. They'd go out at night and sometimes they ranged as far as thirty miles offshore, which was always a risk. If they ran out of fuel or if the motor died it would take a lot of luck to get back to land. Every year or so one of those open boats would disappear offshore, and in every fishing town near Salango there was someone who could tell a horrific tale of survival, or of loss. Dower Medina worked this way too, spending his nights curled up in the bottom of a small boat, drifting offshore and waiting for the fish. He had joined The Expedition on the first day I met him, the first day I came to Salango, in 1993.

Dower had lived in the sea since he was a little boy of six. In the course of his life he had seen perhaps as many as three thousand days on the ocean, but these were only his days at the surface. When he wasn't aboard a boat he was swimming across the ocean's floor, spearing and collecting thousands of pounds of fish and shellfish, relying on his casual access to the seabed in the same unremarkable way that a city dweller relies on the corner store. Whereas most sailors must insulate themselves from the ocean, Dower had been immersed in cold salty seawater for most of the days of his life. And even when he had come out of the water, even when he had sought refuge on land and had walked to his home, he was never entirely separated from the sea. From his front doorstep he had an enormous view of the great Pacific Ocean, rising up until it formed a horizon, and inside his house he slept to the sounds of the thunderous waves, curling over and exploding on the beach.

When those waves came in and broke now, they flooded the base of our raft with stark white foam. It had been four hours of dragging and churning, and no let up. The toiling Ecuadorans had moved the behemoth fifty feet by this time and it was finally at the edge of the surf. Below me I could see Dower standing on the front of the raft, preparing for launch. At twenty-six, he was a fit man of medium height, who possessed the aura of a "nice guy" from a "nice family." Relaxed and confident, he had a kind of a spring in his step that always made him appear cheerful. Everybody liked him and most of the women I knew loved him. A friend of mine once wrote in his diary, upon seeing Dower walking through the dirt streets of Salango, smiling at people and waving to all of his friends, that he was like a "bronzed man." Standing on the deck of the raft in a T-shirt and shorts, with his hat on backward, I could see him signaling to a couple of the big wooden trawlers out in the bay, one bright blue and the other bright yellow, motioning them with his hands and arms to prepare for a tow. We would launch the raft from here—we would set up for one grand push, and if the raft broke free from the hold of the sand, the trawlers would go to full steam and pull the raft through the surf. Dower tied two ropes to the front of the raft and then gave them to two men, who swam through the surf and then handed them to the sailors standing on the sterns of the trawlers. These would be our tow lines, and they now ran from the raft, through the surf, to the boats that would launch us—we were almost there.

On the beach, at the side of the raft, a clearing began to grow. A pocket of space opened up as the pushers and well-wishers backed away from where they had been pressed so compactly against hulking balsa logs, and a young woman stepped forward. Her name was Janette, and it had been agreed among us that she would christen our vessel. Behind her stood The Expedition's cinematographer, Chris Buntenbah, twenty-six, a small heavyset man with brown wavy hair and round eyeglasses. He and Janette were now officially an item. About halfway through the construction of the raft a romance had bloomed between them. Lovely and dignified, Janette liked Chris's mild personality, and for the past eight weeks Chris could be seen shooting various aspects of life in Salango during the day, and strolling through the middle of town in the evenings with Janette, drinking Cokes and holding hands.

Chris knew that he was facing the enormous task of filming in isolation for months, and without any support. Though I had interviewed many cameramen for The Expedition, he was the only one that I had met so far who had shown even the slightest inkling of getting on a raft. His shooting experience was limited, and this expedition was the greatest opportunity of his life—if he could do this he'd have the all-important credentials needed to launch a documentary film career.

For the christening, I climbed down from the crossbeam of the mast, and then jumped off the raft and felt my feet plunge into the soft wet sand. The claustrophobia on the ground was intense. The crowd of people seemed like a wall, densely packed and impenetrable. Cameras of all kinds surrounded me like wide-open black eyes, peering intently, watching every move I made. Annie gave to Janette, a heavy green bottle of champagne who stood next to the raft, holding in the air, poised like a batsman at the plate of a big game. It was time to name our raft.

In a way, I was closing the first chapter of a strange, dual relationship with a giant. The old book that had brought me here, that book about balsa rafts that had motivated me to come to this beach, was of course none other than *Kon-Tiki,* and that giant was the legendary Thor Heyerdahl. Heyerdahl had written an anthropological paper in the 1930s stating that in ancient times the South Americans could have voyaged to Polynesia, some forty-eight hundred nautical miles away, by way of balsa raft. This theory of his was highly controversial, and such a fantastic voyage was considered patently impossible. Heyerdahl wasn't a sailor, but he was as plucky an adventurer as had ever lived, and in 1947 he set out from Peru on a balsa raft, together with his crew of five, and then managed to survive 101 days of sailing and drifting with the ocean current before crash landing on a tropical island near Tahiti. With his raft demolished by the crash but all of his friends safe, Heyerdahl had trudged up the beach in Polynesia, triumphant: He had crossed the Pacific by balsa raft, and as the news got out and millions read his book, *Kon-Tiki,* he became a scientific superman, a confidant to princes and sheiks, a global ambassador of science and goodwill with almost no equal. In his era only the names of Jacques Cousteau or Edmund Hillary carried the same prestige as his.

Back before the start of The Expedition, after I had decided to sail to Hawaii, I had written a letter to the Kon-Tiki Museum in Norway in the hope that Thor Heyerdahl himself would somehow help me in my quest. In my letter I included a request to name my raft after his. *Kon-Tiki* meant, loosely, "Sun God," and *Illa-Tiki* meant, loosely, "Fire God." The museum wrote back saying that hundreds of such projects were proposed each year, and that there was simply too much for the aging Heyerdahl to keep up with, in spite of his incredible vigor. But the news somehow got to him that someone had proposed a voyage to Hawaii, the hardest place to reach from South America, and on January 5, 1994, Thor Heyerdahl faxed me. He had hammered out a letter on an old-fashioned typewriter and had sent it to me from his island base near the west coast of Africa: "It is possible to reach the Hawaiian Islands from Ecuador by balsa raft. P.S. I have no objection to you using the name '*Illa-Tiki*' for your raft."

Now, on the beach in Salango, I had built my first balsa raft, and it was *Kon-*

Tiki and Thor Heyerdahl who had inspired me to do it. But though he was my origin, and though I stood on his shoulders to do what I did, it was always easy for me to separate his expedition from his theory. Scientists throughout the world were bitterly divided over Heyerdahl's theories, but I felt little of their passion—on either side of the argument. Like anyone who read *Kon-Tiki* or *The Adventures of Huckleberry Finn*, I was gripped by a simple certainty that I could handle a raft and a great journey. Perhaps this puts me in a trivial light, and I had no doubt come to this beach for little more reason than adventure, but because I was so detached, my mind was fertile for education. Later, for almost a decade, Thor Heyerdahl—this giant and his legacy, would confuse and confound me, until finally I evolved.

Janette, small and thin and holding the champagne bottle in the air, paused for a second, waiting for the cameras to move in, then sucked in a lungful of air and bellowed out, "FOR GOD! FOR OUR FATHERS! FOR OUR COUNTRY! YOU WILL BE CALLED *ILLA-TIKI!*" Then she swung like a champion, aiming with precision at one of the hardwood crossbeams, and the heavy green bottle exploded into white foam. It was finally time for the big push.

By now, the tide had crested and was starting to recede. Fatigue was taking over. We had to launch the raft right now; if we didn't we'd be chasing the receding surf, exhausted and falling behind. I quickly climbed back to the crossbeam of the mast, working hand over hand up the rope ladder, and then stood on the hardwood pole. From my position in the middle of the A frame I looked out over thousands of exhausted, burned Ecuadorans. They radiated out in every direction from the rectangular vessel in the center and sweat and fatigue showed heavily on their faces. I knew that a well-coordinated push would launch the raft, and to steady myself I now leaned back against the mast pole and reached around to hook it with the crook of my arm. Below me, they were preparing again, readying the *wancas* for a hard push. On the other side of the breaker line, two hundred feet from the raft, the two trawlers throttled their diesels, sending out clouds of black smoke from their stacks. I looked at the Salangueños, they locked eyes with me, and then I drew in the deepest breath I could and yelled, "LET'S GOOOOOOOOOOOOOOO!"

"HAAAUUUUUUUUUUUUUGGGHHHH!" And then hundreds of people near the raft bowed down in unison. Their heads dropped and their shoulders thrust forward in an immense surge of human strength. The raft began to slide. I could see that it wouldn't stop this time. It accelerated steadily and then broke free and sped down the slope of the beach. Our creation—our *experimental* ship—was going into the ocean for the first time; and just offshore, only a hundred feet ahead of it, an enormous wave was coming in. My heart leapt. *Illa-Tiki* was heading straight for it. We didn't even know if the raft would float . . . maybe we had done something wrong during the construction . . . maybe we had over-loaded it with supplies . . . maybe there was something we *didn't know*. I felt the dread of watching an inevitable crash—we had launched the raft at the worst moment and there was no way of stopping it—the front tips of the nine logs were already in the water and we were gathering momentum—we were totally committed and moving fast. The raft was racing toward the wave and the wave was rearing up like a ram standing on its hind legs preparing for a massive blow. I felt *Illa-Tiki*'s bow rising up steeply as it climbed the face of the wave. The wall of water grew and grew and I could see the entire raft—all thirty-thousand pounds of it—slanting upward. The breaker reached its climactic point. It curled over. Tons of seawater plunged forward. The two forces—raft and breaker—slammed headfirst into each other, and then the ocean exploded. It was as though a boulder had been flung into a bathtub. The impact of the raft seemed to blast a hole in the ocean, shattering the face of the in-coming wave and throwing sheets and geysers of water in every direction and flinging people into the air. *Illa-Tiki* staggered under the concussion and then came to an abrupt halt—stopped cold by the breaker—and then it seemed to disappear under the foam and chaos. For a long moment it appeared as though it had sunk; below me I could see only the roof of the hut surrounded by swirling seawater and white foam and human bodies radiating from the explosion like shock waves. Then the water level around the little bamboo house seemed to drop sharply. The raft was coming up. The bamboo canes of the deck surfaced with thick masses of seawa-ter pouring and draining off to all sides. *Illa-Tiki* emerged from under the surf with an enormous bounce. The balsa logs shot up through the surface and then sank back down softly. I could see the two trawlers clawing forward like a dogsled team, straining to drag the bulky wooden barge from the breakers. The towline was taut, and the trawlers were churning dark black smoke from their stacks. *Illa-Tiki* crossed over the breaker line, plowing water, and then it rolled hard over on its right side. The hulking raft then seemed to bounce back, recover its composure—shedding the masses of water off its back—and then settle up-right. Thousands of drops and streams poured off the mast and the hut like the remnants of a monsoon. But the *Illa-Tiki* was floating well now, and obviously at home in the ocean. Pulling away from the beach smoothly and confidently, it be-gan to leave its first wake, a slight trickle, behind its logs.

Illa-Tiki, a balsa raft, tan and sharp, now cruised into the Bay of Salango. Cheers and shouts of joy from the beach filled the air. "This is the greatest day in the history of Salango," Enrique told me later. "People will always study the ancients—they'll look at things in The Museum and so on—but they will al-ways remember today. No one will ever forget what happened here today."

2

Life Aboard a
Balsa Raft

The minute the raft hit the water, the ropes swelled. The dry manila rope gorged itself on so much seawater that every line below the water inflated, shrank in length, and squeezed *Illa-Tiki* into a solid block.

From launch, we were towed out to a mooring buoy lying fifty yards off-shore. Roughly thirty Salangueños rode out on the raft, and as we moved away from land they dove off, one by one, and swam for shore. Dower tied the raft to the mooring buoy, and then boarded a small boat and left. The crowd on land, utterly exhausted by the sun and spectacle, disbursed within a couple of hours. The scorching day had finally mellowed into a lazy tropical afternoon, and I was now alone on the raft, standing near the doorway of the hut.

I wasn't conscious of it at the time, but this afternoon was my "first day of school," and I began to take an unconscious tour of the vessel that would be my home for many weeks to come. *Illa-Tiki* was a tan ship, floating calmly, bathed in sparkling turquoise. The entire raft still dripped from our explosive launch. There were streams and pools of seawater everywhere, even inside the hut, where our gear lay strewn on the floor. The interior of the little bamboo room could best be described as a world of poles: You sat on a floor of fat cane poles while perfect rows of thin poles stood on all sides, surrounding you in a world of parallel lines. And because it was a house of poles it was also a house of hundreds of slender gaps, and therefore it breathed. The air inside, circulating around the bamboo, smelled deliciously of vegetation, of something freshly cut, like cut grass or tree limbs. From the doorway of the hut, I walked forward to the end of the deck, a distance of about eight paces, and under my feet I felt the rows of parallel bamboo canes bending down under my weight like a trampoline. The cane poles were roughly the same width as a human foot, and as I placed my feet on them they moved independently of each other, sinking a couple of inches with each step. I was now discovering that aboard the raft you experienced much of the world through the bottoms of your feet. It was as though a new sense of perception had suddenly been added to the other five: Each step would be unique, and my feet would be reading the surfaces, interpreting the thousands of independent spring-loaded steps like the ridges and patterns of braille.

But the deck didn't cover the entire raft; it stopped short, and so I stepped down and stood on the balsa logs themselves. Below me the world changed from brittle and spring-loaded to fat and solid; my feet gripped the balsawood like soft earth. The massive logs did not move or give, but they were almost completely submerged, and I now stood just four inches above the surface of the ocean. Clear seawater bounced up through the gaps between the logs and then fell back down, busily flooding and receding through every little opening in the base of the raft, and occasionally bathing my feet and ankles in warm saltwater. All around me I could hear the faint clatter of tiny wavelets, gently slapping fat timbers. In front of me lay the heads of the massive balsa logs, which narrowed to a point. Eight of the nine logs were cut at a swept angle, but the center log had never been touched; of the nine, it remained the longest by far. It was a massive beam, far larger than the others, and somehow we had taken to calling this big log in the middle "the Pope": It was sturdy and solid— something to cling to—something you could put your faith in during a perilous journey. It was forty-four feet long, the center of gravity, and it jutted out in front of the raft like a semisubmerged diving board. Moving outward from the center, the logs got progressively shorter, until the beam logs stuck out only a foot. When seen from atop the nearby hills, the raft looked like the palm of an outstretched human hand: one long middle finger, with each contiguous finger getting shorter, until you reached the thumb and pinky at the sides.

Walking farther out, all the way to the nose of the Pope, I stood for a moment in the warm tropical air. Looking aft, *Illa-Tiki* seemed like a caveman's idea of a houseboat. It may have been a balsa raft, but had you seen it that day you'd have thought it made of bamboo. Practically everything above the waterline was made of bamboo canes. During the building of the raft I had gone to Enrique's house every night, and he had made lists of building materials for the raft, and almost invariably that list read something like: ". . . six dozen heavy bamboo canes, seven dozen thin canes, five dozen fine canes . . ." along with a separate list of the names of woodsmen and of which villages to go to, to get the best prices. And looking aft at this bamboo platform you noticed immediately that there were no railings, sides, or walls to block your access to the sea. Unlike a conventional boat, where bulwarks and railings separate the sailor from the water, the deck of the raft opened directly to the ocean, and unlike a conventional boat's hull, which blocks the water below, the bamboo deck was defined by hundreds of narrow cracks and crevices through which you could easily see the bright blue sea below.

Walking back from the nose of the Pope, I took the fifteen-inch step up necessary to stand on the deck and then walked eight spring-loaded steps back to stand under the two mast legs. Above me, the A-frame of slender beige poles narrowed to a peak, arching over the center of *Illa-Tiki*. The mast was held erect by four heavy manila lines, each descending to a separate corner of the raft. The ladder, a manila and bamboo concoction that hung down from the center of the mast, would give us access to the mast's crossbeam at sea, which would serve as our look out.

It was getting dark, and as daylight began to drop, I walked to the edge of the deck, turned sideways toward the hut, and sidestepped my way toward the back of the raft. The hut had eleven storage barrels lashed to its bamboo walls, and the combination of the two, house and barrels, took up most of the space behind the mast. The barrels were made of blue industrial-grade plastic and ranged in size from twenty gallons to thirty-five gallons. Some contained food, others held fresh water, and a couple of the smaller ones contained equipment. Bulging outward from the walls of the hut, the barrels crowded the side walkways until they were narrowed down to twelve-inch catwalks. Working my way back required that I hold on to the tops of the barrels and shuffle along a walkway no more than three bamboo canes wide. At the stern, the catwalk ended abruptly and I stepped down onto the exposed balsa logs. As they had at the front, my feet now found a fat, solid surface. The logs' ends jutted out five feet, forming a platform that was easy to stand on. Once at sea, we would spend many days here, watching the raft's course, fishing, and swimming in the warm Pacific.

We had loaded most of our equipment on *Illa-Tiki* before we launched her, but there was still a great deal to bring aboard. For the next several days, we made repeated trips through the surf in our cargo-laden dinghy, a six-man inflatable boat with a rigid floor. There was no pier in Salango, so the town's ability to remain an active port relied on the Salangueños's uncanny skill to come and go through the breaking surf. They knew the window of opportunity, the split second when there would be an interval in the seemingly endless series of waves. They and their forefathers had been timing the waves on these shores for eighty centuries; we had not. When Dower wasn't around to time the waves we frequently crashed in Salango's breakers. We'd be coming back from the raft, paddling wildly through the surf, and a wave would pick up the dinghy and hurl it into the air. The waves at Salango stood only about ten feet at their highest but they broke with incredible force. Frequently, when launching the dinghy, we'd run out into the surf, pulling the dinghy along until the water was thigh-high, jump in, paddle, and arrive at the breaker line at the same time one of the waves was beginning to rise up. The horizon would disappear and for a moment we would see directly into the wave. Then it would break on top of us. Tons of water would flood the dinghy in less than a second and the momentum of the wave would launch the tiny boat backward, throwing everyone out. The wave surge would yank paddles out of people's hands, tear their clothing off, and scatter debris over a fifty-foot area. The wave's collision with the beach would stir up so much sand that the water would instantly turn from clear to cloudy brown. We'd find ourselves underwater, blinded and crushed by thousands of pounds of water, and then inadvertently brought to the surface, choking and blowing seawater out of our noses. Once, at night, after we had been dumped out into the water, I came to the surface and saw the empty dinghy actually airborne, flying toward the beach like a Frisbee! One man who was working with us refused to go through the surf anymore because of repeated capsizes. Nevertheless, we managed over eight days to transport the remainder of our gear and supplies out to the raft.

Meanwhile, a problem was brewing. Salango was of two minds: They loved the raft and they loved us, and they always treated me personally like I was one of their own; but while those feelings were all very real, there was also a pervading fear that was spreading throughout the village too. Many believed that the raft wouldn't survive the sea. One night during the construction of the raft, over dinner, Dower's sister had said to me in a smooth, even tone, "I love my brother. I don't want to see him killed."

Her husband then leaned in toward me and said, "Sincerely, John, the raft will never make it on the high sea."

"What?"

"I'm telling you the truth for your own good," he said. "I have been sailing all my life. Your raft will survive maybe two weeks, maximum. The people of the village are very scared. Dower's mother cries every day when she looks at that thing."

Brock and I gaped at each other. Shocked is an understatement. He was pale and so was I. Our happy little world had come to a screeching halt. The truth was they liked us, but they also thought us completely naive. The consensus among some in town was that the raft was certain death. Their view was that my inexperience and Dower's well-known optimism were orchestrating a disaster. Enrique's legendary reputation was now being openly questioned for the first time in his long career, which disturbed him. In response, he added more reinforcement to the raft, in the form of cocobolo wood. Weighing sixty-eight pounds per cubic foot, cocobolo is the second-most dense wood in the world. It couldn't be used for floatation or buoyancy because it was guaranteed to sink in the water like an anvil, but it could be used to hold our raft together because it possessed a freakish strength. "Cocobolo is strong," Enrique said to me once, and then rubbed his forearm, awed by the wood: "*Very* strong."

"Strong?"

"Yeah. It will bend"—he bent his arm at the elbow—"but it won't break." He then waved his palms back and forth in the air, wagging his meaty forearms, and said, "It *never* breaks."

The *Illa-Tiki* now contained a formidable array of cocobolo crossbeams. But still, Enrique was disturbed by all of the talk. He wandered around, chin down, cradling his right forearm in his left hand, rubbing it slowly, thinking about the raft and the upcoming voyage, and then one day at dusk he told me to come to his house and talk with him that night. When I got to his house that evening, it was obvious that he had relaxed into that special certainty that only *he* could have about seaworthiness. He had been more than just a shipwright to us: He exuded such wisdom and such confidence from his slightly rotund figure that you couldn't help but think of Buddha, and after someone started calling him our "spiritual leader," that image of higher wisdom just stuck. He had been infinitely patient, had never raised his voice, and he had always known what to do. None of us ever called him "Enrique"; he was always called *Jefe* ("Boss"). "Look, John," he said, "you have to keep the ends together, right? Together." To demonstrate his point he held his hand out flat, palm down. His flat hand was the raft, and his hard brown fingers represented the logs. "Look," he said, and then spread his fingers out so that I could see the spaces between them, "that is bad, very bad." He then reached up with his other hand and clamped the fingers of the hand-raft together. "Everything else can go wrong—everything—but you can't allow the ends to open. Never open, understand?" He made his point by squeezing the fingertips together until they turned red and bulged. "If you can keep the ends of the logs together the raft will float for a long time, very long. Front and back—both points—squeeze the ends, squeeze."

"Yes sir."

"When you're out there, way out"—he pointed to the sea—"check the ends of the raft—always the ends." He had a loop of string, which he now slipped over the finger raft in place of his hand clamp. Threading his pencil into the loop, he began twisting, round and round: it was a tourniquet. He slowly turned the pencil until the loop of string cut off the circulation in his fingertips, then he said, "If you get into trouble, right? Serious trouble. Take the strongest rope you have on board and put in a tourniquet, front end—back end. Both ends."

"Yes, *Jefe*."

"If you ever allow the ends to come open—that's *it*. Understand? You're finished."

With just a few days to go before our departure, Dower's mother and family, still fearful, came to the *Illa-Tiki* in one of their open boats. They had brought a priest with them and Dower's mother was beside herself with anguish. She boarded the raft and immediately went inside the hut and sat in the center of the floor with a look of bewilderment on her face. Her billowy baby blue dress took up half of the single-room hut, while behind her stood all of the children, like a family portrait. On the mother's behalf, the flamboyant priest began an impassioned appeal, quoting great rambling Bible verses to me in slow, unnaturally enunciated Spanish. He seemed to be both blessing the raft and at the same time trying to convince me that I was going to kill the favorite son of the village.

The town feared for the vessel, but the voyage was intimidating too: No one had ever navigated a balsa raft to the North Pacific. Thor Heyerdahl had proven that floating across the South Pacific was like pushing an automobile down a hill: A vessel, no matter what the size, could easily travel the length of the South Pacific because the currents and winds went in only one direction. If a raft leaving from South America could simply stay afloat long enough, it would eventually bump into Polynesia. After Heyerdahl, several other expeditions had duplicated his feat. But sailing *north* of the equator was a completely unexplored idea, and the Hawaiian Islands, the only islands never reached by a raft, were the "unconquered mountain." The goal of my first expedition wouldn't be to prove a theory, but to climb the most difficult mountain I could find. If the voyage of the *Kon-Tiki* could be compared to the summiting of Mount Everest, this voyage would be tantamount to attempting K2: Though the length of the voyage was basically the same, the technical challenges were vastly greater. To get to Hawaii the raft would have to function as a *sailing* vessel; it couldn't just drift, it would have to be *navigated*. It would be a primitive boat, trying to find its way to a very small place in a very large ocean. There were hundreds of islands spread throughout the South Pacific; reaching any one of them would constitute a crossing. The North Pacific, however, was a vast, comparatively uninhabited place. If I sailed north, trying to make it to the Hawaiian Islands, but instead I missed that lonely archipelago, there was a good chance I'd never make landfall anywhere.

This problem with Dower's family was serious. His sisters, especially, were very protective of him. He was currently in love with a girl, the smoldering Carina, who lived just down the street from his house, and I don't know what his family thought of her, but over the years his sisters always seemed to lecture me about the same problem: "Dower is a sensitive guy; You have to look out for him. You do! Women will always try to take advantage of him!" The sisters of Dower Medina stood in the hut now, waiting for the priest to finish, glaring at me in advance for killing their brother. By strange coincidence the roof of the hut was built so low that I couldn't fit my entire gringo body under it, so I had little choice but to bow my head in reverence the whole time. At the end of the sermon, however, I could only reply that Dower had volunteered, that he was an adult, and that I was happy to have him. As the family left they filed out of the little doorway cut in the canes, and though we all liked each other I was now seen as something of a bad influence.

But that scene shrank to insignificance when compared to the demonstration Dower's older brother made on the day of the launch. Benigno Medina-Urdin, Dower's brother, had a face like granite. He was always courteous to me out of deference to Dower, but that didn't hide his stern personality. He boarded the raft on the day of the launch and stayed while all the hangers-on swam back to shore. Then he cried, sobbing with his entire body, his muscular torso shivering violently as though he was suddenly very cold. I remember taking a moment to admire such a profound love. His brother and I were preparing to sail a balsa raft to Hawaii. Benigno, who was a veteran mariner, had gone from having misgivings about the voyage to collapsing into real fear. He just stood there crying and working a rope in his meaty hands. After a minute or so he looked down, then looked up, then wanted to say something to me, and then finally looked out to sea, staring mournfully. The two brothers had fought the ocean together for years; that is a ferocious bond. Standing next to him, I spoke to break the silence: "I will bring Dower back alive. I swear it—"

"—Hurry!" he blurted out, then put his head down and asked, without words, for privacy.

By now it was almost April. We had been in the field for almost three months, and in those last days before leaving Salango for our voyage we were going broke. This is hardly a rare problem. Contrary to popular belief, money for expeditions is always scarce and being underfinanced is the life of an expeditioner. Most expeditionary grants are for less than ten thousand dollars, and even expeditions that are high profile and are broadcast on television are frequently financed by their participants. In almost all expeditions, money limits you in some way. Because of that fact you are always faced with choices, instead of abundance.

Over the previous two years, I had built an expedition from scratch. The biggest break had come when I met Annie Biggs. It was she who had legitimized The *Illa-Tiki* Expedition. Shortly after she volunteered, things started happening fast. Annie seemed to leap on top of problems, as though physically attacking them. She taught me how to network and how to build an organization; her film office became our expeditionary office and she went to Ecuador to solve shipping problems, customs problems, and financial problems. The two of us, along with Chris and Brock, had built a respectable organization, made of patrons who admired the voyage of the *Kon-Tiki* and who oozed integrity. Whether one feels commercialization is good or bad for expeditions, we felt little of its influence. The people who backed me asked only that I build a balsa raft and sail it on the ocean sea. But though we had numerous generous sponsors for equipment, a large cash infusion had always eluded us. More than that, practically all of the cost estimates I had been given before The Expedition had been wrong.

Annie had gone back home by now, back to her responsibilities, and financially I was going to have to make some hard decisions. We were going to be short food, rope, and an adequate anchor. "We're going to have to spend our last few dollars wisely," I said one night to Brock, Chris, and Dower, "and I want to use it all on extra rope, which means we're going to be a little short on food out there. Every other meal that we eat will have to come from the sea." They all agreed with resignation. What else could be done? The raft was held together by rope and rope alone. Without enough of it, what would we do for repairs at sea? Theoretically, the ocean represented an endless supply of food. We could produce food at sea but we could not produce more rope once we left land. Not having an adequate anchor, however, was a big risk. It was our plan to do as *Kon-Tiki* had done: Simply have a boat tow us far offshore, raise sail, and then cross the open sea. Once we approached Hawaii, we'd have a vessel come out and tow us in, like a tug might do with a modern freighter.

Out in the bay, the press and public boarded the raft every day. It was becoming increasingly difficult to remain moored so close to the beach. We were exceedingly busy in our last-minute preparations, and if we were ever going to get ready we'd have to cut down on some of the boarding. With only a few days to go before leaving, we were towed out to Isla de Salango, about two miles offshore, by one of the small open boats. The Ecuadorans called these fifteen-foot boats *fibra,* or "fiber," because they were the only boats on the coast that weren't made of wood. Our tiny *fibra*'s outboard motor strained for about an hour, slowly tugging the bulky raft offshore, and then we finally came to our new anchorage, about fifty yards from the massive island. The *fibra* left, and we held on for a while, but within an hour the situation became untenable. The wind and current were much stronger near the island, and our inadequate anchor was dragging across the bottom. We were drifting out of control, so there was only one choice: Raise sail.

Piloting the raft—how it steered and maneuvered using its own unique system—was always very easy for me to understand. I started out sailing small boats as a boy, and over a period of sunburned summers I developed the feel of hooking the wind that comes from feeling every part of a sailboat working together. Sailing a raft is very different in many ways, but to understand how it works one only needs to know that *balance* is essential in *all* sailing vessels: The wind's pressure on the sail must be equaled by the keel's resistance against the water. When equality is present—when the two forces are balanced—the vessel moves forward in a straight line. If the wind's pressure on the sail overwhelms the resistance of the keel, the vessel slides, or crabs, across the water. The ancient balsa raft had no keel and no rudder; instead, it had *guaras. Guaras* were long boards—flat planks of wood—that could be thrust down into the water to produce the resistance necessary to counterbalance the effort made by the sail. This was very convenient because the wooden planks could be lowered straight into the ocean through the natural gaps between the balsa logs. Not only could the *guaras* ensure a balance of forces, which produced a straight course, but they could be raised and moved to *upset the balance,* which made the raft turn. The intuitive feeling I had gained as a boy has stayed with me my entire life, and the moment I saw a diagram of the *guara* system I understood it. I spent years studying and mentally rehearsing how to sail the raft, and now, aboard *Illa-Tiki,* we hoisted the sail and began to move under our own power for the first time.

The breeze blew gently, just enough to inflate the canvas, and as it did I called out the sailing instructions that made sense to me. Each time we changed the angle of the sail or adjusted the *guaras, Illa-Tiki* turned nicely. We were sailing—and elated. "Wow!" and "Incredible!" seemed to spew out of our mouths every other minute. The steep cliffs of Salango Island slowly fell behind us and we closed in on the town. Standing on the bamboo canes of the foredeck, we could see the Salangueños pouring out onto the beach, cheering. The raft crept through the smooth water of the bay at less than one knot, and we set course for our old mooring buoy near town. The buoy was a small target, just a floating milk jug really, bobbing up and down fifty yards from the breaker line. The precision of *Illa-Tiki's* steering was truly amazing: We cruised for an hour or so until the Pope drove straight over the mooring buoy, where we tied up without the slightest problem.

When we came ashore in the dinghy, Enrique, who was hurt at having seen only the last ten minutes of our bay crossing, asked, "Why didn't you let me know that you were going to sail it today?"

"I didn't know. We couldn't stay out there, so we just brought her in."

"Well?"

"Perfect. She handled perfectly."

He showed no emotion, other than feeling as though he had missed out. Standing on the beach, he contemplated the raft from a distance, rubbing that forearm one last time.

We had one last problem to solve, and then we could leave: We needed a fifth crew member. We had needed another person ever since we lost our doctor in the first week, and shortly before we launched the raft, a tall Swiss man named Frederick showed up in Salango, and in many ways he seemed ideal. He was in his late twenties, though his slightly orange hair made him look much younger, and he had a body like a board, flat and rigid, with square bony shoulders and long lanky arms and legs. A big fan of *Kon-Tiki,* Frederick showed up at our worksite carrying an old postcard with him from the Kon-Tiki Museum in Norway, where Thor Heyerdahl's famous raft was on display. He then hung around for a few days, helping out, and stayed in Salango after the raft was launched. At night during this time there was much talk in our *cabaña* about the need for a fifth person, and at the end of each discussion Frederick always emerged as the logical choice. I put off making a decision about him for as long as I could because something about him bothered me. In the end though, I ignored my conscience, because, you see, Frederick had *credentials.*

Frederick had "lived in the jungle," a mystique so incredibly awesome in the eyes of North Americans that it could stop any conversation flat. He wielded that statement like a fine rapier. He had worked at one time as a guide in the Amazon and if you objected to his opinions he could quickly remind you: "I've lived in the jungle." That signified his veteran status and the listener's amateur status. It worked, too. The reputation of "living in the jungle" must be the greatest credentials ever presented in front of anyone who has not lived there. "Living in the jungle" made Frederick like steel, as cunning as a black panther.

No other candidate existed, and certainly none with Frederick's aura of legitimacy, so we all agreed that he should go with us. Actually, I felt a little giddy about bestowing something that was so obviously wanted onto someone who so obviously wanted it.

On the morning of March 27, the Ecuadoran navy sent out an exceedingly sharp captain to inspect the raft and give us our clearance. With clearance in hand, I said we'd go the next morning. We were all relieved at the thought of leaving. People continued to mob the raft, which gave us all feelings of claustrophobia.

I was ready at about 8:00 the next morning, and left my *cabaña* to walk down the scalding beach for the last time. Halfway down to the raft I passed Dower's niece, who came alongside me and asked, "Do you know how to swim?"

"Yes."

"How far can you swim?"

"I don't know."

She looked at the raft and asked, "What will you do when . . . ," and then she trailed off into a look of dread.

The town had been waiting around for us to leave for forty-eight hours now, and when I began walking across the beach they massed at the surf line. Hundreds of hands stretched out to me, grasping my clothes and hands. People called out, "Good luck, John!" and, "Go with God, John!" Despite the fears that had been floating around, there was a general sense of pride among the Salangueños. Among the cheerful crowd was an old man whose weathered face now stretched faintly into a happy gaze. He was decrepit in the extreme, having no teeth and only a wispy, scraggly beard. In spite of the heat he always wore his shirt buttoned up to his chin and a tweed cap. Of all those who ever knew the joy of the rafts we built in those years, his happiness seemed the purest. Each day, for weeks, he had slowly crept down to the worksite and had stood there mumbling things like: *"Una balsa . . . una balsa . . . esos muchachos . . . contruen una balsa . . . ah . . . que bonita.*" ("A raft . . . a raft . . . those dudes . . . are building a raft . . . that's beautiful.") The old man could remember the days when they still used huge balsa rafts to transport cargo to freighters waiting off-shore. He always smiled whenever I passed him, and I thought him senile. More than that, he seemed vaguely to haunt me. He looked at me now in the same peculiar way he always looked at me—as though he knew me, or, more accurately, as though he knew better than I what part of my life I was passing through at that moment. A great *balsa* (raft) was going to sea once more, and now, leaning precariously on the stick he used for a cane, his eyes seemed to glaze over, as though his mind was swimming in some forgotten, exquisite, bliss.

The five of us boarded a *fibra* at the surf line and it ferried us out to the *Illa-Tiki*, where we prepared to get underway. The raft felt good and solid under our feet, and all around us on the deck, supplies, boxes, and coils of rope lay on the bamboo canes. Our sail, a bulky roll of white canvas as thick as a balsa log, lay ready to be hoisted. Standing at the edge of the deck, Dower spent a few minutes hand signaling his friends, directing them to set up a tow. He had just gotten his final haircut before the long voyage and he wore a clean shirt and shorts and looked like a yachtsman in his wayfarer sunglasses. At the beach, the Salangueños launched all of their *fibras* and within a few minutes the water around us was busy with blue-green fiberglass boats carrying as many as ten people crowded together in them, standing and waving and cheering. Slowly maneuvering in front of us, a bright blue fishing trawler prepared to take us in tow, and as it did, we had one of the *fibras* take our towline to its crew. The heavy wooden boat throttled its growling diesels, puffed soot into the air, and pulled the line forward until it went taut. The water parted in front of us and then began to stream by. The little armada of *fibras* fell into place by our side and we cruised away from the shores of Salango. All around us there were open boats filled with people laughing and crying, bouncing along under the power of their buzzing outboards. Clean-cut and neatly dressed, the Ecuadoran flotilla gave the scene the look and feel of a church picnic. Every few minutes, a *fibra* would glide next to the raft and Dower would walk a few spring-loaded steps over to the edge of the deck and lean out to accept letters of farewell, presents, and kisses. At the center of the fleet was the *Illa-Tiki*, slowly rolling from side to side like a tired elephant.

The weather was nice: Eighty-degrees Fahrenheit, not a cloud in the sky, and the water a brilliant, crystalline turquoise. Salango was a gorgeous tropical paradise. However unlikely it might seem, I was indescribably relieved to be leaving there. The Expedition had exacted a heavy price on us in terms of struggle and sacrifice, but I stood now on the deck of the raft and felt as though I was finally on my way. At that time, all those associated with The Expedition believed that the hardest part entailed building the raft and getting it out to sea; once there, you were home free—it was all downhill after that. And why not? It had appeared that way in *Kon-Tiki;* their voyage had been a warm, tropical jaunt.

Cruising slowly alongside the raft, Benigno Medina stood in his *fibra* as if there were no sea. That was their way: The ocean did not disrupt them at all; they stood on it and walked on their boats like good pavement. For the hour or so necessary to tow the raft free of the coastline, Benigno didn't move a muscle. Not a legend for his humor, he stood like a silent statue and crossed his arms in front of him so tightly that it appeared as though he was trying to rip apart the fabric of his own shirt.

As we continued cruising away from shore, Chris constantly boarded one boat or another to shoot the raft from different perspectives. Spreading his legs wide to keep his balance, he strained constantly to get an elusive, steady shot. Janette rode in a *fibra* near the raft and was exceedingly upset, hiding her reddened face behind her slender hands and refusing to look at the *Illa-Tiki*. Nearby, Oligia Medina, Dower's sister, stood in her family's *fibra*, dignified, wearing her best Sunday dress and makeup, not moving a muscle or making any facial expressions, allowing her tears to stream down her face on their normal course.

Standing side by side on the raft, Brock and I admired the odd majesty of Salango Island, an immense scrub and brush-covered rock. The wear of the expedition was already showing on Brock. He wore a bandana around his blond hair, which was starting to look shaggy, and his face hung from fatigue. He missed his former life acutely; back home he had a wife and two children, as well as a small business. We had been in the field for what seemed like a long time now, and yet we hadn't even started the voyage. We were far behind our original schedule, and that always weighed heavily on him. Over the course of time The Expedition would wear Brock down completely.

The slow pulling of the *Illa-Tiki* lasted about an hour, and behind us the houses and streets faded away until Salango looked like just another town in the distance. We were passing the island now and the *fibras* were coming close by, one by one, so that the Salangueños could shout out their final farewells, some joyous, some sorrowful. Passing beyond the far side of Salango Island, the Pacific Ocean opened up before us under sunny skies. Surprisingly, the trawler cut power, and then a sailor untied the towline and tossed it into the water. We were now only four miles from shore, which seemed strange to me, so I asked Dower: "Is that all? Aren't we going farther out?"

"Yes, this is it." He and the other Salangueños seemed indifferent.

Aboard *Illa-Tiki*, the five of us gathered on the foredeck and hauled up our square sail. It inflated tightly, and our big wooden barge began to slowly plow through the ocean. Our course would be due west—straight out to the horizon and the high sea. The year-round prevailing winds of this region came from the south, which would make it easy to achieve a westerly course and maintain it. Once we reached a point eighteen hundred miles offshore, we'd turn north, cross the equator, and sail north-northwest to Hawaii. But the wind was blocking us. At the moment, it was uncharacteristically blowing *from the west,* toward the shore. The raft could not sail into the wind like a conventional sailboat, so as a defensive measure we would begin by sailing parallel to the coast until the prevailing south wind returned to help us out to sea. I told the men we'd sail south, where the shoreline fell away, until conditions improved.

Benigno had stood by in his *fibra* until we were underway, and when he saw that we were sailing well he came cruising by on his final pass. His face was swelling and reddening in anguish and he was clearly having difficulty swallowing. He grunted a short, painful farewell to his little brother and then signaled to the man at the throttle of the *fibra* to make speed. They were gone in seconds; we were alone.

Illa-Tiki now sailed southward in the brilliant sunshine at two miles an hour. The buzzing outboards and laughing people had disappeared and around us we heard only the sounds of waves splashing and wind blowing. The Bay of Salango fell behind us and we began paralleling the coast. Off our side, the shoreline stretched southward like an immense highway, disappearing over the horizon. We saw no other vessels of any kind; *Illa-Tiki* cruised alone, the five of us steering the raft and trimming the sail. Blowing directly toward shore, the wind seemed resolute in its wish to drive us in. Within an hour it became clear that the raft was definitely giving up leeway and our safety margin, four miles out, was diminishing.

To avoid the coastal breakers was paramount; a collision with the coast would destroy us. We had to avoid one place especially: The rocks at the base of a village called Puerto Rico, about two miles south of us. The breakers there dwarfed those at Salango, and no beach existed. When the waves came in from the sea they came in hard and obliterated themselves against barren rock, jolting the atmosphere so hard that it vibrated your chest cavity, and spewing foam sometimes thirty feet into the air.

Illa-Tiki continued south under a bulging white sail. The raft cruised slowly, barely making a wake. I stood at the edge of the deck for a few minutes, looking at the crushing breakers of Puerto Rico, assuring myself that we would sail well clear of them. Brock, Chris, and Dower stood on the deck at various places, watching the raft sail and talking among themselves. Frederick had been pacing back and forth on the bamboo deck for a while, watching the raft and its performance, and he now came to my side and said. "Uhm, John, we are going to hit those rocks." But for some inexplicable reason he didn't point downwind, toward the rocks at the base of Puerto Rico; instead, he pointed at Los Ahorcados, two rocks jutting up from the ocean like small towers, about a mile offshore. I listened to his explanation, and then told him that I'd keep an eye on the situation.

Maneuvering around Los Ahorcados would be no problem. They were still two miles away from us and were a very small obstacle. Even if we closed to within one hundred yards of them we'd still be able to turn to avoid a collision. It was the breakers near Puerto Rico that presented the real danger; they were downwind from us, and I was reticent to attempt any complicated maneuvers while we were still vulnerable to them. The raft was well underway and cruising at an acceptable course and speed, but Frederick went to the stern and then came back, very agitated, and said, "Perhaps you didn't understand me the first time. We are going to hit those rocks." Again, strangely, he pointed not to the shore but to the tiny outcropping.

I asked Dower if he thought there was a problem and he said he didn't think so. Frederick was starting to boil. He seemed to stretch inside his own skin, straining to push out—or hold back, I am unsure—a psychological crisis. Soon he began stomping back and forth on the bamboo canes, holding his bony arms up in the air for balance, looking like a scarecrow gone mad. Finally he shouted, "John! You don't understand! You've got to listen to me!" I had never seen anything like this: His eyes widened, his face elongated in panic, and he pleaded with me to change course in a high-pitched voice of desperation. Erupting in his sharp Germanic accent, he screeched, "Vee-are-going-to-heet-zose-rocks!" His panicked voice seemed doubly surreal because a collision with Los Ahorcados could be so easily avoided. When I didn't react, he angrily announced that he was going to start gathering up his personal things so that he could abandon ship.

At the start of the tantrum, I thought he was simply trying to get attention, then after a few minutes I realized that he was truly panicked over what he thought was impending doom. This made me question my own judgment: Why would a person become so completely panicked if there was, indeed, no danger? And so I allowed his hysteria to influence me, which is always a fatal mistake in leadership. I decided to come about. We would simply turn around—that would put an end to the panic. I told Dower what I wanted to do, and he sheepishly agreed. I was going to reverse the course of the raft, a difficult maneuver that I had wanted to avoid while we were still vulnerable to being pushed into the breakers at Puerto Rico.

I shouted a few instructions in both English and Spanish and quickly there came a rush of activity on the deck: Men jumping over huge coils of rope, pulling lines, running from bow to stern on the narrow bamboo catwalks, and in the middle of it all, the wind dropped off. Within ten minutes the breeze died down to a gentle puffing against the sail, not nearly enough to inflate the tall rectangle of canvas. We had no power now and no maneuverability. We looked at each other for a few seconds, then, together, we turned and looked at Puerto Rico: the breakers. For the first time, we were scared. Surely the wind would come back. We dropped our sail, but small puffs of wind continued to push us toward the rocks. We then dropped our pitiful little anchor into the water, but it did no good; we would need an anchor many times larger to stop a fifteen-ton barge caught in the breakers at Puerto Rico.

Ducking into the hut, Dower began frantically calling for help on the VHF radio. He pleaded on all frequencies, but there was no one to hear him. Most local fishermen couldn't afford VHF radio, so they relied on the cheaper CB radios—if they used a radio at all. Then Dower said that he could attempt a landing in the dinghy and go for help. I knew that his plan was to paddle south, parallel with the coastline until he cleared the rocks, and then try to time the waves just right for a landing on the beach. "Go!" I yelled, and he and Frederick flung themselves into the dinghy and began paddling frantically. But it was too late. The breakers were going to destroy the *Illa-Tiki* and everybody knew it.

"Well," Brock sighed, "we gave it our best shot."

This would be the end—defeat, destruction, humiliation, injury, and quite possibly, worse: Fifty years before, Thor Heyerdahl's most desperate hour had come when a wave had sucked the *Kon-Tiki* into the same type of landing on a reef in Polynesia. That landing had demolished the *Kon-Tiki* as though it was made of matchsticks. Eleven years after that the adventurer Eric de Bisschop made the same type of landing in a raft and it killed him. Now it would be my turn.

The breakers kill people in a horrible way. First, an incoming wave picks up the victim and slams him down on the rocks, which are pointed and sharp, like thousands of upturned nails. Then the incredible suction from the receding wave drags him back out. In comes the new wave, which repeats the process with machinelike precision. Sometimes the first slam knocks the victim out, or stuns him so badly that he is utterly disoriented. Regardless of whether they are unconscious or just stunned, even the strongest swimmers cannot resist certain areas of the surf line; once they're in that zone, escape is practically impossible. Dower and I once saw a spear fisherman who could not escape a set of big breakers very similar to those at Puerto Rico. We found his dead body in a horrifying form, pulverized from repeated collisions.

Brock, Chris, and I began to discuss our options for survival. The only hope was to abandon ship. We might be able to get away from the raft and land on the beach farther south, as Dower and Frederick had done in the dinghy. The three of us left on board, however, would be forced to swim for it.

Bobbing up and down, the raft slowly approached the point where the waves started their kamikaze charge—where they committed to an all-out attack on the shore. As a prelude of what was to come, one of the big breakers curled up about fifty yards in front of us and slapped down, exploding with a loud CRACK!

Thinking that it might make the landing a little smoother for *Illa-Tiki,* we hurriedly raised the *guaras* out of the water. As soon as that was done, I looked up and saw that we were only about twenty yards from the breakers now. A sickening feeling settled upon on us. We couldn't do anything to stop our own destruction. We stood in silence, drifting slowly toward the break line, waiting for the end. It was a long wait. Looking at the others I saw a grim resignation. The raft had now drifted a little south of Puerto Rico, and we could see that our crash would come on the sandy beach, not on the rocks. But it was of little relief. We knew that we personally would survive but we also knew the breaking waves—millions of pounds of crushing seawater—were going to destroy the raft once it fell into the breaker line.

Then, out of the corner of my eye, I thought I saw something: I thought I saw a boat coming to save us and I grabbed my binoculars. Fumbling with the focus, I realized it had been a mirage, an act of desperation on my mind's part. Slowly putting the binoculars away, I prepared myself: *Ten yards now. We'll go off the back. We'll scurry down the catwalk, dive in, and swim hard on the outer rim of the surf line. We can go ashore where Dower went in with the dinghy.* Then I saw the mirage again, and I realized it was real. Benigno! In the distance, I could see a tiny gray object: the hull of a long fiberglass boat, jumping into the air, beating itself against the swells, and a blunt figure—unmistakably Benigno—standing at the tiller. He had sighted me and he was now driving his vessel and its motor to their limits. "Hurry," I whispered aloud. Then, a little louder, I said, "I don't know. This is going to be close."

A breaker broke with killing force less than ten feet from us. Benigno cut power as he came near and then he screamed, "John! Hurry! Hurry! Swim!!"

I half-fell, half-dove into the water, holding the rope in my teeth to free my hands for swimming. Another breaker exploded near the raft and around me I felt the ocean move. I thought to turn around and look back but knew that had a wave caught the raft broadside it would have torn the rope out of my teeth. Swimming, full of adrenaline, I quickly covered the ten feet between our two vessels and Benigno reached down, yanked the rope out of my mouth, and then tied it to a cleat. Instantly he throttled his motor and shot a jet of water from his propeller. There was an eruption of power at the surface and the line sprung taught. *Illa-Tiki* slowed; it gave up its suicide march reluctantly. Benigno's outboard motor, whining at full throttle and billowing a bright white smoke, could just barely hold the wallowing elephant and prevent it from being sucked into oblivion. "We have more help on the way," Benigno said, looking down on me as I treaded water. The spectacle at the edge of the breakers rattled him and fear and shock showed on his face. Somebody on the coastal road had seen the disaster unfolding and had alerted Salango that the raft was about to crash. At full throttle, Benigno had made it to us at the last second. We had been voyaging for less than three hours.

A heavy wooden fishing boat towed us back to Salango. By the time we secured the raft to the mooring buoy, it was dark. A small tanker ship, the *Everest,* had come into the bay to anchor, and so Dower and I went aboard and asked its captain, a friendly man in his early fifties, if he could tow us twenty-five miles offshore. He said he would be happy to do so if we could get permission from the woman who owned the vessel, and so we left with her phone number and went ashore.

It was around 8:30 p.m. when we arrived at the nearest town with a phone. We had ridden in on the back of an old truck, and just as we got out and began walking, the electrical power for the entire province suddenly went out. The darkness of the night intensified a thousandfold. Utterly blinded, Dower and I had to feel our way for the last thirty feet to a telephone shack located near some crossroads.

Darkness fell on the inside of my mind, too. I thought deeply. I could feel myself brooding, fulminating. Confusion and doubt questioned everything: Frederick had gone berserk out there. I had never seen someone go into a tantrum like that. I had seen fear in the doorways of airplanes or in the middle of rivers, but I had never seen anyone come apart so completely. And he did it so *quickly,* too. What should I do about him? We needed five people to handle the raft, and if I removed him it might be several weeks before we found a suitable replacement. Not only that, but his instability hadn't caused our near-crash—that was all *my* fault. I had expected to be towed out much farther than had been the case, and when the towing stopped short, I did nothing. If I had had any experience I would have had the conviction to simply ask to go out farther. How could I now say that Frederick was unfit to be aboard the raft when the blame for the near-disaster rested solely on me? As the leader of the expedition I had made a series of bad decisions. How could I now judge the actions of another man? I should have.

That night, when I went against my intuition, I began to learn the greatest lesson that can ever be learned by the expeditioner: The *type* of person you take with you on an expedition is the most critical factor of all. Credentials mean nothing if a person is going to wreak havoc. Those who ignore this lesson condemn themselves to my fate, as well as the fate of all the other expeditioners before me who have made this same, fatal mistake. Unfortunately, I decided that Frederick's temporary loss of composure did not nullify the need for a fifth man on the raft. I regretted that decision more than any other I made over the years.

Miraculously, Dower found over the phone the woman who owned the tanker. She gave her consent and we returned to the *Everest*. The tanker's good captain told us his ship would be at anchor until the next day, and then we'd go.

Shortly before four o'clock in the afternoon, March 29, the towing began. The *Everest,* a stubby blue-and-white ship, cruised out of the Bay of Salango while *Illa-Tiki,* about a quarter of the tanker's size, trailed behind on a long rope. Dower and I stood on the bamboo canes of the foredeck watching the squat blue tanker push forward, while behind us the land's details faded, and then left us. Within a few hours the sun set and *Everest* continued plowing through calm, black seas.

At around 10:30, when the towing stopped, the crew of the tanker untied the towline and hurled it into the ocean. The captain then radioed that he had a bottle of good whiskey and a farewell letter for us. Dower jumped off the deck and into our dinghy and I followed him, plunging into darkness, putting my foot through one of the rigid floor-slats of the little rubber boat and tearing the toenail out of my big toe. The pain was both horrible and trivial in the same moment: We knew this was it; we knew that this moment was our final contact with the outside, with land. Around us there was nothing but ocean, empty ocean, nothing but darkness and the faint glimmer of black water. In a few minutes we would be voyaging on the open sea and there'd be no turning back.

Dower and I paddled the bobbing dinghy through the dark ocean and I felt the warm blood pooling around my left foot. Motionless before us, its engines stopped, the *Everest* looked more like an island than a floating vessel. Our little boat bounced and bucked and slowly the hull of the tanker materialized in front of us like an iron wall. A faint green light radiated from the bridge of the ship, and as we glided alongside I stood up in the dinghy and braced my hand against the *Everest*. The iron beast felt warm and solid, like the wall of a concrete building in the dead of summer. Overhead, the captain appeared at the railing and Dower called up to him, thanking him for the tow; then the *Everest's* skipper pitched a bottle to us with a note tied to it. So far everything was all pleasantness and smiles, but then Dower asked him to turn on his floodlights so that we could see the raft. There was a short interval, and then suddenly there was a brilliant semicircle of light on the ocean and we could see that we were surrounded by thousands of shiny, bouncing wavelets. But in the distance, where the far edge of the light faded into the void, we saw something that we could not understand. It was our lonely little raft. The first sight of it stunned me into silence. It looked impossible. Dower's face widened, and then in a whining, pleading voice, as though begging some supreme force for mercy, he said: "Oh, no . . . no . . . *nooooo* . . ."

The tanker's crew stood above us, assembled at the railing of their ship, staring out across the ocean in silent disbelief. Dower and I stared too. We were looking at something we had made and yet we didn't know what we were looking at. The noble thing that had been pushed into the sea was gone. The straight lines were gone. At the edge of the void lay a menagerie of poles and thatch and yellow strings, a preposterous, dilapidated little outpost in an empty wilderness. For a moment I wondered if I had created something so perverse, so ridiculous, that it was suicidal to go through with it. We had expected the appearance of our exotic, ancient ship. Instead, the tiny *Illa-Tiki* was frantically splashing up and down in the same water that wasn't making the *Everest* move at all. Not only did it seem to thrash around in the water but there seemed to be something *wrong with it,* like it was tangled. The raft's structure appeared to twist and writhe in the water. Seaworthy ships should be tight and compact; they should move as one piece. Our raft didn't seem to be a solid object at all, it flapped and flailed wildly, like a drowning man fighting to stay afloat. It seemed to be half sunken as well; even the small waves appeared to be washing over its deck, and in my mind's eye I saw the vision of a man—one of us—clutching the mast, dripping and desperate, with seawater attacking him on all sides. *I never imagined anything like this. We're out here in the middle of the ocean on a pile of bamboo poles. How will we stay alive? We're going to have to tie ourselves down to stay on. What, exactly, am I supposed to tell the men aboard the raft? Surely they're going to ask! What do I say?*

The faces of the sailors at the tanker's railing looked down on me in fear and somber pity. There weren't any secrets; everyone knew what everyone else was thinking: Once the tanker left the area, the cold darkness of the night would close all around us and we'd be isolated, all alone on the vast ocean, clinging to a little wooden platform. Above me I saw one of the sailors at the railing slowly raise his hand to cover his mouth. Dread was smeared all over his face. He was a skinny, bony man in a ragged shirt, and he acted as though he had witnessed a murder. He looked right at me, still holding his hand over his mouth, and then slowly shook his head from side to side. His face said, very clearly: "Don't go out there."

But I carried with me the knowledge that Thor Heyerdahl had survived the voyage of the *Kon-Tiki,* and it was at this moment that he really helped me. Years later, my research would oppose his. In fact, everything that my expeditions would come to stand for would run contrary to his. But I am forever indebted to Thor Heyerdahl, because the main reason why I did not evacuate my crew from the raft that night—and Dower would have gladly helped me— was because I knew that Heyerdahl had survived, and so maybe I could too. So I told Dower to shove off, and we methodically paddled back to the raft like two men forcing themselves to enter a prison cell.

When I returned I went straight into darkness, as though entering a long, narrow tunnel. Blackness covered me like a coating of hot ink. All things: sky, sea, hands, arms, legs, were colorless and formless. On this and many other nights my eyes and ears could detect only the movement of vague shapes. On still other nights I couldn't even detect movement; I saw only blank black space in front of me. At times like that I would catch myself instinctively changing the angle of my head, trying to focus on the void, trying to cope with the ultimate darkness, but it would do no good. It was as though I had lost my sight completely, as though I no longer possessed eyes.

Consequently, we stumbled and fell over everything. It would be a long time before we memorized the layout of the deck, and in the meantime the wood brutalized our feet. The bamboo canes beneath us, though they bent under our weight, were brittle and hard, like baseball bats. Not only that but the deck was now cluttered with equipment because we had run out of other places to store it all. Here and there, wherever a *guara* had been inserted through the deck, its little bulbous head stuck up above the bamboo canes about a foot and this too was ideal for tripping a man or stubbing a toe. The night air was filled with the sounds of stumbling and falling, of stubbed toes and occasionally loud curses. We were five large men, lost in the dark, feeling around with our hands, trying to walk across a small slippery surface that was rolling and pitching.

When I reboarded the raft that first night, there was nothing to do but "get on with it," so I gathered the crew together at the mast to raise the sail. Teetering like an unbalanced mob, we put our combined ten hands on the halyard and squatted down with all our weight. The ocean clattered and splashed all around us and through the darkness we heard the line straining through the pulley at the top of the mast: *creeeek!* We climbed up the rope, hand over hand, then squatted in unison: *creeeek!* We climbed up again, all of us grunting heavily, and then collapsed our legs to combine our weight: *creeeek!* The massive sail slowly levitated and the creaking noise was now joined by the sharp cracking of canvas flapping violently in the wind. The sail jumped and shook back and forth like a massive machine out of control, but after two or three minutes of straining and grunting it calmed down, and then it stopped—we had hit a dead end: The sail had reached the pulley. Dower quickly tied off the line while the four of us hung from the halyard with our feet in the air. As soon as the line was secured we trimmed the canvas at a good angle to the south wind, and *Illa-Tiki* began to sail under our control.

The raft sailed like a car rolling down a very gentle hill. Almost imperceptibly it would begin to move, and after a few minutes you would be amazed that you had picked up speed and were smoothly cruising at two knots or better. A small boat and even a good-sized one will "dance over the waves" because the boat is jumping and its motion is quick—but the raft did not dance, it lumbered. Its motion was the motion of an enormous animal. You felt as though you were riding on the back of an elephant that was walking across the ocean. It was so massive that no resistance slowed it down, but it was not in any kind of hurry either. Even more, Dower and I had obviously misinterpreted the raft's appearance from a distance. *Illa-Tiki* wasn't loose and rickety at all; it was holding together quite well, and remarkably, now that we were underway, it behaved more or less like we had expected. Within thirty minutes of dropping the towline we were sailing on the open sea with no trouble at all. Everything worked well, so I told the others to get some sleep.

I stood out on the bare balsa logs now, forward of the deck, and steered *Illa-Tiki* as it began its voyage. I raised and lowered a single *guara,* adjusting the course, while a seemingly infinite mass of water sloshed all around me. I was at the very edge of the raft now. I stood on what felt fat and solid, like earth; next to me lay the abyss. You could walk straight into the deep sea if you liked, just like stepping off a sidewalk. With nothing to block it, the ocean flooded straight in on me and washed all around, swirling at my ankles and surging up to my shorts. Every few minutes or so the raft would begin to drift off course and when it did I'd go to work with the *guara,* raising or lowering. The steering *guara* was a long board of heavy hardwood with two holes bored through it, one at the top and one about halfway down. When the *guara* balanced the raft on the course I wanted, I simply inserted a wooden peg into one of the holes and it stayed in place. *Illa-Tiki* would then run on "autopilot" for a while, holding its course and steadily walking across the ocean.

As *Illa-Tiki* splashed forward, it set off a galaxy of tiny lights in the water. Thousands of glowing green specks of phosphorescence filled the ocean around me. Every now and then the nose of the Pope would disappear for a second under an oncoming wave and then in the next instant bounce up sharply with water pouring off in every direction. Warm seawater would flood up to my thighs and leave behind brilliant green and yellow phosphorescent specks, glowing in the dark like fireflies. The seas were small, and so the dousing only came when a steep wave would come too fast. *Illa-Tiki* would be at the bottom of a trough just as a little cliff of overhanging water would break. There'd be a sudden plunge of seawater over the front of the raft and then the mammoth logs would heave upward, fighting to get on top, rising and hissing like an enormous hydraulic machine, sucking and pulling on the surface and draining tons of seawater through the gaps and down the channels. *Illa-Tiki* was now leaving a faint streak of light behind her, an unearthly trail of dying phosphorescence stars that disappeared back toward where we had come. Overhead, the entire universe gleamed in rich, clear perfection. The starlight was immense. A more copious sky has never been seen, none clearer, more spectacular. Every star was out, every galaxy, cluster, planet, and constellation. The universe formed a map over my head and I stood there in the ocean and guided the behemoth toward a star in Orion's Belt. No other constellation in the sky is like Orion; when it is in the sky, it takes over. Standing before me, it was a gigantic signpost. It was headed west, and the *Illa-Tiki* would simply plod after it, a lumbering wooden animal alone on the wide-open Pacific.

I had sailed my entire life, but I had never been out of sight of land before. I wish I could say that the high sea changed my life, but it didn't. For me, being on the raft was like breathing. At sea, I could ask myself if what I was doing with my life was the right thing at that very moment, and I could always get an immediate guarantee that it was. Even later, when I drifted on the open sea for months, I never had the slightest desire to return to land. Seas boarded and vanished all around my feet and for one extraordinary moment among the stars, the warm seawater, and my raft, I was calmed and satisfied. At times I leaned forward and draped my body casually over the *guara,* slouching comfortably, and just stargazed. I asked myself if it was real. I unconsciously made a quick effort to wake up—jolting myself—blinking hard to make sure that my fantastic location wasn't just a well-detailed dream. I asked myself if I would ever see anything like this again. I asked if this was the highest moment of my life, or if any other moment would ever compare to it. I stood there in the dark, alone—standing in the Pacific as though standing in a vast, shallow pool—satisfied, steering a ship that was a thousand years old, and for one moment, I had everything that I had ever wanted in the world.

In a couple of hours Chris came out for his steering watch. He got up very slowly and put on his black wetsuit with great difficulty, then stumbled out of the hut and felt his way across the foredeck until he could step down to the steering *guara*. He stood before me on the bare balsa logs in his black neoprene body suit with his brown hair tangled and matted around his face and his round eyeglasses on crooked. He was miserable and I felt sorry for him. He didn't have any experience whatsoever in sailing and he had just parted from his new girlfriend, whom he cared for very much. I explained how to steer by the stars and he did the best he could. I stayed on the foredeck for the rest of his watch, but I had to fight to stay awake. A blinding fatigue blanketed all of us on that first night at sea, and I went to bed when the next watch came on deck, around 2:00 a.m.

The events in Ecuador had drained me, and I lay on my back in the hut now with my nylon sleeping bag clinging to my salted arms and the sounds of water all around me. The interior of the little bamboo room was completely black; I couldn't perceive anything with my eyes. Frederick lay next to me and Brock lay on the other side of him and yet I could not perceive them in any way, nor could I see the bamboo wall on my other side or the roof over my head. No stress noises came from *Illa-Tiki*—no ticking sounds, no woods creaking. Nature had cut off all of my senses and perceptions and I could only lie there on the bamboo canes and listen to the water.

Just below me, below the canes on which I lay, there existed a series of large, hollow chambers. They were a normal part of the raft's anatomy, and had been formed during the construction of the *Illa-Tiki* when we had lain the bamboo canes over the crossbeams, much like the open space created under a bridge when a road is laid over supporting columns. And much like the empty spaces below any other bridge, these hollow chambers allowed the water to flow through them. But there was a great difference between a bridge suspended over a body of water and the canes on which I now lay: The noises reaching me were not the romantic sounds of water coming from a distance like some nostalgic recording of the sea; instead, my ears rested just ten inches above the mighty Pacific, and tons of seawater roared in and out every minute, rushing through the chambers and exploding against the crossbeams, shattering the air with hundreds of sloshing noises and then sheeting over the sides of the hulking balsa logs. The water sounds would then fall off to a lazy sloshing, a benign repose, and then another ferocious burst would come, a furious flood of ocean blowing through the chambers below me, followed by a long, steady drain-off, that would slow to a tiny trickling. I lay there motionless, opening my eyes sometimes, expecting to see the water, instinctively searching the darkness for the origin of the fantastic noises that were only inches from my head, but there was nothing there. There was no water and no ocean before me; there was only darkness and a vivid, symphonic performance playing directly into my mind as though I had plugged a pair of stereo headphones into the sea. The noises were amplified by the hollow chambers and broadcast up through our floor of poles where they clattered and ricocheted off the brittle bamboo walls of the hut, distorting and echoing, flying around my head, coming at me from random locations in the dark, sometimes exploding below my ears, sometimes surging at my feet, and sometimes muffling back to me from twenty feet away like the sounds of someone taking a bath at the end of a long hallway. This was life aboard a balsa raft, and my memories and daydreams remain filled with this strange noise.

In the morning we awoke to sunny skies and a shining ocean. Land was gone. The raft was now cruising slowly and steadily across a vast field of pointed waves. Had you seen *Illa-Tiki* from a distance that morning you would have seen at first a stark-white sail towering above the surface like a three-story building. Behind the bulging sail you would have seen a bulky wooden barge plodding through the blue ocean with a little bamboo house on its back. You would have had no trouble determining that the craft was built in the tropics. Its superstructure was strictly bamboo architecture, made from scores of neatly cut bamboo poles and bushy palm fronds in typical *cabaña* style. You would have also gotten the clear impression that this was a work boat, not a pleasure craft. Supplies lay stacked on its deck and heavy barrels stood lashed to its cabin, giving it the looks and personality of an ocean freighter—a tropical cargo boat from ancient America.

We were completely isolated now. Though we would have sporadic communications with the outside via shortwave radio, everything of the earth was gone, the people, the conflicts, the commerce, all of it, and all of our attentions and thoughts turned inward. Our entire relationship with Earth and Reality was suddenly reduced to two ideas: the raft, and the ocean. The raft felt solid and heavy under our feet, permanent and unmoving, almost like standing on ground. That gave you the feeling of *living* on the ocean as much as sailing across it, and when I think of the voyage of the *Illa-Tiki* I think of five men inhabiting a wooden island. Eventually we would all come to see the raft as a compartmentalized place, where each small area—the chair between the water barrels, or the galley, or the swimming platform at the stern—as distinctly different microneighborhoods in a tiny wooden village in the center of a blue-and-white desert.

We stood that morning, all five of us on the bamboo canes, and looked at each other in the early light. We were most definitely not five men in a boat. We stood now on what felt like on an open-air stage, flat and wide and slightly elevated above the open expanse of the ocean. All around us the water was turquoise, as it had been in Salango, but darker and richer and louder. Standing there, every mind asked the same question: "What do we do now?" I felt it best to eat well, to dig into our stored rations and create the safe, warm feeling that can only come from a hot meal.

We cooked all of our meals using a crude propane stove. It was a small cast-iron burner that received gas from a tank, using a simple tube-and-regulator system. The Salangueños used the same system in their houses. On this first day at sea we set it up on the foredeck, out in the open, and cooked some canned meat; but within forty-eight hours we had set up an outdoor galley against the starboard wall of the hut. Here we mounted the stove inside a wooden box, which acted as a windbreak, and then placed the propane tank next to the box. The ancient Manteños cooked over stone fireplaces that they installed in the decks of their rafts, and over the years I found that this was a very convenient method, perhaps no more difficult than using gas; but because of our limited storage space we simply couldn't carry the immense stockpile of firewood necessary to maintain such a lengthy voyage as ours. Because the voyage would be so long, we carried four other gas tanks onboard, which we tied to the center of the foredeck, where the seawater ate through their yellow paint and corroded them from the outset. We folded and stacked our spare sail on top of the tanks to make a kind of canvas bench, where we could sit and eat our meals. Our metal pots, pans, and utensils were kept in small wooden crates next to the galley.

Our main foodstuff was rice, of which we carried four hundred pounds onboard. In addition, we carried one hundred pounds of potatoes, fifty pounds of beans, and about twenty-five pounds of carrots. We also carried two large stalks of bananas, which we tied to the outside of the back wall of the hut.

Each stalk held roughly forty good bananas. They were the only foodstuff not subjected to rationing. They could be eaten at anytime, which was encouraged because we knew they would spoil quickly; all you had to do was walk to the back of the raft and pluck as many fresh plump bananas as you could eat. Next to the stalks we tied two large jugs of cooking oil, for preparing the fish and rice, and a fishing net loaded with twenty-five coconuts, which were used for their meat and their milk. We stored about one hundred cans and packages of food, most of which had been sent from the United States, inside the storage barrels lashed to the sides of the hut. These rations ranged from canned vegetables, to canned meat, to packages of spaghetti.

We carried approximately 140 gallons of fresh drinking water in the storage barrels. Strangely, in all the days I was to live on rafts at sea, I rarely saw any person consume more than three-quarters of a gallon of water in a day. Perhaps it was because our diet was so pure: Fish and rice are rich in water content and contain little sodium. More importantly, we rarely drank diuretics, like coffee, soda, or alcohol.

We ate twice a day, once at dawn and once at sunset. We took turns cooking, each one of us cooking an equal amount of meals, and the crewmember whose turn it was to cook also cleaned the pots and pans. No insects or parasites followed us from land or stowed away in our food, so once we were at sea we maintained sanitation quite easily.

After breakfast on that first morning we spent some time arranging the raft. Aboard *Illa-Tiki* we carried a mobile radio station, a mini film studio, a full-time fishing operation, a small library, our personal possessions, and all the food and water necessary to sustain five large men for five months. Storage was always a problem. The barrels were ideal, but they were full. Besides the barrels, no storage space existed for the vast amount of gear, and no matter how much we tried to prevent it, equipment and supplies cluttered the raft. The clutter was especially apparent when you went inside the hut.

To enter our bamboo house you had to bend down a couple of feet to duck into the little doorway in the front wall. Immediately on your left, upon entering, you'd see a small plywood table mounted against the wall. This was our radio station. We carried a small high-frequency unit for long-range communications, and a standard VHF unit for maritime communications. Because the plywood board was flat and convenient, it accumulated hundreds of small items: pliers, hammers, screwdrivers, knives, charts, books, and navigational notes. Under the table we placed two twelve-volt batteries, which powered the radios. Three small solar panels were tied on the roof of the hut, and their cords were run through a window and down to the batteries. Inside, we tied our bicycle-driven generator system to the starboard wall. We'd pedal the bike if the solar panels couldn't charge the batteries completely.

On the other side of the room we stored the film equipment. An open platform on the salty sea was the most corrosive environment imaginable, and keeping the cameras running for months posed a huge problem. Chris's gear included a Hi-8 video camera, two 16mm motion picture film cameras, a myriad of still cameras, a tripod for the video camera, a shoulder mount for the film camera, underwater housings for both film and video, extra lenses, blank video tapes, ten thousand feet of motion picture film, battery packs, extra battery packs, cleaning equipment, which included several thousand Q-tips, chamois, and chemicals for cleaning lenses, electrical cords, miniature tools for making repairs, and hundreds of other odds and ends for various contingencies.

Much of this gear sat on the floor of the hut, but a multitude of small items hung from every part of the ceiling too: film gear, diving masks, clothing, personal items—all of which gave the place the look of a gardener's shed. The ceiling of the hut went up to a peak, making it possible to stand upright in the middle of the bamboo room. If you stood up and looked through the back window you saw a slender rope trailing behind the raft, extending one hundred feet out in our wake. We tied this line to the stern to provide a second chance for anyone falling overboard. The line floated, and with the raft's speed rarely exceeding two miles per hour, the man overboard usually had a full twenty seconds to grab the rope before being left behind in the ocean. Also behind us you'd see our gray inflatable dinghy trailing on a ten-foot line. Keeping the dinghy inflated and ready was important because we were aboard an experimental ship. I never said it to the others, but I always mentally prepared myself to wake up in the dark and find that the raft had broken into two halves, or some other unpredictable situation in which we would immediately need a small boat to recover men and equipment—or to simply make a controlled evacuation. Besides the lifeline and the dinghy you'd see only the horizon out the window, where the curvature of the earth bulged up in the form of a dark blue ocean, and formed a perfect semicircle (real or imagined) against the light blue sky.

Standing in the hut you'd feel under your feet a spongy reed mat. These mats were woven in Ecuador and they covered most of the floor, preventing the seawater from bouncing up into our house. They also made it more comfortable to sleep. We slept in nylon sleeping bags, and because a thin layer of salt covered us all the time the nylon fabric sometimes stuck to our skin. Four men slept in the back half of the hut, lying parallel to each other, and Chris slept on top of his pile of film gear in the front corner. Each day he restacked, reshuffled, and rearranged his mound of stuff in order to wedge his body into a semicomfortable sleeping position. Between the soft nylon bags and the spongy mats, we never missed beds or bunks. Frequently we'd would come off watch, or from fishing or bathing, and collapse on top of our sleeping bags in an exhausted heap. This collapse was delicious.

The occasional nap in the afternoon sometimes produced a freakish occurrence: Sometimes you awoke to the face of a fish. Over a period of weeks the reed mats disintegrated, exposing the bamboo deck and the hundreds of open gaps between the poles. This gave you a perfect, close-up view of the Pacific Ocean, seventeen inches below your face. Triggerfish swarmed under the raft, and when a triggerfish wants to look up at the surface of the water it turns on its side and swims laterally. That meant that if you were sleeping on your side the two of you would meet, eye to eye: In the fogginess of afternoon-nap-heaven, you'd roll over, your face against the floor, and come face-to-face with a triggerfish, madly flapping its fins, utterly perplexed at seeing the large green eye of a human, just inches away. Both animals would blink at each other—both minds, fish and human, equally confused.

At night, however, when the light and the heat vanished, the environment changed. Invariably you awoke shivering. This occurred of course because nothing separated us from the ocean. Heat moves; and if you laid on canes that were not covered over, your body heat would travel to the ocean. You didn't "feel" cold, you *were* cold, literally. While you were sleeping your body temperature would drop to well below the shivering point. You never felt the shock of cold air or cold water on your body; on the contrary, the weather was always very nice, even balmy, but it was entirely possible to be so cold that you could not stop shaking. Heat loss breaks the spirit, and to wake up in the blackness of night with all the heat gone from your body can be a dreadful feeling. Over a period of time we adapted, became raft mariners, and put on as many sweaters as we could stand as soon as the sun set.

For light, we used old-style hurricane lanterns, small metal cages with pear-shaped glass housings that protected canvas wicks, which Brock and Chris had scrounged up back in Ecuador. The lanterns ran on kerosene and were constantly fouled by black soot. Though they were fragile and of low quality, they proved invaluable because their technology level fit neatly into our conditions aboard the raft. We also hung a light bulb inside our little hut, and wired it to the batteries. It drained away our tiny supply of electricity so quickly that it could only be used sparingly, but these few minutes of artificial light each night produced such a positive effect on some of the men that I was always reluctant to turn it off, and we sometimes ran the bulb for as much as an hour. When we lit the interior of the hut, especially with the light bulb, the person going out on watch met a jolting wall of blinding darkness the moment he ducked through the little doorway.

Steering watches, both at night and during the day, usually consisted of moving back and forth from the compass to the steering *guaras*. Our compass sat on top of a balsa stump near the doorway of the hut. The stump was two and a half feet-tall and three feet-thick, and weighed roughly one hundred pounds. It was stable and difficult to move and so therefore functioned perfectly as the navigation station. During your watch you sat behind it, watching the black compass swing back and forth until it inevitably swung too far to one side. To correct the course required a change in the *guara* positions, which required that you now slip and slide across the bamboo canes, step down gingerly onto the exposed balsa logs, and then wade out into the warm seawater. Like all islands, *Illa-Tiki* was surrounded by its own private surf, which washed up on the balsa logs, flooding in and then receding back, twenty-four hours a day. Standing in the ankle-deep seawater, you'd pull the peg out of the hole, raise the *guara,* insert the peg in the other hole, and then wade back to step up on the deck and totter back to the compass for another reading.

We steered by compass and stars, but found position via GPS, the global positioning system. I had fought against electronic navigation throughout the preparations for The Expedition; but like so many other arguments for authenticity, I capitulated when the question of life or death came up. In the event of an accident, especially something like a severed limb, we would be unable to direct an effective rescue unless we knew our exact location.

On that first morning at sea, March 30, we were seventy-five miles south of the equator, steering due west, making about two knots across the mild blue Pacific. If we could hold this westerly course we could sail out to more favorable winds and currents. But the winds and currents were, at present, pushing us north. Our sail was hauled over to one side and we were trying to force the *Illa-Tiki* to sail at a right angle to the wind. The raft gave up a lot of leeway when sailed this way. We simply didn't have enough resistance under the water to counteract the lateral force of the sail. Instead of sailing due west, the actual course of the raft was now northwest, toward the Equatorial Counter Current, better known by its common name, the Doldrums.

Nevertheless, I was relieved to be moving farther away from the Ecuadoran coast. In the afternoon, Brock, Dower, and I stood on the front ends of the balsa logs and discussed the raft's sailing abilities, while Frederick stood behind us, listening. Even though the raft gave up a lot of leeway, it still appeared to have the performance capabilities necessary to get us to Hawaii. Frederick overheard and interjected, "The raft is not sailing well, John."

I told him I understood and that we'd be looking at it over the next few days. Frederick was coming apart again; he was once again going into a frenetic state of mind, exuding a biting, malignant tension. When he became excited again, Brock and I turned to look at him. "Frederick," I said, "just wait a minute, OK? We're working it out."

"This course is just a fantasy!" he shrieked. "Can't you see this?"

"Frederick!" I yelled. "Stop arguing with me! Do you understand?"

He looked at me with fear and disbelief, then said quietly, "OK."

Within just twenty-four hours of being at sea I had publicly reprimanded a person, which is never productive. I hated myself for it, and in the end it was a disaster. Instead of sobering him up, it made him even more nervous and more irrational. A tension was already beginning to build aboard *Illa-Tiki*. Shortly afterward, the raft went out of control, and we fought a hard struggle to regain command of the ship. We didn't know it yet, but this was the beginning of a hellish pattern of awkward physical combat during the day, and running chaos throughout the night, a pattern that would repeat itself for weeks.

We sailed aboard an old-fashioned square-rigger, which meant that our sail was essentially a rectangle of canvas, hung from a wooden pole called a yardarm. This primitive engine was a thing to be reckoned with. It was an energy force strong enough to drag a fifteen-ton barge through the waves, and since there weren't any winches aboard *Illa-Tiki* to help us gain mechanical advantage, we were using human strength alone to try to control it. During times of even moderate wind it could inflict injury. If you have ever snapped a wet bath towel at a person's legs, or have ever felt the painful sting of such a snap, then you might be able to appreciate our beatings. Our sail was twenty-five-feet long, soaked in seawater, and when a canvas wave would start at the top it would invariably curl down and burst at the bottom. When that happened fabric became as hard as steel, and ropes became as sharp as knife blades, slicing through the air indiscriminately. Aboard *Kon-Tiki*, Thor Heyerdahl could lower his sail and drift when it became too much for him and his men. We could not. We weren't trying to drift; we had to sail, and each day, out on the bamboo canes of the foredeck, a variation of the same hellish pattern would erupt:

We are cruising west at one and a half knots. I push the port steering *guara* down. The raft turns too close to the wind. At the top of the sail, a wrinkle grows into a curl, and then the belly of the canvas collapses. The sail convulses in a towering seizure, quivering and billowing, flapping and snapping. I reach out to stop it and it curls down into a snap and explodes on my arm and cheek. Now I am on my side. I've been knocked down on the canes. Brock lunges forward. He grabs a corner of the canvas. His body turns to rubber. The giant sail is shaking him like a noodle. I struggle to my feet and grab the corner with him. We are fighting for control. The angry canvas machine throws Brock down to one knee. His leg bone clatters on the hard canes. I fall down again. I can feel the spring-loaded cane poles bending under my body. The canvas is beating Brock down like a giant hammer driving in a human nail. Dower tries to grab it and takes an explosive snap on the arm. He drops, winces in agony, then tries to reach out and grab it again. The sail goes wild with anger and beats him horribly. He's on his hands and knees trying to cover his face. The sail is in a wild seizure—three stories of energy in a horrible spasm—whipping and beating Dower until he scrambles away in agony. I grab the corner and pull it to the wind. It goes taut, inflates, and settles. Brock and Dower grab the corner too and pull it to one side of the raft. We lean over to tie it in place. We are hanging over the deck, trying desperately to tie down the canvas monster. Warm seawater floods over us in masses, burying our lower bodies, surging up into our faces, nostrils, and eyes, making our clothes cling to our bodies. We tire. Fatigue and dread set in.

And that dread was exacerbated by the unavoidable fact that we were consuming our stored rations at almost twice the rate we had expected. Our rationing plan had been based on the assumption that half of our meals would consist of fresh fish, supplemented by rice or one of the other staples. Heyerdahl had written that fish practically jumped aboard his raft. Perhaps it was the region we were in or perhaps it was the era in which we now sailed, but fish were *not* always near our raft. My memories of those first days are dominated by the same scene, one that repeated itself every night:

Dower and I are standing at the edge of the deck, shining flashlights into the dark ocean. There is nothing there. Dower can't understand it—at least when he shines his light over the side of his *fibra* the squid come up, but this is a deep, black, emptiness. We're both wearing rolled up pants and layered sweaters and we're both bored and cold. We stand and wait for something to swim through the light. We wait and wait for hours, but nothing, not one thing, swims to the light. It is as though the stories and pictures of schools of fish are romantic fiction. It seems as though all oceans are empty, as though we are floating in an empty pool of water.

When we did see fish, they proved exceedingly difficult to catch. I had expected Dower to be able to catch fish at will, and to be skilled in survival at sea. But his job in Salango entailed using a twentieth-century motorboat and a long line with perhaps as many as three hundred hooks on it. Under these conditions he roamed a radius of twenty nautical miles or more. In fishing for sustenance under our balsa raft, however, that radius shrank to one hundred feet. Aboard *Illa-Tiki* you had to catch the fish in the water near you—*those particular fish*—out of all the fish in the sea. This presented a completely new problem to him.

Also, there was no way to preserve any excess meat we might have, and fish spoils quickly. Curing the meat can slow this spoilage down. You can salt it, boil it lightly in vinegar, and other such ways, but that lowers substantially the quality and edibility of the fish. This was seldom a problem, however, because our tiny supply of meat rarely lasted longer than twelve hours. We simply weren't catching enough, and in the end, you must catch fish at roughly the same rate as you eat it. Again, this was a new problem for Dower. He saw fishing as a business: If he had a bad night or a bad month, the only negative repercussions he faced were financial. On the raft you couldn't afford two bad nights in a row; if that occurred, hunger set in, and hunger starts desperation—aboard a raft you must catch the fish in the water near you, and you must catch them *now*.

To catch fish we used a hand line attached to a small plastic hand reel, or "hoop." The hoop was a ring of strong black plastic, about a foot in diameter, which had a wide channel molded in its outer edge. This channel made it easy to wind fishing line around the hoop quickly. When you wanted to cast, you simply held the hoop in one hand, and slung the line out with the other. The heavy lead weight at the end of the line pulled out the slack, and holding the hoop at a certain angle allowed it to pay out quickly and smoothly.

We fished every night, all night. We were trying to catch the dorado, sometimes known by its Hawaiian name, "mahimahi." We also pursued smaller fish like tunas, amberjacks, and groupers—if they swam near the raft—but a single dorado could feed the five of us for one day. A dorado is a dolphin fish (of no relation to the gray porpoise, which is a mammal), averaging four and a half feet in length and weighing roughly thirty pounds. They frequently grow much bigger though, and some recorded specimens have weighed over eighty pounds. Their bodies radiate bright green and gold, and they can be seen in fifty feet of water by a trained eye. They are immensely powerful swimmers that can reach speeds of thirty-seven miles per hour when jumping. Fishermen abhor their jaws and teeth in the same way they abhor the snout of a swordfish. Injuries are seldom, but dorados are known to be fanatically aggressive, and bites from their razor-sharp teeth cause infection to start immediately in humans. Their strike at the end of a line is unmistakable. Dorados lunge at anything near them and they slash and jump in a mad frenzy the moment they are hooked. Sometimes they simply take off swimming, making as much as twenty-two knots through the water.

Aboard the raft, a dorado would hit on the line, and then we'd scurry up and down the deck and catwalks for half an hour in our underwear, stubbing and breaking toes, falling down and tearing out toenails, fighting the fish. And we were fighting them in a minefield. At unknown spots, randomly dispersed throughout the deck, the floor would fail. A certain cane pole or a section of cane poles would break and give out under your weight. Your foot would suddenly fall through, sometimes all the way up to the knee, and on the way down the splintery bamboo would scrape all the skin off your shin, and worse, trap your lower leg. At times one misstep could mean a broken leg: In the middle of the night, as you're scurrying across the deck—all of your body weight committed in one direction—your leg breaks through and you stop cold. This breakthrough in midstride was the equivalent of jamming a stick into the spokes of a spinning bicycle wheel: The motion stopped instantly, caught fast between two immovable objects.

Brock and Chris still could not speak enough Spanish to communicate with Dower. Anytime he said something, it had to be translated. The translation, along with the noise of the waves and the suffocating darkness, all compounded to block communication. Against this backdrop, catching dorados became a desperate fight. We openly discussed the possibility that we might have to call for an evacuation because our food would run out long before we reached Hawaii. We were fishing neither for sport nor commerce; we were fishing for survival. Dower would cast out a line into the night and get a strike, the hoop would whir from the sound of hundreds of feet of line unwinding at high speed, and then the desperate game was on:

"He's taking it out!"

"What?"

"Com 'ere! Com 'ere! He's got one!"

Dower is standing at the edge of the deck in his underwear and bare feet. He has the hoop in his right hand. He holds it out in front of him to ensure that the line goes out at the maximum rate. Somewhere out there in the dark, a predator is speeding through the water at two thousand feet per minute. The fishing line feeds out frantically, oscillating into a blur in front of the hoop. Then it stops. The line hangs limp. Dower runs aft, stops before the mast, cocks his head, then reels in the line as fast as he can. *"Ya viene!"* ("It's coming back at us!")

"What?"

"He says it's coming back!"

"What's happening?!"

"It's coming back! It's coming back! It's going to go under the raft!"

Dower drops down on his stomach and holds the line down in the water to prevent it from dragging against bottom of the raft. If the dorado swims underneath the raft it will take the nylon line with it. If we allow the line to scrape against the barnacles that cover the bottom of the raft, they will cut the line and we'll lose everything: Hook, line, sinker, bait, fish, and precious opportunity: "Help him!"

"What?"

"It's gone under the raft! Keep the line off the bottom of the raft! Take it around front!"

"Around front?"

"He's on the other side now!"

I seize the line and walk it around the tip of the Pope, letting out hundreds of feet of line per second as the fish swims for its life. Brock and Chris are behind me, asking me, "Is he still on the line?"

"I don't know! I don't know!"

Dower is somewhere back by the hut. I can hear his voice in the dark, *"John! Deme la liña!"* ("John! Give me the line!")

"He wants the line! Give Dower the line!"

Chris edges forward and takes the line and hands it to Dower, who begins reeling it in slowly, cautiously. If he uses too much tension, the line will break. Everyone is silent for a moment, watching the line come in, one foot at a time. The line extends from the hoop out into the darkness where somewhere, maybe twenty yards out, it disappears under the surface. The sloshing noise of water is everywhere. It is 3:15 in the morning. We need food. We are a group of barefooted men, some in their underwear and others in shirts and long pants, standing silently on a bamboo platform and staring at a single strand of nylon line. Every man carries an instrument in his hand: a spear, a gaff, a machete, a knife. Then: *Whirrrrrzzzzzzz!* The line goes rocketing out of the hoop! The dorado takes off toward the stern!

"Cuidado! Cuidado!" ("Look out! Look out!")

The line gets caught in the mast stay as Dower's trying to get back to the stern and in two seconds the spindly plastic line tangles around Dower's arm, a mast stay, and the mast itself. He fends it off like swatting at a swarm of mosquitoes. It stretches out; it's going to snap! His arms flail wildly!

"It's going to break! Help him untangle it! Untangle it!"

Dower untangles it and then runs down the catwalk to the stern. *"Que ves-tia!"* ("Good Lord!")

We scurry behind him like a mob in the darkness. Our bony feet are clomping on the hollow poles like a horse team crossing a wooden bridge. Before me I can see only black forms of men, vague human shapes moving clumsily in the dark. We are fumbling hand over hand to get to the back of the raft. Ten hands are feverishly grasping and clutching the brittle thatch. The crispy leaves crinkle and crackle and our bony feet clomp and then we stop at the stern, huddled together, hungrily looking out into the ocean: "Is he still on the line? I think he got away!"

"He got away?"

"No! We've still got him!"

Again Dower reels in slowly. The big fish is tiring; he's been fighting for forty-five minutes now. Dower patiently reels him in, one foot at a time. Just below the surface we see a flash of green and gold: "That's him! He's right there!"

"We got 'em!"

"Cuidado. Me voy adelante." ("Look out. I'm going forward.")

"He's coming forward. I think we've got one. Get ready on that gaff."

Dower pulls the exhausted fish up alongside the foredeck. It surfaces—a long, flat fish, dark green and hideously ugly. A gaff hooks its gills and hoists it up on deck. Frenzy! It's alive and flapping all over the bamboo! It's springing three feet into the air! It's kicking its way to the edge of the deck!

"Stop him!"

"Don't let him get away!"

Brock is kicking it and Dower is clubbing it.

"No! No!"

Its jaws are working like a hideous machine, biting at air and legs and feet. Frederick grabs its slimy tail fin and then loses his grip. The dorado thrashes wildly. It kicks hard and goes over the side with a splash. We rush to the edge to see a flash of gold shoot out of sight forever. We stand in the dark and stare. Each person exhales, one at a time, releasing his pent-up breath. Mouths hang open in disbelief.

Like all fishermen throughout time, we dreamed of landing "The Big Fish." At times, Dower would turn misty-eyed and talk about the possibility of three hundred-pound tunas somewhere out there, just beneath the surface. For several days, at dusk, we took an enormous fishing hook—the largest one we had, and stabbed it through the center of an amberjack, a flat fish about the size of a large dinner plate, and then threw it over the stern. It trailed behind us on fifty feet of line, and had a white milk jug—our "buoy," attached to the end. Throughout the night the buoy, hook, and fish, were towed behind the raft in the hope that something big would strike. Every hour or so the person on watch would work his way back to the stern and check the buoy. Standing there, you saw a long thin line extending out into the wake of the raft, and at the very edge of your night vision a white milk jug, bobbing across the surface. If, however, the buoy was submerged, something big had hit on the bait.

Several nights passed with no luck. Then one night I went to the stern to check the buoy. The others were asleep and I was alone with the monotonous sloshing of water and the gentle rolling of the raft. Standing on the back ends of the logs, the water swirling around my legs, I peered out into our wake but could see nothing. The darkness made it impossible to tell whether or not the buoy had gone under, and so I took the line in my hand and began to slowly haul it in. It was unnatural work at an unnatural angle. I was bent over the sea, working hand over hand, steadying myself every few seconds, trying not to get pulled overboard by the drag of the buoy while my toes and feet curled and flexed, trying to grip the wet balsa logs. The more I pulled the easier it got and my hands sped up. Obviously there was nothing on the hook. Then the form of a hammerhead shark materialized on the surface of the water, a streamlined gray fish, like a miniature submarine, with our heavy fishing line disappearing into its mouth. It measured about five feet in length and it didn't thrash or fight. *Is it still alive?* Alive or not, it had swallowed the amberjack, and I had to get it off the hook so that we could use the fishing rig on the next night. Instead of bringing it aboard at the stern, where there wasn't any deck to stand on, I left it in the water and walked forward with the line in my hand, towing the shark through the water.

On the foredeck, I pulled the gray fish up on the bamboo canes. *How do I get the hook out?* Just to make sure there weren't any surprises, I put on some work gloves and then stepped on its head. Frenzy! It was alive! It thrashed around on the foredeck as though it had been, up to that moment, asleep! It was threatening to go over the side, so I grabbed it by the tail. Heyerdahl had said that holding a shark up by the tail paralyzes it. *Fine. I'll just hold it upside down until it stops thrashing around.*

The minute I got it up in the air it tried to bite me. It weighed no more than forty pounds, so I held it out to one side with my right arm. It could, however, turn its head at a right angle to its body and almost reach me. At full-arm extension I could just barely separate myself from its gnashing teeth. Then it started twisting its head back and forth, swinging its whole body like a pendulum, and at the end of each long swing it would grind its teeth. It wasn't terrifying in any way, but thank God no one saw me: a lone man in the dark, dancing around in his underwear, holding a snapping shark out at arm's length.

It went on interminably; the fish wouldn't die. My right arm tired quickly, and I had to pass it out in front of me to my left hand, changing my dance step dramatically. *Why doesn't it die?* After a few minutes I gave up, thinking the whole paralysis theory hopeless, and just let it flap around in the center of the deck. In the morning, we ate it.

3

Madness at Sea:
Aboard *Illa-Tiki*

The wind died in the early hours of April 1, our fourth day out from Salango, and when the sun arose we awoke to total calm. During the previous three days we had moved roughly a hundred nautical miles to the northwest. That was not the course we wanted. The voyage to Hawaii required us to sail due west, staying south of the equator until well out to sea. But the ocean current had now taken total control. Sitting in the still air, unable to fill our sail, we drifted helplessly past the equator and toward the Equatorial Counter Current.

Our fishing operations had been almost completely futile. While underway we had run into a group of fishermen who's home port was a town near Salango. They were working a patch of ocean like farmers might work a flat field, going back and forth on their "land," casually walking on their boats, checking their lines, and harvesting their catch. We sailed by their fishing grounds, and when they spotted the raft, they sent a *fibra* over to check on us.

Three small wiry men came gliding alongside us in their *fibra,* gently bumping the balsa logs with their fiberglass hull. They wore ragged working clothes and two of them had tied T-shirts over their heads to protect themselves from the radiation. The smallest of the group reached inside the *fibra*'s hold and pulled out a beautiful dorado. He handed it to me and said, "Fry it or fillet it or whatever you want. Enjoy." Besides this fortunate incident, the quantity of fish aboard *Illa-Tiki* had been meager. We were now on a strict rationing program, trying not to dig into our stored reserves.

After breakfast on the morning of the first, Dower and Chris went out about two hundred yards in the dinghy to do some filming of the raft. It was hot and bright out and the sea was exceedingly calm. The rest of us stayed aboard to work on the radio. The marine VHF unit had been working before we left port, but the high-frequency unit, or shortwave, had not. I sat at the radio table, testing the shortwave unit, and in the afternoon I stumbled across a gentleman named Owen, operating his radio from Pine Island, Florida. "Owen," I said into the little plastic microphone, "can you get on the land line, call an operator named Dick Hoff, and have him call me on this frequency?"

"Roger. What is your location?"

"I am off the coast of Colombia, floating on a forty-four foot balsa raft."

". . . OK," he said. There was a pregnant pause. It was April 1—April Fool's Day. It must have taken a lot of trust for him to say: "I, I, I'll call him."

We worked on the raft for the rest of the day, tightening ropes, stowing gear, and modifying the sail, which had been made too long and was dragging on the foredeck. The calm continued throughout the night, and on the next day I made radio contact with Dick Hoff, The Expedition's radio coordinator in the United States.

I was elated that the radio station was working. It raised the spirits of the others too, but by that evening our plan for sailing due west was starting to fade, and with it, our buoyant sprits. We continued to drift in an unfavorable current. *Illa-Tiki* was a very slow vessel, so an unfavorable current of even just one knot could play havoc on our desired course. Calms—when we could not get underway—could destroy our course, and our plans, completely.

For the next five days, from the second to the sixth, we traveled 130 nautical miles to the northwest in a series of short winds and calms. We drifted hundreds of miles off course, we fought desperate battles against the cruel sail, and we were hungry and losing weight; but it was Frederick's mania that now dominated every aspect of life aboard the raft. Written in my notes from this period is, simply: "Desperation of Frederick."

"Desperation" encompassed the entire personality of this strange man. Frantic nervousness radiated out of him and catastrophe threatened his life every day. Every problem, regardless of its significance, held the seeds of doom, and he felt that only a fool could not see this. There was always a tension in his speech, and natural laughter eluded him. He forced his laugh, straining his neck and throat to force out air—the type of laugh that was no laugh at all. He was unable to relax, and sometimes I let him do things like put extra holes in the *guaras* for no other reason than it kept his nervous mind occupied for a while.

Frederick had infected sores on his hands, arms, and feet. He had "lived in the jungle," and told us that the sores were the effects of a rare tropical disease. He had worked out an elaborate explanation to justify his belief that he was infected by something so complicated that it confounded all doctors. According to Frederick it caused "holes" to form in a person's flesh, and if the doctors he had gone to had been unable to identify it, then that was only natural—it was the first of its kind ever discovered, an original, completely unlike any other in the history of diseases.

Normal activity on the raft produced a variety of cuts and scrapes on all of us, but Frederick obsessed over every break in his skin. These cuts and scrapes became part of his "tropical disease," which gave him an excuse to use his masochistic ritual for dealing with them: He'd pour hydrogen peroxide on a scratch or a cut until the tissue softened, and then tear out the flesh with a pair of surgical pliers, or hemostats. This quickly caused trauma and infection all over his body, which reinforced his theory that he must continue to eradicate the "disease." Working around the sharp bamboo canes produced plenty of new wounds to torture.

Each afternoon, during this time, Frederick would sit on a large box in the middle of the foredeck, and I'd sit in the hut at the radio table, looking at him through the doorway. The raft would be sailing in the sunshine, lazily rolling back and forth, and Frederick would sit, minute after minute, concentrating on those raging sores. He picked at them with nervous intensity. He'd bend his long body over to get a close up view of an ugly sore on his hand, hunch up his shoulders, and then carefully pour peroxide into a wound. Once the peroxide had bubbled up and spilled out, he'd shake it off, and then meticulously pour in more. This would go on sometimes for more than an hour. Then the ripping would start. Taking a pair of gleaming steel hemostats, he'd clamp down on his softened, whitened flesh, and then slowly pull. His face wouldn't quiver or shake as he did this, not as you might expect; on the contrary, as the flesh would elongate and stretch into a strip and then snap out he would seem to be at his calmest, or, better said, at his most Frederick. *Illa-Tiki* would roll on, the sun would beat down, and slowly, meticulously, he'd widen and deepen each wound until it was the size of a dime, and half an inch deep. In just a few days he exhausted our copious supply of hydrogen peroxide. Unfortunately, and almost unbelievably, I rationalized it all away, and tried to concentrate only on moving forward.

By April 7, ten days out from Salango, I knew we'd have to pass close to Central America if we were to reach Hawaii. We were now in such a position that if we continued to move west we'd enter the worst part of the Equatorial Counter Current: The Gyre. To avoid it we'd have to sail north and pass near Costa Rica. This would circumvent an area notorious for its impossible sailing conditions. In The Gyre, calms sometimes lasted for several months.

On the eighth, we were reported missing. Both the U.S. Embassy in Quito and an Ecuadoran television station received reports of a mysterious radio message saying: "We're breaking up . . ." The only way for anyone to communicate with us was through scheduled radio contacts, and frequently several days passed between these contacts. The shipwreck was reported thirty-six hours before our next scheduled contact, and in the meantime it set off a chain reaction of events on land, which we on the raft did not know were occurring.

At eleven o'clock on Sunday morning, April 9, Dick Hoff called my mother. He had bad news. My mother received the news as calmly as she could, then drove to Dick's radio station. At noon, she and others, including Annie, gathered to hear whether or not we were, indeed, still intact. Dick tuned up the radio, the antenna, and his transmitting tower out back. Then he called across the airwaves. There was nothing but static. He called for fifteen minutes with no response. Dick was a businessman from middle America, a radio aficionado, and he had innocently volunteered to work on The Expedition just because he wanted to help—now he would have to turn around and explain to our families that we were gone. Trying every trick he knew, he adjusted knobs, called some more, and then made more adjustments. Each time he called, the families crowded him more and more. At times he thought he heard me through the static, but he couldn't be sure. His dread increasing, he at last became desperate and said into the microphone, "John, if everything is OK, say, 'Roger, Roger, Roger.'"

Aboard *Illa-Tiki,* we were fighting the sail, which made me late for the scheduled radio contact. By the time I tuned to the right frequency, I heard only: ". . . say 'Roger, Roger, Roger.'" It was definitely Dick's voice, so I said, "Roger, Roger, Roger." From two thousand miles away, over the radio, I could hear my mother gasping with relief.

Dick communicated our position to the Ecuadoran navy, and within half an hour, two aircraft appeared on the horizon. They came roaring in at low altitude, two airplanes over a wide-open, flat sea. One was a small jet, which made a pass over us and then left. The other was a large turboprop transport that flew a series of wave-top-level passes. When it swooped by the last time we saw the pilot, in helmet, visor, and mask, signal "Thumbs up." Then he climbed and headed over the horizon.

While in radio contact with Dick Hoff, I explained Frederick's condition: He had approximately five sores on his hands and arms and we needed to talk to a doctor about it, but there was no emergency. Regardless of my suspicions of masochism, Frederick *did* have horrific boils all over his body. *What if he's really infected by a "rare tropical disease?"* Even if he didn't have a disease, I couldn't just let him self-destruct; the welfare of the men was my responsibility. Evacuation could be as far away as two days or more, and if I didn't take his condition seriously I'd be responsible for a serious illness, or a death. The circumstances seemed to justify collaboration with a highly dubious situation. You must understand that this was my first expedition—I knew nothing of strange behavior in isolation and confinement. But because I mobilized the entire expedition to treat his "disease," I perpetuated the problem. My actions reinforced his mania, which motivated him to try to convince me and everyone else that we had it too. He even volunteered to demonstrate his special method for dealing with our cuts and scratches. I said I might be willing to take antibiotics, but like the others I wasn't willing to be a part of his masochistic obsessions. When he offered to perform the procedure for me, I declined.

During the radio contact, there was a suggestion by someone that Frederick try putting "moistened tobacco over the boil until it comes to a head." That horrified me and I quickly tried to suppress the idea, but for Frederick, it provided all the license he needed. He immediately went into the hut and began rummaging through his personal belongings, then ducked out of the doorway with several bottles of evil-looking chemicals in his trembling hands. Sitting down on the box in the glaring sunlight, he got started. For the next three days he hunched over his hands and feet, nervously torturing himself by slowly pouring brown and black liquids directly into his flesh. His sores mutated into hard black pockets of dead tissue. The one at the base of his thumb was his favorite. He widened it into a hideous crater, large enough to fit a quarter inside it and half an inch deep. None of the sores developed into normal infections because he was taking antibiotics, but they couldn't heal either; his torture regimen was too disciplined for that; he kept them alive and angry through cold-blooded efficiency.

The tropical disease story had worked well on land, but now that he was creating new sores out on the sea he needed a more elaborate explanation. The new explanation went like this: You simpletons! You can't understand! This disease isn't simple! It's complex! His cuts and scratches looked just like ours did when they were fresh, yes, but that meant nothing! He explained to us that his tropical disease fooled its victim into believing that it wasn't really there.

A cut or scratch appeared harmless simply as a disguise to throw you off the trail. One could say that the thing had a mind of its own—that's why it was so successful! It couldn't be trusted, and it couldn't fool Frederick. He would dutifully dig down into his flesh until the thing was exposed, and eradicated.

But I am telling you my story with the benefit of hindsight. During that insane voyage of 1995, I knew nothing. If someone would have come to me at that time and said, "Beware," I might have scoffed. I would have reasoned that maybe he was just nervous about being on a raft, maybe he had just lost his head a little near Puerto Rico on that first day, and maybe his "tropical disease" was serious. This type of rationalizing is exceedingly dangerous. Herman Melville, in writing his masterpiece *Moby Dick,* knew full well of this danger when he described a ship's company's reaction to the first stirrings of pathological behavior. Melville had himself made long voyages into isolation, and so when his fictitious crew was faced with the freakish Captain Ahab, he made sure that their reaction was denial and rationalization—they too were made to say, "Maybe just this . . ." or "Maybe just that . . ." Then, soon, a ship's crew is following the pathological man because they want to appease him, to keep the peace, and because it seems like a small matter. This is precisely what happened to us. By appeasing this man, by giving into his mania, we were essentially *following him.* We seemed to simply spin around Frederick like a whirlpool, with his mania sucking us in like a vortex. Had he been a total idiot or obviously crazy from the beginning it would have been a different matter. But Frederick always acted as though he was the most knowledgeable, and I can assure you that it is entirely possible for a crew of stable men to follow an unstable man if he plays his role of "most knowledgeable" well enough.

Frederick did many things well—or so it seemed. In the first week he repaired our sail by sewing it into a more functional shape. He established an air of erudition and superiority early on by claiming that he was a marine biologist and speaking vaguely about his "research" on seabirds. He played his role of "veteran" very well, and at various times he referred to individuals onboard as "lazy," "childlike," and "stupid." Sometimes he would entertain us with proud stories of how he liked to antagonize strangers until they started fights with him. These stories were designed to show how he could always get the best of people with simple minds. He condescended well, but it went deeper—there was a darkness. He was a cold, hollow, cynical man, who felt that any sign of brotherhood was in reality a sign of childish romanticism. When he caught me pushing a tiny portion of my rice onto Chris's plate one day he launched into a five-minute harangue about how honored we should all feel to be in the presence of such a great martyr! In this atmosphere I played the role of journeyman. And why not? This was my first expedition, and I had never made an ocean voyage. We were silly, romantic amateurs, but he had "lived in the jungle."

Shortly after the reporting of our shipwreck, we caught a dorado. The catch relieved the hunger for a while, but soon the tension rose to catch another.

From the ninth to the thirteenth, we sailed and drifted 150 miles in a clumsy course to the northeast. Again we stumbled through a series of light air and calms. The wind changed direction every day and sometimes several times in a twenty-four-hour period. For a week we drifted, sailed, and floundered in the unpredictable currents and searing waters of the Equatorial Counter Current. The fights with the sail intensified. Each day the canvas monster knocked down or threw someone overboard. There was no adventure or excitement in any of it. It horrified us to watch each other being cruelly beaten by the giant canvas machine. We'd be cruising along, the sail tightly inflated and pulling the raft well, and then the sail would unexpectedly go wild in the changing winds.

Suddenly the canvas is a piece of steel the size of a house, flapping, snapping, cracking. It spits out a malignant crackle, acidic, almost electric, like the crackling of a blown power line. I grab a corner of the canvas and it shakes me violently. It is like trying to hold back a steel machine. It flaps my body like a rag. My feet come off the ground and my body slams down on the bamboo canes. Chris tries to grab the sail but it hits him in the neck and shoulders and flings him overboard. "Grab that line!" Brock grabs it with his right hand. He looks like a man trying to hold back a very powerful animal on leash. He squats, then sits. Dower runs up and sits down in front of him and grabs the line. The line is dragging them. They are sitting down on the deck to maximize their resistance. They are spreading their legs and leaning back onto the bamboo canes, trying to make their bodies like anchors. Dower loses his grip, and Brock is dragged to the edge and almost overboard before he lets go. The sail flies out of control! I am standing in the center of the deck, looking up at a three-story canvas monster that is angry and shaking and beating the little men. I grab the sail with one hand and cling to a crossbeam with the other. A gust of wind inflates the sail, stretching it out taut. It surges away. *Oh, God, I'm being pulled apart!* The sail rips my arms to their limits! The fibers in my body stretch to dismemberment! I am calling out for someone to help: "Help me! Help me!" The line breaks out of my hand at the moment that I think I'm going to be pulled apart. Now it's out of control again. It cracks like steel. It vibrates the world around us. Out of the corner of my eye I see a black knot shoot through the air, making a low, bass hummmmm. Thwock! The solid thud of a heavy rock hitting a hard container. Brock is down.

He's lying on his side on the canes. He can't get up. His trembling hands cradle the side of his head. His eyes go blank, then come back, then blank, then back. *Did it split his head open?*

"Jesus. He's hurt."

"Brock? Brock?"

The heavy knot, soaked in seawater, has hit him between the temple and the ear. His eyes are blank. He struggles to get up, but we hold him for a minute. He gets up, then appears to be about to kneel down, then stands upright, wavering. "I can't hear," he croaks. "I can't hear out of my ear." He stands for a moment, propped against a water barrel, bewildered.

Brock's head injury was questionable. He wasn't clearheaded for the next twelve hours, and as those hours passed we became more and more concerned. It had been a hard blow, and dreadfully loud. He struggled to function, but in the morning he said he thought he could keep going.

We were now fighting the Equatorial Counter Current and the Pacific Ocean. Fighting a vast entity that does not sleep is demoralizing. It was ugly, physical combat, and we were losing. For a week we basically went nowhere. Each day when we looked at the GPS receiver, it presented us with a new, strange, inexplicable position. The currents pushed us east, then west, and then south—*backward,* toward Ecuador.

Frederick radiated more desperation and more chaos every day. He multiplied our difficulties by being uncooperative. If I told him to raise a *guara* at a critical time, he frequently lowered it. If I told him to pull in on a sheet, he would let it out. I sometimes had to stop what I was doing and walk to some other part of the raft to demand that he cooperate. His sores still raged. One day during this hellish period a Colombian fishing boat appeared on the horizon, coming toward us. Frederick said that we must ask them for medicine.

The *Oyster* was a fast fishing boat. Dower had heard it while it was still on the other side of the horizon, and when it came over the curvature of the earth, it was making better than twelve knots. When it stopped, about fifty yards off our port side, Dower and I paddled over in the calm sea.

Six men, ragged and skinny, gathered at the railing to help us come aboard the *Oyster*. Their vessel was a sixty-foot long-liner from the Port of Tumaco, two hundred nautical miles to the southeast, in Colombia. A plethora of green sea grass grew on its hull and gray primer showed through a thin top coat of white paint, as did a good amount of rust. The trappings of a typical long-liner lay on its quarterdeck: lines, hooks, bait buckets, buoys, and flags. Upon boarding we immediately asked the crew how the fishing was and they immediately replied, "Nothing," "Very bad," "Nothing at all."

Their captain walked astern and met Dower and me on the quarterdeck and shook our hands. He was a large man, well groomed and serious looking, and obviously concerned for our safety. Our two vessels drifted near each other in the calm water while I explained The Expedition to him, and then dutifully asked for medicine, which made me very uneasy: The Colombians sailed aboard a modern vessel, but the crew was essentially poor. The captain gave me a bottle of antibiotics, which were expired, and I thanked him, left the *Oyster,* and boarded the raft. The crew waved at us and then left as quickly as they had come, making good speed with their purring diesel engine. Dower noted that Colombian fishermen in this area have a reputation for being *buena gente* ("good people").

The pain was starting to overwhelm Frederick. The new level of brown and black masochism produced a positive result: The relentless picking slowed a little. We also made two short-wave radio contacts with doctors during this time in which they told him to wash the sores with soap and water and then leave them alone. Each of us aboard had given him the same advice, and now, cornered by so many who were telling him to stop, he had to relent a little. He was still, however, unwilling to cooperate whenever we tried to handle the raft. A miserable tension had developed aboard *Illa-Tiki,* and I sat some days and thought of only one thing: how to cope with this man. I had prepared for this expedition for years, but I had never prepared for Frederick. I had made contingency plans for many things, but havoc aboard the raft had never occurred to me. The *Illa-Tiki* Expedition had worked through every obstacle and had solved every problem in a relentless two-year push to make the dream a reality. We had always moved forward, but now, just seventeen days into the voyage, we stopped: I was paralyzed. I was like an adult who had never had any kids of his own suddenly put in charge of a large, emotionally disturbed child. But more than that, Frederick was inside my mind now, torturing me. More than just the screaming tantrums, more than the refusal to cooperate, the freakish disease, and the masochism—more than all these, the *darkness* of the man had begun to drain my blood.

I had become an expeditioner because of a brilliant, unquestioning idealism: I would do a thing that would make my life great. Regardless of what they claimed at the time, this was precisely what drove explorers to circumnavigate the globe, to journey to the poles, and to stand on the moon. Hopefully it will put people on Mars. When even just a tiny shred of this idealism is present, then all things can be endured—the beatings, the hunger, even the failed plans. It is this mentality that makes the suffering worthwhile. But it was gone now. Frederick had methodically crushed it with the same relentless wrenching that he used to eradicate his disease. The fall from idealism to disillusionment was much like the grim reality that comes over soldiers who go off to war believing in a great cause and then experience a series of dirty little murders. Suddenly, the fight in them is gone. Thor Heyerdahl's *Kon-Tiki* had been a voyage into paradise, and on some level we had all thought that the voyage of the *Illa-Tiki* would inevitably develop into the same paradise, into a deep breath of fresh air—the fullest life that a human being can live on this earth. It was nothing like that. It was not paradise. Frederick's mania suffocated me. I felt a cancerous presence crawling all over the raft. He told me once, with a look of blissful malice on his face, "I love catastrophe: people screaming—things breaking—I *love* it." I slept next to him in our tiny bamboo room and each morning my first image upon waking was his hollow face. Other than the death of my father when I was twelve, the voyage of the *Illa-Tiki* was the darkest moment of my life. My expedition had degenerated into drifting on the ocean with a venal, pathological, antihero.

On the fifteenth, in the morning, I awakened to more trouble. I vaguely remember hearing Frederick's voice and something that sounded like a radio contact. I came out of a foggy sleep knowing that something was wrong, but not really comprehending what. Getting up quickly, I went out on deck—out into blinding sunlight—and saw off our starboard side an enormous white freighter, the 15,700-ton *Santiago Star*: Frederick had stopped a ship.

I was mortified. He had radioed them and told their captain that his situation was serious. By the time I awoke, they had already agreed to stop, and the giant white ship was already starting its two-mile slowdown. I stood now at the doorway of the hut and stared at the colossal *Santiago Star*, just one hundred yards away, sitting on the sparkling blue water like an enormous white castle. The spectacle stunned me for a moment, and then I looked over at Dower. He could only shrug. Like me, he was unsure; like me, he wavered: Regardless of whether Frederick was out of control, the way he was going he would soon exhaust his supply of antibiotics. He had pulled a radical stunt, but it would be irrational to refuse assistance now that they had stopped. Rational thought now dictated that we must go through with it.

Ducking back into the hut, I picked up the microphone and called the captain of the *Santiago Star*, apologizing profusely for the inconvenience, and then asked if we could do anything to speed the process. He said no, told me he was happy to lend assistance, and then told me to stand by for him to make a pass, at which time he would send over a buoy with the antibiotics in it.

I was incensed, but remained silent. Frederick was burdening professional mariners, and I hated being dependant on their sense of seamanship (and fear of liability). Moreover, the *Santiago Star* was a food carrier, which meant that its cargo (probably bananas) was highly perishable. A vessel of this type must run on a rigid schedule because delays ruin the cargo. The *Santiago Star* had probably been near its maximum cruising speed, twenty-two knots, when Frederick had stopped it. He was forcing its crew to slow down, change course, come about, and make a pass close to us. They would then have to lend us assistance, make sure we were all right, and finally waste a huge amount of fuel pushing their heavy ship back up to cruising speed.

Santiago Star was a beautiful white ship, with tan trim on its superstructure and royal blue below the waterline. It had a fine, high bow, and eight masts towering from its deck. As it majestically passed us, a tiny-looking man at the railing threw an orange object overboard. I wanted to retrieve it myself because it would give me some time away from Frederick, but I sent Brock and Dower instead. They launched the dinghy and immediately started paddling at full strength. I stayed behind and stood in the doorway of the hut, between Frederick and the radio.

Measuring 568 feet in length, the *Santiago Star* was almost one hundred times larger than our dinghy. As Dower and Brock approached the freighter they were dwarfed by its size. We could see them paddling frantically in the little boat, climbing and bouncing over the enormous bow wave that the ship had kicked up. Bright orange smoke was now billowing out of a marker grenade attached to the "emergency" package, and they headed right for it. The timing of the drop and rendezvous had been good; the smoke grenade began to die out just as the dinghy reached the buoy. We saw Brock and Dower lunge over the side of the inflatable boat, grab the package, haul it aboard, and then hurriedly grab their paddles. They turned around and began digging water, their heads bowing down in the rhythm of each hard stroke. It was a clean transfer and they returned to *Illa-Tiki* within ten minutes.

We had now taken medicine from two vessels on the high sea. This weighed heavily on me. No amount of antibiotics could reverse the ravages of Frederick's self-inflicted, self-destruction. But we lived on a raft, adrift in a vast ocean. We were an isolated group of desperate men with very little connection to the outside world. In this environment I couldn't afford the luxury of smug certainty. What if, by chance, Frederick's hysteria was legitimate? What if a rare tropical disease indeed threatened his life?

As we drifted on the open sea we began to see that the raft was changing; the vessel itself was growing. Primordial things emerged out of it. Bright green sea grass sprouted from the massive balsa logs and then grew until it hung down like stringy moss in a prehistoric swamp, with long brown barnacles dwelling inside it like ugly Pleistocene worms. A community of creatures now inhabited *Illa-Tiki*'s sides, its cracks, its little pockets and tunnels. Juvenile fish lived in the splits of the logs and tiny crabs lived under the little tentlike shelters created by the crisscrossed ropes. Sometimes when you swam alongside the raft you saw a dozen or so little creatures ducking back into their houses all at once, like the frightened inhabitants of a city street. At times I couldn't help but notice that a steady series of beady little creature eyeballs were watching me when I swam past their homes. Farther below, when you went under the raft and looked up, you saw the Black Barge, the Leviathan. Underneath it was a different world, a private, silent world, lit by soft, cool light. The incessant equatorial sun had plagued us for months, but when the massive *Illa-Tiki* cruised overhead it suddenly disappeared and you momentarily entered a dark netherworld. At various places, where the sun leaked through the raft, brilliant shafts of tropical sunlight shot down and disappeared into the depths of the infinite Pacific—Chris called them "God rays." No technology had ever been in this place; underneath the raft, Nature was starting all over again. A lush ecosystem of primitive plants and animals was forming, and that had attracted a nation of fish. None of them were what we, the Hungry, could eat; but we now owned and even lived in an awesome aquarium.

Layers upon layers of fish congregated below the *Illa-Tiki*: One layer at a depth of three feet, and then another at six feet, and another at ten, and so on. They were following *Illa-Tiki*—following it but not imitating it. They continuously shot back and forth under the raft, swimming two miles for every one of the raft's. I can only describe them as like a happy group of small children on a playground, running in random directions, barely organized, expanding in size and collapsing in size and never moving in a straight line. Sometimes the crystal-clear seawater vibrated with thousands of wiggling yellow tailfins. There were schools of blue-striped and gold-striped snappers, orange and yellow angelfish, amberjacks, tan-and-black or yellow-and-white, with sharp black lines across their faces as though wearing masks over their eyes, and of course there were the ever-present triggerfish, black and hard and small, slicing and flitting around the periphery, scavenging for our leavings.

But the little creatures weren't the only inhabitants of the raft. We five now lived a daily life atop thirty-eight parallel bamboo canes, while all around us the eternal surf washed against our little wooden island. Thousands of pounds of seawater flooded in and ebbed away every minute, hissing and sloshing. In every direction there was nothing but endless blue ocean, the only feature being the earth's curvature, its edge. On a typical day a light wind would blow and the raft would lilt forward under gray-and-white clouds. Each man would usually be occupied with his own interests, bathing, reading, or sailing the raft. Wet laundry now hung all around the front of our little bamboo house, swinging gently and slinging drops. Dower could usually be found sitting on a wooden box with his back against the hut, watching the compass and singing absent-mindedly. Almost invariably he wore only his underwear, and looked completely at home on the sea. He sang to the ocean, sang to us, and sang to himself. His voice would drift around the deck, mixing with the monotonous sloshing of water and the creaking of taut ropes. Dower was, in reality, trying to keep up the morale on the raft. This was his heroism. He sang, danced, told jokes, made hilariously sarcastic remarks, and always avoided confrontation. He would also try to accentuate any positive development, regardless of how small, like the catching of a fish or fair weather, and he always tried to engage all of us in warm conversation, as though we were just on any other voyage. In this way he saved me, and the others. His songs, which he sang at all hours of the day and night, were an off-key hodgepodge of salsa favorites, romantic classics, and hilarious spontaneity. They always ended with some message for his beautiful Carina, back in Salango: "O beautiful Carina, I love you so, but you probably don't love me anymore because only a moron would get on a raft and leave you alone! Ah ha ha ha!"

By now a routine had set in on the raft. We awoke to the same weather every day: sunny and hot, the seas rarely higher than five feet. We usually checked our position on the GPS in the mornings. I posted the positions on the radio table, and we talked about them all of the time. Everyone onboard kept a detailed journal, especially Chris. He spent many hours making extensive notes and entries, and over time he developed into the record keeper of The Expedition. He was good at it, and he always knew any minor detail that you asked.

Much of our fresh food was gone by this time. The banana stalks hanging from the back wall of the hut were now wilting and turning brown. A few yellow bananas still remained, and in a few days we would cut the stalks down and hurl them into our wake. Our supply of carrots grew patches of dark brown mold within the first ten days of the voyage, but we had eaten most of them by then. The potatoes lasted longer, but by the fifteenth they had either been eaten or had gone bad. Soon the beans began to rot. Frederick sat on deck every few days and meticulously picked out the moldy, fuzzy beans out of the bunch, one by one, and threw them overboard. Brock and Chris, especially, enjoyed eating and drinking the coconuts. They'd chop off the tops of the nuts, insert a straw, then spend twenty minutes trying to slurp up the abundant milk inside. We of course fished all of the time and usually there was a large plastic bowl on deck with various fish meats in it: Vanilla-colored dorado steaks, low-grade shark steaks, and sometimes whole amberjacks. The dorado was excellent and the amberjacks satisfactory, but the shark meat usually turned gray quickly and was difficult to get down.

One day, while we were cooking, the water next to the stove solidified into the form of a whale. It surfaced next to us like a massive submarine. Water cascaded off of its sides and it blew out its enormous breath, releasing it in the same way a human might if he had stayed down a little too long. Then it drew in a deep breath of fresh air and released it in a long sigh, spraying little drops out of its blowhole and making a tiny rain shower all around us. The drops sprinkled down onto my arms and my skin prickled from the sudden, icy shock. Feeling the drops on my arm proved to me that the experience was real: I was standing next to the greatest animal in the sea. There were at least two of them near the raft now, and we could hear their vacuous lungs inhaling and exhaling, making a remarkably humanlike noise—breathing in and out, in and out. Their black skin shone and glinted in the sunlight as they cruised by at less than two miles per hour, surfacing for a moment, looking at us, and then arcing back under in shallow dives. The one that surfaced next to the stove was clearly examining us, and our raft. Its enormous eye, black and white like a billiard ball, rotated in its socket, looking up and down and back and forth, as though memorizing the raft's measurements.

The whales stayed no more than five minutes. Throughout all of my voyages I always noticed that whales always seemed to be on their way somewhere, as though they had an itinerary—a schedule to keep—like people on their way to the office. The other inhabitants of the sea always scurried about, either following something else or completely confused, but not the whales; they were very businesslike: They stopped by, examined us, and then went on. Those that cruised next to us that day were roughly the size of the raft. A few days later, more appeared, and Chris and I went over the side to swim with them.

The visibility of the seawater that day was roughly a hundred feet. *Illa-Tiki* crawled along at less than one knot and Chris and I hung back behind the raft, holding onto the lifeline, our bodies slipping smoothly through the soft, salty water. Every few seconds we'd pull the snorkels out of our mouths and yell at each other in fabulous excitement: We were alone in a vast ocean, swimming with the greatest animals in the sea. After about a minute or so of this, a whale passed within a hundred feet of me, and so I hurriedly swam out to it, pulling my body through the water as fast as I could. I wanted to see it underwater of course, but it maintained its distance from me. I am unsure whether it was swimming away from me in fear, or just returning to its business, but on my next-to-last dive I finally saw it. It was in front of me, less than seventy-five feet away. The whale I saw that day through the seawater was like a pointillist painting, or a digital image, not fully completed. But I could make out many important features, especially its huge tail. Its massive body was upside down—its nose pointed toward the bottom of the ocean and its tail toward the surface. Then I ran out of breath and had to surface. When I dove again I saw the enormous animal make a singular kick with its tail and rocket downward into the depths of the sea. It disappeared in less than one elapsed second. If I had not witnessed it with my own eyes I would not have believed its velocity through the water. Unfortunately, I can only compare its sudden movement through the water as being like animation—like a cartoon. It didn't seem to swim away or travel as a living animal might: With one mighty kick of its tail—in less than the blink of an eye—the eighty-thousand-pound animal simply disintegrated into the blue abyss.

Other animals visited us, especially sea turtles. They would come swimming up from nowhere and mistake *Illa-Tiki* for an island, where they'd try to "come ashore." Picking them up and examining them was no problem at all, and occasionally we'd hoist the heavy animals up by the shell, gripping them in both hands like boulders, straining under their weight to hold them out in front of our bodies so that we could examine them. They made no effort to fight and usually seemed calm in our presence. Invariably green and black, they sometimes also had bright red stripes on the tail end of their shells. They usually weighed no more that fifty pounds, although occasionally we saw some that were larger. When we'd put them back in the water they'd swim away lazily, gliding, breast stroking down into the infinite blue, back to their life in the open sea. Years later, a friend of mine would describe them as "the loneliest animals in the world."

Chris and I spent many nights looking down through the canes at the schools of mackerel and snapper that lit up the glittering green phosphorescence in the dark seawater. These schools of small fish would agitate the ocean's phosphorescence so much that they would create a sparkling cloud directly under our feet, which was a new and surreal experience. Thousands of tiny lights would orbit the raft, silent and moving as a single unit, constantly changing shape in the black water, sweeping in wide arcs underneath us, turning sharply and spinning around their own axis like a swarm of ghostly green bees. This was one of the most entertaining things about being on night watch, and even after we had been seeing it for weeks, we still stood for minute after silent minute, watching the green ghost, just below our feet.

Chris and Brock were now standing many of their night watches together, during which they could be heard laughing and talking. I can remember many nights, waking up in the dark, exhausted, preparing myself for my watch, lying there in the little bamboo room just above the surface of the sea, listening to the sounds of our little isolated world: Water sloshing, small wavelets breaking into whitecaps, the squeak of the pulley atop the mast, the *"tick tick tick"* of a hundred lines straining and relaxing, and the sounds of two men, obviously friends, talking and laughing, their voices muffled and floating, as though coming from a dwindling campfire.

Their friendship had started back in Salango when they had taken a series of trips to various towns on the coast to gather equipment. During those trips they bought hundreds of small items for the voyage. At sea, they always had that little part or device that was indispensable. You have, no doubt, taken trips with these sorts of people yourself. They were the ones with massive amounts of luggage and an endless assortment of equipment, all of which seems highly suspicious—until you're in trouble. Week after week Chris and Brock magically produced that one tiny thing that instantly removed an impossible obstacle: Extra fishing gear, extra light sources, tools and equipment to clean the electrical gear, medical supplies, and much, much more.

Dower of course sang when he was on watch. When he stood there at night, looking out over the ocean and watching for ships, he seemed to accept the darkness and emptiness before him as though he were completely unimpressed. In the course of his life he had lived and worked on Boston whalers, fishing trawlers, midsized long-liners, small freighters and tankers, sailing yachts, lighters, tenders, inflatables, and canoes. And it was when he stood out there at night that he clearly defined himself, and when I really came to understand him: I never felt that he loved the ocean, not consciously anyway—he had never studied it and it certainly held no romance for him—but the years of sleeping on the vast Pacific, of living at its surface and of swimming along its floor, had installed so many memories in him and had so thoroughly educated his subconscious mind, that being on the sea was as right to him as being on the land. And that had given him a certain type of posture. Dower had the unmistakable posture of a person who had waited on the sea his entire life.

He also possessed uncanny abilities. While others stumbled and fell, Dower always darted across the decks of boats using quick steps, all of them lightly placed. He rarely lost his footing, and he always handled rope beautifully, coiling giant bundles of it effortlessly and untangling massive snarls in just seconds. He never erred in forecasting the weather either, or so it seemed, and after we had been at sea for a while I simply accepted that he could predict the future. Whenever I would ask him about the weather, he would immediately launch into a perfect forecast: "It'll blow from the west for about ten hours, then it will be calm for twenty hours, then . . ."—and say all of it as though it was completely obvious. But these things were small compared to the scene that played out almost nightly aboard the *Illa-Tiki*.

At sea, Dower could hear ships while they were still on the other side of the horizon—long before they could be seen. There were times at night when we'd be asleep in our little bamboo room and suddenly, inexplicably, his mind would awaken. When that happened it would be as though something had shocked him. He'd be sleeping peacefully one minute and then in the next his whole body would shoot out of his sleeping bag in a violent jerk, as though there was an emergency somewhere on the raft. But I'd hear nothing. Startled awake and unsure, I'd sit up just in time to see him rushing to the doorway, stepping over the other sleeping men and calling out over his shoulder, "A ship is coming!"

"Dower? What is it?"

"A ship!"

By this time he'd be standing out in the night air in his underwear and bare feet, staring into the vast Pacific. Ducking through the little doorway in our bamboo house on the sea, I'd call out to the night watchman, usually Chris, "Hey! Did you hear something? Have you seen lights?"

"No! Nothing!"

All around us the ocean would clatter and slosh, a thousand pointed waves washing over massive balsa logs. Unmoved by the ocean's length and breadth, Dower would stand on the bamboo canes relaxed, his mind casually focused on a single point in the infinite darkness. We'd stand for moment after moment, waiting in the darkness, and then I'd have to break the tension by asking him, "You're sure?"

"Of course I'm sure."

"A ship is coming?"

"Yeah," he'd say, and then he'd do a strange thing; he'd invariably point out into the ocean as though pointing at a specific object: "It's *right there*."

But there'd be nothing out there—no light, no movement, no noise—just waves and emptiness. He had heard something that only he could hear, something coming toward him, probably a big iron freighter, coming from as far away as twenty miles across the sea. But he had *felt* something, too, and over the years I came to believe that whenever a big ship came close to him—a ship that could run him down and kill him—he could detect a disturbance in the atmosphere, a change in the air. But we wouldn't hear anything, Chris and I, or feel anything, or perceive anything; we'd just stand there watching Dower loiter, unhurried, like a businessman awaiting the arrival of a scheduled train. The lonely, monotonous sloshing of the ocean would now be joined by Dower's singing voice, cracking and breaking and dipping down and shooting up. We'd wait and wait, and then almost invariably we'd slowly turn to each other and start to smile, chuckling from amazement: It never failed. Sometimes it took awhile, sometimes as long as ten minutes, but out in the black, way out at the very rim of the world, a light would begin to twinkle on the horizon, a single, tiny, pinpoint of white light: a solitary ship, crawling over the curvature of the earth.

I am unsure, even to this day, what Frederick did during his watches. It is possible that he was changing the course of the raft each night, while the rest of us were asleep. Frederick always argued with any course we set during the voyage, regardless of what it was, and many times we would awaken in the morning, check our position, and find ourselves in an inexplicable location. This was not necessarily unusual; I have been on other vessels when an unusual or uncharted current has pushed the boat in a way that was not expected. Frederick later admitted to changing the course of the raft while we slept, but that was during another part of the voyage. Whether or not he was sabotaging our course during this time remains unknown.

I worked around the clock, even while on watch. I had to raise morale, so I spent several days just cleaning and arranging the raft. Within ten days I was fatigued, but I loved the raft nevertheless and I loved being at sea aboard her. When the wind was constant, the *Illa-Tiki* could cross hundreds of miles of ocean effortlessly. It wasn't a vessel made for going across the bay; it was a vessel that went across the earth—less a sailor, more a voyager. Sometimes it rolled at a predictable rhythm for hours, maintaining a good course, and I'd stand at the back of the raft, holding onto the mast stay, my feet awash in the warm seawater, and watch the whole vessel in motion. It was such a flat, stable platform that I sometimes felt like I was riding on the top of a railroad boxcar, rambling across a wide-open plain. In every direction there was good, open sea—millions of square miles of it. Visibility was usually unlimited, and sometimes we would watch as long rows of saltwater dunes rolled in from miles away, creeping toward us at a slow and constant speed. At times like this I'd stand in the warm Pacific sunshine and ride the massive raft across the open ocean. I'd forget the madness for a moment, and my mind would know the exquisite pleasure of living a dream.

.   .   .

From the fifteenth to the twenty-third, we sailed in a wide semicircle: first west, then north, then east. We had been at sea for three weeks and were now trying to cross the Equatorial Counter Current. Our only option was to try to sail north, pass by Central America, then head toward Hawaii.

Frederick's sores were getting a little better. He had used up our supply of hydrogen peroxide in the first few days and his own concoctions had proven a little too painful. The doctors had told him over the radio to leave himself alone, and he had complied, reluctantly. The sores were now starting to heal. Within a few days they turned a nice, healthy, pink.

He obsessed over other things though, especially the sail. In the first week he had demanded that we cut off the bottom of the sail, or foot, to make it more functional. He supervised this modification himself and did extremely well, but then he started obsessing over each individual stitch. He harassed me about it every day, insisting that minor modifications were urgently needed. Saying no or asking him to wait agitated him greatly.

We had all grown beards by now. We were moderately sunburned, and the tropical sun had bleached the hair of the three fair-complexioned men. Our feet swelled from walking on the bamboo canes, and we continued to have problems catching enough fish to feed five men.

For each meal we ate a piece of fish, ranging in weight from one-half to three-quarters of a pound, cooked in vegetable oil, combined with a cup of cooked rice. There are several ways to calculate our food intake and energy output, but in the end, one mathematical reality always emerges: We were consuming roughly two thousand calories a day, but were burning more than four thousand. This is nothing like the deficiencies that many other expeditions have faced, but aboard *Illa-Tiki* some of the men were, for the first time in their lives, subjected to hunger.

Hunger, in its initial stages, creates an urgency that antagonizes its victim every waking moment. It starts slowly, and when the need can never be filled, your life revolves around waiting, unbearably, for something to happen. The tension squeezes your mind harder every day. The clock ticks; you wait; the hunger gnaws.

I was hungry on the raft but it only distracted me at night, when I was on watch and bored. The main reason why hunger did not antagonize me as it did the others was because I had prepared my mind in advance for hardship. Being mentally prepared is critical: If you are expecting hardship, you feel no injustice when the hard times come. If you are expecting good times, hardship feels insulting, unfair, and unjust. Chris, Brock, and Dower had all come from a good home life where they ate well. When there was not enough food to eat for days and days, the hunger slowly broke them down. Their emotional state—their will to carry on—collapsed.

I especially worried about Chris. Hunger crushed him. He had lived an easy, sedentary life back home, and he had been twenty-five pounds overweight when he had come aboard the raft. He was now losing weight at an alarming rate, perhaps as much as twenty pounds in the first twenty days. Now, entering our fourth week, the food supply dwindled even further. Brock kept Chris's spirits up by befriending him and standing watch with him, but he was sleeping twelve hours a day and sometimes more. It was harder and harder to get him to do his work. Within just a few weeks, his spirit had died.

Brock had come aboard with a small layer of fat around an otherwise skinny body. He quickly used up that layer. It was a small amount of weight compared to Chris, but he was now nearing emaciation. Worse, Brock sometimes refused to eat altogether. He said that he didn't like fish that were cooked *au natural*: the head and fins still attached. A week after telling me this, he scraped a tuna steak off of his plate and simply waved his hand, meaning he would eat no more. His beard grew long, like an old man's, and his face sank. He had aggravated his injured ear during a dive under the raft and now he couldn't hear a sound out of it. During the early days of the voyage he had slept little; now he slept like a dead man. The image of Brock that remains with me is of a skinny, bony man, lying on his back in a dark bamboo room. Above him hangs a metal lantern that casts a dim yellow light on his face. His mouth is hanging open like a corpse. He is sleeping the deep, deep slumber of an underfed, exhausted man.

Dower was growing tired of the meager fare as well, and on the afternoon of the nineteenth, after we had been unable to catch enough fish over the previous twenty-four hours, he opened the storage barrels and dug deeply into our reserves. When I talked to him about it he became defensive, saying only, "I have great hunger, John! My stomach is completely empty!" Then he put the cans of food down and went off to be alone. Seeing the normally heroic Dower this way really put the problem in perspective: I had felt only disgust up to that point, disgust for the weakness of the others, because I felt that if I could endure, then they could too. But seeing Dower suffer made me ashamed of forcing hunger on another man. I was suddenly and acutely ashamed of being in charge of an organization that could not feed its people.

These men, especially Chris and Brock, were *declining emotionally*. Their motivation to endure eroded more each day. The hunger, the beatings from the sail, and the madness of Frederick, all combined to shrink down their life force until it couldn't be seen. It was like watching wind-up toys slowly grind to a halt. Chris had all but given up. Brock's refusal to eat seemed to be a signal that he would give up soon as well. Perhaps after years of experience an expedition leader can prevent this, but during The *Illa-Tiki* Expedition of 1995 I could not. I could only endure through grim determination, as did Dower.

But this only explains the behavior of four of the five men on the raft. Frederick's psychological chaos is the chief danger that can be faced by a group enduring *isolation and confinement*. This was made clear in 1957 by the actions of the U.S. Navy's expeditionary team that wintered over at an Antarctic research station near McMurdo Sound. The team worked for months in isolation, and slowly, one man began to exhibit strange behavior, which started as paranoia and ended in "psychotic ravings." It is important to point out that in the end, an entire unit of hearty servicemen became so fearful of this single, pathological man, that they built a special padded cell to cage him in—and soundproofed it so that they wouldn't have to listen to his screaming episodes. They went so far as to tear out the electrical wires in the walls because they feared that he might sabotage the entire station by short-circuiting the wiring. This incident motivated the U.S. Navy and other organizations to begin long-term research into the special problems of isolation and confinement. One of the more comprehensive works to come from this research is Dr. Jack Stuster's *Bold Endeavors,* published in 1996, and widely read among the astronauts of NASA. In his book, Dr. Stuster points out that after decades of study it has become apparent that if an expedition team member isn't unstable before he or she goes into isolation and confinement, being there probably won't destabilize him or her. Perhaps they might decline emotionally, but isolation and confinement alone probably does not create pathological behavior. Based on my own experiences, I believe this conclusion to be accurate. Chris, Brock, and Dower were declining, yes, but they were in no way *unstable*. On the contrary—in spite of the stress, they remained calm and sane. In fact, over the years, I would see many people decline while trying to survive on a raft at sea: They'd eat too much or they'd eat too little; they'd sleep too much or they wouldn't sleep; they'd become sarcastic, depressed, distant, despondent, hopeless, and finally catatonic; they'd go into denial, or into a childlike state, or into any one of a number of other coping states. But no other person on any of the rafts ever showed even the slightest *inclination* toward Frederick's pattern of bizarre behavior, or his frenetic state of mind.

How Frederick felt about the problem of hunger on the raft can only be estimated. It didn't really seem to bother him at all, and then one day he proudly announced that he would eat a triggerfish. Some species of triggerfish contain a neurotoxin called Tetrodotoxin, or TTX. A single milligram of TTX will kill an adult human. Aboard the raft we had no way of knowing which triggerfish were poisonous and which were not. Frederick said it was no problem, then lectured me about having "lived in the jungle." I thought it was beyond him, but then I came around the corner of the hut and saw him nervously eating a triggerfish he had thrown in the frying pan. When nothing happened, he put a piece of its leathery skin between his teeth and skinned the fat off it like you might skin an artichoke leaf. Perhaps it was the look on my face or perhaps he realized that it was unnecessary and insane, but he did not ingest anymore triggerfish for the rest of the voyage. He suffered no ill effects.

Dower and I were now spending entire days trying to catch fish. Together we worked well, but caught only small fish, like jacks and tunas. Sometimes there weren't any fish in the water around the raft at all. We lost several of the large dorados who hit on the bait and then swam straight under the raft, severing the line on the barnacles of the logs. Sometimes a fish would strike and Dower would pull too hard and the line would break and we'd never see that lure again. Several of our best lures were lost this way. The deck of the raft was an open stage, and on two separate occasions we had a fish onboard—actually got it on the bamboo canes—when it wrestled itself off the line and managed to fight its way back to the water. Most of the time the dorados wouldn't hit on the bait we were using, and our homemade lures didn't entice them either.

The jacks and tunas made for meager eating. A single man needed at least four or five jacks a day to keep going. There was still some food left in the barrels, but if we dug into our reserves we'd exhaust them in a month. Between the five of us we had now lost at least eighty pounds. The desperation of a slow, burning hunger now pervaded the raft. We had to catch some big dorados.

Dower told me one day that lures made from a white bird feather were a sure thing. Dorados are attracted to anything white, and a feather shakes and vibrates as it's pulled through the water, just like a wounded fish. White sea birds occasionally landed on the raft, and Dower suggested capturing or killing one of them. I had killed a bird once in the countryside near my home and had immediately felt such a self-disgust that I decided would never kill anything again; but I said I was willing to do this if it meant ending the hunger. Frederick promptly walked out to the bow of the raft and began throwing coconuts at a seabird, shouting: "Fly away, you stupid bird!"

From the doorway of the hut, I yelled, "Frederick! Stop doing that!"

The second I yelled at him I knew I was on the wrong side of a moral argument. He turned around, stuck his head out, and shrieked, stretching his vocal chords past a scream—flattening his face and giving vent to some brittle, glassy noise that came from deep, deep inside: "We're not going to kill any bird! Did you hear what I saaaiiiiiddddd?"

The moment he exploded I wanted his explosion to end. I worried less about the ethical question and more about the picture of the man before me. I understand outrage, and I am fully capable of it; but this was more. This was not a man involved in a typical argument; he *looked* like a madman. There was both anger and fire in eyes, yes, but his eyes were also in a strange way empty—blank—like there was no one home.

There was nothing to say, so I said nothing. But I was also scared. I knew that this was a person who would not be able to stop escalating, a person who would not be able stop his own madness before it went too far. Brock, who was sitting down in the hut, said calmly: "John, we're catching fish. We have a barrelful of food. I don't want to kill a bird; I'm just not a killer."

No bird was killed, and the matter was quickly dropped. It had been a bad idea, dreamed up by desperate men. But the fact that I had *considered the idea* scared me. The madness aboard *Illa-Tiki* had degenerated to a new low. I went to the back of the raft to do some thinking: Hunger? Desperation? Madness? On the opposite side of an unethical argument with someone like Frederick? Was I unstable too? These questions would have seemed incredibly far-fetched just a few days ago; now nothing seemed far-fetched. Frederick's latest episode had been the worst so far, and bone-chilling in its intensity, but ethically he was *right*—herein lay the problem: Five minutes ago I had been willing to consider an act that I would normally consider morally repugnant, and so when Frederick went into a frenzy I once again rationalized away his freakish behavior. The difference between his reaction and Brock's was obvious, but I didn't understand its significance. It was only after years of voyages and experience that I began to really understand what had happened to us aboard *Illa-Tiki*. I didn't realize it at the time, but Frederick was indeed the worst-case scenario: a pathological man in isolation and confinement.

By the twenty-third, we were just two hundred miles from Panama. We knew we would be making land somewhere in Central America, but our main goal was to sail out of the Equatorial Counter Current—the Doldrums. Calms came every day now, and when wind did come it didn't last long enough for us to escape. If we drifted too deeply into the Doldrums, we might remain becalmed for months. We needed to travel just sixty nautical miles—just one degree of latitude—to escape.

Frederick demanded, as always, that we make modifications to the sail. After the sores, it was his favorite obsession. He had demanded to modify it every day of the voyage; but now that there was no wind with which to sail, I couldn't see any harm. For two days Frederick and I sat cross-legged on the bamboo canes in the burning tropical sun, slowly stitching up the white canvas that lay strewn across the foredeck. On the second afternoon, Frederick's hands trembled and his face flattened, then his thin neck twisted backward and he cackled into the air, "I haff another howl!"

He had been washing his "holes" for the last few days as the doctors had told him; but like a chain smoker who has given up the habit cold turkey, it was just a matter of time before he found an excuse to start again. When the sores turned pink and the pain decreased, he switched to using saltwater to clean them, rather than soap and freshwater. Chris and I had seen him dipping seawater out of the ocean. The saltwater helped keep the "disease" alive by inflaming the sores and preventing them from healing, but it wasn't nearly as rewarding for him as his previous level of meticulous carnage.

Finally, in the evening of the second day, we stopped sewing. One small line of less than a dozen stitches remained unfinished, but our hands were exhausted. At dawn on the next day, the wind began to blow. It was a steady wind: Finally, the wind we needed. I looked at Dower and said, "Let's sail—"

"Let's go," he said, simultaneously, and then jumped up and went to work.

Dower and I wrestled the canvas, gathering up billows of it in our arms and sweeping mounds of it with our legs and feet. The raspy clatter of the heavy material folding and bending and crinkling drowned out the sounds of the sloshing ocean. We jumped around the deck in our bare feet for a few seconds, readying lines and canvas, and then we met at the halyard. Standing under the arch of the mast, we reached up, grabbed the halyard, and immediately fell into a rhythmic hauling, hoisting with our weight and then climbing up hand over hand.

Just as the sail inflated nicely and we began to sail, Frederick emerged from the doorway and asked, "What are you doing?" Then he snapped. His personality shattered like a plateglass window exploding into a million pieces on a concrete sidewalk: "Aaaagggghhhh! It's not finished yet! It's not finished yet! It's not finished yet! It's not finished yet!" He sat down in the doorway of the hut and split the air with shrill screams, rocking his boardlike body back and forth like an autistic child. Thick veins bulged from his neck, his skin turned red, and then he reached up with his fingers and began acting as though he was clawing his own face, screaming, "It's not finished yet! It's not finished yet! Aaaagggghhhh!"

"Frederick," I called into the hut, "it's OK."

I don't think he could hear me; his mind had blocked out the outside. "We're going to sail for a while," I said. "Then we can take it down and finish it. It'll be alright."

I was lying about the last part, and it showed. I didn't think it was going to "be alright." I was aghast. I couldn't believe what I was seeing. *How can this be happening?* It was the most disturbing behavior I have ever witnessed. I thought he might lapse into permanent psychosis. He bobbed back and forth, his fingers "clawing" his face, shrieking brittle screams, "It's not finished yet! It's not finished yet! Aaaggghhhh!"

Frederick's screams were a loud release of negative energy from a dark region of the mind that doesn't speak English, or Spanish, or German. They were so brittle and shrill and high-pitched that they penetrated everyone who was there that morning, slicing deeply into our minds, invading and assaulting a place where we kept our own sanity, protected and safe. I could see the other men withering in the face of his hysteria. Brock's face sank and turned ashen. Dower turned away, then looked back at me over his shoulder; like me, he was scared. Frederick's episodes had been spectacular in the past, but I think we all knew, at least subconsciously, that he had just flirted with insanity.

This screaming lived in isolation. By now the outside world had completely dissolved. We were five men on a small platform in the middle of a desert sea, floating alone in a bamboo village, having no human neighbors, spending no money, and knowing nothing of world events. My single remembrance of these days is of a sickened ship. I remember wilted men, traumatized and exhausted. I can still see their faces full of fear and disillusionment. I was firm about one thing, however: Frederick wasn't going to take the sail down. We had to escape the Doldrums. If we didn't sail now, how long would it be until we had another chance? Shortly after Frederick's freakish tantrum over the sail, Brock told me he wanted to leave The Expedition. He wanted to return to his life in the modern world. I told him I wouldn't argue with his decision. He had been miserable, was eating little, and it was clear that something very disturbing was happening aboard *Illa-Tiki*.

Frederick's psychotic outburst made me sick inside, but there was no time to feel sorry for myself: He was starting again. Now it was the dinghy, which we towed behind the raft. He accosted me every day, demanding to bring the dinghy aboard and stow it. He claimed that we would eventually lose it if we continued to tow it behind the raft. This claim wasn't completely irrational. Towing a dinghy behind a sailing boat is usually undesirable because it causes drag and other complications. But our dinghy caused no such problems for *Illa-Tiki*. The little gray boat, tightly inflated and bulbous, trailed behind the massive raft with no trouble at all, gliding smoothly on the flat water in our wake. Dower and I talked it over and neither one of us could see any urgency in bringing it aboard. It created no appreciable drag, and the line wasn't in any danger of parting. There was no place to stow it aboard the raft if it was inflated, and deflating it was a bad idea. So far, two instances had occurred when we had needed the dinghy ready-to-go at a moment's notice. If we awakened in the night to find *Illa-Tiki* coming apart, we probably wouldn't be able to inflate and assemble the dinghy in time to save ourselves. I talked to Frederick several times about it, finally telling him that maybe we could find a compromise. That answer was probably the worst one I could have given him: A vague solution to something over which he obsessed.

More and more, Frederick fixated on the little rubber boat. He went back and forth on the deck, going astern, then coming forward, then astern, then forward. Each day he nervously questioned me. I went to elaborate lengths to appease him without making a commitment. Each day, when I didn't end the obsession, he fidgeted a little more and shrieked a little louder. Again, the tension was growing.

It was starting to rain on us every day now. We had entered Panamanian waters, and the relentless rain showers that keep the Panama Canal full of water were now pouring through our roof. Inside the little bamboo room it seemed as though water hung in the air. Thin columns of rainwater streamed down at various places and gusts of wind slung drops through the crevices in the walls. The sleeping mats were disintegrating under us and sometimes when an ocean wave passed below the raft it would momentarily come up through the floor a few inches. We five men twisted, contorted, hid under sleeping bags and jackets, and rolled ourselves up into little balls to dodge the incoming flood. The dripping seemed especially cruel on Chris. He lay hidden in his dark corner of the hut, with drops loudly pelting his various nylon gear covers, bags, and clothes. In this environment electronics were bound to fail. Water vapor seeped into the radio and the GPS. During the twenty-fifth, twenty-sixth, and twenty-seventh, they started to falter. Soon the radio no longer functioned. We were now cut off. Then the GPS went dead, and I began calibrating my sextant.

One day, during a steady rain, we sat inside the hut with the door and windows closed. Outside it was a dim, gray day. The sea was calm and flat. Cold drops fell straight down through dead air, thumping and crackling on our roof. We had worked a little in the morning, but now, tired and cold and knowing we wouldn't be sailing, we took a moment to rest. Brock read, as did Dower. They lay on their blue sleeping bags, holding their opened books suspended in the air to catch a little shaft of light seeping through the bamboo poles. Chris disappeared into the darkness of his corner, presumably to sleep, and I looked at a chart for a while, lying on my back like Brock and Dower, then closed my eyes and felt a welcome moment of relaxation. I did not realize it, but I had just given Frederick his opportunity. He got his umbrella and went outside.

After a few minutes Frederick called me. "Uhm, John," he said, ducking his head in the entryway. "Uhm, you had better come here, uhm, and see something. Uhm, I mean right away."

I knew by the sound of his voice that something was wrong. I got up, and went out into the downpour. Frederick led me back to the port beam, where he proudly pointed to a small gray object, floating in the ocean about a hundred yards away: the dinghy! The dinghy was floating away from the raft!

"Oh, God," I said.

"The dinghy has broken free—"

"Goddamn it!" I exclaimed, and then looked at him. It was impossible to tell what was going through his mind, but the moment he saw my reaction he stopped talking. Standing on the canes, his face elongated, Frederick had the look of a child who had spent the morning playing with matches, and now, with the house in flames and the fire-truck sirens screaming all around, he suddenly realized that maybe he had gone a little too far.

I pulled my shirt over my head and prepared to swim.

"What are you going to do John?" he asked.

"I'm going out there to get it."

He started to quibble, incredulous that I was willing to swim that far from the raft, but I didn't care at that moment. I dove off the edge of the deck and started swimming through the warm ocean, taking two breaststrokes at a time and then surfacing to get a breath of air. It was good to tire myself out, to rid myself of the anger I felt at that moment. There was no wind and the sea was calm, and because of that the dinghy drifted away at a leisurely rate. By the time I got to it, I had swum about 150 yards from the raft.

Pulling myself aboard the little boat, I began to row back in the rain. The cold drops pelted my bare back, and I sat in the bottom of the dinghy, slowly rowing myself back to the raft. Around me raindrops steadily crackled on the plastic boat and the glassy surface of the water.

The moment I came gliding in through the drops, Frederick began nervously chattering, telling me that this was bound to happen. He held up the end of the line that had been tied to the dinghy. The line had been cut through by vigorously rubbing it against the sharp ends of the bamboo canes. We occasionally used this method to cut lines when we did not have a knife handy. For a moment he tried to convince me that natural forces had been at work, but then lost confidence. He was unable to look at me. I didn't say a word.

Later that day I sat on the side of the raft, between the water barrels, and wrote myself the following note: "I must resolve to make this my finest hour. I can go one of two ways: I can degenerate, or I can rise above all this." I am ashamed of that note. I was romanticizing without knowing it. I was still trying to reason with insanity. It seems improbable now, but fully a month after we had been voyaging I still assumed that I had caused all of the problems on the raft. I reasoned that I was a novice expeditioner and a landsmen, that the people on my expedition were suffering, and that if I had done a better job of things then none of this would have ever happened. All of this was true and rational, but it had little to do Frederick's mania. I saw it as a choice between an escalation of hostility, or short-term appeasement with little long-term consequence. I was wrong. Pathological behavior in isolation and confinement only gets worse with the passage of time. Whether chasing whales in the 1800s, sailing experimental rafts in the late 1990s, or confined inside a spacecraft for eighteen months on a voyage to Mars, this type of behavior is the greatest disaster that can beset an expedition. It is so dangerous that the American polar explorer Admiral Byrd took only two coffins with him on his 1929 Antarctic expedition, but he took *twelve* straitjackets. Eventually the pathological person will sabotage the team's mission or its equipment. Abnormal behavior is part of that individual's personality, and he or she therefore reacts to stressors abnormally. The neurosis makes the person believe that the simple things, the small things, the things that do not threaten others in any way, mean *peril*—a threat to his or her emotional and even physical life—and such a person will do *anything* in the realm of human behavior to protect him- or herself. Dr. Stuster, whose work is oriented toward preparing astronauts for the long voyage to Mars, shrewdly points out, in *Bold Endeavors*: ". . . a case of severe psychosis could be catastrophic on future expeditions. . . . there exists the danger of a manic or paranoid individual disabling key equipment or essential systems of a spacecraft . . . or planetary outpost."

In the history of expeditions, there is a corresponding history of extraordinary behavior. There are mysteries surrounding those extraordinary events that will be debated by historians for the rest of time. Did Frederick cut the dinghy free that day on the high sea? Did he put the crew of the *Illa-Tiki* in jeopardy just to satisfy one of his obsessions? The mechanical forces of the scenario say "yes": We had been sitting becalmed on a flat ocean, so there had been no strain put on the line holding the dinghy. Even if the rope was in danger of chafing through, it would still require at least a small strain to rip it apart. No such strain existed that day. What *did* occur was that the other four men on the raft stayed inside the hut with all of the windows closed, and could not see outside. Therefore, I cannot claim that I witnessed Frederick in the act of sabotaging the dinghy. And I did not question him about it—not that day, not ever. But I am certain, however, that he waited until the little boat had floated away before telling us. I believe that risking the loss of the dinghy was entirely acceptable to him if it helped to satisfy one of his obsessions.

Regardless of whether he cut it loose or simply waited, I was now frightened of turning my back on him. It was horrible to watch his hysteria and his panic; but those things were small compared to this: Losing the dinghy would be an unqualified disaster. After the radio and the GPS receiver, the dinghy was our most important piece of safety equipment.

In May of 1995, my understanding of the realities of expeditioning was very crude. My mind was guided only by a clear sense of immediacy: If Frederick obsessed over something, it meant serious trouble. We stowed the dinghy.

But then things got a little better. We were now making good speed, heading for Panama. This was the best stretch of sailing we made. During those days I got a glimpse of what a workhorse the balsa raft can be. The sail inflated fully, we set the *guaras,* and the raft made a constant 2.5 to 3 knots for about four days. Chris dried out the GPS by sealing it in a waterproof camera case with a handful of moisture-absorption packets inside. Then, after the rains let up, the radio began to work again.

On the twenty-seventh, a small sailing yacht approached us from astern. It was the *Glory Glory,* skippered by a woman named Suzanne. She had picked up our radio transmissions and had set course to rendezvous. When her pointed, triangular sails came over the horizon behind us, I sent the others over to greet her. I stayed aboard to mind the raft and talk on the radio to the United States. When the others returned from *Glory Glory,* they were cheered up. Suzanne had been a gracious host, and generous. She had given them chocolate, peanut butter, and wine.

Our fishing operations improved, too. The ecosystem below the raft had evolved in sophistication to the point of attracting and supporting groupers, dimwitted fish that were so slow they could be speared by hand. About the time the groupers started appearing, Dower and I had a talk. We sat in the corner of the hut, on my sleeping bag, exhausted and hungry, and I said, "We must catch more fish. Got any ideas? I'll listen to anything."

"I could make a spear," he said.

"Will that work?"

"Maybe. It's worth a try."

For the next two days Dower filed down a small metal rod that had been a spare part from the bicycle-driven generator. He sat on top of the gear and canvas stacked in the center of the deck and patiently worked, humming and singing a few words here and there while the blue ocean sloshed all around him. He didn't look at all like he had when we left Salango. He was noticeably thinner, had a black beard, and a maze of tangled, salted hair. When he started filing, it seemed like idle futility. The rod was made of a very hard metal, and to grind it he had only a small hand rasp, made of what felt like a very soft metal. Nevertheless, he sat in the sun and rubbed and filed for hours and slowly, methodically, he ground the rod to a point. On the second day of filing, in the afternoon, he held the metal point up to examine it in the sun and seemed satisfied.

To make the handle he took a stick of scrap wood and aligned the little rod on it so that it was straight, and then began slowly wrapping a thin metal wire around the two, binding them together, concentrating steadily, winding one hand around the other. The finished product was roughly three feet long and consisted of a flat stick of scrap lumber with a metal rod protruding from the end. It was the crudest instrument I have ever seen; even the spears we made as boys were more advanced, but it worked. He stripped, sat at the edge of the bamboo canes, crossed himself, then slipped into the water and disappeared under the raft. Twenty minutes passed, and then the point of the spear surfaced with a plump red-and-gray grouper flapping on the end of it. Our daily fishing with hooks and lines was improving, too. We were moving into Panamanian waters now and the sea burst with massive shoals of silver albacore tunas. Sometimes in the mornings the surface of the ocean would vibrate and wiggle with thousands of bright silver fish. A patch of ocean about the size of a football field would suddenly bubble into a frenzy of flapping and jumping, all of which would drive us into a frenzy and we'd frantically cast out lines, trying to catch them all.

On the twenty-ninth, when we checked our position, we saw that we were near Panama. Dower knew that land was nearby and spent the afternoon concentrating on the horizon. His sharp eyes could see land, but mine could not. On the thirtieth, right after dawn, a large Malaysian freighter appeared off our starboard bow. It was outbound from the Canal. Land now loomed on the horizon in front of us: Panama. I climbed to the crossbeam of the mast, hugged my body against the spars, and looked out across the ocean to see what looked like dark green mountains, rising straight out of the water. I knew nothing about this place. We were so far off our original course that we had no maps or charts of the area and were therefore completely lost. I could not form a picture in my mind, no matter how fanciful, of the land in front of me or of its people.

We sailed toward Panama all day, and by noon a fine green island lay in front of us, beckoning us with its tranquility and its calm. We set course for it, sailing in the warm sunshine, closing in slowly and coolly. The island was massive and mountainous, with tall, angular slopes. It was heavily wooded and richly green, and the sight of it seemed to create warm feelings in all of us. The voyage of madness would soon be over. We would regroup, get our heads straightened out, and make everything right. We had passed through a dark tunnel, and no one aboard the *Illa-Tiki* would ever be the same. But the crises we had faced were over now, and there was finally a little calm on the raft.

In the early afternoon, as *Illa-Tiki* cruised toward the beautiful green island, I made contact with some ham radio operators in North America. Sitting at the radio table, just inside the doorway of the hut, I talked to various "hams" who were now working together as an informal network on our behalf. Brock and Chris sat on the floor nearby and Dower and Frederick stood outside in the sun, looking at the island. Stationed at the little table, and working the various frequencies, I alternated between talking to the ham radio operators, and writing notes. Before me lay a small black radio with a digital read out, displaying the frequency in block numerals, and a clutter of random objects around it: pliers, binoculars, and spare parts. The sea was calm and the sloshing noises around us benign. Radio static streamed from the little black box like the raspy hiss of a strong breeze. Through the hissing static I could hear roughly five "hams" talking to each other and trying to help me. They reported in from all over North America, using disciplined, military-style radio procedures and speaking in a wide variety of American accents. When they were ready, I pressed the key of the microphone and carefully read aloud the coordinates of my position and then asked for confirmation. The "hams" confirmed the data, repeating the coordinates back to me, and then the voice of a friendly but concerned man named Dave, transmitting from Florida, said he knew the area well and could do some quick research on the island. I remained at the little table while he stepped away, and continued my steady conversation with two other operators. Brock and Chris talked softly between themselves, as did Dower and Frederick, out on the deck. Through the bamboo doorway I could see the island on the horizon, growing larger all the time. Over the radio we could hear a ham operator's electronic voice, clearly worried, asking us to carefully describe the island's features so that he and his colleagues could identify it, and then Dave's voice suddenly interrupted the conversation and said, "It's Prisoner Island."

The other electronic voices stopped. Empty radio static drifted through the hut for a long moment. Brock and Chris stopped talking and looked up at me. Their faces seemed frozen; for a long second, neither blinked. Both groups, the "hams" in North America and the five isolated men, were silent. I squeezed my thumb against the plastic key on the microphone, and said, "Please say again?"

The radio crackled, and then Dave's electronic voice explained, "The island in front of you is the Isle of Coiba; it is inhabited by prisoners. It is a prison colony."

4

Panama

Dread. Every thought I had was dark. I was suddenly hot for a minute and felt like taking my shirt off. The Expedition had mutated into a horror: trapped on a small platform with a screaming masochist, sailing toward a penal colony. A U.S. Department of State report on the island during this time would later say, quite dryly:

> ... conditions on Coiba Island Penal Colony remain grim. . . . (the) compound on the island (is) loosely guarded . . . part of the island (is) controlled by rival prison gang(s) . . . rival prisoners (are) captured, tortured, and beheaded . . .
>
> Although national prison authorities had slated Coiba for closure, they have used the island prison colony as a means to relieve overcrowding at the two largest prisons. . . . By moving dangerous prisoners to Coiba, prison officials have attempted to establish order in other prisons.
>
> Prisoners suffer from malnutrition and shortage of potable water, and medical care is practically nonexistent. . . . Escapes from Coiba are reportedly common.

After a pause, Dave's voice came back on, "There is heavy pirating in the area and there have been several killings there recently." Another pause, then, "They boarded a yacht recently and kidnapped the entire crew. I don't think that'd be too good a place to land. Over?"

"Roger that."

For the first time, I realized what a hostile boarding would mean. If they attacked us they could maintain the element of surprise until they were on top of us. Strange vessels frequently visited each other in coastal waters, so there would be no way to know if they were pirates until they were onboard. I vividly pictured a shooting on the bamboo canes of the *Illa-Tiki,* which made me bristle inside and out. Brock had bought a couple of handmade pistols at the outdoor market back when we were in Ecuador. I had protested then; now I thanked him. We learned later from locals living on the mainland that the prisoners sometimes built their own vessels for escaping the hellish island. The vessel of choice? Why, the *raft*—of course.

We turned our raft around and headed east. *Illa-Tiki* now cruised seventeen miles off the coast of the Azuero Peninsula, a block of land jutting out sixty miles into the Pacific Ocean like an enormous diving board. We were now paralleling the southern shore of the peninsula, involved in the complicated problem of making a safe landing in a raft, something few had ever succeeded at. The raft was exceedingly limited in the direction in which it could travel, and in the places it could safely anchor. In the modern day it could be likened to a commercial airliner: it was a big, bulky craft that could only land in very specific places, and if we tried to land anywhere else, we'd crash. To ensure success we would need assistance: a tow. The ham radio operators monitoring our transmissions found a U.S. coast guardsman to come on the frequency and give us the locations of possible landing sites. According to him, our only hope was a small port on the far east side of the peninsula. Shortly after receiving this communication, night fell, and we saw only two navigation lights marking the shore. From where we stood the coast looked like a dark, black, block, with no sign of technology or civilization.

When the sun came up the next morning, we lay ten miles offshore. Freighters and tankers cruised all around us, either inbound toward the Canal or outbound from it. Most of them passed by us at a distance of two to three nautical miles. Standing on the bamboo canes in the afternoon sun, we looked out on a grand, moving gallery of commercial ships: Massive black-and-white fertilizer carriers plowing through the ocean, stirring up miniature storms of white caps at their bows; tired old red-and-orange tankers—probably destined to carry palm oil—empty and floating high in the water, showing their ugly, crusty undersides; well-financed petroleum tankers with fresh paint crisply defining their hulls, making fantastic speed, ignoring everything on the earth, appearing on one horizon and disappearing over the other in less than ten minutes.

Illa-Tiki, wooden and ancient, continued east. We intended to round Punta Mala (Bad Point) within the next forty-eight hours. It marked the entrance into the Gulf of Panama, and lay at the southeastern tip of the peninsula. Once we rounded *Punta Mala* we'd head north for the nearest small port on the east side of the peninsula.

On the third of June, we passed close by two menacing islands, Los Frailes or The Monks, each about the size of a large ship. They rose up from the water like the cliffs of Dover, white and bright, about five miles from shore. Both islands could be seen at a great distance, and I wondered if the ancient mariners might have used them as a marker or waypoint. Birds inhabited them in abundance, and years later a Panamanian friend of mine told me that the guano on top of Los Frailes was as much as four feet deep.

Shortly afterward, Punta Mala came into view, and we began to change our minds about rounding the point. To our mind the Azuero Peninsula acted as an enormous windbreak. If we sailed northward and passed into the leeward side of the peninsula—its wind shadow—we might enter a trap. Rounding the point would require a close pass on the rocks, and once on the other side we'd have little if any wind with which to maneuver. Wisdom dictated that we turn back, retrace our previous course along the bottom of the peninsula, and then sail close enough to land to find a vessel to tow us into a safe anchorage.

I had noticed over the previous four days that the wind had died each morning at about 2:00 a.m. To get within paddling distance of land, I knew we must try to steer toward the shore as much as was prudent while there was wind. It might take another two nights to gently maneuver inside the five-mile mark, at which time we'd launch our dinghy. Night came on the third, and we cruised along in the dark. Frederick started becoming nervous again. "Du yu zee that light?" he said, pointing at a navigational light on land. "It has moved." Lights always appear to "move" because the bearing of the boat is always changing relative to the light; but I didn't want to argue. I was scared of Frederick going berserk or pulling some kind of crazy stunt near land. We'd change course a little, and in the morning we'd go back to closing with the land. *Illa-Tiki* continued to cruise in the dark, six miles offshore. I went to bed, but awakened at around 2:00 a.m. to voices bouncing off the water's surface and echoing inside the hut. Brock was calling to Chris, and Chris was calling back. I could feel the raft turn and turn. *Illa-Tiki* was slowly spinning around and around. I got up quickly, thinking we might be out of control, and went out on deck. In the moonlight I could see Brock's skinny figure standing on the canes. "We've done three three-sixties in the last thirty minutes!" he blurted. "We can't seem to sail in a straight line for more than just a few minutes!" This was always a problem for *Illa-Tiki:* It had no directional stability because it had no keel. Steering the raft in light air required methods other than those we had used out on the high sea in stronger winds. I told Chris and Brock not to worry; their watches ended and I took mine.

It was a fine Panamanian night, warm and clear, with a brilliant moon illuminating the calm coastal waters. The dark shoreline lay five miles off. *Illa-Tiki* cruised quietly, an enormous barge trailing behind a tall rectangle of canvas in the gray light. Standing on the bamboo canes, I steered the raft by controlling the angle of the sail—trimming it to the wind by gently hauling in on lines and then letting them out. In the distance, the warning light atop Los Frailes burned in the dark like a singular red eye. We would pass the massive rock islands within the next two hours and I stood on the foredeck of *Illa-Tiki* in my bare feet, watching the red eye of the monster. Warm air bathed my face and arms and I was happy to be steering the raft we had built in Ecuador.

Los Frailes loomed now off the starboard bow: two enormous blocks of rock, square and flat, like enormous ships. Sounds from their isolated world began to reach me. Breakers curled over into explosions, slamming against the rocks. Higher up, birds screamed as they took off and landed on their overcrowded little country. The burning red eye rose and rose until it reached a height of 130 feet, while I slid silently below it. At the closest point, Los Frailes stood 50 yards off my starboard beam. Then the wave hit me. I stood still for a moment as waves of adrenaline shot through my body. What if Frederick should awaken at this moment? What if he should come out on deck for some reason? He'd fly into a screaming panic for sure! It would be just like that horrible first day back in March—*but in the middle of the night.* For ten nail-biting, sweat-trickling minutes, I hung in moonlit suspense. *Illa-Tiki* cruised by the hulking rocks at a speed of less that one knot. In the dim gray light I could see long cracks and fissures in the sheer cliffs. I stood on the hard bamboo poles, looking up at the red eye, listening to the distant breakers and feverishly glancing over to the doorway of the hut, terrified that Frederick might emerge, fly into a panicked explosion, and send *Illa-Tiki* into chaos.

When the sun arose in the morning, land lay just four miles away. We saw the faces of the green and brown hills now, fence lines, and groves of trees. During the previous four days we had slowly been able to discern some activity on the peninsula. We had once seen a truck traveling to the east at high speed and had deduced that a paved road might exist near the shoreline. Dower and I knew we must get ashore quickly, make contact, and secure the tow.

The day was sunny, with a few puffy clouds beginning to steadily form, which no doubt would bring the afternoon showers. At around noon a white *fibra* came motoring toward us from the sea. It sped across the water with a fierce-looking man standing at the tiller. He was tall and slim, with dark eyes and a black moustache. He cut the power on his outboard motor when he came close, and then drifted off our starboard side. I stood on the deck, looking at him, and he stood in his bobbing boat, looking at the raft in mute astonishment. "We're on an expedition from Ecuador," I said.

He took a moment to think, then, in a quiet, deep voice, he asked, "Are you hungry?"

"Well, yes."

He walked forward, lifted the top off the hold of the *fibra,* and then began rummaging around, digging his long arms deep down until he found and pulled out a plump *corvina,* the best fish in the area. He walked back to his outboard, stone faced, and then eased his boat next to the raft, where he reached across to hand the fish to me. "Here, take it," he said, then turned back to the tiller and sped away. It was my first taste of the towering generosity of Panamanians.

Shortly afterward, we lifted the dinghy from the deck and placed it on the water beside the raft. Dower and I boarded the little gray boat, shoved off, and began rowing toward land. We rowed for about forty-five minutes, taking turns sitting in the little boat and pulling on the oars, heading for a small beach with a moderate surf breaking on its sand. Individual trees were now visible and we could smell the land. Then Dower sat up suddenly and looked around. A *fibra* was speeding toward us. It was the same one that had come alongside us in the morning. A slightly overweight man in his early fifties, dressed in a light brown police uniform, now sat up on the bow. The outboard motor's buzzing dropped off, they slowed, and we threw a line to them. Climbing aboard the *fibra,* we showed our passports to the policeman, and explained ourselves. The officer showed no emotion; he simply took care of his business, carefully recording our names and passport numbers in his notebook, and after listening to our story he told the fierce-looking man to take *Illa-Tiki* in tow.

After about thirty minutes of arduous towing behind the straining *fibra, Illa-Tiki* entered the Bay of Ciruelos. The tiny bay measured only about a half mile at its mouth, and only a few hundred yards near its beach. The *fibra* steadily tugged the heavy barge toward land until we approached a tiny milk jug, floating on the surface, with a line tied to its handle that ran down to an old engine block on the seabed. There were several of these milk jug–buoys scattered about the bay for the fishermen of the area, who numbered about fifteen. Dower tied up the raft and I paid the fierce-looking man for the tow with a couple of spare life jackets we had onboard, a fee he found acceptable. Behind us lay a volcanic reef, roughly fifty yards away, with a moderate surf hitting it. After tying up, we climbed aboard the white *fibra,* and the fierce-looking man ferried us to shore. Thirty-eight miserable days after we first set sail from Salango, we stepped off onto a beach made of black volcanic sand: land.

At the police officer's direction, we walked up a little road and climbed aboard an old Chevrolet truck that was already waiting for us. The truck eased onto a pockmarked road and began lumbering to the east. The air around us seemed especially soft and tranquilizing. Barbed wire lined the road, as did cattle and cowboys. After half an hour of twisting and turning through the empty countryside, we entered the little town of Pedasi and drove straight to the police station, a small cinder-block building surrounded by immaculately kept grounds.

Stepping into the modest building, we were met by three, tough-looking National Police who wore blue jeans and sport shirts and carried pistols jammed in their belts. There was a counter there, like at any other police station, and Dower and I stood at it, explaining our improbable story to the armed men. Though they seemed a little on the cold-blooded side, they didn't try to actively intimidate us; on the contrary, even though this was an interrogation and they were obviously serious, they listened quietly and seemed unwilling to pass judgment on us. Nevertheless, Dower and I were tense: Night had fallen, we were isolated, and these were men whom we could not afford to upset. When there was a little break in our presentation, one of the plainclothed policemen, wide-eyed and a little stupefied, looked at the uniformed man who had brought us in as if to ask if our story could be true. "Yes. Yes—it's a raft," the uniformed man said to the others, "but you should see this thing—it's *huuuge!*"

The men looked at each other incredulously, and then, for the first time, they seemed to examine us, top to bottom: In front of them stood two lean men, both deeply sunburned and wearing shirts with white salt streaks at the armpits, both with thick, matted hair, and shaggy, salt-encrusted beards—both completely sincere and obviously telling the truth. The plainclothed policemen nodded gravely, still not completely convinced, and ordered us into a small, windowless, cement room.

Dower and I now sat on wooden chairs in front of a fat man, who sat behind a wooden desk with a single lightbulb hanging over his head. He began by asking, "Now: Where did you come from?"

"Ecuador," Dower said.

"Yes, we know that you're Ecuadoran, but where was your last stop, before you came here?"

"Ecuador," Dower said.

"What stops did you make along the way? Galapagos? Colombia? The Pearl Islands?" he asked, like he was talking to an idiot.

"We didn't stop. We came from Ecuador." He looked at me and asked: "How far is it?"

"About five hundred nautical miles," I said.

"About five hundred nautical miles across the sea," he said to the interrogator, "more or less."

The interrogator stopped the official business for a moment, squinted at us as though looking into a bright light, and asked a question of human interest, "My God! What makes a man *do* such a thing?"

Dower seemed to realize for the first time that what he had done was a source of awe for others, and smiled a little smile of pride: "Adventure."

That did it. Nobody could make up a lie like that. The fat man seemed to relax a little. The rest was more an interview of sympathy than an interrogation. At the end, the policemen asked if there was anything they could do for us. We said no. Then they asked if we had any firearms, and I told them about our pathetic little pistols, which they found both humorous and also perilous. They warned us about the dangers of their waters, then they asked if we had any money, to which we replied that we didn't have a dime. They passed the hat around and collected twenty dollars for us, plus several offers of food, which we declined. Afterward they became official again and told us we'd have to go through immigration just like anyone else. We shook hands all around, and I said, "Thank you for having us in your country."

We returned to the anchored raft in the darkness, and slept well, resting heavily after the long passage.

The next morning, Brock boarded a bus and headed for Panama City. He'd lost at least twenty-five pounds, had almost been knocked out in a fight with the sail, and had lost his hearing. He looked like a shaggy, haggard weed, a tuff of hard grass that survives through the relentless summer sun only by sheer obstinacy. Chris, desperate for a little civilization, went with him as far as the first town.

In the afternoon I went ashore and had my first beer in Panama. We landed on the beach in the dinghy and walked up the little hill that overlooked the bay. The fierce-looking man who had towed us in lived there in a nice cinderblock house with a tin roof and a cement floor. No electricity existed there, but the coastal road ran right behind the house and you could reach a phone by foot in less than two hours. Next to the house stood a cantina. I walked up to the bar and asked for a beer, and the fierce-looking man introduced himself as "Memo," then served me an ice cold *Atlas*. The air was sweet and tranquil, and it felt good to be in Panama.

The next day, aboard the raft, Frederick explained, "I have been changing the course each night while we have cruised along the coast." He mentioned only the coast, but the question in my mind was: How long had it been going on? Had he changed it while we were out on the high sea? Was that the reason we had "gone backward" on several nights? But I didn't ask or quibble; I just wanted him to be gone.

In a few days Dower and I left for Panama City with only one thing in mind: Find the biggest anchor around and get back to the *Illa-Tiki,* quickly. A single van passed by Memo's house each morning at seven o'clock, headed down the coastal road, and on that warm morning in May, Dower and I boarded it.

We packed in with the locals and went swaying and bouncing down the lonely, pockmarked road. After we had been traveling a few hours, I broached a question to Dower that had been on my mind since the beginning of our voyage: "What would you think of assuming the captaincy?"

"What? Absolutely not," he said.

"But I'm not doing so well, and you know everything about the sea."

"You're doing fine—let's just stick together."

Then I asked him about Frederick changing the course. He made a hilariously animated gesture of jamming a sock into Frederick's mouth to get him to shut up, and after that, I just let the issue go.

When we arrived in Panama City, we went to the national telephone office, where Dower called a cousin in Ecuador. He wanted to send word to his family that he was alright, but when he got off the line he was somber. "Three guys from a nearby village were lost at sea for sixteen days," he said.

"Were?"

"Yeah," he said. "They picked up the boat in Panamanian waters a couple of weeks ago."

"Did they survive?"

"Yeah. People are saying one of them went crazy and tried to drink battery acid."

"What?"

"Yep," he said.

Dower was completely resigned. I thought it must be a rumor. Regardless, neither the report of a vessel lost at sea nor a battery-acid-drinking story impressed him. He was sincerely sorry for the fishermen, but not shocked. Why?

Because he and his people were always resigned to their fate. They were mariners, Manteños, and the Pacific Ocean had been stranding them and swallowing them and crushing them since before the great pyramids of Egypt were conceived. I remembered back in Salango when Enrique had once talked to me about the ocean in a way that only they talk. He was sitting on *Illa-Tiki* in the hot afternoon, rubbing his forearm and looking out toward Salango Island, when I said to him, "Tomorrow I might swim out to the island."

"Good. That would be nice."

"Did you ever swim out there?" I asked.

He smiled. "When I was young."

"I'll bet it's farther out there than you think," I said.

"On the sea, everything is farther than you think. Much farther."

"Without a doubt, *Jefe*," I said.

He then explained the law of his culture to me. "The sea will reign forever, John. You may go out there many times—maybe everything will work out—but she will always be the Queen." He pointed to the Pacific, then to the raft, the sand, himself, and then finally to me, because I, too, was now living under their rules: "She is the Queen of *everything*."

Later that day, in Panama City, I met Frederick in the lobby of a hotel, where he gave me his official resignation. I was relieved but remained in shock. Of all the things I had planned for, this type of problem was not one of them, and because of that I had no way to deal with him. He paralyzed me, which paralyzed the expedition. In the annals of expeditionary history, standing up to danger pales in comparison to the problem of a destructive man among a team. A single human personality gone awry can produce an almost unfathomable chaos. But more than that, I have to admit that I felt what can only be called a "touch of evil." In all the years of struggle, Frederick was the most demoralizing influence I faced. I felt as though I had consumed a fifty-gallon barrel of black ink—actually *drunk* it—so that had you cut me open I would've bled black. In him, I had encountered something profoundly dark.

The next morning I had some "emergency money" wired to me, and then Dower and I went to the various yacht clubs around the Panama Canal until we found and bought an anchor. While there, Dower accidentally bumped his thumb against a table, which caused him great pain. He had cut himself while aboard the raft and now the cut was starting to become infected. That night, we went to the main hospital in Panama City to see if they could prescribe something for the infected thumb. We sat in the overcrowded lobby for hours, and when they looked at Dower's cut they deemed it "not serious." Disgusted, we left and checked into a foul hotel nearby, where we spent the night.

I had received news from the United States that my family wanted to come to Panama to see me, my mother especially. On the eleventh, Dower, Chris, and I went to Tocumen Airport, on the outskirts of Panama City. My mother arrived, as did Chris's mother, as did Annie Biggs, who was now running The Expedition's operations in the United States.

Annie was the most charismatic person I had ever known. Two years before, I had stood in the waiting room of her office, not knowing what to expect, when she had blown into my life. She flew into the room in the same way she always entered any place: striding forward as though in a tremendous hurry, and then she offered me her hand warmly, saying, as though she was welcoming me into her own private amusement park, "Hi, John—I'm Annie Biggs." I have never felt such an immediate chemistry with any other woman. "You don't have to explain yourself to me," she said. "You should try being a female director—and an independent filmmaker!" We were allies within a day.

When they landed in Panama there was a warm reunion between all of us. My mother had made up her mind to come see me, no matter the difficulty. She was the type of person who had known practically nothing but hardship in her life. She had grown up in abject poverty, and she was a hard woman when I was a boy, sharp minded and sharp tempered, but after the untimely death of my father, whom she deeply loved, she had begun to mellow. Over the last few years, we had not been especially close. I lived only a few miles from her, but I had always been wrapped up in my own world. When The Expedition came along, it seemed to separate us even more. She believed it suicidal, and had chosen not to come to the airport to see me off when I left for Ecuador. I thought that wise, since an overtly distraught person at the airport would have cast a pall over The Expedition. But after we were reported shipwrecked, she wanted to see me "just one last time," in the event that I might meet an unfortunate end. It is interesting how over the years The Expeditions brought out the intervention in so many mothers. This is exactly what had happened to Charles Lindbergh right before his historic flight across the Atlantic. The press had scared the wits out of his normally-calm mother and she had crossed the country by railroad just to see him one last time. Ironically, my mother arrived in Panama just in time.

Dower's hand was getting bad now. His infected thumb was swelling, and his ability to fight the infection was evaporating. On the twelfth, we drove to the Azuero Peninsula, and by the night of the thirteenth, Dower was in serious trouble. The infection inside his thumb, which we referred to as the "tropical abscess," starts when bacteria from the sand in the region gets inside an open wound. Within forty-eight to seventy-two hours the infected tissues swell to three or four or five times their normal size. It is excruciatingly painful. Watching your tissues exploding before your eyes sickens you and causes traumatic shock. Fever follows quickly. The victims rarely worry about that though, because the furious agony overwhelms them. This is a serious problem in the rural areas of Latin America. Back in Salango an American zoologist once told me the story of a young pregnant woman who had developed this condition. It killed her within a week.

When we arrived at the raft, I stayed to take care of several problems, while my mother, Chris's mother, and Annie, drove around the Azuero Peninsula trying to find medical care for Dower. The facilities appalled them. Each time they entered one of the hospitals, flies and the smell of death greeted them.

That night I joined up with them and checked into a little hotel in Pedasi. Dower was going out of his mind in pain. His hand was hideous. The skin on the back of his thumb expanded as though made of rubber, and when it split open the flesh bulged through it as though the muscles had turned inside out. It was now grotesquely possible to look inside his tissues, which quickly turned from red, to brown, to a revolting, angry, yellowish brown. More and more, Dower rolled back and forth in the bed, gritting his teeth and laughing nervously and kicking his right leg as though stomping the ground. As the night wore on, the abscess expanded the thin strip of tissue behind his thumb until it was roughly half the size of a baseball. His bronzed face turned gray and he was now occasionally calling out in pain. He was holding up as best he could, but it was grotesque that the human body could live with such a hot angry thing growing inside of it.

At around eight o'clock that evening, my mother and I stepped away for a moment and went out to the road to have a talk. We stood in lower Panama, my mother and I, and discussed the amputation of Dower's hand: "I can't leave him in one of the hospitals here," she said.

"It's getting bad," I said.

"I know. He's better off with me than in a hospital here. The conditions are horrid."

"We can't wait much longer."

"If I can't find a doctor tomorrow, I'm taking him to the United States," she said.

"Jesus. I'm scared they're going to want to amputate that hand."

"Uh—me too. I—"

"Good God, Mother, he's a *fisherman!* If he loses a hand—that's it! He absolutely cannot lose that hand."

"I know. I'll find a way."

During the night, Dower went temporarily insane from the pain and the fever. It was hard to tell when he was sleeping or awake. He hallucinated and talked to people who weren't there. Annie described him simply as "gone mad." In the morning my mother went to the hotel owner and asked, desperately, if he knew where she could find a doctor. "I am a doctor," he said.

Dr. Vera looked at Dower and then explained to the others the detailed method for stopping the abscess. They were to acquire a variety of soaps and then clean the wound every four hours. Dower would also take an antibiotic, engineered especially to stop the abscess, but which was sometimes difficult to get.

The three women stayed by Dower's side for the next three days, meticulously cleaning the wound over and over again. During those tense days I saw the remarkable effect that battlefield nurses have on demoralized soldiers. They brought to Dower what he needed: care, not just medication. Working in shifts, they slowly, methodically, saved his hand. When the fever broke, they brought him out on the cement porch in front of the hotel and sat him down on a metal chair. He had the same look that a new mother has after a hard labor: soaked in sweat, drained from the fight, inexpressibly relieved. He sat there for half an hour just blinking, bewildered by his lapse into insanity.

The next day Annie and I drove my mother to a landing strip, where she caught a bush plane to Panama City. Later, I wrote a letter to her, in which I stated, simply: "Thank you for saving my friend." What I meant to say was: "Thank you for saving my friend"—*whom I might not have been able to save.*

Annie and I spent the next two days on the peninsula. There were romantic moments between us, many of them, but more than that she and I seemed to fit together. You must understand that when you are an expeditioner, and perhaps an independent filmmaker, you are always on the verge of appearing farcical, hopeless, ridiculous. When I had first begun, the public reaction to the voyage had been absolute rejection from all quarters. A dream is only beautiful as long as it stays hidden inside the dreamer; show it to the world, and it becomes an eyesore that is so ugly that the dreamer is embarrassed of ever thinking it. After you've been at it for a few years you will slowly accumulate allies, but in the beginning you will be met by an onslaught of naysayers, and unfortunately, the probabilities are on their side. People, who are "really acting in your own best interest," will stand in a line a mile long to lecture you about all the failures that await you. Expeditions are "epic" when they are made into films, but they are "crazy" in the development stage. Back when I had first started The Expedition I had called around to various film experts, looking for advice, and after several rejections I had finally come upon a particularly condescending "director" who had said, "Truthfully, I can't think of anything as boring as the thought of watching a film about a bunch of people on a raft, but there may be one person who would be interested in this kind of *thing*." He gave me a phone number, begrudgingly, and I girded myself for yet another negative conversation. After one ring, the secretary connected me with the only person who would be interested in such a *thing*. But this time it was different; I had accidentally run across a real adventurer. "I'm going to cross the ocean on a balsa raft," I said to the woman over the phone, "and I want to shoot a film about it."

"Really?"

"Really."

"How will you power the cameras out there?" she asked.

"Bicycle-driven generator."

"You're kidding."

"No. It's for real."

"Do you know how to get to my office?"

Annie never blinked. She lived her life and fought her struggle with a type of high morale that was infectious. It was good to have her in Panama after the voyage of madness; but after our very short interlude, she drove to Panama City, where she caught a flight back to the States.

When I returned to the raft forty-eight hours later, I explained to Dower that Frederick was gone. A smile came on his face and then we broke into peels of laughter.

But in the afternoon, things began to change. The waves began to build around the anchored raft. Chris came to me while I was standing on the bow, looking out to sea, and said, "Memo's waving at us. I think he wants us to come ashore."

We went ashore to find Memo standing on the cliff that overlooked the bay. He was openly worried and started talking as I was walking up. "The raft is moving, my friend."

"Are you sure?"

"*Sí*," he said in the closing darkness, "and I think a storm is coming."

"Are we going to crash tonight?" I asked, feeling that deep down he knew something I did not.

My blunt question shocked him. He recovered, took a deep breath, and then released it slowly, creating a deep sigh. The character of the bay had

changed completely by now. Although no wind blew, massive rollers were pil-
ing in from the sea and multiple lines of white foam now streaked the dark blue
water. "I don't know," he said, clearly preparing himself for disaster. "Be very
careful tonight."

We hurried back to the water's edge, and launched the dinghy into the oncoming waves. Chris sat out front and I sat on the back. Night had just fallen
and three lines of heavy breakers stood before us, blocking our way to the *Illa-
Tiki* like advancing white walls. Just as we reached the first line, a wave crested
and hit Chris in the chin. Water exploded in his face and he shot backward six
feet, crashing into me with his full torso. I teetered backward, scratching and
clawing at the walls of the dinghy. I could feel the inflatable boat flexing and
shaking under me. Saltwater and sand splashed everywhere. I was blinded for a
moment, then pulled myself up and blurted out, "Come on, Chris! Get back up
there! Paddle!" Grunting in determination, he lunged forward to the bow of the
dinghy, dug his paddle in, and pulled water frantically. We got the boat under
control and cleared the breaker line, then began making our way through the
darkness, paddling hard toward *Illa-Tiki*. We were going up hill and down hill
now. One moment we would be on the crest of a wave looking down on the raft
and in the next moment the raft would be above us on top of a watery hill.
Once alongside the *Illa-Tiki*, the dinghy suddenly became like a small gray
membrane on the belly of a huge beast, flapping and flailing wildly. Chris struggled in the darkness to pull himself on deck, and once aboard, he held the
dinghy for me and I got aboard.

Illa-Tiki was like an elevator gone mad, rising up, stalling, then dropping
back down. The commotion had awakened Dower, and he came out of the hut
holding his bandaged hand in front of him and looking as though he had sweat
out his last fever. Standing on the deck, he wrinkled his face up with curiosity,
and then looked at me as if to ask, "What happened?" Scrambling past him, I
asked how he was doing and heard him say, behind me, "I'm terrific." Sitting
down on the bare balsa logs, I began hauling on the anchor line. It should have
been a slow struggle; instead, the line did not resist at all. Dower stood behind
me, and as the anchor came up through the murky water we saw that the hook
had snapped off. All that was left at the end of the line was the steel arm, or
shank, of the anchor. "Now," Dower said, "I'm scared."

A rush of nauseating adrenaline shot through me, making my fingertips tin-
gle. The only thing that could keep us from shipwreck had been ripped apart by
the massive pull of the raft. We had tied off to an engine-block buoy before
we had anchored, and so far that had prevented disaster. But it wouldn't hold

forever: *Illa-Tiki* was clearly pulling the engine block across the seabed. The raft pointed directly toward the waves coming in from offshore, and from our vantage point we could see that twenty footers were starting to come in now. Because of its incredible buoyancy the raft couldn't cut through the water like other boats could. Instead, it would rise up twenty feet in one second and then drop down just as fast when the wave passed under it. One hundred feet behind the raft lay a reef of black volcanic rock, a massive, jagged surface that would slash to pieces anything that hit it. Each time the raft rose up on top of a wave it plucked the engine block from the seabed and placed it down a little closer to the reef. *Illa-Tiki* was steadily marching toward shipwreck.

Ninety seconds had ticked by since we discovered the anchor was gone. The ocean was rising up out of the darkness like a herd of elephants, completely overtaking our field of vision. For three or four seconds at a time nothing existed in front of us but a giant wall of water. Then, off our starboard side, we saw a nearby fishing boat suddenly rise up into the air. A giant wave seemed to grab the eighteen-foot Boston whaler by the bottom and shove it right at us. The long white boat came barging out of the darkness and crashed down on our foredeck with an enormous "BOOM!" Its fiberglass walls quivered and shook and a crack opened in its hull. We stumbled back toward the hut in fear and felt *Illa-Tiki* vibrating under our feet from the impact. The four-hundred-pound boat was now beached on the bamboo canes. Walls of water continued to come in and *Illa-Tiki* continued to climb them, pitching and rolling and tilting, sending the Boston whaler careening around on the deck and crashing into the mast poles, smashing equipment, and making the raft shake. Stumbling forward, holding his hand up, Dower suddenly called out, "Help me! Help me with the boat!" In an instant I realized that he wanted to try to tie the fishing boat aboard the raft to keep it from going overboard and sinking. We threw a line around the whaler and tied it to the deck, but it did little good. We didn't have the rope or the manpower to secure it permanently, and it was still moving and sliding around. Looking at Dower, I asked, "Do you think Memo could make it through the surf (in his canoe) to get his *fibra* and tow us out of here?" We both then turned around and looked back at the beach where the fisherman left their canoes for the night: The waves breaking there now were monsters. A landing might work in an inflatable boat like ours—you'd probably crash in the surf—but you'd make it to the beach alive. The return, however, was simply impossible. "No," I said to Dower, answering my own question.

"No es posible, Señor." he said, and then sat down for a minute with a hopeless look on his face.

Illa-Tiki was closing the gap with the reef; nothing could stop her. "Chris," I said. "Get ready to abandon ship. I want all of the equipment inside the hut."

At the rate the raft was moving toward the reef, we would have to make a decision in the next half hour: stay aboard the raft during the shipwreck or be away in the dinghy. In that short time *Illa-Tiki* would reach the line where the rollers curled over and exploded. Chris and I wouldn't have enough power to paddle the dinghy out of that area. The surface of the water would be warping and changing shape so fast that getting a good grip on it would be next to impossible for two men. If we wanted to leave the raft, we'd have to leave before then. Regardless of when we left, we'd be running white water. We'd have to go down the barrel of the waves, skimming along between the parallel crests of the foaming breakers, then turn and try to surf the dinghy to the beach, somehow, under control.

If, instead, we stayed aboard the *Illa-Tiki* during the crash, we would have to evacuate the raft by jumping onto the rocks in the dark and running to land, an uncertain plan, to be sure. I feared a broken leg or serious gashes in our feet from the razor sharp rocks; and worse, if a man somehow managed to become trapped between the reef and the raft, the huge vessel would act like a thirty thousand-pound hand, crushing that man against the horrible surface.

Chris and I quickly stowed everything in the hut. Dower sat on a balsa stump in the middle of the deck. His whole body drooped; the situation seemed hopeless. I couldn't bear to just stand there, so I told him to tie one end of a coil of line to the bow of *Illa-Tiki*. Standing up, he looked at me in disbelief and asked, "What are you going to do?"

"I'm going to tie off to every buoy in the bay. If we crash tonight we're taking every one of these engine blocks with us."

"OK," he said, as though slightly resuscitated.

My plan was to take the coil of line with me in the dinghy, reeling it out as I rowed, and head toward the other milk jug–buoys. I got in the dinghy, put the oars into the oarlocks, and rowed around to the front of the raft. Dower, working laboriously with his one good hand and substituting his teeth for the other, threw the line aboard the dinghy, and I took off rowing.

I was sitting in the bottom of the rubber boat now, wearing only my swim trunks. At my feet lay a tall coil of blue rope that paid out as I rowed away. Water sloshed around my legs and buttocks and raindrops sporadically pelted my back. Lightning flashed constantly, but strangely the wind was only intermittent and light. The waves elevated the dinghy one moment and dropped it the next. I pulled on the oars with all my strength, and I made it to the nearest buoy within a minute. I had to stow the oars now without being driven away from the milk jug, but the moment I stopped rowing a wave rose behind me and I surfed twenty feet away before bringing the little boat back under control. I went at it again and was again pushed back. What was going on back at the raft I did not know; I was in a water world, narrowly focused on reaching a plastic jug—a clammy man in blue swimming trunks, sliding around in a little rubber boat in the dark. Finally, I became desperate and gave up on the oars, stowed them, then draped my body over the bulbous head of the inflatable boat and began digging the ocean like a dog. I clawed handfuls of water in the dark and when I had splashed to within a few feet of the little jug I lunged forward and grabbed it around the neck. The line from the jug to the seabed was slimy with sea grass and it slipped out of my grasp when a wave came under me. I splashed back to it, grabbed it again and finally got our blue rope knotted around it. We now had two engine blocks dragging in front of *Illa-Tiki,* but it was still moving.

Overhead, the silent lightning continued. I tried to row out to the next buoy but the line behind me was developing too much drag. It curved in a wide arc back to the raft, dragging in the water like a parachute. I was pulling on the oars so hard that it was only a matter of time before I tore the dinghy apart. The vinyl bulwarks flexed and contorted under the strain and I just hung there, ten feet away from the next milk jug, rowing and pulling with all my strength, sliding around on the plastic floor of the dinghy. The drag was too great; I had to turn back. When I reached the raft, Dower asked, "Why did you give up? We're still moving! What happened?"

The fishing boat still ricocheted around the deck. We couldn't control it. A wave came at us, we shot up in the air, and the raft threw the fishing boat off like a toy. It went overboard into the darkness and hit the surface with hollow thud. Water collected slowly in its bow and it began sinking. Within a few minutes, its bow dropped, its nose sank under, and the brass propeller of its motor began to protrude up from the surface of the water.

"Come on, Chris," I said, "we've got to go back out there and tie off to that far buoy." He dutifully complied without complaint, but he did not relish the idea of going out in the fury. I couldn't blame him; I didn't want to go either.

Boarding the dinghy, we paddled out in the dark. After fifty feet we stopped. The drag on the line held us like a leash. We couldn't overcome it. "We have to go back and try again!" I shouted, and turned the dinghy back toward the raft. A giant wave rose up behind us and the dinghy tilted down. I felt the little boat lose its grip on the water and then surf down the side of the wave. The stern of the dinghy rode high and I was looking downhill at Chris in the bow; then I was looking up at him, then down again. The dinghy spun and surfed through the darkness, picking up speed and heading toward *Illa-Tiki*. I paddled backward in a series of short strokes, furiously pushing back piles of seawater. *Illa-Tiki* materialized in front of us: A gray balsa raft shrouded by raindrops and darkness. We were still out of control and speeding in. The bulbous head of the dinghy struck the side of the Pope, glanced off sharply, and slammed into the propeller of the sinking boat. The bronze blades sliced through the plastic and the dinghy deflated instantly. The little boat lost its shape, water poured in over the sides, and for a moment I had the sensation of sitting down in very shallow water. I rolled over the side of the sunken dinghy with my paddle in my right hand and the dinghy in tow in my left. Chris went in face first, fending off the water in front of him with his hands and feet like a dog. We both drank mouthfuls of warm saltwater and treaded water furiously with our legs. Wrestling and towing the dinghy through the water, we managed to get it to the other side of the raft, where we could bring it aboard. The dinghy was now just a pitiful clump of deflated plastic; when we hoisted it out of the water it lay there like a dead animal.

Chris had gained some experience working with plastic while making housings for film cameras, so I shouted over the cracking of an incoming wave, "Do you think you can repair this?"

"I don't know," he said, bewildered. "I'll try."

Without the dinghy, we wouldn't be able to abandon ship.

While Chris went to work, I went to the back of the raft and waited for a flash of lightning. When one came, I saw every detail of the rocks and the breakers. We had closed the distance to the reef by more than half. We were less than forty feet from the breaker line now.

Working my way up to the foredeck, I came to a grand spectacle: a gallery of advancing waves. Something—some distant event far offshore, either a hurricane or an underwater earthquake, was generating enormous wave heights. When the lightning flashed it would briefly illuminate twenty-foot hills of black water, glittering like emeralds. Dower and I stood and watched as mountains of water rose and rose and rose. The slopes of the waves weren't steep, not at all like typical breakers near a beach; they were like long sloping hills—and their growth wasn't sudden, like the typical waves that come in to curl over and burst on the sand. They grew slowly, surreally, agonizingly, as though superpotent seeds had been planted in the sea. They weren't waves as much as simply an immense growth in the ocean's surface. In front of the raft, what was once a flat surface would suddenly swell, rising up and expanding, growing and growing and growing until it formed a long, massive structure that blocked out the horizon like a hill or a river levee or an entire block of three-story apartment buildings that had suddenly started moving toward you, traveling across the earth, advancing with finality and rolling over everything in its path. When they finally elongated into a crude peak and curled over and slapped down in front of us they made sounds that were horrible—long, cracking noises like wooden logs fracturing under immense pressure. Each time a wave broke, the horrible crackling noise would split the air for three or four heart-stopping seconds and our faces would change from determination, to astonishment, to involuntary, recoiling fear. Looking up at the advancing hills of water, Dower croaked, *"Que tremendo!"* His voice cracked and his mouth hung open, and then to himself he whispered aloud, as though he needed to confirm to himself what he was seeing, *"Que tremendo!"*

By now, Chris had ducked into the hut and returned with a tube of glue and a strip of plastic. He dried the ripped area of the dinghy, smeared some glue down, and then placed the patch on it. Kneeling on the deck as though praying, Chris bowed his body down until his face was almost on the canes, and began gently blowing on the glue, pressing on the patch with the heel of his hand. Dower stood and watched. He was speechless. He knew better than any of us that disasters on boats sometimes occur like a series of falling dominoes: one thing after another in an unstoppable, deliberate motion, and in the last hour a storm had ripped apart our anchor, another vessel had collided with us and sunk, and our dinghy had been destroyed by the biggest waves that he had ever seen.

In a few minutes Chris said we could try inflating the dinghy. Miraculously, it held air. We again launched into the storm and paddled out about thirty yards from the *Illa-Tiki,* towing the line behind us. From that position I looked back on a sight that was even more freakish than the one I had seen on the raft: Every time one of the waves came in, the *Illa-Tiki* disappeared from view as though the ocean had rolled over it. The lightning over the bay silently flickered and was sometimes exceedingly bright, illuminating every detail for a split second as though lit by sunlight. When that happened you could see Dower standing alone on the deck of the *Illa-Tiki,* trying to feed more line out to us with his one, usable hand. He looked like a character in an old-fashioned horror movie: appearing as a flickering image, black-and-white, hunched over and cradling his sickened hand, shuffling back and forth on the deck, pulling and rearranging lines—his face twisted in extreme effort and agony. Sometimes I could see him hand signaling me to do different things: "Take the line out," or "There's another buoy to the left," or "We're still moving back."

Chris and I made it to the third buoy and tied up. *Illa-Tiki* could pull one block and it could pull two, but the third slowed it down. The raft, pulling a dog sled team of engine blocks across the floor of the ocean, had finally begun to give up its suicide march. We had been fighting the storm for three hours now. Still, strangely, there was no wind. Then the tide started to flood in and that lessened the waves heights considerably. Near dawn, the sea finally calmed down. By that time we had less than thirty feet between us and the reef. We were utterly exhausted; it had been a horrible night. When Dower said, "I think we're going to make it," I collapsed in relief.

That night, in May of 1995, we dragged three blocks across the Bay of Ciruelos. The ancient Manteño had dragged them as well: In the year 1619, the Dutch explorer Spilbergen made one of the first drawings of a balsa raft at sea. The sailors aboard this raft can be seen operating their *guaras*. Lying on the deck next to them are three anchor stones, each shaped like a primitive wheel: a circular block with a hole chipped through the middle so that a line can be tied to it easily. How many times had the men in that drawing been through what we had just been through?: Three or four blocks out in front of the raft and the whole apparatus, raft and anchors, leaping across a bay like a gigantic frog.

Every boat in the bay was swamped or sunk that night and many good-sized hunks of the shore were carved off and carried away. In the morning we swam over to Memo's boat, the *fibra* that had towed us in. It was submerged just below the surface and barely hanging on. We helped Memo paddle, tow, and swim his vessel to the shallows near the beach, where he salvaged what he could.

A few days later we received news from the United States that a sailor had volunteered to go with us to Hawaii. I knew him only vaguely, but he was well qualified, with lots of experience at sea. I went to Panama City to pick him up and then escorted him back to the raft. When he and I arrived back at the bay and went aboard *Illa-Tiki*, I saw the unmistakable look of a person who had no earthly idea that conditions could be so primitive. I sympathized with his predicament. If I hadn't gone through primitive technology indoctrination back in Salango, I probably would not want to live on the raft either. Shortly afterward we went ashore in the dinghy and walked to the nearest phone, a two-hour journey through the empty countryside. "John," he said, as we walked, "you know what? I've been thinking: I don't think I can go with you on this thing."

"Really?"

"Yeah," he said. "I've been thinking; I'm really starting to appreciate my life. Maybe I had a good thing going on back home."

"OK."

"I don't know—maybe I should get married or go back to school."

"I totally understand. Don't worry about it," I said.

"Thanks for not being an asshole."

"No problem," I said. "I have learned one thing: It's better to decide now that it's not for you than to discover it out there. You have to be absolutely mentally prepared before you get on that raft."

He returned to the United States in forty-eight hours, but gave us his best equipment before he left, which helped greatly.

We had been in the field for over twenty weeks now, and in Panama for three. Living in a bamboo houseboat anchored near the shore, we were completely self-sufficient, and more isolated than we had been in Salango. We continued to talk to the United States twice a week via shortwave radio. After about twenty days of constant rain and overcast, the solar panels could no longer charge the batteries, so we used the bicycle generator during this time. No one could peddle the contraption for very long, but it developed such an enormous amount of electricity that it did in a few minutes what it had taken the panels days to do.

The tropical rain showers that came every day were causing greater problems for us than just dead batteries. Freshwater and tropical heat breed mold. Had you ducked inside the hut during this time you would have been greeted by the strong smell of mildew. All things reeked sharply. This smell, like the inside of an unclean shower, but a thousand times more intense, was quite frequently the day-to-day smell throughout The Expeditions. The sails were especially vulnerable to this problem. We spent hours and hours wrestling with the heavy canvas, hanging it up or putting it under cover, vainly trying to keep it dry. This was a serious problem. The tropical mildew was so aggressive that is caused the fibers of the canvas to rapidly decompose. Later, during other voyages, we developed various potions from boiled tree bark that could be painted on the sails to slow this decomposition, but keeping the canvas dry was always the best way to prevent mold. This meant that furling the sails and stowing them was out of the question. Unless the canvas was kept open and aerated it was just a matter of time before the mold rendered it useless. A furled sail, even one that did not appear wet, would rapidly develop a massive mold culture that would make the canvas so brittle that it could be broken up into a powder by just working it between your hands.

Each day, the rain would start early in the afternoon, build, and within an hour become a heavy downpour. Then there was little to do but sit in the hut and wait for it to end. Looking out the door at the heavy rain and listening to it crackle and pound our thatched roof, I began to understand for the first time a little of the heartbreak of being marooned. On all sides of me were parallel lines of tan poles and slivers of sunlight, dripping drops, and the smell of acrid mold. Through the door, framed by the bamboo canes, I could see the great Pacific Ocean, rising to the horizon like a barrier, and through the back window I could see the Azuero Peninsula, a sparsely inhabited, disconnected wilderness. I had been forced to a place that seemed like the farthest place from Hawaii, and home. I was living—trapped, really—in a place that I had never known existed before. I had never dreamed of this place, had never expected it, had never fantasized about it, had never taken into account its existence in my mind. While it was true that we could make the arduous journey to Panama City and leave via the airport, this never entered our minds. Our only way home seemed to be through Hawaii, and so a modern method of escape meant nothing to us. We were stranded. We lived now, basically, as castaways. In the mornings we fished in the bay for albacore tunas and dove to the seabed to spear lobsters. In the afternoons we foraged on land for mangos and coconuts. We drank the fresh rainwater that filled our tanks and sometimes bathed in tropical showers. It was no wonder that when Homer chose a punishment that the gods could inflict upon his hero Odysseus—a punishment that would be godlike in its severity—he chose to maroon him: Even being marooned in paradise would cause pain. To block a person's ability to get home, to prevent them from getting to a restful end of a long journey, must be one of the most heartbreaking fates that anyone can face.

We went back and forth to land several times a day. We'd land on the beach below Memo's house, walk up the little dirt road, and enter the peaceful, domestic world of rural Panama. Memo's family accepted us as their own, and we roamed freely on their land and in their house. This place seemed like Utopia to me. The soft tropical air tranquilized everything that passed through it and the people radiated kindness and warmth in everything they did. I could hardly walk past a Panamanian without waving. It was as though we had lived there our entire lives.

On the Azuero Peninsula, they ranched; it was cattle country. The Spaniards had left behind a deeply rooted tradition of prancing horses and cowboys who worked the herds across the rolling green hills. Hundreds of head of cattle were driven down lonely back roads by machete-carrying cowboys who frequently tipped their hats to passersby and who never allowed a horse to open its gait. In the towns, cowboys could be seen at all hours of the day, sprinting through the streets on beautiful brown horses that clipped along on the tips of their hooves.

As the days went by, and we lived our marooned life, my admiration for Dower grew. He had been heroic during our thirty-eight-day spiral into madness at sea. During the night of the storm, when our anchor broke, he had been as concerned about the boat of another fisherman—a man like himself—as he had been about his own safety. He was, like me, desperate to see some other part of the world. He once told me: "I just can't let my entire life pass here (Salango). All I do is exist here. Sometimes I go out to work in Galapagos, but then I always come back. I've never seen anything but this."

Dower and I knew we must escape Panama, regardless of our love for its people. We knew we must try to continue to Hawaii. He possessed a valid passport and a U.S. visa, and we talked often about the idea that he would accompany me back to my home. One day, while we were standing on the beach, burning some trash, I said to him, "There isn't any racism here. Have you noticed that?"

"Yeah," he said.

There seemed to be a complete lack of racism in Panama. Families included all races, and the contrast of color faded. In Memo's family there was African, European, and indigenous blood, all happily blended. It seemed to increase the inherent good a thousandfold, which increased the mellow calm. Dower and I stared at the little fire on the sand for a minute, and then I said, because I felt I had to warn him, "It's really bad in my country. I hope you know that."

"My country, too."

We stood on the beach, marooned, two middle-class men from completely different worlds, wanting, essentially, the same things from life.

One day, two Panamanian men, both in their early thirties, came to the bay. One carried a large video camera and the other a microphone. They were from CNN South America, and they asked to interview me aboard the *Illa-Tiki*. I happily agreed, and Memo ferried us out to the raft. When we got aboard, they milled around for a while, then one asked me to stand on the Pope for the interview, and just as the camera started rolling I asked them to pause so that I could put down the knife I was carrying. I bent down to the Pope, stuck the knife in the side of the log, and felt it sink up to the handle. The log was no longer solid; it was hollow. I looked over the wood for a moment, and realized that the underside had been completely tunneled through.

I put up a brave face and finished the interview quickly, but inside I was sick. Obviously, the raft was completely worm-eaten. When the news crew left, I dove under the raft to look at the other logs. It was awful; every log was honeycombed. I had heard about worms eating wood, as well as the problem of termites, but none of the popular books about balsa rafts had ever said anything about it being a problem, and I certainly had never imagined devastation like this. Fully one-third of the wood mass, some ten thousand pounds, had been consumed. *Illa-Tiki* was sinking.

I was sick with depression and came ashore to take a walk in the hills near the bay. I had been unspeakably relieved to get rid of Frederick, save Dower's hand, and survive the night of the storm. I had begun to believe that I might actually accomplish what I had set out to do. Now it seemed all was lost. Eventually I reached the nearest telephone and called Annie to tell her the bad news. It caused a massive surge of energy in her, and she assured me that we could, somehow, fix it.

In a few days we received word from Annie, via shortwave radio, confirming that we had been attacked by *Teredo navalis,* the common "shipworm," and how we should go about treating it. This parasite is in reality a mollusk that is exceedingly well adapted for boring into wood. *Teredo navalis* look like white worms, except that they have two bits of shell at the front of their bodies, which—if closely examined—resemble a drill bit. They range in size from microscopic to about four inches in length. The *Teredo navalis* were boring into the soft balsa wood of *Illa-Tiki,* and slowly consuming it. In order to kill them we would have to expose the underside of the raft to the air for a period of twenty-four continuous hours.

Four weeks after anchoring in Panama, we intentionally grounded *Illa-Tiki* on the sand, hoping to rid her of the *Teredo navalis.* When the tide rose, we brought the raft up on the beach and tied it in place. In an hour or so, when the water ebbed away, a fifteen-ton balsa raft lay on the sand like a beached whale. From a distance the raft showed no obvious signs of decay. It sat there on the beach, enormous and completely intact. Up close, its "hull" showed all the signs of a sea-going ship in dry dock. Bright green sea grass and dark brown barnacles hung down, and underneath, hundreds of thousands of holes could now be seen on the bottoms of the logs. The *Teredo navalis* had bored in under the waterline—which had been masked by the sea grass and barnacles—and had then run down the grain of the wood, consuming everything in their paths.

We continued our castaway life, hoping that after a few days the *Teredo navalis* would die. I spoke to Brock over the phone, and he volunteered to come back; but I told him no, I wanted to bring in someone new and fresh. A young man from Memo's family volunteered to go as well, but his mother intervened, and it hurt her so much that I simply couldn't accept him. More time passed, and it seemed we'd never escape Panama.

Then one sunny Sunday afternoon, shortly after we grounded the raft, a small group of locals gathered at Memo's cantina. Some had come out expressly to see the raft, but most were there to drink and have a good time, as they usually did on Sundays. Music squawked from the radio and one of the cowboys danced around the cantina happily. A friend of Memo's was there, and we talked to him awhile. He was a fit man in his late forties, wearing a modest, button-down shirt, and—we were led to believe—moderately wealthy. He showed us his rare 35mm camera from Russia, as well as his attractive wife, also from Russia. We wandered through a conversation until we got to the subject of fishing, then things perked up. The man was a spear fisherman, and he always brought his gear with him whenever he thought he might be near the ocean. Dower and I talked with him some more, and then we said we were going fishing in the bay for our dinner. He was very eager to go, saying he had heard of Dower's reputation as a diver from Ecuador.

Twenty minutes later we met at the water's edge and swam out from the beach. The sky and water were gray, but it was pleasant out. The ocean was calm and nice, and the three of us pushed through the water, talking back and forth and making little wakes in front of our bodies. The man indicated that he wanted to go to the front of the reef, near where the rolling waves came in from the sea, so that he could look for some big fish. Dower and I, on the other hand, wanted to stay in the shallows, to dive for lobsters. We had no use for trophy fish; we just wanted to eat. As the man swam away, we both became worried. "I don't know," Dower said to him.

"Yes," he said over his shoulder, "it's fine."

"Uh, I don't know. It's rough out there," Dower said.

"No problem," he said, and then swam out to the front of the reef.

In twenty feet of water, Dower dove to the seabed below while I waited at the surface with the collection bag and an extra spear. We fished for forty-five minutes and then came in, empty-handed. I spent an hour or so doing some housecleaning on the raft, and then Dower came back from the cantina and we went fishing again. Thirty feet offshore, treading water, we were both struck by an ominous feeling. "Have you seen that guy?" I asked Dower.

He furrowed his brow and let out a worried, "Noooo."

Looking back toward land I saw Memo standing on the cliff, signaling us to come ashore, just as he had done on the night of the storm. When we swam ashore, he asked, simply, "Where is he?"

"What?"

"Did he come back?" he asked. "Did you see him come out of the water?"

"What? You mean you think something happened to him?"

"I don't know," he said.

"We'll go out in the dinghy," I said, "and look for him."

Dower and I went back to the beach and launched the dinghy, and then paddled out past the head of the reef. We sat up on the sides of the little boat and called out: "HELLO! . . . HELLO! . . . HELLO!" We saw no sign of anything. Emptiness engulfed us. The waves pounded the reef as they had done for thousands of years and the world seemed to turn especially gray. An acute feeling of loneliness came over me, and when we turned to come in I saw Memo on the cliff again. He stood like a pole, skinny and motionless. Without showing any outward emotion, he simply reached up with his pointer finger and slowly drew it across his throat like he was drawing a knife.

They found our fishing partner washed up on a beach about a mile away. By the time we arrived a group of ten people had already gathered. They stood looking at three black boulders near the waterline. We came up from behind, weaving our way through the crowd, and then stopped, stunned, muted. His body had already begun to sink into the sand. He lay on his stomach, with his head jammed between two angular black rocks. He had been wearing long pants when he went in, not unusual in rural Latin America, and they now clung to his legs, drenched and torn. The surf washed up by his bare feet and receded back, and he looked so lonely. He lay face down, so that his wife, who had just arrived, was spared from having to look at him. He had probably been killed by a simple knock on the head, but later we learned that his body had been badly beaten and torn by the reef. Dower and I stood there for a moment on the sand, staring in disbelief: He had been killed by the same forces that we had escaped on the night our anchor broke.

The man had told us his name before we had gone out, and then later several people retold it to us after his death, but I think we blocked it out because of the utter morbidity of the moment. We simply referred to him as "The Man," which, in conversation between us, seemed to always come out in a stammer, or in a low, foreboding voice. They held his funeral two days later and afterward Memo milled around the cantina in disbelief. The following day I came back from town to find a group of four National Policemen standing on the cliff, looking down on *Illa-Tiki*. They were in their thirties and forties, some wore uniforms and some were in plain clothes. "The Man" had been the father of a senior police co-mandante. I saw Dower talk to Memo for a moment, then wander around the area in shock: The son was sure that we had been hired by someone to kill his wealthy father. That seemed so fantastic to me that I told Dower it was ridiculous, to which he replied, "In my country, somebody has got to pay in this kind of situation. If three men set out in a boat and the boat comes back with only two, then those two guys are in serious trouble." He then slowly drew his finger across his throat: "Nobody cares what their explanation is."

That afternoon, the son angrily ordered the body exhumed. The National Police had not brought any formal charges on us yet, but the local police suggested that we could be arrested for murder. The situation was exceedingly tense and I worried about trouble in the middle of the night at the hands of the National Police. Dower was scared and so was I. Then Memo came and told us that we had to report to the nearby police station. When we arrived we sat in a small hot room with the town's clerk, a middle-aged women behind an old-fashioned typewriter, who took our "statement." In it we said that we knew nothing about "The Man's" death—he had simply disappeared. When we had finished, the town's clerk said, as though saddened about giving us horrible news, "You cannot leave here (Pedasi)."

While awaiting our fate, I spent several nights walking down the coastal road to the nearest phone. Crossing the open countryside at night scared the local people, and they frequently asked me, "You walk out there in the dark by yourself?" I think some of this fear came from the bats that flew near your head in the dark. I'd walk for hours in the night, the only sounds being my feet crunching on the road, and then suddenly weblike membranes would flap against the heavy air. "Screeeeech!!" Then the nearsighted little animal would make a hard, banking turn past my cheek and flap madly into obscurity. By the time I'd ducked down and thrown my hands in front of my face it would be long gone. That is my memory of those days: a sickened vessel lying on the beach, bats flying near my head in the darkness of the back roads of rural Panama, and Dower, small, frightened, and waiting.

A week after the police first arrived, the tension began to ease. The grieving son started to regain his senses and ended his informal investigation. My family had notified the Ecuadoran ambassador that Dower had become the target of the police's inquiry, and around this time, he came to Pedasi.

The Ecuadoran ambassador may have been the smoothest thing that had ever come through these parts. He cruised into the quiet little town in a spotless 1973 Cadillac. It wasn't a limousine, but it was one of the biggest luxury cars ever built by Detroit. The minute the ambassador stepped out of his car I knew everything was going to be all right. He was pure gold, and had the most disarming smile that can be imagined. He was a slim man, warm and urbane, exceedingly well-groomed, wearing thin black pants and a tailored shirt, open at the collar. You could see why this guy was a diplomat. He strode into the police station and told everyone, without uttering a word, that there was not now—nor had there ever been—any reason to worry. He was the ambassador of The Democratic Republic of Ecuador . . . His Most Honorable, The Most Excellent, The Unbelievably Lovely, etc, etc, and he was here to ensure that his fellow Ecuatoriano wasn't going to have so much as a hair moved out of place by all of this unfortunate, innocent, "completely regrettable," silliness. Afterward he would have a cocktail at the beach to demonstrate how innocent the matter really was. Then he and his driver would retire back to Panama City, never hitting a bump.

Illa-Tiki had been sitting on the beach for two weeks now, exposed to the air. We had waited long enough, if the *Teredo navalis* were going to die from this method, they'd be dead. When the tide rose, Dower and I collected Memo and some cowboys and together we all pushed on *Illa-Tiki's* stern, easily launching it through the moderate surf. Then Memo boarded his *fibra* and towed us out to our old mooring buoy, the one we had been attached to during the night of the storm.

It did not appear that the *Teredo navalis* were dying. The infestation was already too advanced and the tunnels too deep. Since leaving Salango more than eighty days previously, the raft had sunk down about four inches. The tops of the logs that had protruded above the surface at the beginning now lay submerged under an inch of water. Our only option now would be to use a modern pesticide to stop them, but that would cause an environmental disaster in the bay: This, we simply could not do. Therefore, to elevate the raft, we poured some of our excess drinking water into the bay. Just emptying two tanks raised the logs back to their previous level, but I knew it was of no use. All the delays in Panama meant that we would have to sail the now weakened raft right down "hurricane alley" in high season. On the afternoon of the seventeenth of June, I told Dower that we'd never make it to Hawaii. The news crushed him. He had left his country as a hero; now all was ruined.

Dower and I agreed that we could make an attempt to sail *Illa-Tiki* back to Ecuador, where the raft could be inducted into the raft mariner's museum, Museo Salango. It was a desperate plan, but the idea of letting the great *Illa-Tiki* waste away was just too horrible to contemplate.

On the eighteenth, we prepared to leave the Bay of Ciruelos. Overcast skies clouded the morning, and Dower, Chris, and I stood looking out to sea, preparing to return to Ecuador. According to our plan, Memo would tow us out of the bay, where we would raise sail and make way as best we could back to Ecuador. Memo boarded his *fibra,* and as soon as we were ready he began pulling the chord on his outboard. When the motor fired he reached back and turned the throttle. He sped forward, the outboard coughed smoke, and then stalled. Looking back at the motor in consternation, he pulled the chord again, restarted the motor, and throttled it again. Again it stalled. We stood on the foredeck, waiting in angst with our sail furled at our feet. In front of us lay the gray sea, open and barren. Memo labored and cursed and then couldn't get the motor started at all. He pulled and pulled, working over the outboard in futility. Then Dower signaled another fisherman in a *fibra* to come over and help. The second fisherman tied up to the raft and began to pull. His *fibra* strained and strained. The weight of the raft overloaded his outboard motor, and he gave up. Dower then turned to me and said, very sincerely, "God doesn't want us to leave."

At that moment I had roughly the same feeling, and so I said, "OK, that's it. We're going to beach it."

And that was the end: No great climax, no cymbal crash at the end of the symphony, we had simply reached a point where only disaster awaited—a common fate for expeditions. I gave the order to unload all of the equipment and to beach the raft permanently. We ran it onto the sand at high tide and tied it to the land. The voyage of the *Illa-Tiki* was over.

In the afternoon a fish truck came by Memo's house, and Chris boarded it, heading for Panama City. I spent the rest of the day unloading equipment from *Illa-Tiki,* and when a fish truck pulled in the next day to pick up the catch, I boarded it. Climbing on the tailgate, I began working my way forward via the hand railing until I was at the cab. My family had given Dower a little money to ensure his safe passage back to Ecuador, and he stood now on the grass next to the truck, looking at me. He would be leaving in the morning for the journey back to Salango. He was happy at the thought of returning home, and relieved. He smiled warmly now, his face crinkling up in heroic optimism. "Good-bye, Captain," he said. He waved. "Good-bye, Captain." The driver started the truck, we pulled away, and Dower stood there waving, smiling heroically: "Good-bye, Captain. Good-bye."

I made it to Panama City and then boarded an airplane bound for the United States. At the Miami International Airport I walked down the concourse, headed for my connecting flight. The cavernous walkway was practically empty, and I felt alone. A feeling came over me without warning or premeditation. It surprised me, but it did not confuse me: I knew that I had just survived my first expedition, and that being an expeditioner was no longer a far-fetched idea that I would only dream about. Being on expedition had given me a feeling of self-realization, a filling of a void, the void that exists between your wished-for life and the life that you must lead, day to day.

5

The Body of Knowledge

Back in Salango you could buy old clothing from the United States at a lonely shack on the coastal highway. The Salangueños always told me that the shirts and pants had been pulled off of corpses in the United States—that was the only way they could be so cheap. I heard a lot of tales back in the rural areas of South America over the years, but this one actually possessed an air of plausibility. The shirts cost only fifty cents, so I bought a faded blue one sporting the logo of a pool-cleaning service somewhere in Virginia. I landed in the United States wearing that same faded blue shirt. Everything else that I owned had been destroyed or rendered worthless by a combination of misadventure, tropical heat and humidity, and a flood of corrosive seawater. My body and clothes reeked sharply of mold, my skin burned from the equatorial sun, and my face hung from exhaustion and psychological injury at the hands of a dark, venal, freak. I walked off the airplane wearing "dead man's clothes," and not much else.

I had been on expedition for six months and on a primitive raft for three. Then modern transportation instantly transformed my surroundings. Annie met me at the airport and we drove to her home in suburban America, where I rambled around the halls as though I had just awakened from a deep sleep. There was then and is now a missing part—a gap—in my recollection of life in twentieth century North America. For months I had lived by ancient technology, by spear and bamboo cane, and it had grown on me. For a long while, I did not fit in the modern world.

For three years afterward, I planned, researched, and prepared. The madness of my first expedition stayed with me, both in my waking hours and in my sleep. I searched for answers to what had happened to us out there, and I found them in Ernest Shackleton, the legendary leader of The *Endurance* Expedition. I had read books about expeditions before, but now I recognized the truth when I ran across it. Shackleton selected his expedition team by considering the *type of person* they were first, and he never took anyone with him who violated his intuition. I had ignored my intuition back in Salango, both when we decided to bring Frederick aboard and after his panic in front of the rocks at Puerto Rico. This had been the beginning of disaster: *You simply cannot go on an expedition with someone who violates your intuition.* Many people can have friends of that sort for years, perhaps even live with them and sleep with them—and that's fine—but don't ever take them with you on an expedition.

But the bizarre behavior of Frederick couldn't explain the behavior of the others. Their decline was to a certain degree my fault. I went on that first expedition believing that everyone would naturally bear up under the strain. I believed that everyone would embrace the challenges—the hunger, the suffering, the uncertainty—as simply a part of being on expedition. But most people aren't ready for the levels of risk and suffering that invariably come on expeditions. They do not necessarily bear up heroically under the strain. When faced with truly dangerous or hellish conditions, they discover that they have lost their appetite for adventure. My first reaction to this was the same that many others have: I was shocked, appalled, and dismayed. Perhaps this was a completely human reaction, but to lead a desperate struggle you can't afford such a luxury. Shackleton knew the grave consequences of this. When he saw signs of emotional decline in any of his men, he brought them under his wing, influencing them and supporting them, giving them hope and help. He knew that you had to *give to others that thing inside you that prevented you from declining as quickly as they did.*

Being an adventurer wasn't good enough for expeditions; staying cool under fire only went so far. I wasn't an expedition leader at all; I would have to change; I would have to learn. Shortly after my return to the United States, I wrote an apology to the Salangueños in the form of an open letter. In it I said that the vessel that Enrique had built was of the highest quality, and that I was at fault for the failure of the expedition. I mentioned Dower's heroics and his great spirit, and that they should be very proud of him. Chris went back to Salango to see Janette, and before he left I asked him to post the letter throughout the town. That winter, I gave Chris a copy of *Kon-Tiki*. Inside the book I wrote: "Change what is bad, remember the good. I remember the night of the danger, you did well." (I was referring to Panama, when the anchor broke.) And that was it. I didn't see him much after that. Brock and I talked about The Expedition some, but I was now on my own. Throughout the last months of 1995 I did odd jobs to get by, and slowly, by degrees, my views and my goals changed radically.

Living in Ecuador had changed me permanently. I had lived with the coastal mariners and had learned much of their culture, and I had come to see that the people of coastal Ecuador defined themselves in a very subtle way: I remember one afternoon during the days of hunger aboard *Illa-Tiki,* when Dower and I discussed the enjoyment of fine fish. "Sometimes when you walk into a restaurant in Ecuador," he said, "they'll tell you anything to get you to stay and eat."

"Tell you anything?"

"Yeah—like they serve the freshest *dorado,* or the best *corvina* (sea bass), when really it's crap."

"That's true. They always say everything is *corvina.*"

"But not to us," he said, proudly pointing to himself. "If they can tell that you're from Santa Elena, they keep quiet."

"Santa Elena?"

"Yeah," he said. "They can't fool us. The mariners of the Santa Elena Peninsula—my people."

Geographically, the Santa Elena Peninsula is the spit of land at the southwest corner of Ecuador, but Dower was speaking of a culture—a mind-set more than a geographical boundary. It was the region and the mentality and the culture of the ancient balsa raft, and the Manteño: One hundred eighty miles of sand, turquoise waters, ancient fishing towns, *fibras,* free divers who can go to the bottom on a lungful of air, and mariners who could be seen standing in their boats off the shores of southern Ecuador. These people carry inside them what the historian Clinton Edwards called an "ancient familiarity of the ocean." Human culture began there at the very dawn of The Americas, as early as 6000 BC, and it slowly rose in sophistication until around 2400 BC, when the people of coastal Ecuador took the critical step that would make them legendary: They began to voyage offshore. The precise beginning of the era of the great sailing rafts is still unknown, but what is known is that this steady progression in the sophistication of societies led to the rise, in AD 800, of the Manteño-Huancavilca, an entire culture of voyaging merchants. At its height, the Manteño culture spanned some 180 miles of coastline—the coast of Santa Elena—Dower's "people."

The Manteño were a "league of merchants." In the modern day they might be called a cartel. They organized mainly for commercial gain rather than military or strategic advantage. Their business was the highly lucrative *Spondylus* trade. *Spondylus* is a conch shell, about the size of a small melon, that lives on the seabed at depths of forty to eighty feet. When the shell is chipped away it reveals a red and purple coral-like substance that can be worked, like ivory, into jewelry and ornaments. It was marketed throughout ancient South America, and when the Spaniards first arrived they noted that *Spondylus* had "as much value to the natives as gold, and in some cases, more." The Manteño were known throughout the ancient world as great shell divers, and they were experts in obtaining the precious *Spondylus*. That ability had survived in one form or another until today. Most Salangueños that I knew could easily dive to a depth of eighty feet, and Dower could dive to the ocean floor and stay there for so long that it seemed flatly inhuman. In ancient times, *Spondylus* lived in abundance in the home waters of the Manteño, they had the skill to dive for it, and they had the ships—the balsa raft—to move their merchandise. Their market was practically unlimited because everyone in their ancient world wanted the precious shell, especially the Incas, and for seven hundred years the Manteño ranged up and down the coast of South America, buying and selling, trading in *Spondylus*.

But then one day in 1526 the Manteños sent out one of their balsa rafts, and the history of the Americas was altered irreversibly. At sea, they spotted an unusual ship coming over the northern horizon. It measured fifty feet in length and it carried the flag of the Crown of Spain: The conquistadors had arrived. It was the end of everything. Nowhere in known history has the meeting of two ships at sea heralded cultural change of such unimaginable, unthinkable scope. Within ten years of this first meeting the Inca Empire had fallen, 90 percent of the Manteño had died of European disease, and the Spanish Empire controlled the entire Pacific Coast.

The giant raft the Spaniards overtook on that first fateful day in 1526 was a freighter from Salango. It carried gold, silver, fine cloth, and *Spondylus*. The Spaniards noted that the raft carried "sails like that of our own ships," and that the raft was sailing north on a trading voyage, looking to accumulate more *Spondylus*. Before my first expedition this first contact had meant nothing to me. It was a historical event that occurred in a foreign land, involving a people I knew nothing about. But in March of 1995, I, too, set out from Salango aboard a balsa raft. I, too, sailed the waters of this first contact. I, too, eventually, sailed north.

Archaeologists and historians had always theorized that the Manteño sailed north to Central America on trading voyages, perhaps as far as present-day

Mexico, but it was hard to prove. Attributes of the two cultures—Ecuadoran and West Mexican—were similar in many ways, but you could always argue that this was because of "independent invention." Independent invention says that we are all human, and it is not uncommon for two cultures that are great distances from each other to develop similar art forms, or tastes in architecture, or agricultural technologies. All of these things originate from the same place: the human mind. The argument for independent invention was always good enough to cast doubt on the theory that the Manteño had been to West Mexico.

But then in the 1980s, two metallurgists at the Massachusetts Institute of Technology, Dorothy Hosler and Heather Lechtman, began running tests on a peculiar little artifact called an ax money. These were tiny slices of bronze, shaped like miniature ax heads. Typically they were found at archaeological sites, wrapped up in packets of five, ten, and twenty, like packs of dollar bills. Ax monies were produced in both ancient West Mexico and ancient Ecuador, and both cultures used a precise recipe of arsenic and bronze to create a unique color in the thin slices of metal. This color was critical: It gave the ax monies authenticity, much in the same way intricate engravings give authenticity to our currency today, as a way to prevent counterfeiting.

In 1990, Hosler and Lechtman, with the help of the preeminent Danish scholar, Olaf Holm, published their landmark paper: *Axe-Monies and Their Relatives*. It was a short, stunning demonstration that the axe-monies produced in West Mexico were precise duplicates of those produced in Ecuador. They weren't accidental and they weren't produced by independent invention. The ax monies produced in West Mexico were of the same, precise composition as those produced in Ecuador. It was an exact match, like a fingerprint: It was the unmistakable fingerprint of the voyaging Manteño.

On an afternoon in early 1996, I lay on my back in the San Francisco Airport, waiting out a fog, reading *Axe-Monies and Their Relatives,* wide-eyed, my mouth agape, stopping every two minutes to frantically scribble notes, then reading and rereading. The authors, along with many other prominent archaeologists, were confident that there was only one way that all of this could have happened: As early as AD 1100, four hundred years before the Spanish conquistadors arrived, the Manteño had reached Western Mexico *by balsa raft.*

After reading *Axe-Monies and Their Relatives* I walked around aimlessly for two days, lost in thought. You could say that it stunned me into silence. I had accidentally stumbled into one of the most important research problems of the Americas: I had departed from Salango and had sailed the first five hundred miles of this ancient voyage to western Mexico. Archaeologists were convinced

that an established seaway—an entire *trading route*—might have existed between Ecuador and West Mexico, and now, in modern times, I was the only
one who had done anything like it.

What should I do? Frankly, I tried to ignore it; I tried to rationalize away a
very unpleasant idea: Try to sail the Manteño Trading Route—try to navigate
a balsa raft—a freighter from Salango—all the way to West Mexico. That type
of expedition would be astronomically high risk, and there would be no glory
in it. But if I didn't attempt this voyage, who would?

So I considered my options: The first was a voyage across the Pacific Ocean.
If I built another balsa raft and then had it towed out to the Humboldt Current,
I could drift across the Pacific for a few months and I'd be a big hero. All I'd
have to do is hold on and the ocean would push me to the South Pacific Islands.
From 1947, the year of *Kon-Tiki,* to 1973, there had been at least eight rafts
that had successfully "crossed the Pacific Ocean." They were towed offshore,
entered the mighty Humboldt Current, and ran downhill all the way, pushed
inexorably to Polynesia or Australia by the eternal trade winds and currents.
Even if my new raft got the *Teredo navalis,* I knew how to keep a balsa raft alive
for one hundred days or better—more than enough time to reach Polynesia.
Just like *Kon-Tiki,* I'd have "crossed the Pacific on a balsa raft"—and it would
erase some of the horrible failure of The *Illa-Tiki* Expedition. But what would I
have really accomplished? Nothing.

But if I attempted the Manteño Trading Route, I'd be risking shipwreck all
the way. To make it through the Manteño Trading Route I'd have to steer a balsa
raft around landmasses, peninsulas, islands, rocks, breakers, tidal currents, coves,
river mouths, other vessels, and pirates. Coastal piloting requires quick, precision maneuvering, but we'd be sailing a slow, wallowing elephant, and if we got
into trouble we'd have no alternative propulsion like motors or oars to pull us out
at the last second. The wind and current would be unpredictable too. Out in
the Pacific, where the other rafts had sailed, the wind blew in only one direction: from east to west. Up the Central American coast the wind would hit us
from every direction. I'd be sailing an experimental ship through an eighteen-
hundred-mile obstacle course, trying to dance my way around collision. If I
made a mistake on the Trading Route it could mean annihilation. I was well
aware of the previous disasters: Thor Heyerdahl's balsa raft *Kon-Tiki* had sailed
through forty-eight hundred nautical miles of open ocean without a scratch, but
one thirty-second meeting with land demolished it. The explorer Eric DeBiss-
chop had sailed *ten thousand* miles across the open ocean in his rafts, only to be
killed by a single collision with land. In 1955, a Canadian named Henri Beaud-
out had been driven into the rocks aboard the raft *L'Egare,* and it was only

through luck and nerve that he and his crew had saved themselves at the last second. Their vessel, on the other hand, was utterly obliterated. Even in the era of satellites and electronics, ships sank every day because they collided with something, most often the coast. The ill-fated *Exxon Valdez* did not meet disaster at the hands of the high seas, but because it hit the coast due to a piloting error. Every week it seemed there was the same bleak news: "Russian-flagged tanker . . . split in two and partially sank overnight after running aground in heavy winds . . ." "Norwegian catamaran/passenger ferry . . . struck a rock . . . 13 people were killed, and 5 are still missing, presumed dead . . ."

There was a second problem, perhaps greater than that of collision: The balsa raft attracted all kinds of erroneous beliefs, legends, and misinformation. Every time I tried to isolate and confirm a fact about the vessel or the route to Mexico, that "fact" proved erroneous. Heyerdahl claimed that the reason *Kon-Tiki*'s balsa logs didn't waterlog and sink after 101 days in the ocean was because he cut down his balsa trees and then put them in the water before they had a chance to dry out. The sap inside them kept the seawater out, he said. But the first thing that wood engineers told me was that balsa logs don't waterlog! I constantly heard conflicting tales of how to deal with the *Teredo navalis* too. But none made any sense. We were told by some people that in the early twentieth century some balsa rafts made voyages to Panama; but whenever we asked around on the Santa Elena Peninsula about these voyages, we received answers that were quite vague. These voyages were undoubtedly made, but no one could actually give us any details. A balsa raft expert once told me that the voyage would take two weeks. Based on what? He had no answer. In the end, *nobody* knew. The trading route had slipped through the cracks of history. It wasn't like an artifact—it couldn't be dug up and then analyzed under a microscope; it was a vital piece of history that could only be known through experiment, and unless we understood the Trading Route—the greatest achievement of the Manteño—then we'd never really know the history of "Dower's people."

Back in 1995 I decided to undertake The *Illa-Tiki* Expedition in five minutes, and without the slightest hesitation, but it took me a year to decide on The *Manteño* Expedition. I was exceedingly reticent, but that reticence was overwhelmed by my desire to undertake an expedition that would have real scientific value. In 1997, I committed to navigating a balsa raft to the mouth of Rio Balsa, sixty miles north of Acapulco, the farthest-known reach of the ancient Manteño. If that could be completed, then I still wanted to try for Hawaii. I still relished the idea of crossing a great stretch of ocean, but now, that was secondary. I immediately had a feeling of foreboding about my fate, but for the first time I felt the pride that comes from working on an expedition that would contribute to "the body of knowledge."

Thankfully, miraculously, my patrons would stick by me. They risked lawsuit, damage to reputation, public embarrassment, and, in the end, the possibility that all their efforts might come to naught. It is remarkable that any of them ever threw in their lot with mine. Their loyalty to me can be summed up by the words of one gentleman, a successful businessman named Bill Kress, who said, "Well, these types of expeditions are very important, and we don't want to see you go out there poorly equipped."

They asked nothing of me, except that I try again. Their camaraderie was difficult to believe in such a cynical era. Most were small businessmen, well-seasoned in the area of hardship and setback—more afraid of giving up than of taking a risk. One of the first to help me back when I had nothing but a dream was Bill Lockhart. He had built a profitable little empire by manufacturing beautiful documents—the type of expertly prepared presentations that made others take The Expedition seriously. He was a man two generations removed from me, a man who had probably never left the office of his small business for twenty years, but he was gratified that there were still people who explored, who still went on expeditions, who still tried. I went to see him in late 1995 to tell him that I had failed, and it was agonizing. But when I had finished he said only, "Oh . . . well, don't worry about that, you know—I had my fair share of hiccups when I was starting out—just keep going—you can have whatever you want—just talk to my people."

It might be easy to think that I was relieved when he said that to me, but I wasn't; it was very hard. There is a feeling, one that has been shared by every expeditioner, and perhaps one that can only be understood by expeditioners from Shackleton to Heyerdahl—that feeling when you walk out of a patron's office with a lump in your throat that you cannot swallow—regardless of how hard you try, you simply cannot get their generosity down. There are few who can understand the enormous burden of knowing that you can never repay those brave ones who've stood by you—like Marion Jett, the engineer who built the generators for our bicycle-driven electrical system. When I tried to explain the expedition to him, stumbling through the story, he asked, "How did the generators work?"

"Fine. Just fine, well—there was a little corrosion on one of them near the end."

"I'll take care of that."

When I called him the next month, he said, "The generators are sitting on the floor of my office. They won't corrode; I've gold-plated the wires."

Then there was the affable, irrepressible Henri Kohn, who owned balsa farms in Ecuador and had helped us get our logs safely and legally. He was my first patron, whom I had called back in 1993. In 1995, after the failure of The *Illa-Tiki* Expedition, I made an agonizing phone call to him, explaining that we had had a lot of problems. At the end, when I said, "I want to try again—" he blurted out, "Well you *have* to try again!"

When I went to Ecuador a couple of years later I called on one of Henri Kohn's lieutenants in Quevedo, where we would get the balsa logs for our next raft. Henri's representative there was an engineer named Jose "Pepe" Chang. Quiet and soft-spoken in the extreme, Pepe Chang was a highly respected man who dressed plainly and wore a tape measure on all occasions. I explained that we had had problems, and that we'd need his help again. Sitting behind his desk, he played with his tape measure for a second, took a puff on his cigarette, then smiled wryly and said, "When you're ready, just let me know. I'll take care of everything."

"Are you sure?"

"I'm sure," he said. "We believe in what you're doing."

On a rainy morning in March of 1996, in a small, civil ceremony, I married Annie Biggs. I had always assumed that I would never marry, but Annie was perfect. When I had come home from The *Illa-Tiki* Expedition, demoralized, wearing "dead man's clothes," I had gone to her house planning to stay for just a few hours, but I had never left. Neither of us had any money, but we had "The Struggle."

In late 1995, Annie and I had returned to Panama, back to the little cove on the Azuero Peninsula. When we walked down to the beach, we were met by an astonishing scene: The wrecked hulk of an enormous Manteño sailing raft, abandoned in a sparsely inhabited wilderness, five hundred miles from its home. No other image can stir the soul like that of a marooned ship on an empty beach. The *Illa-Tiki* was slowly sinking, bow first, into the black sand of a foreign shore. It was still completely intact, all of its timbers and canes still straight and tied into place, but now you could see only the top part of its logs, where they peeked above the sand. As it had back in Salango, the *Illa-Tiki* seemed to transport you for a moment: It looked just like what it would have looked like to a marooned mariner from ancient Salango, a Manteño. I couldn't help but wonder—indeed, at times I have been *beguiled* by the question: Was it among company? Was it simply joining other Manteño ships, sunken into the sands of Central America? Standing on the volcanic sand, looking at the *Illa-Tiki,* all of the old feelings came back. It was hard for me to take. But Annie was there, and as always she knew we must move forward—we must keep going. It was at times like these when she was at her best. We spread out a remnant of one of the sails and cleaned all of the equipment that could be salvaged, while the acrid smell of mold and mildew made our eyes water. It took us an entire week to organize what we had, and then roll the mass of gear into the sail. Once the packing was finished, we tied the canvas up so that it looked like an immense, ungainly sausage, and transported it home.

It was an emotional exercise for me and I was moving forward on grim determination, but now I was doing everything with Annie. And in an era when I had seen people wilt at sea, her resolute refusal to stop moving forward was what saved me. Together, we were living a double life. We were making reconnaissance trips, gathering data, and continuing to build the infrastructure needed to put an expedition in the field, but we also lived in suburban America. We were building giant rafts and salvaging them—disappearing to remote areas under the most fantastic of circumstances, and then the next week sitting at dinner parties, among polite company, where some unsuspecting, well-meaning soul would invariably look at Annie and me and ask, "So! Now . . . What do *you two* do?

We were working night and day on The *Manteño* Expedition now, wading through a mountain of paperwork, and we were accumulating the expeditionary team. In those years there were several catastrophic expeditions, catastrophes in the field that I could not ignore. I once had a phone conversation with a well-known expeditioner who was coming off a failed expedition where there had been casualties, including a death. I remember that his persona—his entire life—was a manifestation of bitterness. Then we began hearing news of a fantastic disaster atop Mount Everest. When I went to Washington, D.C., in 1997 to address The Explorers Club, it had been almost a year since Everest, but the pall still remained. Throughout the weekend veteran expeditioners talked solemnly about the loss of friends. What would I do if this happened to me? Losing a person was so horrible an idea that I vacillated from cool calculations of how to stay alive in every scenario to mind-bending flashes of terror. I had no delusions of safety. I interviewed many people who wanted to volunteer for the expedition, and none of them seemed to realize what they were getting into; the few who did, once I had bluntly explained the dangers to them, wanted things changed.

The first to join was David Moorer, a medic from Oakland, California. I met him in September of 1996, when I was invited to speak at the Grand Gathering of Explorers in San Francisco. He was in his early thirties, tall and friendly in a folksy kind of way, and he immediately volunteered to go on the next expedition. He was a highly qualified person, with experience in emergency medicine, swift water rescue, and high-angle rescue.

Then, after months of fruitless interviews, I asked Scott Siekierski to join. He was just out of college and had no expeditionary skills to speak of, but his clearheaded enthusiasm impressed me. Unlike all those before him, my detailed explanation of the dangers did not send him into an emotional retreat.

In March of 1998, I met Cameron MacPhearson Smith. He was a professional archaeologist, with years of expeditionary experience. He was the type of quiet unassuming guy who did everything well, and he always met a tough situation with a long, loud, hiss. He'd suck in whole lungful of air through his front teeth: "Hssssss. Man, we're in a real fix." We loved that hiss.

In May of 1998, Annie and I held four days of briefings at our home. The new team sat through hours upon hours of lectures on primitive technology, raft design, piloting, geography, expeditionary operations, hazards, the options open to us at each step of the way, and more. When the four days were over, I worried that I had told them only half of what I knew.

I signed a deal with a film company in July of 1998 to make a two-hour documentary television program. In the package I got another member of the team: Martin Johnson, the cinematographer. Martin was in his middle twenties and an experienced climber. He was a guy who made people feel comfortable, and I was very glad to have him.

Shortly after meeting Martin, I began keeping a diary.

24 July 1998
I have never before felt the pressure that I feel now. I can never repay the people who have helped me. For every one day in the field there are three in prep. Keeping technology off of the raft is a constant struggle. I will miss my wife terribly.

The team began assembling at my home a few days before our scheduled departure to Ecuador. Cameron brought along his climbing partner, Chiu-Liang Kuo, who would help the expedition for the first two weeks, then return home. This brought the field team up to six.

We broke down the entire expedition into parts, none larger than seventeen inches in size, and packed them into duffel bags. We did this to avoid shipping our gear in, where it could become stalled in Ecuadoran customs. If the gear wasn't illegal or hazardous, then they would let it through at the airport—theoretically. We could buy the rest of the gear in Ecuador, especially the hazardous objects, like aerial flares. In the early hours of the twenty-ninth of July, the six of us sat in the airport, exhausted, waiting to go into the field. Over the airport intercom the official voice announced the last call for our flight: Time to go. Annie and I drifted toward the Jetway. "I love you," I said, "but I have to go." She looked at me and squeezed my hand tightly. Tears poured down her cheeks.

The last days before an expedition are always somewhat morbid. There are parties, but the worry builds and the noise subsides until there is a tense silence among your loved ones. That morbid silence had built up, and now, as I walked onto the Jetway, it had manifested itself in Annie. We parted and I walked forward, then turned around to look at her for the last time. She was distraught; it was as though a storm had come over her face.

6

On Expedition in Ecuador

We landed at the Guayaquil Airport at 9:30 in the evening, and were met by an elderly Ecuadoran woman of great prestige. She politely explained to the customs officials that we had come to build a great *balsa*, and they waved us through, wishing us good luck in our endeavor.

29 July 1998
". . . Finally, we are on the ground in Ecuador. We have landed in Guayaquil with 2700 lbs. of expeditionary gear neatly packed into 27 green, military-style duffel bags. After three and a half years of preparations, the six of us are crammed into two, foul-smelling, $3.50 a night hotel rooms in downtown Guayaquil with a gigantic mass of green canvas . . ."

We went out for a drink that first night, walking through the streets of Guayaquil, a group of happy gringos, fresh from their world. At the Oro Verde, the best hotel in the city, we lounged at the air-conditioned bar, talking and laughing. The second team had come on The *Manteño* Expedition completely innocently, as had the first, on The *Illa-Tiki* Expedition. But I had changed. I knew what lay ahead, and I emitted a deep respect for the upcoming difficulties that the new team couldn't understand. I knew that there would be some among us who might break under the strain. At the bar, Martin said, "I'm really impressed with the way you've handled the expedition so far."

So far?

30 July 1998
. . . Martin leads the way. He possesses humor, gamesmanship, a sense of
the scheme. He smiles under pressure—a quality I have always wished for.

In the morning we spent a little time getting organized. Though we were now
working out of a cheap hotel in a foul part of downtown Guayaquil, it felt good
to be back in Ecuador. Guayaquil is very much akin to New Orleans: hot, humid, frantically busy, musical, unafraid to drink, and wide open. Ecuador pro-
duces and exports more bananas than any other country in the world, and
banana leaves, branches, and occasionally whole trees, can be seen floating past
the town, day and night, coming down the rivers from plantations as far away as
two hundred miles. And from all of this fruit and all of this activity comes the
greatest concentration of odors and smells imaginable. Guayaquil's air is completely unique: Walking down the street you are struck by one highly concentrated odor after another: First, women's perfume, then suddenly sewage, then
rotting vegetation, then fresh tropical flowers, then rotten-egg-smelling standing
water, then smog, then a thick, tropical wind coming off of the river, then a
strong mix of cheap aftershave and roasting chickens. Sitting at the junction of
the tropical rivers Guayas and Babahoyo, Guayaquil is by far the largest city in
Ecuador. The official population is quoted at 1.6 million people, but the surrounding sprawl is more like 3 million. At the north end of town lies the only
bridge across the rivers for twenty miles. Twenty-four hours a day, seven days a
week, the banana trucks come in from both sides of the river to be off-loaded at
the Port of Guayaquil. From the port it's another forty miles downriver to the Pacific Ocean. Guayaquil is the bottom of a gigantic funnel through which the
world's bananas must be forced.

In the evening we had dinner at a restaurant on stilts over the river Guayas.
When the tide floods in at the mouth of the river, forty miles south of the city,
the level of the river in Guayaquil rises nine feet. In ancient times skilled balsa
mariners used the tide's effect to pilot their rafts up the river, sometimes as far
as sixty miles inland. We now intended to pilot the river ourselves. We
planned to cut down the balsa logs deep in the interior, build the base or "hull"
of the raft there, and then float sixty miles south, where we'd land on one of
the bushy islands at the mouth of the river, and finish construction. If this
plan worked it would eliminate all of the arduous overland transport that had
plagued us during The *Illa-Tiki* Expedition. But it would be no easy feat. To
make this journey we would have to first survey the river to be certain that no
obstacles blocked the way.

Twenty-four hours after our arrival in Ecuador, Scott was already impatient. At dinner he said to all of us, passionately, "We can't just sit around. We've got to get to work."

31 July 1998
Scott's entire personality is based on what might be called "traditional" masculine strength. He is taut, physically and mentally; rigid, linear, upright. His mind is muscular. He communicates like a Russian gymnast: An unembarrassed display of power, but a draconian slavery to form and efficiency.

Today the entire team spent their first collective day in Guayaquil, tropical metropolis.

In the morning, we boarded buses for the four-hour journey to Quevedo, where we prepared to survey the river. The river survey would entail all of the miseries of working in the tropics. All expeditions know misery: In the desert you face heat and dehydration, in the polar regions cold and storms, and in the tropics, the first misery you face is disease. I learned this during my first week in Ecuador, in 1993. While on the banks of the river Quevedo, I ate a sandwich made of an unknown meat, and within two hours it gave me a full-blown case of dysentery, my first official expeditionary disease. But dysentery can be treated if you act quickly. It was the others that worried me. The Armed Forces Preventative Medicine Recommendations Survey warns of the following as common occurrence in the Ecuadoran interior: malaria, typhus, typhoid fever, yellow fever, dengue fever, rabies, bubonic plague, the *entire* hepatitis series, onchocerciasis (river blindness), brucellosis, cholera, and paragonimiasis (lung worms). Malaria scared me especially. In the 1990s, they still had the big billboards up by the highway showing a giant mosquito with blood dripping from its sucker and a changeable number panel, like a lotto board, to show the number of victims for that month. They also still had the malaria eradication service working in various areas, suppressing the mosquitoes with DDT and fire. Upwind of a village they'd park what looked like a small street sweeper that would dump a cloud of pesticide into the air in the form of a white powder. The powdery wall would drive the mosquitoes out of the village, making them flee like a panicked mob. I saw the eradication service burn a bamboo house once, just north of the town of Santo Domingo. It must have been infested. As our bus bounced by the scene, a middle-aged woman in front of me shed a tear and her daughter crossed herself. But the family who lived there, standing out by the road with the possessions they were allowed to keep, didn't seem emotional at all. Perhaps they were all cried out. The eradication service evidently stopped the harsher methods between 1997 and 2000, but as of this writing they are back at it, because the malaria epidemic has descended once again.

We had taken malaria pills during the first expedition, but now, with David Moorer aboard, the expedition developed a medical conscience. We had finally graduated to the medical standards necessary to cope with tropical conditions. We instituted "National Take Your Goddamned Larium Day." Larium, malaria medicine, must be taken every seven days without fail to be effective. Each Sunday, we religiously, publicly, took our Larium. It is a weird drug that frequently causes nightmares and other disturbing psychological side effects.

1 August 1998
We are in Quevedo to survey the river. My love for these men, Martin, Scott, Cameron, and David, grows daily. Scott and Martin are kind and brotherly toward each other. The Ecuadorans are a (closed) culture; they are mesmerized by our presence here.

. . . The weather is mild here, yet sweating is mandatory in this environment.

. . . The River Quevedo is a mud menagerie. Between this base of operations and the sea lie 17 hair-pin turns, 5 bridges, and perhaps a hundred sand bars that could permanently ground the raft. In a raft made for the open ocean, navigation of the confusion (the river) is quite possibly impossible.

To ground the raft (somewhere on the river) would mean disaster. The suction that the mud of the Quevedo develops, combined with the massive weight of the (raft), might be too much for man or machine to overcome. This is a complicated decision.

On the morning of August 2, the six of us left our low-rent hotel room in downtown and tramped through the bustling streets of Quevedo, dodging people and cars and carrying our equipment in our arms and on our backs. A block away we turned left and walked down to the bank of the river Quevedo. The river was half a mile wide here and flowed silently past the city at about one mile per hour, headed southward toward Guayaquil. The water before us was horrible. It was brown and gray and smelled of sewage. Standing at the riverbank was like standing in the alley of the city. Though we were still surrounded by the traffic noise and the honking of horns from the busy streets, most of the buildings of the town faced away from the river, as though trying to ignore it. The riverbank's only inhabitants were an ungainly group of local children and filthy homeless men, who quickly gathered to stare. They stood

Illa-Tiki on the open sea. The spare sail is drying on the roof of the hut.
Photo credit: Chris Buntenbah

The author with Maestro
Enrique Guillen, shipwright.
Photo credit: Chris Buntenbah

Manuco working on the
starboard mast step.
*Photo credit: Elizabeth
Eckstein*

The first raft, *Illa-
Tiki*, sitting on the
beach in Salango,
almost ready for
launch, March
1995
*Photo credit:
Elizabeth Eckstein*

The launch of the *Illa-Tiki*: "The impact of the raft seemed to blast a hole in the ocean...."
Photo credit: Sandra Sykes

Brock Haslett sitting on the forward deck of *Illa-Tiki*, exhausted from fighting with the sail.
Photo credit: Chris Buntenbah

Chris Buntenbah in Panama. "We lived, basically, as castaways."
Photo credit: John Haslett

Manteño at sea.
Photo Credit: John Haslett

Dower Medina-Urdin, standing on the forward deck of the *Manteño,* at dawn, with a product of "the fishing watch."
Photo credit: Cameron MacPherson Smith

The bare balsa logs, forward of the bamboo deck.
Photo credit: Chris Buntenbah

The catwalk—our only way to reach the stern of the raft.
Photo credit: Chris Buntenbah

David Moorer steering the *Manteño* into Bahia Solano. The rocks that we piloted the raft through are on the horizon, at right.
Photo credit: John Haslett

Cameron MacPherson Smith. In 2004 he crossed the ice cap of Iceland in the dead of winter, alone, and on foot.
Photo credit: John Haslett

Scott Siekierski on night watch. Just behind him stands the steering *guara*.
Photo credit: John Haslett

The infamous Camp Hardcore: Refitting *Manteño* in the wettest place on earth.
Photo credit: John Haslett

Annie Biggs in Salango, 1998
(with Dower's son), shortly before
the launch of the *Manteño.*
Photo credit: John Haslett

Alejandro Martinez sail-
ing *Manteño II,* shortly
before it entered
The Gyre.
Photo credit: John Haslett

Cesar Alarcon, with sea
snake. "He yearned,
always, to catch one."
Photo credit: John Haslett

An unusually windy and wild day in The Gyre.
Photo credit: John Haslett

The Remarkable Colombians: Alejandro Martinez (in foreground), and Cesar
Alarcon, preparing for a day's work under the raft. Note the *guaras* at right.
Photo credit: John Haslett

around us with their fingers in their mouths, scratching their faces, exchanging jokes, and shrieking in astonishment.

There was a small park of cement and grass at the riverbank, and the team dutifully walked over to it, laid two inflatable boats on the ground, and prepared to get underway. The first boat was a dark gray river runner, ten feet long and shaped like an oval. Martin leaned down, connected the plastic hose of the foot pump to a steel fitting in its side, and began stomping air into to it. It was worn and weathered and had several patches glued to its sides, but was of very sturdy construction. It would carry the six men. The second boat, which was much smaller, would carry our gear. It was made of plastic and was much flimsier than the river runner. Fending off questions from the kids and the homeless men, we steadily took turns stepping on the mechanical pump. This was the beginning of field operations for The *Manteño* Expedition: a group of groomed, glowing, gringos, working fresh muscles under clean clothes, their skin shining from waxy cleanliness under the equatorial sun.

When the boats had stretched tight, we carried them to the river's edge and set them on the surface. The water was a brown and gray soup. In a way, I was glad: This would give me a chance to observe each man's individual reaction to bad conditions. There were a few strained jokes among them, but mainly an attitude of acceptance. We quickly took our places on the gray boat, straddled over the gunwales, three to a side, and shoved off from the bank.

Riding on top of the hard rubber wall of the boat, I reached forward and began to dig water. We were already in the current, moving at about two miles per hour. David sat in front of me, on the bow, and like the rest of us he wore a T-shirt and a baseball cap and had a milky film of sun block smeared over every inch of his bare skin. Scott sat opposite him, also on the bow, with Chiu behind him. We dug deep strokes of brown water while Martin sat on the stern, steering. Cameron, sitting opposite Martin, took notes and measurements. Months later, in distant waters, the inflated walls of the river runner would be soft and saggy, making the boat hard to paddle, but on this first morning we sat on a sturdy structure with a hard surface that held up well under the working movement of six men.

Once clear of the foul shore near downtown, we headed downstream at a good speed, and within a few minutes came upon a large sandy island in the middle of the river. We landed, took a few minutes to get better organized, and then launched again. Once more we made good speed in the current. We seemed to find our rhythm now, our heads and shoulders bowing a little with each stroke and the bulbous head of the gray boat pushing smoothly across the water. We were finally leaving the city, making a constant speed and steadily towing the supply boat behind us. The noises from town faded and within ten minutes they were gone and forgotten. Around us the heavy tropical atmosphere seemed to settle, as though quieting the world with its weight. Silence rested on the river now. Our paddles splashed softly. We were alone.

We were now paddling through a tropical basin—a trough between the Andes and the coastal highlands—a region where heavy rains, oceans of mud, decaying plant life, human and animal excrement, and pesticide all slide into seven main rivers, all of them wide and muddy. It is somewhat like a giant aquifer, like the Everglades in South Florida. It is a vast sea of mud and muddy water, melting off to the south, emptying out into the Pacific Ocean. Sometimes called *Los Rios,* or simply "The Rivers," it is where the world's bananas are produced—one thousand square miles of concentrated fertility, where hundreds of tons of bananas flow south, like the rivers, twenty-four hours a day.

From our perspective in the boat the Quevedo River was wide and steady flowing, like a highway, working its way southward in a series of long straightaways and smooth turns. Banana plantations lined the river, sometimes stopping at the very lip of the muddy bank. When that happened the river turned into a long corridor, with high walls on both sides. Sometimes it was possible to travel for miles and see nothing on either side but rows upon rows of green banana trees like bushy scarecrows, standing silently on both banks, their arms hanging over under the burden of the heavy fruit.

After five miles of solitude we passed a bamboo house on stilts above the mud and filth. It undoubtedly housed the family that took care of that particular section of the plantation. At the edge of the water, a lone woman in her thirties knelt down in front of a rock and did her laundry. She soaped up her clothes and then beat them sharply with a paddle. The hollow "whop! . . . whop! . . . whop!" of her striking her laundry could be heard from a mile away. As we passed, she paused for a minute and looked at us, then went back to work. We cruised steadily down the center of the river, the six of us straddled over the walls of the gray boat, about one hundred yards from her bank. A single rope shot straight back to our supply boat, which we were towing smoothly, and together the two boats left behind a slight disturbance as they pushed across the slowly drifting brown water. Then the woman at the bank was overcome by curiosity, looked at us again, and returned once again to her work. As we cruised away the entire river corridor echoed with a hollow "whop! . . . whop! . . . whop!"

At midday we reached the banks of the Ecuadoran government's experimental forest, eight miles below Quevedo. The logs to build our raft would come from this place. I went ashore with David and Cameron and told Scott to stand watch at the boats. We spent the rest of the day talking to the locals, making friends, and scouting the location. Drinking cane liquor with the men who tended the experimental forest, we established ourselves with them—an important ritual in Ecuador—and when we took our leave they promised to help us build and launch the raft from their land. We returned late, and passed the night quietly on a sand bar in the middle of the river.

In the morning, Scott was angry and complained very loudly about having to stay behind the previous day while we went ashore and drank. He felt spending an entire afternoon talking and making friends with the locals was an enormous waste of time. He felt the expedition wasn't moving fast enough, and said that there was "no excuse for it." The rest of the team launched the boats in silence.

Aboard the boats, we paddled in unison. After one day in harsh conditions, a tension had already started to build. Martin, in his clumsy way, defused it. He had been a river guide at a tourist attraction somewhere in Colorado, and he seemed natural as pilot of the riverboat. He sat on the stern, awkwardly guiding us down the river, sometimes sending us far out of our way and occasionally letting the boat turn completely around so that we floated down backward. I was loath to remove him though because he seemed to need to prove himself in front of the others, and more importantly, he was funny and cavalier in his position of authority. To Martin, being a pubescent boy was the greatest experience of his life; everything afterward had been a letdown. He entertained, shocked, and appalled us with his pubescent humor until he was told, first discreetly, and then overtly, to stop. But it broke the tension.

We were surveying the river now, working with laminated topographical maps and handheld compasses. In order for our new balsa raft to float down the Quevedo, the river would have to be at least three feet deep and forty feet wide and free of obstructions, all the way from the experimental forest to the sea. We carried with us a sounding pole, marked at various depths, which we used to probe the bottom of the river and record its depth. We used our paddles as well, sinking them into the murky water to measure the depth of the river. As we sounded for depth, I kept a running conversation with Martin, who was steering: "Two feet. Not good enough. Martin—take us to the other side . . . two feet . . . two feet . . . three feet . . . four feet . . . four feet . . . four and a half feet. Martin—let's go back and forth in this area."

Cameron sat on the stern of the boat and wrote down measurements as they were called out. He also made notes and drew sketches of important features and the general shape of the river. Expeditionary documentation was a specialty of his, and as we worked our way back and forth across the brown river he wrote almost continuously, his head bent down and concentrated on his notebook. Physically, Cameron was much like Dower: of medium height and weight, fit, and exceedingly streamlined. He had black curly hair and a thin beard, and he wore a faded black T-shirt and a plastic compass around his neck on a nylon line. Tropical sun beat down hard on his nose and ears, as it did everyone else's, and he spent a lot of time looking up and down the river and then looking back at the map, squinting hard to overcome the glint of the plastic lamination.

Even though the Quevedo was as much as half a mile wide in some places, it was rarely deeper than six feet. We worked our way downstream, crisscrossing the river, plunging our paddles into the water, adjusting our seating positions, readjusting, bending our backs and legs, working hard in the equatorial sun, sweating and burning, trying to get comfortable in our sweat and mud-encrusted tub. In the afternoon we cruised through a narrow channel with a strong current and had to land and resurvey it. Cameron and I walked up to the head of the channel and waded out into the murky water. The current immediately grabbed our bodies, and we ran down the riverbed, calling out approximate depths to each other.

In the evening we landed on a mud flat, half a mile from the nearest settlement. It was a defensible campsite, and secluded. Here, the new group received its first bathing in mud. They slogged and fought their way from the mud flat to the boats and back, the earth sucking at their boots every step of the way. The flats near the river were made of mud just thick enough to hold a shape and yet so thin and mushy that it was impossible to walk in it without sinking. As was the case everywhere else on the Quevedo River, it was a grayish brown and exceedingly sticky. It was also, invariably, very deep, and walking in it always degenerated into futility. There seemed to be an endless supply of it, too, as though there had once been, throughout the earth, a great flood of mud. At our campsite we put down tarps to prevent sinking in, and then set up the tents. As the light faded I told the others that they could stand their watches inside, but they had to be awake and on guard. I did this because, in the position our camp was in, I feared a mosquito swarm more than an attack by humans.

I had been through a mosquito swarm during the first expedition. Dower's brother-in-law Marlon and I had been out in the countryside one evening at dusk, waiting for the bus, when they descended on us. There were some muddy river flats nearby, and when the sun set the mosquitos swarmed by the thousands. We slapped as fast as our hands could move from one hot spot to another, but there were so many that it was futile. Growing more frantic and disoriented each minute, we looked like two men performing some kind of crazy dance on an empty highway. They were penetrating our eyes balls by sticking their suckers through our eyelashes, and I was sucking two or three at a time into my nostrils every time I inhaled. Every few seconds I'd blow them out of my nose and try to breathe out of my mouth, but that only meant that I now sucked dozens of spindly little insect bodies down my throat. We began shivering, as though extremely cold—as though all of the heat had been suddenly sucked out of our bodies. Then, coming over a hill, we saw the lights of a truck. Standing in the middle of the highway with our hands in the air, signaling frantically, we felt our bodies shaking violently. The sensation of hundreds of tiny suckers puncturing our skin was triggering convulsions in both of us. The truck slowed as it came near, and the four guys standing in the back—who obviously knew exactly what was happening—yelled, "Come on! Come on!" and we leapt onto the back of the truck just as the driver accelerated. The wind blew the swarms off us instantly. Sweet relief! Within two minutes we went from pure hell to complete calm.

Now, on the banks of the Quevedo, we stayed inside our tents after sundown, and avoided the mosquitoes.

In the morning, we set out in the boats and continued our silent tour of the muddy river. I noticed a subtle change in the group. The mud was creeping up their legs. It had jumped to the arms on a couple of them. Cameron and I were now painted head to toe from sounding the river with our bodies.

We were thirteen miles below the experimental forest now, working our way down, steadily recording the condition of the river. Occasionally we'd call out to people on the banks, asking them what was around the next bend or how far it was to the next settlement. They'd stare at us in silence, sometimes forcing out a few words in spite of their shock. Almost invariably the information we received made no sense because most of them had never been around the next bend.

At midday we landed at the base of a steep embankment and walked up. From the top of the bank we could see the entire corridor of the river, extending southward for miles—a wide brown chasm through a plain of rich green banana plantations. At the embankment we were met by some boys hunting with rifles in the tall grass. Their father came walking up and we talked for a while, then went to his house. It had a mud floor and a single table in the middle of the front room. The man's wife and small daughter stared at me as I talked to him about the river. It was obvious they had rarely seen anyone from the outside before.

On the way back to the river, the man turned misty-eyed and spoke to me in a reverent tone, assuring me that there was a sandy beach at a village somewhere down the river—he couldn't remember the name or its distance—where the women sometimes bathed in the nude. I nodded reassuringly, unwilling to crush heaven. He was so grave and so sincere I told him that if I found it, I'd send word.

In the afternoon, as we pushed the rubber boats downstream, we came around a quiet bend and saw a man sitting on a balsa raft. He was floating in an eddy, studiously casting a hand line into the river, silently fishing for perch. He was in his late forties, had deep lines in his face, and wore a plaid shirt and long blue polyester pants. His raft was made of five slender poles and measured no more than eight feet long by four feet wide. To keep his pants dry he sat on a tiny block of wood, about the size of a chalkboard eraser. A boy was there too, probably the man's son, and he was also floating on a balsa raft. We came by at one mile per hour, passing to within twenty feet of the man, and gently asked him questions about the geography of the river. He looked at us like we were a bunch of maniacs screaming obscenities at him from a red convertible, and by the time he managed an answer, we were already behind him and on our way.

In the afternoon of the fourth, we landed on a mud flat and made camp. For the group, the initial coating was complete, and the mud was now creeping inside their bodies. I saw Martin wincing and opening his jaw, working his tongue around, trying to rid himself of the muddy paste inside his mouth. Cameron spent a few minutes lost in thought, working his fingers around in his ears, trying to dig out some of the mud. David stood motionless, reaching up to delicately remove the little globs that hung from his eyelashes. I spent a few moments snorting loudly, but the gooey mud was too deep inside my nasal cavities, so I just swallowed it.

On the morning of the fifth, we got underway and immediately hit a mud shoal. The river there was less than two feet deep. We had surveyed many other areas of the river that we could list as "sketchy," but the bar at this point in the river was clearly impassable. Thirty-three miles below the experimental forest, we decided that it was simply too risky to bring the logs out by the river. In the afternoon, as we approached a village that we thought might have bus service, we decided to leave the river.

We landed, broke down the boats and gear, and walked up a hill to a waiting truck. The group looked nothing like it had just a week before. Mud covered every inch of our bodies and equipment. It was the type of coating that would never wash off. The new team was no longer a virgin.

It was hot in Guayaquil when we got back. David had been irritable on the way in and some of the guys told me they thought he was in trouble. Once inside our hotel rooms the air was foul and dank, and all of us labored a little to breathe. David was in a very bad mood and said that he felt tired. Shortly afterward, he fainted in the shower. His six-foot body crashed hard. We moved him to a bed, where he quickly came to. As I left to get some water, I heard someone in the hallway of the hotel say, "I think Dave's got malaria."

6 August
. . . I do indeed love this place, (Ecuador). . . . The River Quevedo is a brown streak running right down the middle of the world's largest banana factory . . .

. . . I can describe our survey of depth and width as a losing battle with a relentless flood of mud.

David never developed a fever, and in the morning he was back up to full strength. We never established what had made him pass out.

With the river impassable we'd have to truck the logs overland, as we had done during the first expedition. This wouldn't be easy. An earthquake had hit Ecuador just a few months back, and many of the roads were gone. Boarding buses in the afternoon, we began a survey of the roads between Quevedo and Salango. We found most of them were satisfactory—except one narrow passage through the mountains where the quake had caused ten feet of the road to fall away. The flatbed trucks, heavily loaded with the balsa logs, would be able to make this pass only if their drivers did not lose their nerve as they approached it. If they did, I wouldn't blame them. When we reached the coast, however, we discovered that the previous year's *El Niño* had washed away several bridges. In their place the army had laid down provisional bridges, simple iron beams that were narrow and precarious. We later measured the width of these and determined that they would allow the trucks to pass with a clearance of one inch to spare on either side.

8 August 1998
I return to Salango. I have absolutely no idea what to think. The men are in good spirits in anticipation of arriving in a clean dry place.

Perhaps the Salangueños have their imperfections, but their spirit put that raft (*Illa-Tiki*) in the Pacific; they gave us their hope. Whatever nobility that a simple fishing culture can have was given to us in good faith and trust.

I dreaded my return to Salango after the failure of *Illa-Tiki*, but the Salangueños accepted me back as though I'd only been away for a few weeks, and was now home. On the morning of my second day in town, I put on my best shirt and made the long walk to Enrique's house.

Rain drizzled down and I walked up slowly, accompanied by the new team. Enrique met me warmly, and we sat down together. In one minute we were back to our old partnership. We talked about everything, the wise old *Jefe* listening patiently to the new things I had learned, absentmindedly rubbing his forearm, and then he handed me his sketch pad and pencil and asked for examples. He loved to draw and he loved drawings. During the first expedition he had built a scale model of *Illa-Tiki,* and had a collection of sticks and strings that corresponded with the *wancas* and ropes we'd used in construction. Any person with a new idea had to be able to demonstrate it by using the model. Once the idea was brought into the discussion based on illustration and example, Enrique would then comment on the idea's merits and faults. If your idea was better than his, he changed his mind.

Just inside Enrique's house there were two pictures on the wall. The first was a picture of a small wooden boat that he had built, and I asked him once, "How many have you built like that one?"

"Those? Those are without number."

"Pardon?"

"I don't know how many I have built. They're without number. Who knows? Hundreds? Without number."

The second picture was one I'd never seen before: It was a photograph of that strange old man, the one who used to come down to the raft site and say, "How beautiful. Look at the raft. Those dudes are building a *balsa*. That's marvelous."

As we were talking, I said to Enrique, *"Mire."* ("Look at that."), and pointed at the picture.

"Sí. Mi Papa. Buena persona, muy buena persona," ("Yes. My father. Good guy, very good guy.") he said.

"That man is your father?"

"Yeah. He's sick now, very sick."

"Sorry to hear that."

"Ah, what can be done? He's old, very old."

As we spoke, the old man appeared, wearing a faded evening jacket and hat. He came up feebly, leaning heavily on his stick, and sat down on one of the wooden benches in front of Enrique's house. He recognized me, and then I saw a distant memory shoot through his mind. He seemed to awaken from the twilight of age and realize what was going on around him. He smiled and nodded his head approvingly. The young men had returned to build another *balsa,* like the ones he remembered from his youth.

·   ·   ·

The new raft would be built in Salango, following the same plan as the first expedition, but unlike that first expedition the group would at times split up. David and Scott usually toiled alongside Enrique's men, as did Martin sometimes, working in the sand with the *wancas,* while Cameron spent a lot of time in Guayaquil, sewing the canvas sails. I crisscrossed Ecuador, coping with operational problems and chasing down logistical headaches.

There were a million things to do and sometimes I logged as much as three hundred miles a week in buses. This was what it was to be "on expedition in Ecuador" as much as anything else: traversing a small country on the bus system, sometimes mountaintop-to-coast in one day. I went to the capital first—to Quito—climbing the switchbacks of the Andes aboard the express bus, disappearing into the clouds and finally arriving on the cobble-stoned streets of that mountaintop city. Martin accompanied me on this trip. I of course didn't know it at the time but he and I would see some strange adventures together over the next year. Martin was a wiry guy with an enormous grin of white teeth. There was so much of the playful child in him, so much of the gamer, that I couldn't help but like him. For some reason he seemed to spasm every few weeks. It wasn't so much a physical malady as a manifestation of his hilarious life. From time to time his arms and legs shot out from his body in all directions like a cartoon character. We went to a meeting with representatives of Freddie Ehlers, the famous television personality who sponsored us in Ecuador, and all went well, except that Martin had a crash on the way there. He was walking along just fine, and then his body hit the pavement with a meaty SLAP!

"FUCK!"

Back on the bus, crisscrossing the switchbacks of the mystical Andes, Martin's contact lenses dried out and he put on a pair of eyeglasses that were . . . unflattering. They were made like World War I flying goggles, but not in a warm and nostalgic sense. I think I muttered, "Yikes," because they conjured up images of bunkers and nuclear blasts. There was something so offensive in their overengineering that they made you wince, like looking at bad meat. I was slowly getting the feeling that this guy had probably been picked on unmercifully in high school. Winding our way up and over the coastal highland, and more switchbacks, I said to him in casual conversation, "My little sister had braces, boy—thank God I never had to endure that. Did you ever have to have them?"

"Are you kidding?"

"Bad, huh?"

"Oh, man."

"Head gear?" I asked.

"Head gear!" his eyes widened. "Head gear? I couldn't even *move* my head!"

We arrived back in Salango to overcast skies and drizzle. The purple radiation was gone, and now Enrique and company toiled under a gray sky—the Ecuadoran winter. The logs were down on the beach and the new construction was moving along quickly. After I had been in Salango a few days, Scott and Martin told me that they wanted a young man named Francisco to sail with us. Francisco was from Salango, and I had known him vaguely for quite a while. I went to see him and told him that he could go if Dower decided not to. Francisco was a good guy, and strong, but I had my obligation to Dower, the hero of The *Illa-Tiki* Expedition, who was now living in Galapagos. Nevertheless, Scott and Martin lobbied hard for Francisco. I sympathized with them because I had been in their shoes once: When they looked into the eyes of their new friend, Francisco, they saw, essentially, *themselves*: a young, middle-class man who wanted the same things from life that they wanted: escape, adventure, and opportunity.

Then one day, as I was walking down the steps of our *cabaña*, Dower was suddenly there: the "bronzed man." I had not seen him for more than three years and when we embraced, he spontaneously shed a tear. That caught both of us off guard. He quickly wiped his face and we stood for a moment just looking at each other. A few wrinkles now lined his eyes where his face crinkled up when he smiled, but other than that he looked the same: a slim man, clean-cut, wearing the same clothes that I'd wear if I lived in his world. I awkwardly broke the mood by showing him a 145-pound Danforth anchor that I had bought for emergencies—I didn't want any more nasty surprises in the middle of the night. We both laughed nervously, like two men walking past a graveyard. The rest of the team stood by, watching us, unable to appreciate the weird adventures that Dower and I had been through together.

Twenty-four hours later I was back on the bus, back into the switchbacks, and back winding over the coastal highlands. On August 19, I arrived in Quevedo, where we had left for the river survey. I checked into a hotel in the middle of town just as a long steady rain was starting to fall. Night came and I sat out by the street, having a drink, while streams of water fell from the tin roofs. Annie was in Ecuador, and I was waiting for her. She had been in the country for two days already and we had missed each other several times. In an emotional phone call she had said, desperately, "You just stay where you are and I'll come to you." This meant that she would have to navigate across Ecuador at night, as well as cope with the Ecuadoran bus system. Saying she didn't care—as long as it meant that we could be together—she had boarded a chicken bus in Guayaquil and had set out to find me.

In Quevedo, the banana trucks cruised by steadily for hours, one after another, and then shortly before midnight, I saw Annie's bus pull up under a

distant streetlight, two blocks away, and stop. The doors of the bus parted
and she jumped out and began running. Annie had been through a lot with
me. Our relationship had never known anything but expeditions, Ecuador,
and ancient ships. It had also always had something of a pall over it: Years
ago, when I had walked into her office, she had been married. Strangely, that
wasn't really the problem—she would've divorced even if we had never met.
The problem was that the man she was married to had been ideal, handsome
and good in every way—her parent's dream. To leave that conventional life
and come to these dirty streets had broken a lot of hearts. Annie had risked
everything, publicly, and now she was running through the rain in Ecuador—
something that all those broken hearts could never understand. But what else
could she do? It was as natural to her as Dower waiting for a ship in the night.

It was a muggy night in Ecuador's center of fertility, and the tropical rain
was pouring down on the dark streets and clattering on the tin roofs. I could
see her coming, sprinting down the dilapidated sidewalk like a bullet, her body
flashing at steady intervals—glimmering under the streetlights in brief images,
her auburn hair shooting out like a flame. It had only been a couple of months
since I'd seen her, but I felt as though I had lost a little piece of her, as though
being immersed in Ecuador had erased part of my memory. Her powerful little body sped through the streets of Quevedo and then shot from the darkness
and rain and into my arms like a wild animal. A gust of her sweet perfume
washed over me and she grabbed me around the neck and kissed me deeply. I
could feel her panting, her arms trembling as she held me close to her. We
stood, embraced, our throats choked, with the smell of the rain and the loud
sizzling of the drops on the cement all around us.

We stayed up late that night, talking and laughing and telling each other of
all the events we had missed in each other's life, and in the morning we made
the fourteen-hour bus journey to Salango.

The new raft now sat on the beach, ready for launch, but upon our arrival we
received somber news—Enrique's father had died. A writer and friend of mine
named Elizabeth Eckstein, who had come to Salango to help The Expedition,
both in 1995 and 1998, wrote of the funeral of Enrique's father, in her diary.

20 September 1998
. . . Enrique, who had on his best clothes and a bit of cologne for the occa-
sion, walked behind the casket. The casket was hoisted onto the shoulders
of four young men; ahead were children carrying flowers; following were
weeping women of the family. As the procession made its way through
town, it grew to 250 people. (Trucks) stopped for the crowd of mourners on

the road, and the people crowded into the white-washed cemetery to hear the eulogy, to lay the casket in a vault, seal it, and paint his name on it . . ."

I said to Annie that it would be best for us to pay our respects right away. It was long past dark, and so we walked through the silent town with our feet squishing in the mud. It was cold and wet out and all things dripped. The tiny mom-and-pop stores that dimly lit the street corners had closed up, and the rows of cinder-block houses appeared cold and dormant. Salango's church, a rectangular building of cinder blocks with an enormous A-frame roof, was dark and still. On nights like this, in the wintertime, you felt the breath of the sea in Salango. The ocean air streamed straight in and circulated through every house. It was as though the Pacific was breathing through the town, as though the homes and hallways and kitchens were all connected in a vast maze of cells, like an enormous lung. No house in Salango was completely sealed, nor was any room. Wherever you went, in every bedroom, in every kitchen, in every bathroom and in every closet, the deep salt air circulated freely there. This was the way it had been for eighty centuries. Every aspect of life, from lunch in the afternoon to a midnight kiss, had always been accentuated by the breath of the Pacific, and the eternal rumble of a crashing surf.

Coming up the low rise that led to Enrique's home, we could see that the house was closed up and dark, and so we would wait until the morning to talk to him. His house was at one end of Salango, and at the other end, roughly a mile north, lay the cemetery. The long dirt street that connected the two was now red and brown and as slippery as ice. I remember the Salangueños trudging up and down it in the winter in muddy work boots, sincere and humble. I had been down that street hundreds of times now too, many times humbled. Soon, I would be departing Salango for the last time.

The next day, in the bright afternoon, I met Enrique as he was ambling through the middle of town. I said I was sorry to hear about his father. Standing before me, he cradled his right forearm against his powerful torso. The lines in his face deepened, and his curly hair seemed especially white. He gazed for a long time down the road toward the cemetery. He said nothing to me directly, but for his own benefit he was able to choke out, *"Mi papa era bien bonita."* ("My dad was really beautiful.")

"I'm sorry."

We were standing next to each other in the dirt street, and around us, people went about their daily lives. I was a foot taller than he was and painfully aware of towering over him. "Dower is going to sail with us," I said.

"Good. There is no one in town more qualified to make this voyage. No one."

He peered around my body, looking in the direction of the cemetery, then he was lost in thought, playing with his tape measure. "Great guy—my dad."

Enrique's father, Eugenio Guillen-Pincay, loved the *balsa*. He was a mariner and a boat builder. His father taught him, he taught his son, and he had built boats "without number." His generation was the last to see the big rafts at work, an era that spanned at least eleven hundred years.

7

Voyage of the *Manteño*

We had researched the *Teredo navalis* for three years now. None of the popular books offered a valid solution. Various experts, some credible and some dubious, had suggested covering the logs with all sorts of various concoctions, credible and dubious. None guaranteed success. We had talked to companies that used balsawood to build fiberglass boats, but in tens of thousands of boats, they had never seen a single case because the balsa was insulted between layers of fiberglass. We had experimented by suspending blocks of balsa wood in seawater with various solutions and compounds on them and all had gotten the *Teredo navalis*. On August 25, 1998, twenty-four hours before launch, I finally gave up on finding a historically authentic solution. I was out of options. Reluctantly, I acquiesced to painting the bottoms of the logs with modern antifouling paint, and Cameron dutifully recorded the painting in our expeditionary records. I considered it a grave blow to our research, but it seemed to be the only logical way to cope with *Teredo navalis*. I felt that if we kept having rafts sink out from under us, we'd never learn anything. I could not have been more wrong: The opposite would prove true.

On the morning of the twenty-sixth, we prepared to launch. The new raft sat on top of its roller logs, and under overcast skies. It differed from its predecessor, the *Illa-Tiki,* in many ways, and it was a product of our changing views. The new vessel was still a barge, but now it was long and thin, almost sixty feet in length, which would make it faster than *Illa-Tiki*. It carried two masts, as well. Instead of using an A frame as we had on the previous raft, the new masts were single poles, tall and slender. In many ways it was still akin to *Illa-Tiki*, especially in the spring-loaded canes and the bamboo architecture.

As launch day progressed, the tide rose. I had chosen this particular day to launch because the highest tide of the month would occur in the afternoon. The sea would rise up and cover the beach in front of the construction site, and when it did, we'd go. I wanted the raft to travel the shortest distance possible to enter the ocean because I feared trouble on launch.

The epic launch of the *Illa-Tiki* in 1995 had been a fluke. We had been able to launch that raft in spite of destroying the launching mechanism underneath it in the process. For five hours, thousands of people had muscled a giant sand plow across the beach without knowing it. Only after the raft was launched did we determine what had happened. The crushing weight of *Illa-Tiki* had fractured the bamboo launch track and roller logs early on, turning them into a mangled wooden snarl that burrowed into the sand as the raft was pushed. If something like that happened again we wouldn't have the manpower to get the raft off the beach. Enthusiasm for the new raft was warm, but it's launch wouldn't attract the massive crowds and passion that *Illa-Tiki* had. Like those who attended Woodstock, those who witnessed the epic launch scene in 1995 knew that it had been a "cosmic accident."

Not only did I fear getting the new raft stuck in the sand before it reached the waterline, but I feared crashing it as well. Launch is one of the most dangerous operations in primitive shipbuilding and popular books abound with stories of the destruction of primitive vessels on land. A few have been totally wrecked before they have even reached the sea. After the launch of *Illa-Tiki*, Enrique spent a lot of time rethinking the process. He put in wider rollers, and removed the bamboo track. His improvements worked better than either of us could have ever been expected, and we were shocked by the ease with which we launched the new raft. Our newly completed vessel was launched in roughly ninety minutes, using fewer than 150 people. At the end an earthmover showed up and gave it the last push, but that was really only to speed the process. The raft slipped sweetly into the Bay of Salango on the afternoon of September 26, 1998. We christened her *La Manteño-Huancavilca*, in honor of the two great civilizations of the Santa Elena Peninsula.

Two weeks later, we prepared to leave Salango. Getting *Manteño* ready for sea had been an arduous process. The new design complicated the rigging enormously; it was like sorting out the toy box of a giant. Whole days had been used up just moving things—whole days of grunting and pushing and "one, two, three, heave!" and then "Hold on! Hold on! Hold on! Put it down." Most of it was just the reality of rigging a boat, but *Manteño* had a lot of structural problems, too. Enrique had been devastated by the loss of his father, and his mind hadn't been on construction, especially near the end, when the superstructure was built. Also, for various reasons, construction had been rushed, which is *always* a mistake when using ancient technology. Sitting at anchor, *Manteño*'s hut developed a depressing lean. Yardarms broke all of the time, and frequently the masts became unstable, swinging violently from one side to the other because their manila stays stretched like elastic. Nevertheless, the raft had performed satisfactorily in two trials. Our new vessel had more than twenty-five *guaras,* three times the number on the previous raft. *Manteño* grabbed the water in a way that the *Illa-Tiki* never could. On the eleventh, in the afternoon, after we had just finished the second trial, we agreed that we'd leave on the next day.

In the morning, the Salangueños built a small raft and prepared to tow and sail it around Salango Island. It was the day of the annual Balsa Raft Festival. They dressed a young man and a young woman in traditional clothing and they celebrated their forefathers, the *Manteño* and the *Huancavilca.* In the middle of it all we worked to load the raft with all the last-minute items. At 2:00 p.m. a boat towed *Manteño* to a point northwest of Salango Island, and then released us to sail. There was no parade and no grand escort this time. Our towboat quickly took leave of us and we were left alone, two miles offshore. Conditions were excellent. The wind was blowing in just the right direction for us to get underway, all we had to do was raise sail and head out to the high sea. In the ship's log, I wrote:

12 October 1998
Scheduled departure. Fix near Isla de Salango @ 1442

In Ecuadoran waters, it was the end of winter. It was cold out but not blustery. Overcast skies were moving in, turning the sky gray and the water dark. Aboard the *Manteño,* six ordinary men, ages twenty-three to thirty-five, prepared to get underway. The cool winter light grayed their faces, making them appear ashen. Their bodies hulked from layers of sweaters and baggy rolled-up pants, and if there was a common denominator among them it was that they all moved like marionettes, clomping on the bamboo poles with stiff limbs. Scott was the youngest, blond, muscular, rigid. Next came Martin, skinny and jerky. Cameron Smith was in the middle at thirty-two, but looked older with his Viking beard and curly hair. Dower, relaxed and fit—"the bronzed man," looked around at his gringo mates and wondered what kind of seamen they'd make. David was my age, thirty-five, tall and lanky, and struggling a bit. I was on my second balsa raft voyage, and proud to show my new friends some adventure.

Clear of the towboat, I said to the others, "OK, everybody on this," and we gathered into a semicircle at the base of the main mast. All around us the ocean sloshed and splashed noisily. Salango Island, the four-hundred-foot monolith, towered off our port beam, and before us the open sea stretched out to the horizon. Bunching tightly together, we spread our feet out and bowed our legs for balance, and then a swarm of bare hands reached up and grasped the hairy line and began hoisting the sail. We worked as a group, collapsing our legs and sinking down, then climbing the line and sinking down again. Unlike aboard *Illa-Tiki*, we now hoisted sails that were triangular, not square. Based on Cameron's analysis of the conquistador's sightings of balsa rafts we felt sure that this type of rig was much more authentic. The new raft's foresail levitated slowly upward, an immense triangle of canvas attached to a forty-foot-long bamboo cane. We could feel *Manteño* beginning to slide slowly on the water. The pointed peak of the mainsail climbed until it reached a height of almost fifty feet above the deck, and at the signal, Dower tied off the halyard and we backed away from the mast. Going astern as a group, we hauled up the mizzen sail—a much smaller triangle of canvas—in the same way, and when it had cleared the roof of the hut, we tied it off and trimmed it. *Manteño* was underway now.

If you'd have stood atop Salango Island, four hundred feet above the bay, you'd have looked out over a cobalt-colored ocean and seen a solitary wooden boat, just leaving, slowly and deliberately pushing out into an empty sea. From this vista you would have seen two sharp triangles protruding up like the spines on the back of a dinosaur. You'd have seen less a "raft" and more a slim sailing vessel made of tan-and-brown wood. If you'd have lived in AD 900, the era of the *Manteño*, perhaps you'd have seen a friend's boat, and worried privately about their uncertain return. More and more, this is the way I viewed things as well; more and more, I saw the ancient rafts as they once were.

Cameron and I had spent many months now pouring over *The Spanish Chronicles*, the official logs and records of the conquistadors' expeditions in the New World. Since the Manteño didn't have a written language, most of the descriptions of balsa rafts that we have today come from *The Chronicles*. Unfortunately, these documents are four hundred years old, and interpreting them is a tricky business. Because of that, it had been a relief to work with Cameron. Whereas I had no formal education, he was a disciplined scientist who could determine what we were allowed to assume about the Manteño and what we were not. The main problem we faced at this point was that *The Chronicles* only gave us an outline of what the raft looked like, which forced us to fill in the critical gaps with the knowledge we gleaned from popular books, and my own experiences aboard *Illa-Tiki*. This mishmash of knowledge had many flaws in it, as would be seen later. Cameron and I were certain, however, of one thing: We'd approach our problem not as mavericks but as researchers. We didn't care about theories and we didn't want to prove anything; we simply wanted to learn. Our sole motivation would be to increase the "body of knowledge."

Aboard *Manteño,* we stood on the bamboo canes and watched the long nose of the Pope dip into the waves. The wind blew from the south and the rolling swells broadsided us. It was just the sea state necessary to cause the raft to roll. *Manteño* swayed back and forth, back and forth, back and forth. Crowded together on the foredeck, we stood with our backs to the hut and to the land. Above us, the pulleys that held the sails to their masts squeaked at a slow rhythm, and at the end of each long roll of the raft they let out a rusty *"creeeeak."* Then the raft would roll back, splashing and sloshing, and then lean over again to another *"creeeeak."* Looking out to sea, we felt its cool air on our faces, and each time we glanced behind us the details of Salango faded a little more. The tan sand and the cinder-block houses and the snarls of scrub brush all merged into gray. Land turned into a dark band on the horizon, which thinned and floated away. *Manteño* was now patiently trudging out to sea at a speed of 1.5 knots.

We were now living and working on a platform of thirty-seven parallel canes. *Manteño's* deck was like a narrow bamboo stage. To walk across it usually required about ten spring-loaded steps. Its defining feature was that it was populated by a wide variety of primitive objects. First, there were the tools, which lay stacked in a pile at the center of the deck and looked like they had come from a medieval torturer's workshop: Long knives with dirty gray blades in various states of corrosion, several machetes of varying length—also gray and horrible, several *wancas*—heavy wooden poles with blunt points like stone-aged war clubs, and an enormous iron ax, which we called "the Caveman." Then there were the coils of rope. Though we had always enforced a strict authenticity in the construction of the raft, I wanted every line I could get my hands on in case we got into trouble. Every fiber was represented on the deck. Coils were stacked on top of coils: shiny blue polypropylene on top of white nylon, on top of dirty and hairy manila. Next, there were the standing objects. The largest and most commanding was of course the mainmast, standing in the very center of the bamboo deck, a solitary, forty-foot pole of blond *piñuelo* wood. Surrounding it at random locations here and there stood the steering *guaras,* five-foot-tall boards with bulbous heads that looked like wooden soldiers. When they weren't in use, which was often days at a time, we left the *guaras* half-inserted in the deck, so that they stood upright. At night you sometimes felt as though you were standing next to small wooden men who stared forward resolutely, like enormous pawns from a giant's chessboard. Farther back, closer to the doorway of the hut, stood what looked like a caveman's idea of office furniture. This was the watch station. The centerpiece was a balsa stump, which was the ideal stone-age table, solid and heavy and unmoving, and in the center of it sat the ship's black-and-white compass, slowly rotating back and forth as the raft felt its way forward. Behind the big stump table sat a bench, created by laying a board across two smaller stumps. The two people on watch would sit on the bench, reading the compass and piloting the raft.

Standing on the deck in the gray light, among our primitive tools, the six of us heaved a collective sigh of relief. We were finally on our way, and in my diary, I wrote, simply: "We are at sea now." We set our course, reviewed the watch system, and headed out to open ocean. Both sails were working perfectly. Our new rig was well balanced and *Manteño* sailed beautifully. "Wow!" Cameron said, shocked at his own accomplishment, "Raise the sails and she just goes! Incredible." After ten minutes or so it was clear that the raft would hold a course and that there was nothing to do but set the watches, and wait.

Dower, familiar with his home waters, fretted terrifically about pirates. Right before we left he pleaded with me to the point of using the expression: "I'm begging you" to sail out to high sea, away from the coastal thugs. Never at a loss for a little drama, he now told the crew: ". . . they will kill you for one, teeny, tiny, shrimp!" That didn't send the group into panic, but it got their attention nevertheless. We of course had discussed pirates among ourselves back in Salango. My memory of these discussions are quite surreal: A group of sincere, sober men, discussing the possibility of robberies, kidnappings, shootings, and gunfights on the bamboo decks of a balsa raft. The pirates in this region had a reputation of boarding *fibras* and stealing the outboard motors off of them and then leaving the fishermen aboard to die a slow, hideous death, adrift on the endless ocean with their tongues black and bloated from dehydration. Understandably, Dower wanted to sail due west, until we were fifty miles offshore. I respected his concern over any matter concerning the sea, plus, pirating was my own favorite fear.

We settled on a course of northwest, for twenty miles out. That would have us passing close to the sacred Isla de La Plata, twenty-two miles from Salango. This island had been a Mecca for the Manteño. They had considered it sacred and had built special areas there for religious ceremonies. A research zoologist once told me, "We've found the charred remains of some big fish out there on La Plata Island." His eyes widened and then he added: "We're talking *huge*. You have to have some serious boats to bring in that type of catch." Once we passed Isla de La Plata, we'd turn north and head for Panama, five hundred nautical miles away.

Manteño now made two and a half knots through the water. The conditions were ideal for seasickness, and slowly, our faces began to hang. We were fatigued from the intense work of preparing the raft for the sea, and fatigue is seasickness' greatest ally. The sun set, and *Manteño* continued its slow rolling in the darkness. Cameron and Scott took the first watch and did well, in spite of the seasickness. David and I took the next watch, midnight to 4:00 a.m.

It was my first time to be seasick. In the dark, David and I agreed that we'd take turns lying down. I lay my body down on the bench behind the compass table, put my arm over my face, and David sat next to my head and watched the course of the raft. Water sloshed loudly below me and I lay there in the cold, asking him about our compass course, which he constantly checked with a penlight. To our left, ocean swells rolled in from the darkness. Every few seconds a little hill of water would pass through and the raft would lift its logs up to skirt over it. In front of us stood the mainmast, a nine-hundred-pound column, balanced precariously on its end. It was now alive and swaying back and forth in the darkness. It pulled hard on its manila stays, stretching them taut and then relaxing. After each long stretch, the rope stays drooped a little more. More and more the pole was developing a humanlike motion, like a drunk or like a marionette on strings, falling and jerking in all directions and constantly catching itself at the last second. It was now definitely alive and jumping wildly. If it fell on the hut it would crush it like a giant foot stomping on a cardboard matchbox. I listened to the mainmast jump for a few minutes, but then couldn't take it anymore and sat up in the night air and said to David, "We have to tighten the stays."

"Maybe we should wake up the other guys."

"No," I said. "I want them to sleep. We can do it ourselves."

We got up from the bench like hungover drunks and stumbled across the bamboo canes, dizzy and nauseated, wet and cold. After feeling for the way to the end of the deck, I stepped down onto the bare balsa logs, while David stood at the edge of the deck, towering over me. Like me, he was a tall, lanky man. In the darkness I could only perceive his silhouette over me, which seemed to droop noticeably from the fatigue and seasickness. As I had so many times before, I stood knee-deep in the loudest part of the ocean, its surface. Cool seawater flooded up my legs and into my shorts and tons of water sloshed all around me. I had torn a good portion of the skin off of my hands a few days before while working with the ropes, and the saltwater now burned deeply, scorching the open sores on my palms. In order to tighten the stay we took a small pole and twisted the manila rope around it like a tourniquet. The idea was to crank the tourniquet pole around until the fifty-foot rope was taut, and then tie it off. When the mast leaned way over and the rope drooped, David and I hurriedly turned the pole, frantically twisting tourniquet to take up the slack. Waves foamed and hissed and tiny wavelets clattered and broke. Then the raft counterrolled and the mast flew back to the other side, violently spinning the tourniquet out, which narrowly missed our faces. We waited in the dark, felt the raft roll back over, and then cranked over on the pole again. It held for a split second, then snapped out. We stayed at it in the darkness, cranking over desperately and then ducking out of the way when it snapped out. The mast was now swinging over the deck in a wide arc. Finally, after forty-five minutes in the dark, it swung over, I cranked the pole, and David seized the tourniquet shut with two short lengths of rope. The violent motion suddenly stopped. The mast was secure.

With about twenty minutes to go on our watch, a tiny white light flashed in front of us: Isla de Plata. We handed the watch over to Dower and Martin at 4:00 a.m., and I estimated the island to be seven to ten miles away. It was Martin's first night at sea, and that was precisely the scenario that had motivated me to make sure that Dower sailed with us. With him on board, I could sleep well. And I was glad to sleep; I was tired, seasick, worn out.

At 5:00 a.m. Martin came into the hut and woke me. He was worried, but in control of himself. "We've got a real problem," he said. "I think you'd better come have a look."

"What . . . huh?" I was disoriented, my head still spinning from the seasickness.

"We're not going to be able to sail around La Plata Island."

"No way, Martin. Just take it easy. Dower will handle it."

Frederick's various panics had jaded me. During the voyage of the *Illa-Tiki* I had endured thirty-eight days of needless hysteria. Moreover, it was Dower's watch, and he was the best on the raft. If there was a real problem, I figured Dower would come get me himself. We were still at least five miles from the island, and at this distance Dower could simply drop the mizzen sail and the raft would turn and run down wind—easy maneuver, problem solved.

But in half an hour Martin was back. This time there was real fear in his voice. "John, you've gotta' get up," he said. "We're in trouble." I started to tell him that Dower could handle the boat better than I could when he blurted out, "I'm not kidding damn it, get off your ass right now!"

I got up and went out on the deck in the gray dawn of early morning. Martin was not Frederick. The island stood in front of us like a massive barrier, just a mile away. It was an enormous white-and-gray rock, two miles wide, with patches of green scrub hugging its steep walls. I could see the killer breakers hitting the rocks at its base; they were thirty minutes away. Even at that distance we could already hear the explosions. We had to escape right now or lose the raft.

For a moment I was incredulous. I turned to Dower, "What happened?"

"I don't know! I don't know, *Capitan!* I've been trying to turn this thing for *two hours!* I can't get it to sail any direction but directly at the island."

"What?"

"*Sí.* We've tried everything I know. Every time we do something, it just turns right around and sails directly toward the rocks."

The raft pushed straight for the surf line as though guided by an automatic pilot. Dower looked at me and we both thought of that first day, three years ago, when we had narrowly missed spectacular destruction at Puerto Rico. I instinctively looked back to make sure the dinghy was in the water, under tow. *Good. If we have to abandon ship, we have that option.*

The seconds ticked by. The sound of the exploding breakers intensified. "What do you think we should do?" Martin asked calmly. Then Dower began telling me all of the turning methods they had tried over the last couple of hours. I was starting to look at the rigging when Martin said, "I'm waking everyone up." He was nervous again, but not out of control.

The raft's ability to maneuver—what it could and could not do—was based largely on the speed at which the crew could move the sails and the *guaras.* Each time we wanted to force *Manteño* to make a sharp turn, the rigging and the *guara* placement had to be reconfigured. This might take as long as fifteen minutes. This meant that from the time we decided on what to do, to the completion of the turn, the raft would need at least a quarter mile lead time. During that delay, between decision and action, the wind and current would be pushing the raft toward the rocky shores of Isla de la Plata. Most of the men already knew, at least intuitively, that the raft could not be maneuvered out of a space smaller than a thousand feet. Once inside that point, the raft would be more or less committed to crashing.

The wind ran parallel to the coastline of the island. Ideally, we wanted to turn ninety degrees and run alongside the shoreline with the wind at our back and let the island fall off to our side. If we could do this, we'd have open sea in front of us again.

The crew, sick and exhausted, piled out onto the deck. Standing in a group at the doorway of the hut, they were a disheveled-looking rabble, ranging from David in full gear, including gloves and baseball cap, to Scott, barefoot and shirtless. I told Scott and Cameron to drop the mizzen sail, which meant that they would have to climb on top of the hut to reach it. They were the smallest and lightest, so there was little chance of them falling through the roof, but as they crawled around on all fours the brittle thatch crinkled loudly under them like the crispy sounds of men walking on dry leaves in a forest. As they began to disconnect the rigging there quickly came the sharp tinny *"clink!"* of the carabineers opening and snapping closed. On deck, David and Dower worked to raise the forward *guaras,* pulling the flat boards smoothly out of the ocean. Conventional thinking dictated that when the drag created by the front *guaras* disappeared, the mainsail should be able to pull the raft downwind. Dower had tried this technique without results, but I had to try it myself because it seemed a mechanical impossibility not to work. The *guaras* came up—and we stayed on course, closing in on the rocks. Minutes wasted away. The window of opportunity was closing and still we maintained a suicide course. The massive island was growing in front of us. We were closing in on half a mile and we could see all the details of the waves and rocks. The place where we would probably crash now had a face and a personality: At the base of the island lay a line of jagged little peaks, sharp black rocks that stood just above the surface of the water as though guarding the barren shore—they were La Plata's first line of defense, and they would rip the guts out of anything that tried to pass by them.

We probably had time for one last decision. For some reason our vessel would not turn right, so we'd turn left until the raft arrived at the course we wanted. Instead of turning 90 degrees to the starboard, we'd turn 270 degrees to the port to arrive at the desired course. I decided to round up—turn directly into the wind, then switch the mainsail to the other side of the mast, hook the wind, and fall away from the island.

I started giving new orders. Scott thought it was a bad idea and started to question the decision. Dower looked at me, puzzled, squinting his eyes and letting his mouth drop. But I ignored their reactions and just kept telling people what to do. We pushed the *guaras* down at the front, and hauled up the mizzen sail at the back. *Manteño* swung slowly around, like a giant door on a hinge. We had turned into the wind. We were now parallel with the coastline of Isla de la Plata, coming up to the quarter-mile cutoff. We rushed to the base of the mast, all six of us, and gathered up the canvas of the mainsail as it lay on the deck. As we were doing this, I glanced around. Mouths hung open. Eyes widened. *Hurry, guys. This time there won't be someone to show up to pull us out at the last minute.* But they were awake now, working as a team, and I felt them gaining confidence in the maneuver. The six men standing on the canes now held in their arms a long bulky roll of heavy white canvas, and slowly, methodically, they carried it to the other side of the mast. The raft was still turning, but it was losing momentum. Again there came the sharp snap of the carabineers locking into place, and when the complicated rig was ready, Dower said: "Let's go!" Ten hands reached up on the halyard and pulled. The long bamboo yard arm jumped off the deck, stopped, then jumped again. Heavy canvas dangled down now; the massive triangle opened up, filled out, and hooked the wind. *Manteño,* as though begrudgingly changing its mind in the face of overwhelming impossibility, slowly turned its nose away from the island, and began to walk away.

For most of the men the thing to do was to simply maintain that course—get some distance from the island. But what if the raft became unbalanced? What if it suddenly lost power, like *Illa-Tiki* did in front of Puerto Rico? *No. We must get downwind from La Plata right now, while there is wind with which to maneuver.* I tightened the sheet on the mainsail and raised the forward *guaras,* which caused the raft to turn all the way around. Now we were sailing downwind, running just offshore, parallel to the island. Standing at various places on the deck, we looked all around us, watching the raft crawl. *Manteño* sailed downwind for a few minutes and then passed by the island's north end. *Isla la Plata,* barren and desolate, slowly fell behind us. "Bloody hell, man!" Cameron said. "It turns! Whew!"

"Uh, we're still in trouble guys," Scott said.

"No we're not," Cameron said. "Look, man, the rocks are passing us."

Cameron understood piloting, and the decision I had just made. That was a relief, because no one else did, not even Dower. It was no surprise: Our raft was an untried mix of lateen-rigged sails and multiple, moveable keels—a rare combination to be sure, and if we thought about what "ought to happen," we were going to collide with something eventually. Cameron looked at me: "Whew!" he said, then laughed, ". . . hsssssss—that was close." Everyone else had just had a serious scare, but not Cameron Smith, he loved danger.

We sailed north for thirty minutes or so and then Dower began to tell me once again that he was afraid of the coastal pirates, and wanted to go farther out from the coast. We turned to the northwest and began to roll once again in the swells, which caused us to remain seasick for the rest of the fourteenth.

Now that we were offshore, Dower produced a surprise: a GPS receiver. He held the unit in his hands and smiled at me sheepishly. I wanted to keep technology off of the raft, but Dower's nerves had gotten the best of him. For him it was simply a matter of not wanting to die. GPS technology was still a great rarity among the small fishermen of Santa Elena. Knowing your exact position at the press of a button mesmerized them. After getting over the shock and dismay of losing another battle to the armies of technology, I had him check our position and record it.

I spent the rest of the day watching our course and stepping in and out of the hut, from time to time, to check the sea charts. The new hut design was also an 'improvement' over *Illa-Tiki*. It had a sleeping compartment built on a second floor, where the crew could be elevated above the surface of the ocean. To get into the compartment, which was easily discernable by the mound of blue nylon sleeping bags, you had to climb up and crawl around on all fours. There was only room enough for four men to sleep, and the puffy clump of nylon bags made you feel as though you were sleeping on an old-fashioned, over-stuffed mattress. In the very center of the sleeping bags was a thick post: our mizzen mast, a blond pole of *piñuelo* wood that disappeared through a hole in the roof.

In the afternoon of the fourteenth, two days out from Salango, I wrote in the log:

14:00 (2:00 P.M.)
Sea state picking up. Last night very hard . . . all suffering from motion sickness.
    SS (Scott Siekierski) has back problems also.

Conditions are indeed picking up. The raft is alive. Both sails are inflated and taught. *Manteño* knifes through the water. It rolls over, pitches down, then recovers. The pulleys creak and the water sloshes. Tiny white ovals of foam trail behind us. We are making a wake.

(3:30 P.M.)
Moving quickly . . . Small whitecaps, rain to W(est) and SW. Rollers directly on port beam.

We are making speed. Men clomp back and forth on the bamboo canes. Scott stands up from the bench, steadies himself, then leans forward and walks like a stick figure toward the port steering *guara*. "Dave," he calls, "give me a hand with this." Three men converge on the *guara*. Their skin is blue and gray in the winter light. Their faces are drawn but determined. David's hair hangs down in his face like string. Cameron holds a four-foot pole that is like a large stake: It is a *wanca*—a lever that has a flat point carved in one end. He wedges it in between two canes and levers it over, spreading open a hole in the deck. David bends over, grabs the bulbous head of a *guara*, and then pulls it up until the bottom pinhole comes through the floor. Seawater cascades down the sides of the flat board. Scott inserts a wooden pin in the hole to hold the *guara* out of the water. Cameron releases the *wanca*, the canes clamp down, and the *guara* is now standing up by itself in the middle of the foredeck. I stand for a moment and admire these people: They are learning to sail a balsa raft on the open sea. They hold their arms out to balance themselves on the rolling deck. They stumble backward to the bench, the spring-loaded bamboo canes sinking under each step.

At dusk, I sit on the bench and bend forward to write in the ship's log, which lies on the stump next to the compass:

> *(6:00 P.M.)*
> . . . relatively strong wind from S(outh). Seas picking up . . .
> Change course to 030 . . .

We are driving north now. The seasickness is gone. We are in following seas. The waves come from directly behind us. They roll up from the horizon and slam the back of the raft, finishing with a wallop against the back wall of the bamboo hut. I write in my personal diary:

> The violence of the following seas is incredible . . . (they) come rolling along at incredible speed and absolutely explode against the back of the little bamboo house. The explosion sound is modified (by) the hollow house, and the overall exploding noise can be nerve-racking.

Inside the hut, the back wall jumps each time the waves slap it. Then there is silence for half a minute, then another watery explosion against the back wall. You can feel the sea out there; it is alive.

> *15 Oct. 1998*
> (7:00 A.M.) Swells from astern.

It might be possible to duplicate the bizarre commotion of a following sea, as it is heard from inside the hut, by imagining the following scenario: Picture yourself sitting on a small stool at the end of a long hallway. It is completely dark; you can't see anything at all. You are calm and the hallway is silent. Then you hear a muffled noise from the far end, but it barely disturbs the peace. In a few seconds the sound changes from harmless to aggressive. A group of men are beating their fists on sheet metal. The hollow rumble comes to you from the other end of the long hallway, and as soon as you can make it out, it's clear the men are running toward you. Hundreds of heavy boots shake the air as they run. Now they're angry. The sheet metal thunders in the dark; boots and bass drums are rumbling; they are sprinting down the hall now. The mob is psychotic and running full blast, but you see nothing, there is only darkness. The floor vibrates; the stool vibrates; sound is violence. The mob is everywhere for a moment, pounding, beating, shaking, rattling. They shoot past you—then—absolute calm. Tranquility. You're alone again, sitting quietly in the black silence. That was a following sea.

(8:50 A.M.)
Large swells . . .

We are maintaining good speed. Cameron and I stand facing each other in the first-floor compartment. The hut is dimly lit in the morning light. It is like being in a shallow cave. Each time a following sea passes us it squirts twenty geysers through the gaps in the bamboo canes. The splashes come from every conceivable direction. The walls are alive around us. A following sea clatters against the back wall and everything jumps. Cameron falls backward for an instant, grabs a cane to hold on to, then the ship counterrolls and stands him back up. Without any effort he finds himself back on his feet with a look of momentary confusion on his face. We smile at each other. "Water up the nose," he says.

"Wild and woolly," I say.

"Hsssss. Beautiful."

Another wave pushes from astern. The stern rises up and the floor tilts sharply down. We fall backward for a moment, grab each other, are splashed, curse calmly, swing back forward and upright, then glance at each other with smiles on our faces. We are two grown men in a small bamboo room, involved in a friendly wrestling match.

I step out into the early morning light. Martin and Dower are out there on watch, sitting side by side on the bench. They are bundled up in layers of sweaters. Martin is staring at the compass. Dower is looking all around, watching for ships. The raft is maintaining constant speed. We are a working, voyaging ship. Night comes and there is no break. Throughout the night we watch the water stream by us like a river.

16 Oct. 98
(1:26 P.M.) . . . rollers from dead astern.

Afternoon watch. I step into the gray light of the front room compartment. The walls clatter. Geysers splash up my pants. The cool water spikes my inner thigh. I step close to the chart board and hold on. The raft is working hard. I can feel it around me like a breathing animal. A wave pops the canes below me and an arc of water shoots through a gap and strikes me below my nose. I inhale a noseful of saltwater and snort it out. I lean in toward the chart board to get a better look. We slow down. We've lost power. We're coasting. The raft stops.

(2:30 P.M.)
Yardarm broken on mainsail. Drifting.

Men stare up at the broken limb. It hangs down from the mast, defeated. Splinters and fibers protrude from the fracture. It made no sound. There was no great struggle of forces; it just folded. We grudgingly unlace the sail from the arm. It is slow work. The sun sets. We are working by flashlight now. Cameron and Martin are mountaineers. They are used to working with rope. It is good to have them aboard. We raise the new yardarm and sail. I look at my watch. It has taken us roughly five and a half hours. The raft gets back to speed. We are cruising in the night.

(9:00 P.M.)
Underway with new yardarm. . . . Heavy swells.

I sleep deeply. Scott awakens me. I can hear his voice in the darkness. Or is it Cameron? I know it is their watch. I'm lying half sunken in the nylon puff pile, as though I'm drowning in fluffy pillows. Darkness blinds me. I raise my left arm and steady my wrist at my eye. The glowing numbers read 4:05. I'm in a small bamboo room suspended above a great sloshing ocean. I can see nothing at all in the darkness, but I can hear Cameron's calm voice muffling in from outside on the foredeck. Something's wrong. A faint noise rises from a hundred feet behind the raft. It builds and climaxes with a wallop on the back wall of the hut. Everything jumps. *Following sea.* I struggle to sit up in the nylon menagerie. There are soft whooshes and zips from the nylon bags. Scott is back. We've got a problem. I slide off the second floor and onto the bamboo canes of the forward compartment. I feel my way toward the doorway. I can perceive nothing with my eyes, but I can feel the spring-loaded canes under my feet. The air is filled with the musty vegetable odor of freshly cut bamboo cane and the roar of thousands of pounds of water sloshing all around me. I step out into the outside. Cameron is standing at the base of the mast. His head is tilted way back. He is looking at the rigging.

17 October 1998
(4:30 A.M.) Eye on mainsail is broken. Adrift.

Wake everyone up. We're going to have to drop the mainsail, prop it up on bamboo sawhorses, untie all of the rigging, and then rework it. Slowly, one man after another, the crew emerges from the door in the bamboo house like surly cavemen. It is 4:30 in the morning on the Pacific Ocean. There is no moon and the overcast blocks the starlight. The impression of being on the open ocean is gone. Blackness crowds in all around us. We cannot see the ocean, but we can see black water lapping at the sides of the raft. It feels as though the edge of the deck is the very edge of the earth—to step off would be like stepping into the vacuum of space: for us, there is the raft and only the raft. On the canes of the foredeck it is now a world of flashlights. Glaring beams of light ricochet everywhere. Each individual flashlight has its own personality: Weak yellow beams dimly illuminate small, localized areas. Harsh white beams splash light all over the raft, glaring and blinding. Men can be heard from all parts of the deck, calling to each other, talking back and forth, trying to communicate over the loudness of the waves. Before one thing can be done, three others must be done first. The complicated repair demoralizes the puffy-faced men who have just awakened. There are no heroics. We could just as easily be a group of guys milling around a campsite on a windy night. Flashlight beams illuminate working hands that fumble with broken ropes. You can hear men talking in the dark but their voices are muffled. They are struggling to communicate with Dower in unnatural Spanish. They struggle to make sensible sentences. The sloshing of the ocean and their halting Spanish fills the black air around the platform.

(7:30 A.M.)
Back underway with new eye on the mainsail. Continued following seas
and heavy winds. . . . continued overcast.

We are making way again. It is the gray morning of October 17. No sign of
sun, just the gray light of winter. The ocean is a hard blue desert. We are driving north toward Panama. We are 210 miles from Salango. I check my dead
reckoning figures against Dower's GPS. I am off by two miles. But we are having trouble steering the raft north. We keep angling to the east.

(4:50 P.M.)
We have been running around 40–50 (course in degrees) for the last two
hours. Goal is 20 (degrees) but is very difficult (because) we are so close to
the wind.

(6:40 P.M.)
Still not able to (steer) 20 (degrees) consistently.

(10:05 P.M.)
Swells more or less from astern, but also port quarter, and occasional
chaotic seas.

It is 11:00 at night on October 17. The ocean is still sliding by us at good
speed. David and I are on watch. I lie on the bench, sitting up every minute or
so to look at the compass heading. I'm boiling with fever. Some kind of infection is incubating in me. The waves are squirting up through the canes. It is
like being in an intermittent rain shower. David is miserable. He does not
want to be on the raft, but he rarely complains openly. We have a tiny flashlight with a red lens. We shine it into the glass bubble that houses the compass. I say to David, "I'm going to raise that *guara* a little."
   "No," he says. "I'll get it." He labors up and clomps forward.
   He'll need help. I get up and slip across the slick canes. David jams the little
wanca in a gap, cranks it over, and I grab the *guara* by the head and hoist. I stand,
holding the flat board out in front of me, and feel cool seawater dribble out of
the soggy wood around my fingertips. David slides the peg into the bottom hole.
A wave breaks behind us. Saltwater shoots up like tiny geysers. We are two men
alone in the dark; we are raising and lowering *guaras*, steering a lonely boat out
on the ocean at night; we are headed north, trying to make Central America.
   Dawn comes on the eighteenth, and we are still cruising.

18 Oct. 98
(11:08 A.M.) . . . Rollers from dead astern.

(8:00 P.M.)
Clear skies, warm wind, . . . calmer seas.

We are beginning to slow down. Our speed is dropping off rapidly. Men are beginning to relax. I can feel a calm on the raft. I am hanging over the side of the deck and fumbling with a rope. The black ocean is streaming quietly by me. Surges of cool seawater rise up and soak my arms and body. Behind me, flashlight beams splash and spray uneven light on the foredeck. Martin is standing in front of the doorway of the hut telling Dower something ridiculous in broken Spanish and Dower is squelching a smirk. The rest of the guys are milling around inside. I can hear them talking and laughing, and I can see dim yellow light glowing in the little bamboo windows as though the hut is a cozy cabin, deep in the woods. Then something moves in the water. Or is it my imagination? There it is again. There's something out there in the water. "Martin," I call. "Come here." Martin emerges from the darkness, be-bopping in his underwear and knee-high jungle boots—a stick figure with a headlamp protruding from his forehead. I point out into the black water: "Shine your light down there."

"Huh?"

"I think there's something down there. Shine your light in the wa——."

"Dorados!"

"Good God!"

There are thousands of them! Dower stops what he's doing and hurries over. *"Que vestia!"*

Our eyes are glued to the spectacle, and I ask Dower: "Have you ever seen anything like this?"

"Hell no!"

It is like we have truly struck gold. We hold up lights and lanterns and stare at a fabulously gaudy spectacle. As far as the eye can see the ocean is layered with long, flat fish, glittering like polished gold metal. We have discovered the mother-lode at the end of a long mineshaft. We snap out of our trance—all of us at the same instant—and scurry around in the dark, frantically grabbing tools to mine the gold. Dower casts lines out. Martin loads a harpoon in the spear gun. I get a flashlight and walk around the perimeter of the raft, shining the beam into the water. As far as the beam can penetrate there are golden dorados. They are all swimming steadily in one direction and in formation, like a vast, disciplined unit. *Manteño* is sailing over an enormous school of fish. Clearly, they are migrating north. *Good Lord! I wonder what the Manteño thought of this!*

Dower gets a sharp strike, but loses the fish. Martin spears one on the first shot, but it takes off under the raft and almost takes Martin with it. Dower casts frantically, but none strike. Martin can't get off another clean shot. The dorados have dropped down to a lower level. We can still see them, but they are now out of reach.

Throughout the evening of the eighteenth the wind weakens, and we continue to slow down.

19 October 1998
(7:59 A.M.) Calm seas and little swells . . .

(10:00 A.M.)
SUNSHINE CALM SEAS

On the morning of October 19, Scott Siekierski sat on the bench over the gleaming wet canes and shaved his face. He balanced on his lap a small bowl of water with shaving cream floating in it. Around him sunny skies lit up the world and pointed wavelets sparkled on a rich blue ocean. Over the last five days, since turning north from La Plata Island, *Manteño* had sped three hundred miles across the ocean. The raft now lay between Colombia to the east, rife with crime, pirates, and civil war; and The Gyre to the west, a six-hundred-mile-wide area of water inside the Doldrums, where the wind does not blow for months at a time and the ocean spins around in a circle. We were now "threading the needle." To make it to Panama we knew that we must sail through a narrow corridor in the open ocean. If we veered to the west we'd enter The Gyre, and probably never escape; if we veered too far to the east, we'd hit Colombia. The wind was dying, and by afternoon we were floundering on an erratic course. Sometimes it was very difficult to steer in certain directions. At times the wind dropped off completely, and we drifted helplessly.

Around noon we set up the bicycle-driven generator inside the hut. I sat in the soft seat, placed my feet on the pedals, and began working hard. Push. Push. Push. My legs sped up and I looked out the bamboo window at the water streaming by. It felt like I was pedaling the raft forward. My legs churned and *Manteño* plowed through the water. Thirty seconds ticked by. Then forty seconds formed a barrier in my mind, and I tired. At forty seconds my legs gave out, but the raft continued on. How could it be that I was only pedaling a little generator and not the forty-thousand-pound raft? Each of the other men took their turn, churning their legs and watching the ocean stream past the window. Cameron was of course the champion. And why not? Here was a man who practiced polar travel by running through the woods for hours at a time, towing an enormous truck tire behind him on a harness. "I consider myself in ideal shape," he told me once, "when I can get up from the couch and run twenty miles." He set the record for pedaling: ninety continuous seconds.

We recharged our batteries by working in shifts. Even just a short burst of pedaling developed an enormous amount of energy. We were once again carrying solar panels, but they were small and rarely saw any direct sunlight, due to the constant overcast skies.

Each day during this time, we worked busily to repair and strengthen the raft. We labored in clean air and fresh breezes, while our vessel voyaged across the blue ocean. Work crews of two to three men moved around the raft, tackling each job, and in some ways the *Manteño* resembled any other job site: People getting in each other's way, people getting out of each other's way, people measuring holes, people measuring wood, and of course, people breaking the bad news to each other that their idea wouldn't work. But all of this was taking place on a solitary wooden platform, floating on an immense ocean. This busy working environment defines the atmosphere onboard the *Manteño* in October of 1998: The six men got along and they worked as a unit, but they did not develop into a brotherhood. Scott, especially, was frequently unhappy and frustrated. For various reasons, he did not like David, or Dower, or me.

David and Scott were oil and water. David was superstitious and very cautious. Scott was rooted in the physical world and somewhat of a gamer. Because Scott had no experience at sea, he couldn't appreciate Dower. Back in Salango, Scott had developed a solid friendship with Francisco, who was the same age as he. Dower was ten years older and had shown up only at the end of the construction of the raft, and he had taken Francisco's place. Also, Dower had lost a lot of prestige in front of the others when he could not turn the raft in front of Isla de la Plata. Dower, understandably, did not like being disapproved of by a man with only ten days' experience on the sea. Finally, Scott didn't like me because I was too loose in my style. He frequently told me that I had to "crack down." I saw nothing to warrant "cracking down." Even if I had I was unwilling to do so, and my buoyant optimism frequently bewildered Scott. Morale—promoting a general feeling of happiness and adventure— meant everything to me. I could still vividly remember the image of men at sea, wilting under stress. What was important was that Scott did not wreak havoc. He got along with everyone on the raft, even if at times he had to force it. At times his praise was strained and his humor was desperate, but he rarely exchanged words with anyone, and he never lost control.

But this tension was smaller than our exhilaration of being on a raft at sea. *Illa-Tiki* had been survived only through grim determination, but aboard *Manteño* the crew remained zealous. Laughter, joke telling, and storytelling were heard every day. And the private friendships felt better than the small animosities. Scott was very close to Martin, and they spent long hours talking and laughing. Also, like all of us, he had a great respect for Cameron Smith. He stood his watches with Cameron and they did well, despite Scott's continued back problems. His lumbar had seized, and each day he slowed a little more. At times he had to stay in bed and miss work. Caught in the vicious cycle of a nagging back injury, he spent hours lying in a mound of blue nylon sleeping bags, silent and rigid, quietly enduring agony, but it was never long enough for his back to heal.

Martin eventually came to admire Dower, and to understand his sublime seamanship. They were watch partners, and their watch usually consisted of Martin explaining various bizarre pillars of his life to Dower and Dower laughing and applauding as though watching a stand-up comedian who knew only fifty words of his own language.

I stood my watch with David. He was obviously miserable, but did not decline into paralysis. He was sullen and sensitive, but he stood his watches well. After my fever wore off, I stepped on the anchor one night during a blind fight with the mainsail, and for several nights I had to throw my arm around David's shoulder so that I could hobble around in the darkness from one job to the next. As soon as the gash began to get better, a sore in my knee became so inflamed with infection that the knee swelled to twice its normal size. The sickened knee and heel made my left leg useless, and I spent many of my night watches lying on the bench, smoking cigars for pain relief. During those watches I'd look up and see David, gray and drawn, grimly watching the *guaras,* the compass, and the *Manteño*.

Nevertheless, I remained exhilarated. We were eating well, the new sails were easy to manage, and after the madness of *Illa-Tiki,* the small personality differences aboard *Manteño* seemed trivial—almost laughable.

(*9:42 P.M.*)
Course erratic. Almost no wind for the last 30 minutes.

On the evening of the nineteenth we saw the massive dorado school again underneath us. We were sailing on the exact course of a vast migration route in use. For some reason they were impossible to catch. This was hardly a tragedy because we had long since solved the fishing problem. We had plenty of good equipment aboard *Manteño,* lots of experience, and a disciplined fishing operation each morning—Dower and Martin's watch.

Dower had fished for twenty-five years; Martin, never. A typical morning would unfold thus:

Dower is sitting on the bench, watching the course and looking out on the sea with his trained eye. The difference between him and Martin can be seen by the way they hold their bodies: Dower is totally relaxed, unimpressed by his surroundings. He sits on the bench with his shoulders slouched and his hands folded between his knees. Every move Martin makes is an excited jerk, a jump, a scurry, or a run. He stands at the edge of the bamboo canes with a fishing line in one hand and the spool in the other. A lure weighs down the line and he twirls it at his side like a sling, spinning it faster and faster until with a enormous underhanded throw he heaves it out fifty feet into the ocean. Now he's reeling it in, spinning the line around the spool until the line goes taught with a sharp strike: "Got one!"

"Vamos, Martin!" ("Let's go, Martin!")

"SHIT! He got off! Man!"

Dower's stamping his foot. He's laughing so hard that he has to hold his belly. He sings out: *"Muy malo, Martin! Muy malo!"* ("That sucked, Martin! That was terrible!")

"He was huge! Man!"

Dower gets up slowly, still laughing, still holding his belly, and takes the line. He casts. Nothing. Another cast, and then a sharp strike: "Yeah!—yeah!—yeah!—yeah!" Dower is suddenly animated. He dances a few steps, singing: "Dorados! Dorados! Dorados!"

"Don't let him get away!"

Dower is patient now, he has learned a lot about this type of fishing while aboard *Illa-Tiki.* Inside the hut, lying on the nylon bags, I can hear Martin running around on the canes, shouting: "There he is! He's huge! All right! Beautiful! God, I love this!"

20 October 1998
(6:30 A.M.) No wind. But Dower caught a fish.

Dower caught a fish. If you hunt and gather for a living, no other thing can make you feel so good. For one golden moment you know—you are *certain*—that you will eat. Perhaps the ancients assigned it a religious significance, but there was also the emotional and psychological release: It reaffirms hope and builds confidence. Anyone who has ever been through a dreadful time when there are no fish, or no buffalo, or no caribou, knows that tension and foreboding start quickly.

On the morning of the twentieth, some of the men suggested that we might already have the *Teredo navalis*. Cameron and Scott dove under the raft while I hovered in the water near the bow, submerged just under the surface, looking through my mask at the deep blue water. I could see the entire underside of the raft. Nine logs bulged down and the *guaras* hung below like huge knife blades. The sea was empty, except for Cameron, who swam the length of the raft. Swimming face up, his mask just inches from the underside, he slowly ran his eyes along the bumpy surface of the logs, examining them closely, gliding through the shafts of underwater sunbeams, pulling gently on the natural handholds of the uneven surfaces, floating weightlessly in the clear water like an astronaut.

In the bow of the raft I could already see signs of the *Teredo navalis*. Cameron cut a chunk out of the starboard-most log and brought it to me. They had gone around the antifouling paint with little trouble. The balsa logs were such an irregular surface and there were so many hundreds of cracks that modern paint just wasn't appropriate. We had in fact probably contracted them on the very first day, when we were forced to anchor *Manteño*. Generally speaking, *Teredo navalis* can only attach itself to wood that sits in calm water—especially calm water that is warm, as when a raft sits at anchor in the tropics, or when it sits through long periods of no wind at the Equator—the Doldrums, which we had sat in aboard *Illa-Tiki*. If a log is constantly moving through the water, or if the water is very cold, it usually won't develop a serious infection.

We knew all of this before we put *Manteño* into the water, and so for three days after we launched the raft we struggled desperately to put it on the beach, as we had done so successfully with *Illa-Tiki* in Panama. We wanted to avoid anchoring in the placid water of the bay while we were preparing to go to sea. On the first try, the day of the launch, we brought the raft up to the beach and tried to tie it down. The spectacle was amazing. *Manteño* lay at the water's edge, bulky and enormous, while the oncoming waves curled over and exploded on top of it. Trying to get the raft to stay in one place was like trying to tie down an elephant gone wild. The deck turned into a battlefield of saltwater explosions. Breakers curled over and slammed into the raft, kicking the crew through the air like a child kicking a ball. The raft was taking a horrific pounding—too destructive to justify. Moreover, it simply wasn't working, and the reason was because *Manteño* had a serious flaw: It didn't float very well.

We had assumed that *Manteño*'s logs would float as high as *Illa-Tiki*'s, but they did not. During the first expedition, we built *Illa-Tiki* in the scorching equatorial heat, and so the logs lost a lot of moisture—much more than we knew—and that had made them exceedingly buoyant. Those logs had been corklike, and even after the shipworms ate most of the wood, the raft was still seaworthy. *Manteño* on the other hand was built under overcast skies and very quickly: Its logs never dried out. They were so wet and heavy that they barely floated at all. *Manteño* couldn't afford to lose *any* wood to the *Teredo navalis*. Heyerdahl had said that the secret of the raft was to use green, wet logs. Clearly, he had been wrong. We were now learning that drying the logs was, in fact, *critical*. Even with just a small infection of *Teredo navalis*, *Manteño* was already in trouble.

We'd have to take the raft out of the water and repair it. In the afternoon of the twentieth, I wrote in my diary:

We have discovered the *Teredo navalis*. They are boring into the wood. . . . Shortly after the discovery, I had to get sharp with the group for the first time since we began. That is unfortunate, but still, I feel OK about it. The men have moved lethargically about in the last few days, and, at times, have ignored my calls for a few moments. I don't think there is any malice afoot; they just needed a little jolt.

For a few hours the crew was downcast. Martin said, softly, "I think we have to realize that it is unlikely that we will make it to—"

"Bullshit!" I barked—it spilled out. I couldn't let his comment sit. I had learned much from *Illa-Tiki*. Nothing could be allowed to break our resolve. But the group recovered from the blow, and they did it so quickly that I was really impressed. They were showing a lot of resilience.

There were, however, more flaws in *Manteño* than just wet logs and *Teredo navalis*. The new design had been a quantum leap in authenticity, but many critical problems remained unsolved. Some of these I could clearly see; most were still only ideas and suspicions. The new *guara* system was a great improvement over *Illa-Tiki,* but it still had problems. Worse, we were breaking *guaras* at an alarming rate. For the first time in modern history, *guaras* were subjected to the forces they would have had to withstand on a Manteño trading voyage in AD 900. The stress of making three knots and better in rough seas caused them to work back and forth like hinges. This hingelike movement fractured eight *guaras*. When you swam under the raft you could see the broken boards hanging down like chipped teeth. We would eventually lose another four.

At dawn on the morning of the twenty-first, we brought in a dorado. It was a gray day and wet, with long streaks of rain falling on the eastern horizon. Martin was on morning fishing watch, with a line in the ocean off our starboard bow. The line suddenly twitched, and Martin jerked hard, snagging the fish, and then released it to run. He handed the line over to Dower and then grabbed his camera. Cameron grabbed the "harpoon" and followed Dower. There was the usual winding in of line and letting out, waiting for the big fish to tire. More and more, they headed toward the back of the raft, working their way down the catwalks, Dower handling the line and Cameron carrying a slightly crooked tree limb with a trident at the end of it. Soon they were standing next to each other on the bare balsa logs, legs spread and knees bowed outward, for maximum stability. They had, in reality, stepped into the ocean. During the voyage of the *Illa-Tiki* the back of the raft had been a swimming platform, but now it was a sunken place. Water swirled around their legs and every few seconds surged up almost to their waists. The two men looked like they were riding on a gently malfunctioning elevator: Over and over again, in a fitful rhythm, they rose up two to three feet, stalled, then gently dropped down for another dousing in water. Dower maintained perfect tension on the line, carefully following the dorado's glide path with his eyes. Cameron raised the harpoon, sighted down the wooded shaft for a tense second, and then with a sharp thrust lanced the dorado cleanly. The barbs grabbed the fish's flesh and they pulled it out of the sea and onto the deck. It was a twenty-seven-pounder that would feed the crew for the day. Our fishing acumen had finally evolved to self-sufficiency. This is difficult to impart, especially in a modern world, but once you can live inside the food chain, then survival becomes commonplace.

A few days later, in the afternoon, I saw something disturbing the water off the starboard bow: Debris from land. Palm fronds floated by every few hours. Then we saw coconuts; then whole trees floated by, half-sunken and drifting past us with their branches still intact. It was a prelude of the world we were about to enter, and a sobering demonstration that we were not in the waters in which we had expected to arrive. Land was nearby.

The more the debris came, the more I knew something was wrong. On the twenty-fifth, Dower and I checked the GPS. We stood on the forward deck and watched the reading come up on the unit. The moment the numbers materialized, we knew we had entered Colombian waters. "That stuff isn't coming from Panama," I said to him. "It's coming from Colombia."

Dower had a strange way of going into denial, and at that moment he embraced that quirk of his personality. He stared blankly for a minute, then milled around aimlessly on the deck for several hours. Seeing the industrious Dower sitting, staring, or absentmindedly chopping wood with a hatchet, told me that the idea of Colombia was so frightening that he simply would not believe it. Night came and he sank lower. He climbed up on the roof of the hut and laid back, reclining on the crispy thatch, and buried his nose in Gabriel Garcia Marquez's *One Hundred Years of Solitude*. He was in total denial.

"We will see land tonight," I said to him.

"*Sí.*"

We were on the wrong side of the Gulf of Panama, 120 miles due east of where we had landed in the *Illa-Tiki*. To avoid The Gyre, we had overcompensated by navigating too far east. Not only that, but the raft continued to perform badly. We could sail into the wind, but just barely. When both the wind *and* current were against us, however, we could not prevent the raft from being pushed off course. We desperately needed to sail west, but more and more the wind and current were pushing us back. *Manteño,* with its sunken wet logs dragging heavily in the water, was becoming more sluggish and unresponsive by the day. While the *Illa-Tiki* was sinking into the sands of the Azuero Peninsula, we were on the other side of the Gulf of Panama, on the verge of landing on Darien, the Panamanian province that borders Colombia.

Darien is a barrier. It is where Central America stops and South America begins. This can be seen on any map by following the course of Highway 1, The Pan-American Highway. This long road runs the entire distance of the Western Hemisphere, from Alaska to Tierra del Fuego, but it does not run through Darien. The Pan-American Highway comes down from the north, hits the outskirts of the Panamanian town of Yavisa, and then fades into the jungle. This is the Darien Gap. The road isn't picked up for another 120 miles south, near Medellin, in northern Colombia. This great concrete highway—"the Pan Am"—spans two entire continents, North America and South America, a distance of roughly sixteen hundred miles, with but one spot missing; we'd probably sight that spot in the morning, off our starboard bow.

Night came and I slept little. In the early morning hours of the twenty-sixth, I came out on the foredeck. It was still dark and the air was cool and calm. I looked at Dower, he looked at me, and said, simply: "Land," and pointed to the east. A low, smooth, black line interrupted the seascape: the Darien Gap.

As the light grew and we awoke on that morning, we began to realize that the ocean had dead-ended at a green wall. This wall, The Darien Gap, stretched out in front of us in panoramic style and blocked the horizon—indeed, it blocked the earth's surface. I guess I had always thought of the ocean as infinite, never ending, but this seemed to be the End—or more accurately—a dead end. The water seemed to flow right up to the green wall and stop. Where the water stopped, a bushy cliff shot up one thousand feet into the air. Lush green trees and bushes and tangled ivies protruded from every inch of the monstrous wall. Waterfalls flooded down its side, bursting with an abundance of fresh water that fell hundreds of feet at a time and then shattered at its base. I would have liked to be high in the sky during this time, flying overhead in an airplane. Up there I would have seen a green wall, a thousand feet tall and curving around for sixty miles, and before it our raft, a tiny speck, twenty feet wide, sailing toward its base like a flea crawling toward a rhinoceros.

Cameron and I stood on the foredeck in the morning light, awed by our discovery of the End. Like the rest of us, Cameron meticulously scanned the immense green wall with his binoculars, and after an hour or so he concluded: "Hssssss, this is truly—the middle of nowhere."

We cruised toward the Darien Gap all day, standing for hours on the bamboo canes of Manteño and staring at the End. The weather was fine and clear. We walked in and out of the hut, talking to each other and looking at maps as the wall grew and grew. We scanned its terrain with our binoculars and could see that the cliff dropped down and dove straight into the water. It was what's known to sailors as a "steep shore": The bottom dropped off so steeply that it would be practically impossible to anchor nearby, and there was practically no beach anywhere. A controlled landing there would require a lot of luck to succeed.

We hoped all day that the wind would change, allowing us to sail out of our predicament, but at about 2:00 in the afternoon I realized that we were running out of space to sail in. On one side of us, a thick cloud bank dropped down to the surface and formed a barrier. On the other side stood the green cliff, arcing around in a long sweeping curve. The two walls, cloud and jungle, intersected at a point, five miles in front of us. Manteño was cruising into a corner. There was talk among some of the men about continuing our course northward, in order to make Panama. I wanted to go to Panama too, but if we went north and made even the slightest piloting error, or if the weather didn't hold, we'd wreck.

A crash on the Darien Gap would put us in an untenable situation: If we survived the crash we'd find ourselves marooned at the base of a thousand-foot jungle cliff. Clinging to the rocks, we'd face two choices for evacuation: overland or by boat. The overland method would require Cameron and Martin to climb the cliff, unaided, and navigate all the way to a safe settlement or town. Even with GPS, the hazards of navigating through unknown, hostile jungle would almost assuredly bring injury or worse. To make a seaborne evacuation we'd probably have to abandon ship via the dinghy and make a controlled landing on an unknown, uncharted beach. Once marooned we'd probably be confined to using short-range VHF radio to signal passing vessels for help. In this area, you'd never know who you were signaling, the Colombian navy, the U.S. Coast Guard, or pirates. Darkness was coming, and I estimated that if we kept our present course, disaster on the rocks of Darien would probably come that night. We'd have to turn around within the next thirty minutes to have any chance of wriggling out. Cameron smiled widely at me now: "Hssssss . . . we're in a hell of a fix, man."

I assembled everyone on the deck. We went through all the normal motions that should turn the raft around. Nothing happened. The current strengthened, and we closed in on the Darien. The wall continued to climb in front of us, blocking out the sky and the light. Not only did the raft not respond well, but the wind was dying. If it died completely, we'd crash for sure.

I once again found myself in the position of telling a raft crew to maneuver in a way that didn't make any sense to them. I knew that the *Manteño* would have to turn toward land, curve around, and jibe to the starboard—we'd have to move even closer to the rocks if we wanted to turn around and sail out of trouble. It would be a high-risk turn, but it was our only chance. Scott didn't like it, and Dower found it difficult to believe. That spooked the rest of the men for a minute, but I wasn't the same person I had been on that first day aboard *Illa-Tiki,* years ago in front of Puerto Rico: I no longer questioned my own judgment.

Once again, Cameron and Scott, both of them in just their shorts and bare feet, climbed on the roof to handle the mizzen sail. David and I, the two heaviest men, hoisted and trimmed the mainsail. Dower, in his underwear as always, quickly began raising the heavy *guaras* like an Olympic weightlifter, using a three-step movement. As they came up, the raft turned downwind, headed for the rocks. The six of us now grouped at the middle of the deck and lowered the mainsail, furled it, and lifted it off the deck, cradling it in our collective arms like a giant canvas sausage. Moving in concert, our legs and bodies all bowed in the same position—unconsciously demonstrating our evolving experience—we maneuvered it to the other side of the mast, unfurled it, hoisted it, and trimmed it. When the triangle peaked over the raft and bobbed a little in the dying breeze, I walked out on the bare logs, reached up and grabbed the fat bamboo yardarm, and held it to the wind. The canvas triangle hooked the light wind and *Manteño* swung around in front of the rocks. Then it stopped. It came about and just hung there. The sails inflated fully but the raft stayed in the same place, treading water. We stood on the foredeck of *Manteño,* bathed in warm tropical air and soft light, and gawked at the towering green wall just a hundred yards away. The raft pushed forward gently. A small wake streamed past the bow. We could clearly see the water trickling past the logs, but the raft did not seem to move. We were sailing into the current at exactly the same speed as it was drifting past us. We stayed in the same place for minute after minute, sailing on a treadmill. Everyone on board was unnaturally calm. Even after just two weeks on the raft the six of us already looked worn. We stood at various places on the deck, looking disheveled and scraggly, and held our breath collectively, waiting for a sign—any sign—of progress. We did not yet know it but we were moving away from the giant green wall at approximately five feet per minute. In half an hour, we moved fifty yards. It seemed to us like amazing progress.

We were creeping away from certain disaster, but now we faced another problem: Aboard *Manteño* we had charts of every inch of land between Salango and Acapulco—except Colombia. We had agreed long ago that we did not want to land there and had planned to do everything possible to avoid it. Our copy of *Sailing Directions* contained only a few paragraphs about the area, so we now found ourselves piloting a coast of which we knew very little.

Sun set, and we piloted *Manteño* through the dark, calm waters, continuing to move away from the hostile land at less than a mile per hour. No signs of life came from the great green wall—no light, no flickering flames from fires, nothing; it hung over us like an immense, black, block.

27 October 1998
(2:00 A.M.) . . . Storm clouds behind us looming over Darien. Stronger winds(.) Faster sailing. Bigger seas on starboard. Mast sending out moans and creaks.

At dawn, we knew we had cleared the coast—at least temporarily. During the day of the twenty-seventh, we cruised slowly southward, shadowing the Darien. The only sign of life we saw were two dugout canoes, drawn up on a distant beach. Even these seemed abandoned. It was a Stone Age-like place, and when David said, "I keep expecting a pterodactyl to go flying by," he captured the atmosphere perfectly.

In the afternoon, Cameron and I went to the back of the raft for a talk. "If

we land in Colombia"—he said—"and it appears we are going to have to do
just that—and if we are there for a long time, say more than a couple of
weeks—and it appears that that is exactly what will happen—then I must go
back to school to finish my Ph.D."

I felt a shock go through me. I considered losing Cameron to be as bad as
contracting the *Teredo navalis*. He was so valuable that he was irreplaceable.
The first expedition had taught me that all things could be overcome—except
the emotional collapse of the men. Cameron would never collapse, and because of that the people around him would always be stronger. "I've been gone
a long time," he said. "They're not going to like it at my university. I simply cannot screw up my Ph.D. I've been working on it my entire life—and I'm on
scholarship right now. I simply must go back." He was crushed. For a brief
moment, the life seemed to go out of him.

Sun set on the twenty-seventh, and the wind continued to blow us south.

(9:15 P.M.)
. . . not sailing into the wind very well. Found 5 broken guaras today on the
port quarter. Still in sight of land.

On the morning of the twenty-eighth, I made contact with Annie via shortwave radio. I had contacted her the day before and asked her to talk to the
Colombian government about a possible landing on the coast near Darien.
"The Colombian government advises against any landing," she said through
the static. "They cannot guarantee your safety anywhere in that area."

Shortly after receiving that message, Martin and I discussed our options
while standing on the starboard edge of the foredeck. If the west wind continued, we'd have little choice but to land our now crippled vessel on the shores
of Darien. The only rational plan was to enter a sheltered inlet called Bahia
Octavia, make anchor, and set out on foot for the nearest civilization, probably
Bahia Solano, forty-five miles through the jungle. "What if there's no trail?"
Martin asked.

"Then we just go overland," I said.

"That puts us bushwhacking," he said, visibily disappointed.

A few minutes after we came to that awful conclusion, the wind freshened
up and the sky cleared. We sailed well, under control, and we set our course to
pass around the ominous rocks of Punta Marzo. At dusk, with darkness coming, accompanied by its inherent confusion, I wrote down instructions in the
log for the watches to reference:

28 October 1998
Bad point bearing 120 m. Any course greater than 120 is acceptable. We are 8 miles from rocks dead ahead. . . . Light @ Cabo Marzo marking dangerous rocks. Pos. 6 49 N 77 41 W.

The course held and we cruised silently throughout the night. I tried to hide my feelings, but drug trafficking, guerrilla warfare, and the Darien Gap filled my thoughts. I feared kidnapping more than anything. It was a horrible idea and I imagined it vividly. That night I wrote in my diary:

> . . . the blunt truth is that a live American is worth a hell of a lot more than a dead one. In the Middle East they'll kill for the hatred. In Colombia they'll ransom you for the money. My mind, usually skeptical of any sort of blind fear, runs wild. I'd take anything over kidnapping.

At dawn on the twenty-ninth, as the sun rose on a beautiful day, the wind direction changed. *Manteño*'s course began to change as well. By 6:30 a.m. we knew that we were committed to a landing before noon. In front of *Manteño*, a mile off her bow, lay Punta Marzo, a line of bare rocks jutting up fifty feet from the surface of the water like jagged teeth. They were ugly black and gray peaks that had stood for thousands of years, permanent and unmoving. We would not be able to pilot around them and turning back would yield nothing. Dower and I agreed that we could cruise through a quarter mile-wide gap in the massive molars by putting the raft into a wide, sweeping turn to port. From there we'd pilot the raft into the tiny cove on the other side of the rocks, and drop anchor.

Scott didn't like it. He sat in the hut, on the bicycle, with his arms folded. When I ducked inside, he said, "We're going to hit those rocks."

"No way. We're fine. We can make this."

"I don't give a damn what you say, we're going to hit those rocks."

I had to respect Scott. Frederick would've panicked and thrown us into crisis. Scott, on the other hand, sat in the hut with his arms folded, calmly talking to Martin.

Manteño walked slowly toward a gigantic open mouth. A set of five bulging molars jutted up to the right, and a matching set jutted up to the left. We crept into the mouth at approximately one mile an hour, and as we did, it came alive. Dolphins surfaced. Their gray fins passed directly in front of us, two or three at a time. Then they surrounded the raft, joyful and optimistic, coming out of the water in groups, jumping into the air in perfect arcs and dives, shooting up, stalling, and then splashing back through the surface. Dower stood up, seemed rejuvenated, and cast a line into the water. A tuna hit sharply and Dower turned animated. Suddenly he was having a good time, dancing around and singing: "Dorados! Dorados! Dorados!" He caught one fish after another, and soon there were three Albacore tunas, plump and shiny silver, flapping madly on the bamboo canes.

We could see inside the mouth of the monster now, into a world of the most beautiful shade of green. Healthy trees rose up and exploded into bushy beauty. Flat and angular leaves glittered with rainwater. The atmosphere inside the mouth of the monster was tranquil and serene, as though it had never been entered before. This produced a sensation in us on the raft that the human race has lost in the last fifty years, one that will probably never return: the feeling of total mystery, the feeling of entering a mysterious land. Humankind's sudden grasp of knowledge has made it possible to give ourselves a map or outline of every place we will go, and therefore the mystery of exploring new lands is gone. For those of us aboard the balsa raft *Manteño,* that feeling was painfully but exhilaratingly real on the morning of October 29, 1998. We knew nothing of the land we were now entering.

We passed through the rocks without making any adjustments to the raft's course. Waves washed and splashed against the jagged boulders, surrounding them in agitated foam, but we cruised smoothly through them without any trouble at all. *Manteño* was like an old horse, walking slowly and purposefully to the safety of the barn. I felt happy, like I had felt at seeing the unknown coast of Panama in the last days of the voyage of the *Illa-Tiki.* No matter how bad things might get, I felt I had lived some adventure.

The entire crew now assembled on the foredeck and analyzed every inch of the cove with the binoculars. Then, suddenly, Dower pointed into the cove and said, "A shrimp boat!" It was the first boat we had seen in the deserted waters of the Darien Gap. He scanned the cove some more with his binoculars, then said: "*Capitan*—a warship, too!"

"What?"

"Look!"

There, resting in "The Bay of the Hopeless Situation," was a Colombian gunboat, waiting for us like a good watchdog. It was as though it had been miraculously placed there for our protection, and ours alone. I said to Cameron, who was piloting the raft: "Cameron, put us one hundred yards astern of that vessel."

We cruised into the cove at about one knot. The open sea dropped away behind us and we entered a silent, closed world. High bushy hills surrounded us, creating a private atmosphere of stillness. Cameron and David steered the raft to the exact point I had requested and we dropped anchor. *Manteño* now rested in what seemed like a calm green pond. All around us the water was placid. In front of us lay a small gray warship, the sixteen-hundred-ton *Sebastion Benalcazar,* a bulging iron bulldog with a wide nose, like a tug boat. It had come into the little cove the day before to allow its crew to get some rest from sea duty. Measuring 151 feet in length, it was armed with .50 caliber machine guns, 40mm cannons, and a full compliment of Colombian sailors. It was the biggest dog in the neighborhood, and it now sat on our front porch.

The *Sebastion Benalcazar* sent out a boarding party immediately. Six Colombian sailors came gliding up in a Boston whaler, hailing us and asking for our passports. One minute later, just as they stepped on the canes of raft, a dense tropical rain dropped from the sky as though a bucket of water was being poured on us from heaven. Heavy drops cascaded straight down in sheets, forcing us to duck into the hut. I stood in the forward compartment with the boarding officer, a big, beefy man wearing an immaculate brown uniform and a bulging orange life vest, and strained to make myself heard over the frantic crackling of drops on our roof. The officer was very professional and obviously a career sailor, and after I gave him a quick explanation of our expedition, he took down all of our information, straining in the half-light of the hut to copy down passport numbers onto a clipboard, while rain streamed through the roof all around him. After our business was finished, he shook my hand and returned to his vessel. Twenty minutes later the whaler returned: The captain wanted to see me.

Dower and I were made to feel at home aboard the gunboat, and we spent a happy evening talking to Captain Navas and his officers. *Sebastion Benalcazar* was a beautiful gray warhorse, with fine wooden flooring on its bridge and an array of stout storm hatches. It had been built in 1944 and had served admirably in the U.S. Navy during World War II, seeing action in a number of famous battles, including Okinawa. It was now serving in the Colombian navy, and its captain and crew did not know it yet, but it was about to undertake the most unusual tow of its storied career.

In the morning, I went to the back of *Manteño* to examine the logs in private. The *Teredo navalis* infection was moderate compared to what we experienced aboard *Illa-Tiki,* but *Manteño's* logs couldn't afford to lose the slightest buoyancy. I had estimated that a balsa raft with the *Teredo navalis* would remain seaworthy for one hundred days, but I had based that estimate on the voyage of the *Illa-Tiki.* Now, after just thirty days in the water, the *Manteño* was sinking.

The stern of the raft was completely under water. Standing on the back ends of the logs, with the water level above my ankles, I felt the most sickening feeling I had felt since the dark days aboard *Illa-Tiki*. Dread pervaded my mind and ugly waves of adrenaline consumed my body. I didn't dare mention it to the men. They were already fatigued and a little bewildered over our predicament. The raft had started out so low in the water and we had taken so many following seas that I hoped they would be slow to notice the ugly subtleties.

At 10:00 a.m, the six of us boarded the dinghy and paddled ashore through the murky green water and misty, rainy air, and stood on land. At our feet lay a beach of black volcanic sand and rock, and before us stood a dense forest of tropical trees, all of them long and slender. Visibility disappeared about fifty feet back, and then all we could see was a dark green morass. We spent half an hour trying to grasp the geography and terrain of this lost world, then Dower said he had seen a fishing camp near the rocks we had passed through on the previous day. Reboarding the dinghy, we slowly and laboriously paddled up to the mouth of the cove. The six of us sat up on the gunwales of the gray boat and paddled in unison, as we had back on the Quevedo, cruising smoothly across the green water. We maneuvered around waterfalls that burst down from the sides of the lush cove, and as we emerged from around a small point, a fishing settlement appeared in front of us, built right on the banks of the cove.

The people there were African, descendant of those brought by the Spaniards to die in the sugarcane fields. They lived at the water's edge in three open-air platforms made of bamboo canes, which housed a community of three or four families. Smoke lilted into the air from a breakfast fire and we could see a fat baby in diapers sitting on one of the platforms, crying loudly. In Spanish times, they had escaped their capturers and had set up colonies of their own in the hills. When the English privateer Sir Frances Drake had come here in the sixteen hundreds, to raid the Spanish colonies, he had made allies of these people. They were called *cimarrónes* (fugitives), and Drake found them to be a remarkably enterprising group of people. I found them, four hundred years later, to be every bit that description. Their camp and their personal appearance made the entire scene appear as though it was straight out of Africa. We landed, and I walked up the little beach and introduced myself to a man who was obviously the pilot of one of the *fibras* lying on the sand. He said he was leaving for a town, thirty-seven miles to the south by sea, where I might be able to get some transport to Bogotá. It was agreed among us from *Manteño* that I would go to a large city and have money wired from the United States to repair the raft.

The pilot of the *fibra* was a tall slim man in his late twenties. His mate was a bulging little man wearing a blue hard hat and missing an eye. They said nothing to me during the three-hour voyage to Bahia Solano, and it was readily apparent that they were helping us less out of a desire for money and more because, in a profound way, they knew how truly marooned we were.

We skimmed along in the *fibra* at fifteen knots, hugging the coastline, and after two and a half hours we turned into a long fjord. At the end of the narrow corridor lay an arcing beach of black sand and a small town, Mutis, better known as Bahia Solano. On the other side of the town lay the Atrato aquifer, ten thousand square miles of impassible swamp. Bahia Solano was cut off—no roads in or out. Our *fibra* cruised past the town's cement pier and landed on the gritty black beach, sliding to a crunchy stop.

Standing on the sand, waiting for the *fibra,* was a thin man of medium build, wearing a T-shirt and shorts, named Joaquin Cuellar. We shook hands and I was immediately struck by his soft-spoken, cerebral nature. Over the next few months he would become a devoted patron of The Expedition, and like the pilot of the *fibra* he seemed overwhelmed by the hopelessness of my situation. Within an hour he had given me money and had introduced me to some bush pilots who then volunteered to take me as far as Pereira, on the other side of the swamp. Besides boat, planes were the only way in or out.

In the air, passing over the Atrato swamp in a clattering Cessna, I looked out over miles and miles of impassable jungle, a mind-blowing explosion of green. When I finally checked into a hotel on the evening of the of October 31, I turned on the television to see that the guerrillas had hit Mitu, a town on the other side of the Quipdo swamp. They had killed hundreds of policemen and had captured the police comandante. I wrote in my diary that night:

> I tell you: Colombia must be the most beautiful place on earth. My God, what a pity (that there is war here).

The four days I spent in the hotel in Pereira were bad. During The *Illa-Tiki* Expedition, when defeat had come in Panama, it was easy to part with the raft and with The Expedition. I had been so unhappy and so revolted by the behavior of the men that the end had been somewhat of a relief. But those days in the hotel room in Colombia were unbearable because the new group deserved success. The spectacle of my forlorn group sickened me so much that I could barely eat. The thought of losing a second ship to the *Teredo navalis* was so utterly appalling that I didn't sleep for three days. I just lay there hour after hour, filled with shame and self-loathing, waiting for the money to be wired from the United States.

When the money came, I went to the Western Union office and got it. From there I was to take a bus to Medellin, where I could catch a bush plane back to Bahia Solano. The man at the Western Union office assured me that I would die in the process. He seemed especially fond of slowly enunciating the word "as-sas-sin-ate."

There were some risks that I took during the expeditions in the nineties that I am not sure I would want to take today. Traveling through the most dangerous drug country in the world with thousands of dollars in cash in my back pocket was a bad risk, but I saw it as having no other choice. The only way I can explain my mentality about risk taking is that I felt if you took the job you took it expecting some serious risks. This is not to say that I was never scared; I was frequently terrified, but that did not change the inevitable truth that if I wanted to go on expedition, I would have to face dangerous risks. I frequently saw others angry, depressed, and disillusioned over having to endure high-risk situations. I rarely felt any of those feelings, and I was frankly bewildered when others did. I could feel sympathy for them, and I was always willing to take on the worst risks by myself, but this was an expedition: What did they expect?

I made my bus journey to Medellin, caught a bush plane at the airport, flew back over the jungle, landed back in Bahia Solano—finally, and set out on foot to find the raft. I knew little of the local geography, but I knew that *Manteño* had been towed to the mouth of a river at the north end of the town. I also knew that the tow had been rough. The *Sebastion Benalcazar* had inadvertently tried to tow the raft at seven knots. The hull of the *Manteño* was far too sunken for that speed. At six knots, the bow of the raft had submerged under the pressure, and masses of water had flooded onboard, fracturing the mainsail yardarm and dragging equipment overboard. Dower quickly signaled *Sebastion Benalcazar* to stop, but the damage was already done. Nevertheless, *Manteño* made it to Bahia Solano intact, and I wandered into town now, asking townspeople for directions to the *"balsa."* It rained lightly and the overcast sky darkened everything, casting the town in an autumn light. The center of Bahia Solano was comprised of several mud streets crowded with square buildings of cinder block and corrugated metal—general stores and dusty saloons mostly, and the main drag, wide and muddy, which almost always had a good number of people on it.

The more I drifted through town, the more I realized that all of these muddy streets panned out and dead-ended at the bank of a small brown river. I followed one street to the edge of town, and where the lane faded into sand

I saw a thing that looked like a bamboo hut. It took me aback. Stopping in my tracks, I took a long moment to gather myself: *Manteño* was a wreck. It sat on the sandy riverbank, completely out of the water and sitting on land, high and dry. It had been run aground there when the river level rose during high tide. The mainsail yardarm was broken and hung sickeningly like a fractured human limb. The tan-colored balsa wood had faded to gray and the canes to a dull yellow. The manila was no longer supple and wiry; it was hard and stiff, like straw. The Expedition's gear was in total disarray from the tow, and mold grew everywhere and on everything. It could not have been more depressing. *Manteño* looked old and worn out, like a dear friend, unseen for several years, who had gone totally gray.

8

Welcome to
Camp Hardcore

As I walked up to the raft, Martin came out of the pathetic hut and stood on deck. "It's a great site, isn't it!" he said. He was serious and that worried me. The raft was marooned on the banks of a brackish, no-name river. Martin's sincere statement told me that he, and *we* for that matter, had been too deep in the field for too long, and had sunken to subhuman standards. Shortly after he made that worrying statement, I received another emotional shock. He sat on a stump and said, "I want you to know that I am with you until the end." He pulled his legs up to his body and wrapped his arms around them, then said, "The guys and I talked, and we're with you as far as it goes."

And so I left the raft with a ray of hope, and walked down the dirt road that ran through the heart of the village. In the distance I saw the undeniable swagger of Cameron Smith, and the methodical caveman trudge of Scott Siekierski. Cameron beamed: No matter how deep it got, he was always ready for more. We met in the middle of the road and shook hands, and then rain started to fall and we jogged over to the shelter of a grove of palm trees, where I shouted: "We've got the money!" over the noise of the drops on the rubbery leaves. Both said, simply, "Good," and both exuded such hardened cheerfulness that I felt proud of them as people and as men. We were all aware of the hellish work that was coming.

Just the *quantity* of work we were facing was staggering. In the morning, the second-highest tide of the year would occur. When that happened the river would back up, swelling to many times its normal width, and we'd use the opportunity to pull the raft up to the highest part of the beach. Twenty-nine days later, the highest tide of the year would arrive, raising the river just a few inches higher—maybe just enough to relaunch the *Manteño*. During the twenty-eight days of dry dock we'd jack up the raft with *wancas* and replace six of the nine balsa logs. Once the raft floated off the riverbank we'd prepare for it sea, which would take about another month in port. Then, maybe, we'd escape this place.

We now found ourselves at the head of a tropical fjord, six miles long. Steep slopes crowded its sides, bursting with impenetrable jungle. Ideally, we'd get six balsa logs from this jungle, let them sit in the hot tropical sun for three weeks, and install them once they were dry and buoyant. But that would be impossible: We were marooned in the wettest place on Earth. Bahia Solano received at least 524 inches of rainfall per year. The official measurement gauge was in the town Lloro, on the other side of the Atrato aquifer, so no one knew the exact amount of rainfall in Bahia Solano; but people in both towns agreed that of the two, Bahia Solano was "much more soaked." The soakings came for seventy-two hours straight sometimes and they came in a wide variety of styles, some like monsoons and some in light, inoffensive drops, like rain manufactured by an amusement park. Then the sun might break out for a couple of hours, shining brilliantly, making colossal rainbows—sometimes as many as half-a-dozen in one sky. It was not uncommon in Bahia Solano to turn around and see the base of a rainbow starting from the ground next to you and shooting straight to the top of the sky. The breaks between rains were never more than two or three hours long though, never long enough for the dripping from the previous rain to stop. The clouds—and there were every sort—large puffy cumulous clouds, gray smears of clouds, cloud streaks, clouds that looked like smoke—would then close over Bahia Solano, and it would start all over again. This tiny fjord where we were now stranded had the highest level of precipitation in the known world. There were no floods in Bahia Solano, no droughts, no torrents of any kind; in this place, it simply rained forever.

The Manteño Expedition faced problems unlike those of other balsa raft expeditions. Or so it seemed. On the surface it seemed as though no other modern raft sailor had ever encountered the problems we were dealing with—the unique problems faced by the ancient Manteño mariners. Of those problems, *Teredo navalis* was the strangest. Numerous historical texts contained references to it, as did many modern adventure books, but the books about balsa rafts said nothing. I had always looked upon those balsa raft books as authoritative, as absolutes, as "how-to" books, but the results of our experiments simply didn't concur with their stories, and now the inconsistencies were just too much. We were now taking the next step in the evolution of our thinking: We were questioning everything and no longer taking anything for granted—regardless of who said it. Cameron once told me, "You should look upon this research as a detective mystery—we're trying to piece together a puzzle." One of the things that puzzled us the most was a mysterious voyage made by a Spaniard named Vital Alsar.

Thor Heyerdahl may have been the first great raft voyager of the modern era, but Vital Alsar was, unquestionably, the best. Alsar was in no way a scientist or a researcher; he was an anachronism, a Spanish conquistador who had been accidentally born in the twentieth century, a charismatic adventurer who never, ever, gave up. He made three balsa raft voyages, crossed the Pacific Ocean twice, and in the end spent five hundred days on rafts. It was his first voyage that was so mysterious—it was the gap in the research—the thing that confounded us the most: In late 1966, Alsar and his crew set out from Ecuador aboard his first balsa raft, the ill-fated *Pacifica,* bound for the Galapagos Islands, and then beyond. Aboard *Pacifica* everything seemed to go wrong from the beginning. There is little written about this fateful voyage, but Alsar evidently faced some of the freakish problems that I saw on my first expedition. One of the men aboard the *Pacifica* was unstable, and once in isolation and confinement that instability quickly came to the surface. Alsar was able to put the unstable man off on the first passing ship, but then *Pacifica* began to drift slowly northward, into the Doldrums, where there was no wind. With nothing to do but wait for the breeze, Alsar and his crew hung on, living aboard their wooden platform in the middle of a vast ocean. After 143 days of doing everything they could to keep their raft afloat they signaled SOS, and had to be rescued. It was a very weird voyage, and years later Alsar was still deeply disturbed by "feverish images" of his unstable man.

But what happened to the vessel? The *Pacifica* was the only balsa raft on record as sinking. A balsa raft doesn't have a "hull," therefore there is nothing to "fill up," so how does it sink? Years later, writing in his book *La Balsa,* Alsar claimed that: ". . . the raft had begun to absorb water, the balsas rotting from the fermented sap that had gradually spread from the core to the outer surface of each log." He then went on to write in considerable length that the solution to this problem of fermentation lay in knowing secrets of the jungle. According to Alsar, the only way to prevent the raft from sinking was to pick out just the right balsa trees and cut them down at just right time. Thor Heyerdahl had written to me in the same vein after *Illa-Tiki* sank, saying: "I assume that

the Ecuadorans gave you balsa timber freshly cut and full of sap in the correct season." But over the years we cut down logs of every type, in every season, and at every moon phase, and they all got the *Teredo navalis.* Even
worse, neither Heyerdahl's book, *Kon-Tiki,* nor Vital Alsar's book, *La Balsa,*
mentioned anything about shipworms. Heyerdahl had gone to great lengths
to discuss every detail of the balsa raft in many of his other books, but in
nine hundred pages of text there wasn't a single reference to the raft's vulnerability to *Teredo navalis.* In the years between the expeditions I had written to Alsar, asking him what he did to prevent the *Teredo navalis,* but there
was no response. Later, I asked others to write to him on my behalf. Again,
there was no response. I eventually tracked down one of his colleagues and
wrote him too, asking how they prevented the *Teredo navalis.* Again, there
was no response.

Until I was marooned in Colombia I believed in Heyerdahl's and Alsar's
characterization of the balsa raft as a special ship, impervious to conventional
problems and surrounded by secrets. But the more I learned the more I began
to become suspicious that perhaps *Pacifica* had sunk because of the *Teredo
navalis,* and that Heyerdahl and Alsar, rather than admit that the vessel was
exceedingly vulnerable to sinking from this problem, had simply skirted
around talking about it.

And so we plodded forward. Every "solution" the experts gave us became
a dead end. How Heyerdahl and Alsar prevented the *Teredo navalis* was still
unknown to me, but I was now sure that a balsa raft was always a better vessel when it was made from dried logs. But you had to have the right climate.
The climate in Bahia Solano would never allow us to dry out our new logs.
The only way to continue our voyage seemed to be to put a preventative
coating on them. Throughout our research we had heard of coating the logs
with creosote, sulfur, beeswax, resin, tar, pitch, scorching the logs with fire,
bathing the logs in fresh water, bathing them in the juice of the barbasco
plant, bathing them in an organic distillate called Rotinone, and of course,
painting them with antifouling paint. Back in Salango we had used modern
antifouling paint because we were modern people. This modern "solution"
had done nothing. The natives of Bahia Solano used tar on their boats, and
they assured us it could stop the *Teredo navalis.* So, with no other choice, we
would bring in six new logs for the damaged raft and tar them. But we'd have
to hurry. If we couldn't be ready to launch in twenty-eight days—the highest
tide of the year—*Manteño* would probably be marooned in this isolated
place forever.

On the morning of November 7, we began to disassemble the raft. A soft rain fell and we worked in the gray light of an overcast sky. From town, a small blue truck bounced down the muddy street leading to our worksite and then pulled up to the spot where the road faded into the beach. Joaquin Cuellar, the man who had helped me when I had first arrived on the *fibra*, got out and walked up to me in the rain. Through the drops he said, calmly: "You can store your equipment in my warehouse."

The crew stood in a line, hats and clothes dripping, and passed item after item from the raft to Joaquin Cuellar's truck: The bicycle and generator, the radios, the storage barrels, and on and on. Once the hut was empty we began untying the fibrous manila ropes that held our little house together. The villagers of Bahia Solano stood all around, some of them under umbrellas, watching the bizarre scene. Cane by cane we disassembled the hut while the eternal rain fell, soaking our clothes and chilling our skin. Next, we went to work on the deck. Two-man teams hoisted each forty-foot deck cane onto their shoulders and carried them to an open field of sand nearby. Each cane was placed on supports and then numbered in the exact sequence that it had come off the raft. It poured and poured and we slowly disassembled *Manteño* like taking apart an enormous model boat. Hours passed, then days. We untied and removed the six logs we wanted to replace, wallowing in the gray volcanic sand, hammering and pounding and levering apart the gigantic manila knots that held them together. We left the center logs in place, as well as the masts, so that when we were finished the raft had been stripped of everything but its backbone. Then we went to work with the hand shovels. Working for hours in the cold rain, we dug out all of the sand underneath the raft so that we could crawl underneath and paint tar on the balsa logs. After a week of constant work *Manteño* sat in dry dock, stripped down to her skeleton.

By now we had established a camp beside the worksite. We were located on an open plain of sand, where the river flowed through the beach. Nothing stood on the flats around us. Besides the sand there was only the ivy, a lowly, weed-like vine that lived in dense colonies, or patches, and our crude little camp. David and Martin had small tents in their personal gear, which we erected twenty feet from the raft. Ten feet from them we set up a makeshift dining fly by standing up four *guaras* in a square, like crude tent poles, and stretching a blue tarp across their tops. Underneath the tarp sat our dinner table, the enormous balsa stump that we had used as our navigation station aboard the raft. It was already becoming weathered and gray, but it was perfect as our table in the forlorn camp. Several years back, the locals had come to this part of the beach to dump their garbage. The sand around us was full of refuse, which had long since sunken underneath the surface but could be seen any time we dug down even just a few inches. This open flat of sand, where the road faded into the beach, was suddenly our toehold on normality.

Had you come to the end of the road on a day in November 1999 you would have seen the skeleton of a wooden sailboat, its two masts, blond and slender, standing tall by the river, and a crude camp on the open beach. Men, some shirtless and some in jackets with hoods over their heads, would be lurching about on the soft sand, shuffling back and forth between the skeleton and the little tarp over the stump. Large patches of sand would hang from their bodies and they would be slinging black gritty bits whenever they moved. At their feet, half-buried and covered with gritty black sand would be an old shoe, a doll, and an empty bleach bottle, all in various stages of sinking. And everything would drip. The men working on the boat would have a steady stream of drops falling from the points of their elbows. The men standing under the fly, regardless of how long they stood there, would be dripping from the points of their noses. On the other side of these dripping figures would stand what was obviously their home, two mountaineering tents, little nylon pyramids, one blue and the other yellow, sagging under the onslaught, dripping, losing the war of attrition. The dripping men would sometimes stand under the tarp for hours, silently grouped around the enormous balsa stump, assessing the skeleton like stoic mechanics, thinking only of what needed to be done next and how long it would take. The bright blue plastic tarp above their heads would drip. Regardless of what was done a trough would develop in the tarp and fill until it was a lake and then this too would drip, until drained. The wooden skeleton before the men under the tarp would be dripping too. Three massive logs, long and powerful like a massive backbone and topped with crossbeams like the ribs of an unearthed dinosaur, would be dripping under a low gray sky. At the skeleton's side: the river, its surface jumping into millions of drops from the impact of millions of other falling drops, and on the other side of that a tangle of wide green palms on the far bank like a wall that had never stopped dripping since it came into existence. On one such day in November 1999, in a fit of wry humor, I dipped my finger into a can of tar and then spelled out "CAMP HARDCORE" in big black letters on an old wooden plank, which dripped, and then placed it in front of our hellish little home.

From Camp Hardcore it was half a mile to the center of town. On the other side of town lay an airstrip and a small fort, manned by roughly two companies of Colombian marines. Electricity was available for a few hours a day in the town and there was running water, as well as a small satellite-telephone office available to the public. Joaquin Cuellar operated the only commercial fishing operation in town. He was an earnest man in his mid thirties, and during our imprisonment in Bahia Solano we learned to call him "brother." He was one of us. He had chosen to leave his safe life in the big city and eke out his existence in the wettest place in the world. Over the years he had slowly built a tiny fishing business, one step at a time. He reached out to us, and we spent many nights in his home and many evenings at his table.

Once labor had begun, we began putting out the word in the village that we were looking for balsa logs, and after a few days we contracted with a skinny, fast-talking man in his early forties, named Fabio, who lived by himself in the jungle, several miles from town. Shortly afterward, Martin told me he wanted to go to Fabio's camp to film the workmen cutting the balsa. He hired a couple of the locals to guide him through the jungle, and at daybreak the next day, they set out. They were gone the entire day, and near dusk they emerged from the tree line on the other side of the river, with Martin tired and sweating profusely. He said little and went straight to his tent. I thanked the two local guys, and then told them to come back to camp the next day—maybe I'd have some other work for them.

In the morning, at breakfast, Martin said that I had "big problems with Fabio." "I talked to the men up in his camp," he said, speaking softly and sincerely. "They said Fabio's a pirate. He's into cocaine, and I think he's a drug runner. He can't get the logs you want, and he's not going to be able to. His workmen haven't been paid, and they're pissed. They're talking about coming down here and getting it from you." He said this as though he meant by force. "Fabio's working them to death and they have nothing to eat. The guides told me that they were thinking of ambushing me and stealing all my camera gear."

"OK," I said. "The first thing is, you're not going back into the sticks."

"I want to go back."

"Bullshit. You're not going back until I find out what the hell's going on."

Martin's willingness to return to the jungle seemed strange and incongruent, given what he had just told me, but I ignored that. I translated to Dower what Martin had said and then told him that he and I would be going up to Fabio's camp the next day.

That night the two "guides," Lledar and Marcelino, came to Camp Hardcore. In the dark, the three of us huddled together under the tarp, and drank shots of *Aguardiente*. A candle lantern lit a tiny area on the balsa stump table, the drops popped overhead, and I asked, "What happened up there?"

"What do you mean?" Lledar asked. He was a muscular man in his late twenties, intelligent, and gave me a sense of camaraderie immediately.

I began explaining to both of them what Martin had said and they began to smirk. At the end of the sordid tale, they began to laugh, which caused me to laugh too because I realized in the middle of it that Martin had exaggerated.

"We told him that he *wouldn't* be ambushed, because we were with him. Yes, Fabio is *mala gente* (bad people), but he's not like a (full-time) pirate. I think your friend was a little nervous," Lledar said.

"Yes, he was nervous out there," Marcelino added.

"I want you to take me and the Ecuadoran guy up to Fabio's camp in the morning. I'll pay you a day's wage."

The next day I went to Fabio's camp, about a two-hour walk through the jungle, and realized that the "big trouble with Fabio" had been a false alarm. Dower and I returned in the afternoon with assurances that the logs would be delivered soon.

Each morning for the next ten days, we painted tar on the balsa logs. We mixed the blocks of hard black tar in a barrel of gasoline, which acted as an emulsifier, and then applied the mixture with big bushy brushes. The three main logs sat suspended above the black volcanic sand, thick and massive and still tied together, and working underneath them was the hardest part. The crawl space below was just wide enough for a man to snake and squirm under. Once under, you painted a surface that was right in front of your face. Many times, I had to keep my head turned to one side to prevent my nose from sticking to the gooey tar on the freshly painted surface. With three men underneath, all of them slapping and stroking tar, the fumes became overwhelming. At first we didn't mind, perhaps the gasoline smelled like home, but then the tar would start to accumulate on you. It gummed up your fingernails within the first seconds, and then quickly crawled all over your body. By the third day we were tar-covered men, with streaks and black rubbery patches on our arms and legs and torsos. Once it attached itself to you it was practically impossible to get it off. We tried scrubbing off the patches of tar with sand and saltwater, scraping the patches with sticks, scraping them with machetes, scraping them with ax heads, ignoring them, picking at them during meals, picking at them while talking to each other, and picking at them while standing under the blue tarp—the most common method—while watching it pour. The only effective method of removing them was the gasoline bath, of which we took many. The gasoline bath consisted of a man standing in his underwear, scratching his sand-covered tar patches with a gasoline-soaked wad of newspaper until he couldn't stand it anymore. It scorched your skin red, but at least it got some of the tar off, which made it easier to sleep at night.

In a few days, the new balsa logs arrived. Fabio towed them to Camp Hardcore behind a *fibra,* and we ran them up on the beach with the high tide. It was about this time when I received an urgent message from Joaquin Cuellar. He had a satellite dish on the roof of his house, and for some strange reason, he now had a balsa raft on his television screen.

When we arrived at Joaquin's we sat on the floor, smelling of gasoline and tar, and watched a documentary film being broadcast from Bogota. On the television before us was Vital Alsar, captain of that weird voyage in 1966, when *Pacifica* sank near Galapagos. The subject of the film was Alsar's third expedition, when he had sailed across the Pacific with three rafts. Years before I had been able to acquire, with great difficulty, an excerpt of this film. I had examined it repeatedly and nothing I had ever seen had made an impression on me. His rafts looked just like my *Illa-Tiki,* and in front of me now were the same types of images that I had seen for years. But then, for a few precious seconds, there was a close-up shot of Alsar's logs: They were black. "Oh God," I groaned.

I knew instantly that they had been covered with tar. In a film lasting eighty-five minutes, this moment of truth lasted less than twenty seconds: The tar had been painted on the lower halves of the logs so that it was almost always hidden below the waterline. Alsar had briefly mentioned that he had coated the underside of his logs with crude oil as a way to prevent fungus, but it now appeared that he had, in fact, painted tar all over his logs to prevent *Teredo navalis.* Perhaps Alsar used the secrets of the jungle, and those secrets are no doubt invaluable, but it seemed that Alsar also knew that the secrets of the jungle would do nothing to stop the *Teredo navalis.* But hadn't we studied the photographs in the books? Surely we would have seen *something.* Not necessarily. Over the years I had collected a myriad of photos from all of the rafting expeditions and all had been inconclusive. But now, after all those years, I returned to the very first picture: The logs of the *Kon-Tiki.* A chill came over me. Of all the logs I'd seen up to now, these logs were the strangest in appearance: They were black, obviously painted, most likely with tar. But it didn't register. It seemed a little too fantastic. Heyerdahl had written to me after my first expedition, saying, "Your problem with the *Teredo navalis* is a complete mystery to me." A complete mystery? Two years later I wrote to him again, once again asking about the problem, to which he replied: ". . . rafts that sailed from Ecuador . . . never seem to have had this problem." But surely he knew! Surely he knew the truth of Alsar's strange first voyage, when *Pacifica* sank. The truth was that *Pacifica* had sunk because of the *Teredo navalis,* and Alsar had painted his logs with tar on subsequent voyages to prevent the problem. Not only that, but Alsar had indeed pointed out in his book, *La Balsa,* that the *Teredo navalis* was a threat to the raft, and it was only through sheer coincidence—which was no fault of Alsar's—that the historical record had been *accidentally altered.* But why didn't Heyerdahl say that? Why didn't he say that he and Alsar had used tar to prevent the *Teredo navalis?* Or write it in any of his books? Why would Heyerdahl go to such lengths to mislead people? Because he knew that the balsa raft had an "Achilles' heal." He knew that the *Teredo navalis* would sink the balsa raft *every time.* Using tar to stop the shipworm was a "modern solution"—it polluted his experiment. He wanted people to believe that ancient raft technology alone could be used to sail across the ocean, even though he knew it could not.

Or so it seemed to me at the time . . . There were still many lessons to be learned, and connections to be made, but these would come later.

On November 14, Cameron Smith left Camp Hardcore to return to Canada and his doctoral thesis. He had of course told me almost a month before that he would have to leave, but when we said farewell it was as though I was falling off a cliff. For the documentary film we shook hands in front of the camera, and I could see in his eyes that he was heartbroken at the idea of having to go home. I smiled and tried to keep the moment light, but inside I was distraught too. Shortly after he left, an enormous Colombian with Herculean strength, named Benedicto, came to Camp Hardcore, and together with Scott and I, stood under the blue tarp and drank shots of mellow cane liquor, toasting Cameron. It was all that could be done. Benedicto, gigantic and brooding, asked me about Cameron, and all I could say was that he was a good man and I hated to lose him. The huge man sensed the situation perfectly, in all its subtleties. "Then we drink to a good man," he said, and ceremoniously threw back a shot, "Cameron!"

He was the best among us, and after he left Camp Hardcore I didn't see him again for years. Nevertheless, he continued to toil in obscurity, researching the Manteño and helping The Expedition logistically. Two years later, he attempted the impossible: He tried to cross the ice cap of Iceland, on foot, alone, and in the dead of winter. During this expedition he would be a solitary person in a frozen wasteland, feeling his way through the polar night, rarely seeing more than a few hours of light per day. No one, not even the Icelanders themselves, had ever been so bold. While on the ice cap he was hit by a meteorological monster called a *Piteriaq*. A *Piteriaq* is a colossal block of frozen wind that falls from high altitudes, blowing away and flash-freezing everything in its path. In a harrowing retreat, Smith somehow managed to navigate through zero-visibility conditions, hiking, marching, stumbling, crawling on all fours, and eventually clawing across the rock and ice for eleven straight hours in sustained winds of ninety miles per hour. At times he felt his body becoming airborne—lifting off from the glacier for one hair-raising second—trying to fly away into darkness like a leaf on a winter's night. Somehow he reached an isolated town at the foot of the ice cap, had a cup of coffee, and then decided to "have another go at it." It would take him another four years before he finally crossed it.

A few days after Cameron left Bahia Solano, Dower began to falter. He had grown up on a beach, and working in the sand irritated and depressed him. He had endured so much and had been so patient through so many trials that when the break came, it came hard. Bahia Solano was a depressed mud bog, and he knew as well as I did that we were backed into a corner of the Gulf of Panama with a vessel that possessed very limited maneuverability. We had all tried to keep a brave face around Camp Hardcore, but our situation appeared hopeless. For five straight days it rained continuously without any let up whatsoever. We spent hours under the dining fly, just standing and watching and thinking. In front of us, in the gray light, lay our forlorn skeleton ship. It sat on blocks next to a brown river with a lush green jungle on the other side. The drops popped endlessly on the tarp over our heads and we could not paint tar or work on the raft structurally. We could not have been stranded in a worse place. The methodical rain never tired, never wore itself out, never reached a point of being enough. Everything smelled sharply of mildew. Mold crawled across all fabrics, foods, ropes, and other organic materials. Everything: books, mats, clothes, wood, and sometimes even skin, seemed to be slowly growing a green fur. In the face of the wettest place in the world, we felt helpless, and as the days wore on, Dower became increasingly depressed, and worse, resigned. His new girlfriend, the dark-eyed Marcia, had opposed his participation in The Expedition. Dower seemed resigned to the idea that we would never succeed, or if we did it would be a year-long voyage, and by the time we returned, Marcia would be long gone.

On the twenty-second, David shook hands with me as Cameron had, and then he left Camp Hardcore to return to his home in the United States. He left because I had suggested that he do so. He had been uncomfortable on the raft and had never relaxed. But telling him he should leave was difficult because I admired him. During the voyage to Colombia he had showed that he could stand his watch as well as I could, if not better. He had great physical strength and a good sense of teamwork, too. When you called for assistance, David was very frequently the person who reached you first. But I worried that he might decline on the next voyage. I felt that he was like Chris and perhaps even Brock during The *Illa-Tiki* Expedition: He was in no way disruptive and he had caused no great problems, but he did not have a natural appetite for this life and its hardships. This for me was an important point: Toughness was a fine thing, but *appetite* was probably better. Having an appetite for the life, or more specifically the hardship, is probably the telling difference in who will do well in the field and who will not. There have been many tough people who have gone into the field over the centuries who have wilted in the face of hardship because they found no enjoyment in it. On the other hand, many who weren't what one might think of as hard or tough have endured far longer. What separates the two is *appetite*: Both types of people are equally as miserable; but while one feels as though the world has been dropped on top of him, the other wouldn't trade his position for the world. During the balsa raft expeditions, most of the people who went into the field expected *Kon-Tiki,* where there was no apparent discomfort. When the suffering came, they declined, not because they weren't tough enough, but because it was nothing like they expected. In late 1998, in Bahia Solano, I still had great doubts about my ability to prevent the type of decline I had seen during the voyage of the *Illa-Tiki.* David and I talked several times, and in the end he bowed out of the expedition without any resentment. He was a man who understood grace.

Two days later I began to notice that a small cut in my foot was growing more painful by the day. Then it began to swell. Then the pain intensified and I felt a darkness come over me. The tissues at the base of my big toe expanded quickly and stretched the skin taut: I had contracted the "tropical abscess." Without saying a word to the others, I quietly slipped away to the field hospital on the other side of town.

The field hospital was a marvel. It was a one-story cement building, clean and well run, with a good roof and floor. They had an X-ray machine in one of the rooms, and I think a rudimentary lab in the back. When I arrived there they took me in without a moment's hesitation, put me on a table, and brought in a small, balding man in his midtwenties. He had an elderly nurse with him, dressed in full whites, who stuck a needle filled with novocain into the bone of my big toe, then cut the distended skin from around the swollen abscess. The man then grabbed the abscess with both hands and squeezed as hard as he could, trying, I guess, to blow the infection out of my foot. After that produced no results, he began sticking the hypodermic needle in all parts of my foot, trying to deaden it. I think he had in mind splitting the swollen abscess down the middle with a scalpel. Throughout this, which took about twenty minutes, I gasped and jumped in pain.

During the procedure, a very beautiful young woman came in and sat down to watch. I think she was like the man: a doctor of sorts. She sat in a chair by the wall, slowly eating a piece of succulent fruit with her fingers and giggling each time I jumped in pain. When the man pulled a scalpel out of a drawer, I reached over and stopped the madness. "I don't think that's going to help," I said. "May I have some antibiotics?"

"OK, sure."

He looked at me for a moment as though my reaction to the pain was the strangest thing he had ever seen, then said, "You've got to be more careful. This thing in your foot comes from a bacteria that lives in the sand around here. It will kill you." He wrote me a prescription, and I hobbled back to Camp Hardcore.

When Dower saw me come up, he didn't say a word. He didn't need to—the abscess chills anyone who's ever had it. His eyes faded; they dimmed into dullness in just a few seconds, and then he wandered off down the road toward Joaquin's without talking to me. Dower had always blocked out problems that were too horrible to think about. He was the only one who knew what the abscess meant.

I had to lie down in my tent. It was dusk anyway and the workday was finished. Inside, I lay on my moldy sleeping bag. Martin came over, opened the tent fly, and told me he would have to go to Bogotá to retrieve a video camera that had gotten stuck in customs. I tried to hide the pain, which was intensifying, but I couldn't help grunting under the strain. I said that I'd watch the camp, and then he took his leave. After he left I lay there wondering if I had caught the infection soon enough. The visit to the doctor had, at least, yielded some antibiotics, but that alone hadn't been enough to stop Dower's abscess during *Illa-Tiki*.

Darkness came and the rain picked up. The tent I lay in was an old, yellow, forlorn-looking structure that was on permanent loan from David. It could keep out the raindrops because the roof was still waterproof; the floor, however, had rotted. Each night, when the rainfall increased and the evaporation decreased, the water seeped through the bottom of the tent and accumulated. It pooled, forming a pond three to four inches deep. I had a foam mattress on loan from Martin, and if I lay perfectly still on it, the water formed a moat around my body. Gradually, over the weeks, the weight of the water in the moat made an impression in the loose sand underneath the tent's floor so that the sand sank down, leaving behind a six-foot island mound in the middle of the tent. I lay there, night after night, on top of a little dome of sand, with the moat around it slowly filling up.

I read every night. From bamboo cane, I made two small lanterns for candles. There was no place to put them because my body occupied every inch of the island in the middle, so I attached the lanterns to flat pieces of Styrofoam, and they floated. But the candle lanterns rarely stayed in one place; they tended to voyage around the island, and every night it was same routine: They'd get underway at about 8:30, floating down one side, around my feet, then back up the other side toward my head. I set it up so that they revolved around me, but stayed on opposite sides of each other. If one was passing by my feet, then the other would be orbiting my head. I'd follow the light with my open book until it left, then pick it up on the other side.

That night, when the abscess began to rage, I couldn't read, even though I tried. I gave up after a few minutes because I couldn't concentrate through the agony. I descended into despair; my mind wouldn't stop working: *I'm lying in a lake. I've got the abscess. The orbiting lights are playing tricks on my eyes and my mind. More rain; it never ends here. I don't know when or how I'm going to get us out of here. The raft is a wreck, and quite frankly, without Enrique, I'm not sure I can put it back together. We've set up camp in the most remote area. We've set up camp in a landfill. I've got the freakin' abscess! Welcome to Camp Hardcore.*

Perhaps the doctor's methods were dubious, but his prescription was not. The abscess began to calm within twenty-four hours. Thankfully, I did not have to endure the torture and delirium that plagued Dower. It seemed to me like the greatest break that I had ever received.

By the last week of November, we were attaching the new logs to *Manteño*. We persevered in the rain. Soaked clothes and shivers defined our lives. Black volcanic sand coated our fingers and hands. *Manteño* lay on the banks of a no-name river, its masts standing and its logs black with tar, hoping for escape. One evening during this time, around midnight, I decided to go into town to buy a little beer. I told Scott that I'd be back shortly, and then made my way up the main road toward the center of town. People were out walking, drinking, and dancing. I wove my way through the wooden and cinder-block buildings until I heard the squawking of a military radio. Just as I turned the corner of one of the gray buildings, I ran right into a patrol of Colombian marines. There were probably about fifteen of them, dressed in full battle gear, green fatigues, boots, and rifles. They were muddy, like they had just come in from the bush and they were fanned out, as though they were making a sweep through the village. The minute I turned the corner I knew I had made a grave mistake. An angry little man with a submachine gun immediately started yelling, "You! You there! Don't move! Do not move!" He came trotting up, grabbed my shirt collar, pressed my face against a cinder-block wall, and put the muzzle of his gun up to the back of my head. I was very scared. I wasn't at all thinking about being shot, but I immediately had a clear vision of being dragged off and beaten severely by the soldiers. "Who are you! What are you doing! What is your name! You'd better have some identification or you've got a serious problem!"

"I was just walking to town. I'm working on the raft down by the river-"

"Shut up!"

He pressed harder against me, making sure I felt the muzzle of his rifle in the back of my head. I was really terrified. It was either going to be in the jungle or back in some dimly lit room at the fort, but these guy were going to beat me with those hard gun butts. His lieutenant came walking up, emerging out of the darkness with a sadistic smile. I can't say if he was drunk on alcohol or if he was drunk with the sudden power of having an American in hand, but his eyes were red. He reached over and ripped my knife out of its sheath. "What is this! What do you need this for! Why are you carrying this around!"

"I work with it. I . . . I'm a sailor. I'm working on the raft down by the river."

"I don't know of any raft," he said, then looked around at the group of marines that had surrounded me, "Do any of you know of a raft?" They all shook their heads, grinning and smirking wickedly. They were gloating over their golden opportunity. The officer demanded my passport, snatching it out of my hand the moment I got it out of my pocket.

I began name dropping as fast as I could. "I'm here on a scientific expedition.

I am a guest of the captain of the port. Call your commanding officer at the base if you don't believe me. He and I are friends."

"I'm not calling anyone."

He wandered away, his arrogant smile disappearing into the darkness, and left his men surrounding me. There wasn't an ounce of pity in any of them. I knew that they had heard stories from their countrymen of humiliation and degradation at the hands of the American DEA or Immigration. *Why should they show me any sympathy?* I was helpless.

In a few long moments, he returned. "What do you need such a large knife for!"

"I—I need it for my work, honestly."

He made a gesture to hand it to me, and when I reached out to take it he pulled it away and acted like he was going to hit me. His mob guffawed for a moment, then he dropped the knife on the ground and I picked it up. It was a memento from Annie's father; I wasn't going to leave it behind. Miraculously, they gave me back my passport, threatened me a little more, then strutted away.

I thought about the beer. I didn't want to cower. Fear is like flooding water in a ship at sea: You've got to stop the leaks or you will eventually sink. I girded myself up, walked to a small store, bought a few things, then walked nervously back to Camp Hardcore. It was a moment of real terror for me. I could take execution. No matter how unfair, it would be over quickly. But the idea of being beaten—that really got to me.

I thought the whole thing an aberration. I had never seen one ounce of hostility in anyone during the entire time I had been in Colombia, and I admired the Colombians greatly. I was convinced that these were just angry little men who had almost let the situation get out of hand.

On December 5, in the afternoon, the river began to rise. Brown murky water swirled in around the raft. The second floor and hut had not yet been attached, so the rebuilt raft weighed significantly less than *Manteño* had, one month earlier. Tidewater continued to flood in, and with only a few minutes left before the water would begin to recede, the raft levitated gently up from the beach. We dug our feet into the sand, leaned over against the balsa logs, and pushed. *Manteño II* slid gently into the river.

We anchored the new raft in the river near Camp Hardcore and began the arduous process of preparing her for the high sea. We spent several days attaching various parts of the superstructure. As usual, it poured. We sat cross-legged on the bamboo canes, four hooded men, tying hundreds of knots, slowly weaving our fingers and hands in intricate maneuvers like stoic artisans.

Meanwhile, Dower was fading. He had told me, twice, that he really wanted to go back to Ecuador. He had received news from home that his girlfriend had fainted one afternoon while waiting tables. The rumor was she had a heart problem. He also faced a second problem: Suddenly he was a hero in an unheroic position. Our union of equality, which I had been confident would make us an invincible team, seemed to leave him feeling unneeded. It seemed like I had changed from incompetent to expert. But this sentiment was utterly preposterous; if I had in any way become a mariner, it was only because I had learned to imitate Dower. Not only that but there was a continuing tension between him and Scott. Instead of enjoying his heroic status, which had made him feel so invaluable during *Illa-Tiki*, Scott's open disdain made him feel second class, which, considering his remarkable abilities, was a very bitter pill for him to swallow. Then one day I walked into Camp Hardcore and knew there was a problem. "Where's Dower?" I asked Scott and Martin.

"He's gone," Martin said with finality.

"Gone?"

"Yeah. I think he's made a deal with one of the transport captains."

I left without saying a word. I walked the mile from camp to the pier quickly, and when I came to the end of the cement, where the transport ship was tied up, I was still striding with my head bent forward. Dower was standing on the upper deck of an old wooden freighter, hauling a line. The ship was about to get underway. "Dower!" I shouted. Looking at me, his face and body slowly spread into alarm, shame, and embarrassment. "Where's my ax?" I yelled, and then he relaxed, the way a person would if he suddenly realized that he had nothing more to prove.

"I put it in your tent."

"Do you need any money?"

"No, *Capitan*."

"Thank you for helping me. Call me in six months—April or May."

"April or May? OK." Then he looked around, trying to think of something to say—*anything* that might capture our feelings at that moment. "I wish you calm seas," he said, "and, and, and—"

"Fair winds."

"Yes. Yes. *Adios, Capitan*."

"Be careful," I said, expecting his face to crinkle up in that warm smile of his. But it did not. I think Dower had some lingering doubts about my survival.

As I turned away and began to walk, I was compelled to look back at him. It seemed as though he focused his attention on my face and body for a moment—like he was trying to memorize what I looked like. It seemed to me that he thought it possible that I would eventually become someone who "disappeared."

After a few days we towed *Manteño II* to an anchorage near the pier. Scott opposed moving the raft, saying that we needed to keep it near Camp Hardcore until we finished all of the structural work. He was growing more and more disillusioned with The Expedition. He spent many days talking to Martin about basketball games, about school, and about home. He was fresh from college, and he missed his former life acutely.

On the sixteenth, Scott came back to the raft after running an errand to one of the other villages. The sun went down and I sat on a balsa stump, working on some rope, while he sat on another stump, facing me. With the light gone, I could barely make out the features on his face; he was a black silhouette in the darkness. Every thirty seconds or so, during a pause in his words, I'd see the coal on the end of his cigarette rise up and redden. "John," he said, his voice quivering, "I don't think I'm game anymore." He had his legs pulled up next to his body now; his body, face, voice, and persona, were a blond, muscular, knot.

I didn't argue with him. I'd been thinking the same thing the last few days. He had become cynical and sarcastic and had begun to quibble about small things. In the morning he caught the plane to Bogotá, and hooked up with Martin for a few days. Martin was spending a lot of time in Bogotá these days, trying to get his equipment out of customs. The two friends wandered around the city, looking at the girls and not saying much. Martin told me later: "He was so embarrassed and ashamed of giving up that he couldn't look me in the eye." That bothered me; Scott never did *anything* shameful; on the contrary, he had done well. His goodness originated from a strong sense of duty. During the tarring of the raft he had confided that the whole, hot, miserable process was "the most unpleasant experience of my life"; yet, daily, he led the charge: First on the job site, first with a tar-filled brush in his hand, and first under the raft to smear the stinking goo on the logs suspended precariously over our heads. Within a few days so much tar caked on him that washing it off became futile. It just hardened, day after day, covering more and more of his sunburned body. He left it on, slept in it, pulled bits of it out of his food, and continued to paint.

It was too bad that he left, but all for the better. He did not approve of me. He had dreams of glory, which I too had once had. He had come on The Expedition talking vaguely about his desire to join the Marines Corps, and I think he had expected a military-style operation while we were in the field. He needed "Captain Kirk," which I was not. I was too loose in my style, whereas he was rigid and linear. Also, perhaps just as importantly, being lost in this jungle crevice, disconnected from his former life, made him feel as though the world was passing him by.

On December 19, 1998, I wrote to Annie.

My Dearest Love,

Scott left today. I was in the jungle when he left. I had expected to be back, but the jeep got stuck in the mud, and I had to walk a while. . . . I am here in Bahia Solano, alone.

9

The Voyage of
Manteño II

I awakened on the twentieth, alone on the raft. The morning was warm and calm and light rain trickled down. I lay on my sleeping bag, looking up at the thatch, while sunlight reflected off of the emerald bay and lit the interior of my house with a soft, green glow. Off to my right I could hear children laughing and playing in the water. Scott's leaving did not trouble me. I thought of only one thing: I must leave this place.

I was now living alone on a bamboo houseboat, floating in an isolated tropical fjord. *Manteño II* lay fifty yards from shore, anchored in sixty feet of water. For the next week, while Martin was in Bogotá, I concentrated on preparing the raft for departure.

As I loaded the raft with gear, it sank. Thousands of pounds of food, water, and equipment had to go aboard; it was unavoidable. Every day something new weighed it down more: Extra lumber for repairs at sea, 300 pounds of excess rope (also for repairs), 250 pounds of canvas sails, 750 pounds of drinking water, 1,000 pounds of food, 200 pounds of metal tools, our 300-pound, self-contained radio station, and 700 pounds of human beings. The raft submerged five inches under the strain. The water level now came up to my ankles when I stood on the stern, right where it had been when we arrived in Colombia. The new logs had been even more wet than the originals. Two months of hell hadn't given us an inch, but I held out the hope that somehow pontoons could be mounted under *Manteño II* to give it the buoyancy it would need for the high sea. In the state it was in, waves would be surging over the deck the minute we left the safety of Bahia Solano.

I faced a second problem in early December of 1998: I needed to recruit at least two more people to sail with me. During the overhaul of the raft, back at Camp Hardcore, a Colombian man in his midtwenties had come by on several occasions to watch us work. I could tell immediately that he was from the outside. Whenever the subject of finding new people came up, Scott would always suggest this man. His name was Alejandro Martinez, and when I asked him to sail with me, he bristled with excitement. "There are a lot of people who think this sort of thing is insane," I said to him.

"No," he said. "To end your life having never done something like this— *that* is insanity."

Alejandro Martinez was of medium build, had a dark complexion, green eyes, and a mouth full of braces. I was to find out later that he was in excellent physical shape, but when I first met him, he seemed stooped. Everything about him seemed to droop down slightly, especially those green eyes. Later I redefined him from "stooped" to "relaxed." He was currently working as a full-time environmental scientist, and I asked him one day, "What are you doing here exactly?"

"I'm working with the garbage."

"Really?"

"Yeah. They have a big problem with waste management here. Their landfill is full. Every week the ship brings in more stuff—more packages—and they've run out of places to bury it."

"What should they do?"

"Well, in the first place, they could grind up their glass and mix it into the sand here."

"You can do that?"

"Sure. The glass is made of the same type of sand that's in the beaches here, so if you grind it fine enough, it fits right in."

I asked Alejandro to become the expedition's quartermaster, which had been Scott's old job. Scott had disliked being quartermaster, but he had carried on out of a sense of duty. Alejandro, on the other hand, attacked the job with zeal. He collected hundreds of packages, cans, and sacks of foodstuffs— and he attended to every detail: If it could be bought cheaper somewhere else and flown in by the bush pilots, he did it; if a nonperishable could be substituted for a perishable, he got it; if packages or cans or containers could be removed from the items to save space, he removed them.

In a few days Martin returned from Bogotá, and we agreed that we must escape Bahia Solano as soon as possible. We were both suffering from fatigue, perhaps more than we knew, and one evening Alejandro said to me, "The two of you look very, very tired."

"We've been in the field for a long time."

"It shows."

Fatigued or not, we worked frantically to get the raft ready. By now, my attitude had changed. I was no longer sure of anything, and I felt it mandatory to prepare to be lost and wandering on the open ocean for months. To prepare the ship, we cut and shaped ten new *guaras*; inventoried and organized our rope supply; sanded, cleaned, and greased the pulleys; then did the same to our fifteen carabiners; then to every radio and electrical part; and then to all of the tools. We inventoried, repaired, and organized the fishing gear; scrubbed and mounted the massive sails; and then brought on extra lumber and bamboo canes for repairs at sea. Martin inventoried, cleaned, and sanded all light sources, from headlamps to candles. We made extra candle lanterns out of bamboo cane; inventoried all pots, pans, and eating utensils; inventoried and bought all back-up equipment for the cooking stoves; and inventoried all of our medical gear, refilling all of the prescription medicines we could get. We brought on four thirty-gallon tanks of water. We did this by paddling fifty yards to the shore, walking up to the nearest waterfall, opening the tanks, and filling them in two minutes or less, and then wrestling them back to the dinghy and paddling back to the raft.

On December 21, I wrote in my diary:

> Alejandro is shaping up to be a good expeditioner. He is good-humored, intelligent, and well-read; a good storyteller; efficient in his work; and industrious always. He eats little, complains never, and sleeps comfortably in the hut.

But we still needed another person to sail with us. Alejandro knew of a guy who might be willing, and on December 21, he arrived in Bahia Solano. Alejandro's friend, Alberto, was a small, wiry man. The first night he was on the raft, he and Alejandro sat on the foredeck and laughed giddily with excitement. They had not seen The Expedition develop, so it must have seemed as though the ultimate adventure had simply fallen out of the sky upon them. Within a day or so Alberto began to obsess over small matters. When he laughed, it was forced. He was shaping up to be another Frederick—*that* I would never endure again. On the morning of the twenty-fourth, I told him he couldn't sail with us. He cried and pleaded. It was a terrible scene of heartbreak. I explained my education to him, said I was very sorry, and never looked back. Alejandro asked me, when I told him of my decision, "John, are you going to do that to me?"

"No. Absolutely not."

"Why did you fire him?"

"Because I've learned to trust my instincts. Perhaps I'm wrong. Perhaps he can be a better raft sailor than I am. But I know by now that I can tell who will do well out there, and who will not."

He looked at me for a moment, then said, "Alberto's had problems with people before."

"I'll bet. He's probably the greatest guy in the world *on land,* but believe me, if there's a flaw running down the center of a person's psychology, the raft's going to find that flaw and put pressure on it until it splits wide open."

"I believe that."

We continued working nonstop. Christmas passed without celebration, but on the twenty-nineth we received a gift: Cesar Alarcon, our fourth man. He was a friend of Alejandro's, and after Alberto left he came to Bahia Solano. Cesar was a small, stocky man with long curly hair. He had been living in the jungle, living a monklike existence, working with snakes and reptiles. He held no degrees or titles, but he was so well known in the field of herpetology that he frequently lectured at universities throughout Colombia. He was also an expert in cutting and shaping bamboo cane, and his most noticeable characteristic was that he possessed the mentality of a craftsman. He focused calmly on every task with a patient, critical eye. Clean and fastidious, Cesar seemed to do everything well. When he spoke, which was seldom, he did so in measured, intelligent sentences. In this way he reminded me of Cameron Smith, and by the second day of his arrival, I knew he'd be good at sea.

29 December 1998

I noticed (today) that our emergency anchor is gone.

A captain from one of the transports came aboard the raft that day. He told me that he had come over to show his son the raft. His son was unimpressed, and the captain seemed to be examining our gear closely. After they left I had to go into town to get some work done, and when I came back the anchor was gone. I was angry as hell and boarded the transport as it sat by the wharf, but the crew told me their captain had gone into town to take care of a few last-minute things.

We had lost our insurance policy. Our other, smaller anchor was enough to hold us in protected water, but exposed to the open sea, especially if there was bad weather, it would be a gamble. The money had run out again and I was once again faced with choosing one priority over another. Once again, I chose rope.

A breeze sprang up in the afternoon of the thirtieth, and we raised sail and navigated *Manteño II* to a new anchorage, one mile north of the pier. We knew that we'd leave within a few days; the raft was almost ready.

We had hired a craftsman in the village to build two wooden boxes for storage, which he now delivered. They were, to our eyes, beautiful: Two squat boxes made from heavy plywood—a perfect cargo hold for a balsa raft. Alejandro and Cesar packed them to the hilt with the remaining food, spices, and oils. We also built, inside the hut, a library. We installed a singular board, suspended from the roof by two lines, and tied it to the wall. It held approximately twenty-five books. During *Kon-Tiki,* a Swedish scientist named Bengt Danielson had read seventy-two books, many of them of impressive length. Drifting across the open ocean affords such luxuries, but coastal cruising most certainly does not. So far, I had never found enough time to read so much as a paragraph, while sailing.

On the twenty-ninth, Martin and I went to Camp Hardcore to recover the last of the balsa logs, which we hoped to use as pontoons under *Manteño II.* Night closed in and visibility disappeared. By yellow lantern light, we tied the four logs together with some of the rotted rope left behind from the rebuilt raft, and when the tide backed up the river and the murky water began swirling around our legs, we launched our miniature raft from the bank and began paddling toward the bay. *Manteño II* was now a mile and half north of the river, anchored near the mouth of the fjord. We paddled down the river for a while and then realized that the tide was still flooding in and we couldn't make any headway. In the darkness, we tied off to the slimy roots of a tree on the bank of the river, and then collapsed. The ordeal of Camp Hardcore had exhausted us. We had endured over 150 inches of rain. We had worked through a world of clattering drops, a world of drips and leaks, of mold, of damp, dank mildew, a world where there was only water. We could push ourselves no more.

And still it rained. Thousands of drops jumped on the muddy water around us. Martin and I lay there in the dark on our miniature raft, sprawled out in despair and exhaustion. The distant village was silent. The rain clattered on the flat leaves of the jungle and we shivered uncontrollably. Our skin crawled with goose bumps and we felt the despondency that comes when there is no way to get warm. We lay there alone in the dark with cold water dripping off us, one last time in the mud pit of a no-name river, one last time in the ceaseless rain of that hellish place—one last time in Camp Hardcore. After an hour of rest we regained our motivation and labored out to the raft. We'd never go back.

In the morning, we prepared the raft. With only four men to handle all the heavy labor, we teamed up on every task. We pushed, pulled, strained, groaned, and grunted in the throes of the eternal, ". . . One—two—three—HEAVE!" The three-count was our life. Alejandro and Cesar were naturals, and within a few days it became second nature to work as a team. We no longer planned a move; we all knew the complicated maneuvers in advance. If I announced that we needed to lift a yardarm, the other three would automatically gather around it with their legs spread and their knees bent. We'd get a shoulder under it, then: "One, two, three, UP!"

If you'd have stood on the nearby shore and seen us that day you would have naturally assumed that there was only one worksite on the raft: the deck. But there were two. For many weeks to come we would work *under* the raft almost as much as above it. The four of us donned masks and snorkels that afternoon and submerged into our second, secluded worksite below the massive logs of *Manteño II*. Here, we worked in silence—there was lots of action, lots of flapping and flailing, but no sound at all. I can only describe it as though looking at an aquarium, inhabited not by fish but by men in masks and black flippers, struggling in semislow motion, their limbs waving and flailing silently against the infinite blue.

Our first job was to tie the lower tips of the *guaras* in such a way that they did not move. During the voyage to Colombia the *guaras* had bunched together like a collapsing paper fan. Tying them so that they wouldn't mesh together anymore was critical: Only in this way would we be able to benefit from the resistance of all twenty-four centerboards.

We worked for hours, one breath at a time, tying ropes, looking at each other through the empty blue water, wading and kicking and flailing, surfacing and clearing our lungs, then submerging again to wrestle with the hanging boards, then shooting out from under the raft to burst through the surface— back to a place where there was air and sound. We'd gasp and pant, spitting saltwater and saying things like, "Can you get that one?" and "You almost had it—I'll hold the *guara* still and you thread the line!" and then we'd dive under again, pulling lines and hand-signaling each other, silently struggling in our private worksite under the raft. After three hours of work we had arranged the *guaras* in a line, and had tied their tips into a fixed position, so that they hung down like the fingers of an open hand. Now, for the first time, I'd be sailing a balsa raft with an effective keel.

On January 1, 1999, we awoke and agreed that we must leave that day. Time was running out for *Manteño II*. We needed to complete only one more task before we could leave the shelter of the fjord: install the pontoons. We tied two manila lines to each small balsa log and then put them over the side; then we forced them under the raft, where they were tied into place. Slowly, the raft rose; the pontoons were working.

At 2:00 in the afternoon, the four of us grouped together on the foredeck and stood for a moment, looking at each other. We wore shorts, T-shirts, and tennis shoes, and our hair hung down in our faces, still soaked from working under the raft. Martin and I were now lean and deeply tanned. The Colombians would soon be the same. The town of Bahia Solano was more than a mile away now and we were alone at our green, tropical anchorage. Through the mouth of the fjord we could see the deep blue sea, waiting for us outside. The conditions were perfect for getting underway, all we had to do was raise sail. "All right," I said, "let's go," and then took a moment to shake hands with each man. We then went forward and sat down on the bare balsa logs at the front of the raft, and began straining to raise the anchor. When it broke free from the floor of the bay, I quickly stood up and pushed the mainsail over to hook the wind. It inflated perfectly and *Manteño II* turned its nose slowly toward the sea. Within thirty seconds of raising anchor, the raft was cruising with the wind at her back, making about one knot: A long primitive boat with a bamboo hut on its back now headed down the center of the green fjord, alone and cruising for the open sea. Before the raft stood a massive triangular sail, inflated and pulling steadily. It had been four years since I left North America for my first expedition. The *Manteño* Expedition had now been in the field for more than five months.

I told Martin that he could pilot the raft. He seemed to need to impress the Colombians, and this was a good opportunity. He was jumpy but seemed to handle the raft well.

Clouds began to gather in front of us as we approached the open sea. They darkened, changing from harmless white to angry gray. That worried me. If we sailed into winds from the west we'd have a hard time staying off the rocks of the Darien. If we crashed up there, where it was practically uninhabited, it might be a week before we found our way back to any civilization.

The raft emerged from Bahia Solano at 5:30 in the afternoon, and the minute we cleared the mouth of the fjord, the sea piled on top of us. A storm, or multiple storms, had spit out clusters of waves that had charged into the semicircle of the Gulf of Panama and were now ricocheting in ten different directions. Confused seas hit us on all sides. Rain poured down in large, cold drops. The world turned dark gray, and then as the afternoon faded and the unseen sun set, the world turned black. All around us the sea was violent. Seawater splashed on deck, then flooded over in heavy masses. Waves would come out of the darkness and plow into our port beam, which would cause the raft to roll down into swells coming over the starboard bow. The entire fore-deck would disappear under the ocean for five agonizing seconds at a time, then we'd recover at the same instant that a following sea would crash into our stern. Disorganized waves and swells were the raft's worst enemy. *Manteño II* had no rhythm. Under my feet I could feel, very clearly, the raft trembling.

Shortly after the darkness closed in on us, *Manteño II* plunged forward into a particularly meaty wave, right as it was barreling down, and the manila strands that held the deck to the raft parted like a giant zipper ripping open. The air-filled canes were now swinging up and down like a giant trap door. Whenever the bow plunged into the water, the entire deck flapped open, riding on top of the waves, threatening to separate from the raft. Then the masts went. The nine-hundred-pound poles flew into a frenzy, jerking back and forth, yanking and snapping their stays. The forward mast was swinging thirty degrees over to one side and then careening sixty degrees back to the other, its stays stretching like rubber bands, tightening, hanging limp, then snapping tight again. Then the hut began to disintegrate. The mizzenmast, jutting up through the hole in the roof, bullied the bamboo house around like a little toy. The enormous pole was falling forward and jumping back and then rolling to one side, all within three second's time. It was night and we were in trouble. Wall canes were breaking loose. Pieces of bamboo were falling overboard and disappearing into the darkness. We were losing *guaras* and cooking equipment, too. One object would escape its binding, which would loosen an entire line, which in turn would set other objects free. The raft was like a large, complex machine—a printing press or a diesel engine—that had lost an important part and was now shaking itself to death.

To save the raft and ourselves we divided into two teams, English-speaking and Spanish-speaking, and I then asked Alejandro and Cesar to try to tie the deck down. At this, they steadied themselves on the canes, and then walked forward into the darkness. Waves broke over the entire deck now, flooding everything. Alejandro sat at the edge of the deck, trying to thread a rope through the tiny slits in the parallel bamboo poles while Cesar sat beside him, trying to pull the rope up. It must have seemed like an impossibility. A wave, a wall of water coming out of the darkness, would crest and slam into their faces and shoot them fifteen feet across the deck, their bodies sliding as though weightless, the bamboo canes slicing their arms and backs while the sea poured salt into their wounds. Sometimes they were hit so hard that they slid and crashed into the mast or the anchor. They'd struggle back to their feet, and then clomp back to the edge. After an hour of punishment, Alejandro came to me and asked, "Is—is this normal?"

I feared a panic, so I lied, "Yup."

"Oh," he said. He shifted his weight from one leg to another, then back. "OK," he said, then teetered forward, making his way through the oncoming waves. Shortly afterward, a broken melody began to muffle through the storm. It sounded vaguely like singing. Waves and swells crashed and sloshed all around the tormented raft and intermittently, against the watery hell, Martin and I could hear a strange song coming from out there in the darkness. We could make out two straining voices, croaking in the night, sounding out poorly pronounced English words: The Colombians, cold, scared, struggling in the dark, were singing "Let It Be."

Meanwhile, Martin and I worked fast. We tied the hut down with stays, working and fumbling in the driving rain. Darkness blinded us and water poured into our faces. Masses of seawater surged up to our thighs and then disappeared in loud, hissing noises. We were exhausted from months of being in the field. Our minds and muscles burned from overwork. Fatigue gave way to seasickness. Our heads spun and our faces hung from nausea. We tied down the hut in every way possible. Within an hour it looked like Gulliver. Then we tightened down the mast stays by bending the lines, which we had learned from previous rafts, and then gathered up any loose articles we could find on the deck and retied them. It was hellish work in the rain and the cold, compounded by the seasickness. I was dizzy and on the verge of vomiting. As soon as there was a break in the action, I asked Martin to take over the raft while I lay down.

Inside the hut, I lay on my soggy old sleeping bag. The confused seas thundered against the walls. The sounds were awful—real explosions—followed by bamboo rubbing hard against manila, making taut, creaking noises. Martin's and the Colombian's voices muffled into the little hut, surrounding my ears with nervousness and fear. I lay for twenty minuets or so; that was all I could take, but it seemed to help me. Miraculously, when I got up, my head had cleared.

Just as I was going out on deck, Martin and I met at the doorway of the hut. I was going out, and he was coming in. Martin's eyes bugged out and he choked back a hard swallow, then said, "I—think—we might—uh—lose the raft."

"If we completely disintegrate, I think we'll be alright. We've got the life raft, the dinghy, rations, radio, we can handle it—"

"—I'm not worried about us; I don't think the raft can handle the pounding."

I thought for a second he would cry, but then he drew himself up with a deep breath.

"OK," I said. "Let me look at it." I wanted to say, "No way," but the raft looked too sick at that moment to give a guarantee. I offered Martin rest, but he declined. I couldn't blame him—the sounds inside the hut were awful.

Shortly afterward, out on the foredeck, the mainsail deflated, and when it did we lost power and floundered. I'd have to reinflate it, so I now crept forward on the spring-loaded canes and stepped down onto the balsa logs. Under me, the raft rolled and pitched like a wild animal caught in a trap, pushing, pulling, wallowing, thrashing. On my hands and knees, I got down and began crawling, working my way out on the Pope. I was more in the ocean than aboard the raft. Cool saltwater splashed up and blinded me. I tasted brackish salt in my mouth and snorted salt out of my nose. Where the Pope jutted out like a diving board I threw my legs around it and locked my ankles together underneath. Cupping my palms around the fat log, I lifted my body out toward the tip. Inch by inch, I shinnied out. The ocean surrounded me, splashing, sloshing, flooding. I held a line, which ran back to the sail, threaded between the fingers of my right hand. At the very tip of the Pope, a small loop of rope stood up from the wood. We had tied it there to act as a cleat. In the darkness, I threaded the line in my hand through the loop and pulled. The sail swung open to the wind. Turning around and calling to the others over the splashing and sloshing, I tried to calmly shout out instructions in Spanish and English to frightened men who had no idea it was going to be this wild. For various technical reasons, the mainsail would not stay inflated. We'd be able to correct this problem later, but for now, I rode on the center log, reinflating it. Waves hit me from every direction. The bow pitched down and bounced up. Masses of cool seawater poured off of my body and I felt tiny stings on my legs from jellyfish. Clinging to the log with my ankles, my torso twisted and swung, and I fought to stay on top under the surges and smacks of the oncoming waves.

We fought on through the black night. We fought the sail, fought the rigging, tried to shout to each other over the noise, and then went through periods of waiting back at the doorway of the hut, where the first thing you noticed was how much you wanted to lie down. We of course could not; we had to maintain headway. At dawn, as the sky slowly turned from black to gray, the sea calmed a little, but not enough for us to relax. The calming trend continued throughout the day, and by the afternoon we were barely moving forward. We had been through a very bad night, and we needed to rest. The raft, and especially the hut, appeared ramshackle. Few right angles remained. What had been straight was now askew. Lines had ruptured in the night and the walls and doorway of the hut now leaned in sickening angles. We appeared ramshackle too, our faces tired and hanging and our clothes in disarray. Our bodies lay strewn about *Manteño II* as though part of the wreckage.

That first twenty-four hours did much to establish trust between us. We saw what kind of people they were and they saw what kind we were. That is invaluable information for people who are going to be fighting the ocean for months. When the Colombians started singing, I said to Martin, quietly: "I'm starting to grow very fond of those guys."

"Me, too."

Our improvements in *guara* configuration had saved us during the storm. *Manteño II* had a functioning keel—sufficient resistance to counteract the force of the sail—and that singular improvement had prevented us from being driven onto the rocks of Darien. Throughout the third and fourth of January, we moved gradually north, still in sight of land. At about 11:00 am on the fifth, we spotted a warship off our starboard bow. It was a large, gray vessel with a multitude of antennas and radar dishes—a modern cutter with fast, angular lines, made for slicing through local waters at high speed—made for tracking down the quick little vessels of modern-day pirates. I called them on the radio, and they answered me in English, identifying themselves as "U.S. Navy Warship," but refusing to give the name of their vessel. I asked them if they had picked up our radar reflector on their screens, to which they replied, "No." They were two nautical miles away from us, and when I gave them my position their bow shot out of the water. It was an amazing overreaction. The cutter came hard about and closed on us at high speed. I talked to their radio operator about The Expedition, explaining that we were "an experimental ship, involved in archeological and historical research." I then told him that they would be welcome to come for a tour of our boat, even though she was in bad shape at the moment. The operator replied by saying, "We're deciding right now whether or not you will be boarded and searched."

Boarded and searched?

The operator came back on the frequency and told me to have my crew stand on the deck, to not go back into the hut from this point on, and to not make any sudden movements. The boarding unit would be searching the vessel within a few minutes.

They sped over on an inflatable boat. There were six sailors, dressed in black, wearing full battle gear, including body armor, Plexiglas face shields, and machine guns. Staying fifty feet out, they circled the raft slowly, studying the situation sternly, and then came alongside. When I offered to help one of them aboard, a burly, red-haired coast guardsman, he scowled at me angrily.

They questioned us at length, collected passports, and rifled through our belongings. Part of their team stood outside, scowling at the raft and insulting Alejandro and Cesar—who were guilty of nothing—while two sailors, a Panamanian and a U.S. coast guardsman from Puerto Rico, acting as translator, stayed in the hut with me. "Do you have any weapons?" they asked.

"We have an old, rusted-out shotgun."

"Where did you get it?" they asked.

"A peasant in Ecuador sold it to us."

"You don't have any sort of papers on it?"

"Papers? Down here? I don't think they have a registration process in Ecuador."

"We want to see it," the Panamanian said.

Martin had bought a hand-made shotgun in Ecuador, and now we showed them the pathetic thing. They talked among themselves, and then the Panamanian said, "I want to confiscate it."

The coast guardsman started to translate, "He's going to—"

"—I understood him. You're kidding, right?"

"Uh, no," the Puerto Rican said. He was starting to become embarrassed by the ridiculousness of the situation.

"You realize," I asked, "that this is an unfireable weapon, right? It can't even be repaired. You couldn't even get money for it from an antique dealer."

He called his ship, using our radio, and the ship's radio operator came back on frequency in a few minutes: "Advise the captain of the ship that this action is taken by the Panamanian government. We are acting only as assistance to the Panamanian navy. We are advising against this action, but have no jurisdiction."

We looked at each other blankly. I didn't object to any part of it except the general overreaction. They confiscated the old, rusty shotgun and left. I was deeply dismayed and embarrassed. The entire episode, and indeed the policy, seemed to me a fantastically unwise use of my country's military prowess.

The wind increased on the afternoon of the fifth. We needed to travel just sixty nautical miles to the west to escape our imprisonment in the Gulf of Panama. If the wind held for just one day, we'd make it out of the Gulf and into the Pacific. By dusk the wind was blowing fifteen to twenty miles per hour, and during this time it became apparent that the raft had lost its balance. The mizzen sail was the main problem; it prevented us from sailing close to the wind. The original

Manteño-Huancavilca had achieved equilibrium when both sails were raised. Now, aboard *Manteño II,* when the mizzen sail was raised, the raft rounded up. Instead of finding a balance of power, the raft turned all the way into the wind, at which time the sails would deflate and the raft would lose all power.

Lowering the mizzen sail, we ran under the mainsail alone, which was pulling strongly. The raft drove westward and by nightfall I knew it was now or never: We had to cross the Gulf of Panama. I told the others to sleep well and I'd stay up to steer the raft. By midnight the wind had stirred up the sea so much that it was breaking hard over the foredeck. From out in the dark ocean I could see the shining edges of black waves coming in and flooding over the bamboo canes. Before me, the canvas triangle bulged outward, straining the rigging to its limits. *Manteño II* was plowing forward into the waves and shortly after midnight, at the forward edge of the bamboo canes, I saw the deck break loose again. Every cane broke its binding and the whole forward deck seemed as though it might separate from the hull. Twenty-five bamboo canes tied together in a row—our floor—were now swinging up and down each time a wave came in. I thought that the raft might be disintegrating. The crashing waves and the banging canes combined to wake up the men, who came out on deck, groggy and awkward, and stood by the hut.

Then the mainsail deflated again, and I worked my way out to the bare balsa logs and began inching myself out on the Pope: I would have to work my way out to the farthest point forward to reset the mainsail. Tired and cold, I rode on top of the log and could see nothing around me. Masses of seawater flooded over my body. The raft was wallowing behind me like an elephant, causing my log to rotate. *Manteño II* rolled and writhed and I held onto its nose. For a moment it would be easy, like riding a hobbyhorse—a lazy, dipping motion, up and down and up and down—and then it would rotate wildly, flinging me in a wide circle, my arms flailing in the dark. I held on for a while with my ankles but then the raft pitched down hard. A wave hit my left shoulder and my hands swung in the air as I tried to keep my balance. I knew I was going over and then I was underwater, upside down. The ocean forced mouthfuls of saltwater into my mouth and nose. I flailed and kicked my legs, trying to find the surface. It was dark and I saw only fragments in front of my half-open eyes. I knew the raft was above me somewhere, then my face broke the surface and I was surrounded by a loud, chaotic ocean. It was black all around me; the ocean was like a vast pool of ink. The raft surged forward and hit me in the left eyebrow and I thought for a second I'd be pushed under the hull and ripped by the barnacles. I was at eye level with the logs and they were splashing forward wildly, and then I was holding onto them and plowing through the water. Reaching up and grabbing the first crossbeam, I slowly and laboriously pulled myself aboard. For a moment, I just lay there on the bare balsa logs, panting, my eyes closed. I just wanted to rest—I just wanted to lie in the warm saltwater and rest for a moment. How could that hurt?

But I could hear Alejandro and Cesar calling to me. They were upset over my safety. In one second I knew that if I lay there it would spook them. They might think us finished, or at least losing the fight. Struggling up, I crawled back to the Pope on my hands and knees, splashing through the seawater that was flooding over the logs, and then inched back out to reset the sail. Martin was now behind me and to the right, trimming the mainsail. Between us, we finally reset it.

When I made it back to the foredeck, all three said they thought it best to drop the sail and just drift. They weren't saying this because they didn't care about making way, but because they were now genuinely concerned for my safety. I explained that we might not get a steady wind for another week, and that we had to sail that night, regardless of the conditions. Alejandro and Cesar tied down the deck as a temporary solution, then went to bed, as did Martin.

The wind was now pulling on the rigging so hard that I thought it might tear it all down. Perhaps the sea and the fatigue were causing my mind to play tricks on me, but I became increasingly worried that the wind would tear the mast out. I could have reefed the mainsail—could have pulled in some canvas to reduce the strain, but I didn't want to. We had to risk running the raft hard. We had to gain every mile possible. I had no idea how much the rigging could take, but whatever the maximum was, that was what we needed. After waiting for more than two months, I felt the raft could cross the Gulf on this night. If we didn't make it tonight, I felt we might not get another chance for days or weeks. We didn't have that kind of time.

Manteño II pushed relentlessly west, a crippled ship, barely able to make headway. It was the night of January 5, 1999—the longest night I have ever spent on a balsa raft. Alone on the foredeck, I stood in the dark and cold with my left arm wrapped around the mast. I wore only my underwear because I knew I would have to go into the water again. My clammy skin prickled as I shivered. I held a machete in my right hand and I kept reassuring myself that at the first sign of disaster I'd chop the halyard and release all the tension on the rigging. Standing out there in the rain and waves, the minutes crept by and I had time to think: *How did I get here? I am standing alone on the wind-swept deck of a disintegrating ship. I can't remember my former life. I can't even remember who I was before all of this—before I became lost in this place. I hate the darkness. How much more will these men take? What right do I have to put another man through this? How much is too much?*

. . .

At dawn, we looked out on a wild ocean. The surface of the water was the same as that which occurs in a small container, like a soda bottle or a pail of water, when it is shaken violently. The previous night's wind had stirred up the contents of the four-hundred-mile-wide Gulf of Panama and confused waves now collided with each other all around us, forming pointed pyramids of water that shot geysers into the air. The entire seascape was filled with triangles and smears of stark white foam, contrasting against the rich blue ocean.

The raft needed extensive repairs. *Manteño II* sounded dreadful. Hundreds of creaking noises all combined to make the perfect sound-effect combination of something wooden and rickety, like a radio drama from the 1930s about a tall ship. Cesar and Alejandro immediately went to work on the deck. It was now an even bigger job than before, but at least they could now work in daylight. The forward mast needed attention too. Someone would have to ascend the four-story wooden pole and examine the connections of the stays for fatigue. During the night I had decided that we would have to reinforce the rigging by adding an extra stay, and whoever went aloft to check for fatigue would now have to attach this new stay as well, which would not be pleasant.

To attach the new stay, one man would have to put on a climbing harness, which would be attached to the halyard, and the other three would have to haul him up, as though hauling up a sail. Whoever it was would carry the new stay with him: A forty-foot line of wet manila rope. As he'd go up, more and more of the rope would hang down. It would weigh seventy pounds once fully extended. Holding on and keeping one's nerve would get more and more difficult as he approached the peak of the mast. As soon as I had explained the process, Martin said he could do it. I was relieved; he was an experienced climber. He would be suspended, four stories up, holding a seventy-pound weight in one hand and the halyard in the other, while the mast jerked him around in a twenty-foot range of motion, like a giant wooden arm shaking a rag. I had seen Cameron do this on a similar operation involving the mizzenmast. He hitched up his climbing harness and went up four stories. When he reached the top, the mast commenced to thrash him about. The raft rolled and rocked and Cameron's body flapped through the air like a human flag waving in a strong breeze. Each time he regained control, the mast would snap ten feet over and he would momentarily fly behind it, attached only by his harness. It was highly likely that Martin would face the same scenario.

I was exhausted. My decision to stay up all night had been completely spontaneous. The others were anxious for me to lie down, and I didn't argue. Martin said that he would handle the mast with just the help of Alejandro and Cesar, but when I awakened an hour later, he said, frankly, "I can't do it. I got scared."

He said this to me in a tone of one climber to another, a matter-of-fact tone, simply conveying the fact that he wasn't up to that particular task. By that time in the expedition we had nothing more to prove to each other.

"No problem," I said, "just help me."

Martin had shown sufficient nerve more than once, and besides, the sea had wrenched a lot of energy out of all of us over the past three days.

The waves had calmed down considerably since I had asked Martin to do the job, and so I went straight up, threw the loop of the new stay over the mast, tightened it, and came straight back down. Miraculously, the entire job took no more than ten minutes.

With the mast reinforced, we went to work stabilizing other critical areas. Underneath the deck we installed a giant tourniquet around the nine base logs. Then we put in tourniquets on the hut stays, and tourniquets on the ropes holding the gear. To install a tourniquet, around the end of the raft for example, we'd loosely tie a rope around the nine balsa logs, and then kink the line just enough to form a small loop. We'd then thread a sturdy pole into the loop, and then two men, straining every fiber in their arms, would begin to crank it down. The tourniquet pole would develop so much resistant energy that if it slipped out of your hand for one second the whole thing would explode.

The turning of the pole starts. One man waits, holding two small lines, ready to seize the tourniquet the instant the crankers are ready. The line twists and kinks around the pole. The rope creaks—"*tick tick tick tick tick.*" Pressure builds. The hands of the crankers redden. The little pole comes alive and wants to spring out. It feels like we are holding down a wild animal: "OK! OK!"

"Now?"

"No! I"—grunting, breathing—"I can go another turn!" Grimacing. Gasping. Squeezing.

"Now?—"

"—Go! Hurry—I can't hold it—"

"I got it! I got it—"

"—Thank God!" Tremendous relief! You shake the pain out of your hands. For a moment they're paralyzed, molded into the form of the rope.

We labored this way for days, sometimes installing or resetting ten tourniquets in a day. This was now our occupation, our day's work—this and other types of repairs.

. . .

At daybreak on the seventh, we sighted land. Off our starboard bow lay the Azuero Peninsula, the grave site of the *Illa-Tiki*. I had now approached Panama from both the west and the east. In both cases I passed close to the Azuero Peninsula, and this did much to convince me that an intensive search for the remains of balsa ships should be made on the southern tip of the Azuero. This area, for me, was a probable transit point on the trading route of the Manteño. In 1512, the conquistador Balboa had had an interesting conversation with a native chief here: When the subject turned to gold, and the chief became disgusted with the Spaniard's naked lust for it, the chief pointed south—toward Ecuador, saying that down there lived a wealthy trading people, who traveled great distances.

Standing on the canes of the foredeck, I watched the raft cruise toward the Azuero Peninsula, jutting out like a panhandle into the ocean. Tropical sunshine warmed me and I felt that we had finally escaped our two-month's imprisonment.

We were now passing through the intersection of the largest ocean currents in the world. It was a traffic jam of waves. Great herds of them came over the horizon from all directions and collided with each other. At times a rolling swell would gently rock the raft back and forth, and then, from miles away, we'd see an angry mob of white caps running toward us. They'd maintain a close formation, perfectly defined against the placid background, and come splashing up noisily, pass under the raft, and then collide with other mobs of waves coming from other directions. For five minutes the raft would jump and pitch violently amid the traffic jam. Then they'd leave, still together in groups, noisily headed off to the horizon.

By the afternoon of the seventh, we had passed out of the area of the colliding waves, and the wind was beginning to die. By nightfall the raft was sitting in calm waters, twenty miles from land, and drifting in the inbound lane of the Panama Canal. Ships passed close by, which was a serious problem because our mast light continued to be unreliable. It was one of the most impractical devices I have ever purchased, and we frequently had to run flashlights and lanterns to ensure we wouldn't be run over. I think many ships thought we were a buoy or a derelict. That night, as freighters and tankers passed close by, I wrote in my diary:

> The lights of the ship are first spotted when the ship is miles away, formless, but moving steadily. At the last moment the supertanker, the largest moving object on earth, surges out of the black. Suddenly it has form. Without exception this moment always produces a chilling and terrifying

effect. How can something so colossal . . . move so fast through the waves? All other vessels struggle and wallow and plod through the waves. The supertanker ignores the waves and ocean completely. The crests of the whitecaps pound and slam against the black hull without any effect whatsoever, not even the slightest roll. And they hum. The throbbing diesel noise is so powerful that it can be heard from five to six miles away. As the ship passes, it does so very fast. No slow majesty; this is wide-open speed. The course of the ship, its engines, the stiffness of its rock-iron hull are all straight, hard, totally unbending in the face of the Pacific.

On the eighth, we passed close by Coiba Island, the penal colony that *Illa-Tiki* had almost landed on four years earlier. But the danger was now gone. The Panamanian government, in response to the horrific incidents that I cited earlier in my story, had evacuated most of the prisoners from the island.

We were now sailing in the Gulf of Chiriqui, which is populated by scores of uninhabited islands. We drifted aimlessly around Isla Jicaron, Isla Jicarita, Isla Montuosa, and many others. We could see them all around us like big green domes above the surface—some close by, and some on the horizon—but we were unable to land on any of them because there was no wind. The raft, its sails hanging limp, lay just sixty nautical miles from the Panamanian shore, and at times no more than five miles from the sands of these islands. But we could do nothing to reach them. Our wooden barge just floated on the calm water, and we just stood on the canes and looked out on islands that we longed to reach. A stillness had settled on the sea.

For six days we drifted away from the mainland, and then back toward it. We were going in and out of an oceanic gyre, which existed west of Panama and Costa Rica. Technically speaking, a gyre is any body of water that rotates around a vortex. This particular gyre was six hundred miles wide and sat under an exceedingly high-pressure air mass, which enforced total calm upon the sea. During our expeditions, this place was always known among us as "*The* Gyre."

Martin was starting to fade. He wanted "to play," and I had to struggle to get him to do his work. It was the beginning of a long, downward spiral. More and more, he ignored his responsibilities; and while we worked, he played. Whenever a fish was within range of the spear gun, he'd go berserk, running up and down the beams of the raft, firing wildly into the water. The Colombians didn't seem to mind or if they minded they weren't willing to show it. They were incredibly sensitive men; they sensed right away that Martin was showing the effects of being in the field longer than he could stand. He fished all day, every day, and caught more than we needed. Chasing fish suddenly became an obsession with him, and several times I had to tell him to stop. One afternoon I told him that we had to try to maintain some level of excellence on the raft, there was simply too much work for three people. He responded somewhat, but it was clear that a steady decline had set in.

By the thirteenth, I noticed that the raft was more vocal than it had ever been on any of the previous voyages. The ropes were rotting. Either they had been rubbing back and forth under enormous strain, or, exposed to the freshwater onslaught in Colombia for over sixty days, they had started a rapid disintegration.

On the fourteenth, we sighted land once again. Off our port bow lay a five-hundred-foot hill, jutting up from the surface of the ocean, glimmering in front of us like a giant silver point, just twenty miles away. It was definitely Montuosa Island, which was listed in *Sailing Directions* as being "heavily wooded." I assumed it would be uninhabited, too, and those two descriptions led me to speculate that there may be fallen, dry balsa timbers there. "Listen guys," I said, "we really want to go to Montuosa Island. We can get better pontoons than we've got, and we can regroup."

If we made it to the island we'd have something to hold on to. We could drop anchor, wait until the winds were favorable, then make small hops, from one coastal island to another, and not risk going back out into The Gyre.

We sailed for the island in light winds, but *Manteño II* lacked performance. The raft was half sunken, overloaded, and the pontoons increased the hull's drag. And our rig had become unbalanced—the raft could no longer sail with both sails up. We could only maintain a speed of half a knot. After a few hours I realized that we were in a current that was drifting out to sea at half a knot as well. We were just holding our own. If the wind slackened, we'd go out to sea again.

We maintained course all night, but at dawn, when we awoke, Montuosa Island was gone.

10

Life, Death, and Beauty, In The Gyre

16 January 1999
Hopeless and helpless in The Gyre. The idea of another go around (is grim).

I awoke on the morning of the nineteenth to find that the siphon from the main water tank had been left running, and that we had lost most of our freshwater into the sea. In the past we had always had enough water in reserve, and getting more was simply a matter of removing the lids from the storage barrels during a rain shower. But now our reserves were gone. We had only thirty-five gallons left aboard the raft, enough to last for about five days at the current rate of usage. We quickly held a meeting to discuss the situation.

First, we'd have to cut consumption down to five gallons of water per day. If we got down to fifteen gallons left onboard I'd have to call an evacuation, regardless of any other conditions. A decision to evacuate would need a three-day lead-time to ensure total success. At fifteen gallons, I would have to declare an emergency, we would have to commit to an evacuation, and we would have to leave *Manteño II* behind in The Gyre.

I was disgusted with the situation. I couldn't stand the idea of coming this far and being stopped by something as ridiculous as spilled water. But Alejandro was reassuring. "No, John. Don't worry. We'll start a freshwater warehouse!" Beginning with that statement, Alejandro and Cesar established themselves in my diary as "The Inventors."

They began by scrounging around the raft for a few hours, looking for materials. Once they had what they needed, they sat down and drew pictures, discussed plans, talked, laughed, and sang. Alejandro started construction by spreading a sheet of clear plastic on one side of the hut's roof, to create a water-catching plane. Then Cesar took a small bamboo cane from storage, split it down the center, and smoothed out the insides of the two halves. These would be the gutters, which he attached to the eave of the hut. Next, they cut the spout off of a two-liter soda bottle that they had found floating in the ocean a couple of weeks back, and mounted it upside down at the end of the gutter, so that it acted as a funnel. Then they came up with a section of garden hose (from who knows where) and attached it to the funnel, so that they could pipe the rainwater directly into a water tank.

We spent two days in dry air, worrying whether or not we would have enough water to finish the voyage. When rain finally came, it was just a minor shower, hardly enough to make a difference. As the drops began to fall, I asked the Inventors if there was something I could do to help them catch water. "No, *Capitan!*" Alejandro said, exposing his braces in a huge grin, *"Es automatico!"* ("It's automatic!") He and Cesar stood by with their arms folded, talking about women and politics, while the raindrops turned into trickles that ran down the slope and turned into a little brook, which grew to a steady stream of clean water. In just ninety minutes, Cesar and Alejandro manufactured thirty-five gallons of fresh drinking water. On several occasions after that we filled every water tank on the raft, a capacity of 120 gallons. You might be tempted to think that this water system was no great feat, but you must keep in mind that they built it in the middle of the Pacific Ocean, out of debris and scrap. Each part was cut and shaped and installed with patience and precision. Moreover, nothing was ever haphazard or poorly planned—their inventions *worked*.

There was no end to the devices they made from odds and ends. They could design and build anything, all I had to do was ask for it. They even made things that I wouldn't have asked for. They sang and laughed the whole time. To me, catching water was a serious proposition, one that could mean life or death, but the Colombians just grinned from ear to ear. "Noooooo, John," they'd say to me, shaking their fingers and smiling, *"Por un culo grande—un calcon mas grande!"* ("The only solution for a big butt—is bigger underwear!")

Soon we had *running* water. The Inventors took the foot pump out of the inflatable dinghy and used it to generate pressure for a water tap. From our spare-parts inventory, they scrounged up two lengths of plastic tubing, which worked as the "pipes." Air was pumped into a water tank and drinking water came out—all you had to do was put your cup under the spout. It eliminated the unsanitary ladling of water, and the wasteful siphoning. Again, it sounds simple, but how remarkable it was to wake up in the morning, walk out onto a bamboo platform suspended in the middle of a vast gyre, step on the pump twice, and have cool drinking water emerge as though running from a faucet.

Then the hopelessly impractical mast light malfunctioned, so Cesar created a new one out of thin air. He came up with a plastic light housing that was once probably a juice bottle, and painted it with a dye made from cooking oil, flour, and Kool-Aid: Red on one side for port, green on the other for starboard. Shortly after that I mentioned that I missed chocolate brownies, so Cesar—using odds and ends from the storage boxes—produced brownies a few hours later. One night I said I missed having a cocktail in the evening, so the Inventors produced a crude cocktail from rubbing alcohol, cherry Kool-Aid, and something else that they refused to divulge. I said that I liked to play dominoes—and they simply appeared a few days later. Cesar sanded down twenty-eight pieces of bamboo, each one a duplicate of all the others, painted dots on them, and we played dominoes that night by the light of Alejandro's baking-powder-can oil lamps.

Then one day I came out on deck and found that the Inventors had created *scuba*. They unhooked the foot pump from the water tank, fitted the end of the hose to Alejandro's snorkel, and sent air ten feet under the surface of the water. Because of pressure differences, a person cannot pull air through a snorkel much further than a few feet, so Cesar sat on the deck and pumped air down to Alejandro, who swam under the raft. To send air down the hose required just the right amount of pressure. Alejandro submerged, and Cesar, who sat on a balsa stump, counted very carefully, *"Uno, dos, tres, quatro, cinco, seis, siete,"* then stepped down gingerly on the pump, trying not to blow Alejandro's lungs out. Standing on the bamboo canes with my hands in my pockets, I said to Cesar: "I—uh—I'm not sure it's working."

"Relax. When he runs out of air he'll probably come up."

Looking down into the water, I wondered what could be going on. Cesar, folding his arms and dead-panning hilariously, asked, "Well, is he still alive?"

"It appears so."

"Oh well," he said, "too bad."

The Colombians were shaping up to be fine swearers too. I went so far as to call them, in my diary, "gifted." Perhaps it was all in the timing: Cesar and Alejandro blurted out expletives *before the fact*. Somehow they had figured out on an intuitive level just exactly when they were going to fall down on the deck, drop something valuable into the ocean, accidentally stab themselves with a machete, or an ax, or a fishing hook, or when any one of a hundred minor accidents was about to happen. This gave them the ability to blurt out: "Son of a bitch!" *before the event occurred.*

As much as the Colombians were champion swearers, Martin was more and more showing his ability to amaze us with his eating regimen. He guzzled sugar by the ton. Whatever he prepared—fish, pancakes, rice, eggs—it always "needed more sugar." His diet was difficult to believe. He'd swallow great fingerfuls of chocolate paste, have a drink of chocolate syrup, eat three to four chocolate bars—then wash it all down with a couple of tall glasses of hot orange soda, all of which he had brought with him in his luggage.

We developed into a fairly happy group, mainly because of the hearty Colombians. After a few weeks together, we grew nicknames. I gave Cesar the name of *El Diablo* ("Little Devil"). Alejandro was perfect as *Sr. Insolente* ("Mr. Smart Aleck".) The Colombians named Martin, *Cucaracha* ("Cockroach"). And Alejandro started calling me *Alma Negra* ("The Black Spirit"). To him I seemed like a lost man, one who had obviously been wandering in a void for months, and now years.

But they were thoughtful men, the Colombians—and emminently sane. As we drifted on the glassy surface of The Gyre, Alejandro read *The Last Days of Socrates,* the story of a wise old man who maintains his dignity in the face of injustice. When Alejandro was finished with the book he put it down very slowly. I wasn't sure if he actually shed a tear, but I did see him wipe his face. Tears or no, he was deeply disturbed. "This is a very sad story," he said, "very tragic."

"You understood it?"

"*Sí.*"

"In English?"

"*Sí.*"

At this, I took a moment to wonder at him: I was beginning to realize that Alejandro possessed a brilliant mind.

"Why did they imprison Socrates?" he asked.

"He was teaching unpopular ideas," I said.

"Yeah?"

"Yeah. That, and he was a smart ass."

"Ahhhh! How wonderful!"

On the twenty-second, we spotted a school of dolphins directly astern. There were about twenty in all, traveling in what appeared to be two separate families.

They came right toward the raft, driving thousands of fish before them. We noticed this phenomenon repeatedly: Whenever large numbers of dolphins were around they were always preceded by schools of frightened fish. As these two groups came by, we geared-up for snorkeling and went over the side. Diving down, holding my breath, I pressurized my ears and then began kicking steadily with my heavy fins. The ocean was a pale turquoise, with streaks of white highlights made by shafts of sun rays. The water was as clear as that in a swimming pool, and visibility seemed to be unlimited. From one hundred feet behind the raft, I could see them coming: a family of dolphins. Pumping along at about five miles an hour, their muscular bodies bulged, thick and taut, under their rubbery skins. They hovered at ten feet below the surface and soon I was paralleling them, cruising along at the same depth—me looking at them, and them looking at me. I immediately recognized a difference in the way the dolphins behaved in comparison to other types of sea creatures. All the other types of fish I had swum with simply took a momentary glance at me and then scurried off; but the dolphin family *examined* me.

Their family stayed tightly grouped, like a disciplined unit, and maintained a distance of eight to ten feet from me. I could easily distinguish the parts of the family: The young ones sprang happily along, and the old ones labored in the rear. The older ones fascinated me the most: The years and the sea had weathered them in the extreme. Old scratches, nicks, cuts, and gouges had scarred their gray skin. They examined me carefully while I cruised alongside, and I watched them form an opinion of me over twenty minutes of traveling together. The young ones were playful and open and uncritical, but not the old; there was a calm carefulness about them. Clearly, they worried that I was in their domain. I wondered if they had ever seen a human being before. How often would a human suddenly appear in the water out here in the middle of The Gyre? Each time I swam with dolphins I was overcome with the incredible urge to want to talk to them. I emerged from the ocean each time wishing to know their life's story. What had their life in the sea been about? What had they seen throughout the years? What enlightenment had they accumulated?

By the twenty-ninth, the perpetual drifting had caused a routine to set in on the raft. We knew that to escape The Gyre we must be patient. In reality, there wasn't much else to do. For two weeks the sea had been as calm as glass, and wind had been nonexistent. *Manteño II* had been drifting due west in the current at about twenty miles per day, a lonely bamboo platform with a little house on it, resting on the surface of a flat plain, surrounded by thousands of miles of emptiness, stillness. We were on a long circular course that would eventually take us around to the northernmost perimeter of the whirlpool, where we hoped to find wind, and escape.

At night, we had extreme calm and a brilliant moon. There were no sounds of any kind; all was silent. The Gyre lit up fantastically, like the reflection of a full moon on a field of freshly fallen snow. You had all the characteristics of night—except that you could see perfectly. As the days passed, the water of The Gyre calmed even more and now at night it was like a mirror. As far as you could see in any direction the ocean had become a shining plate. The horizon line, the edge of this plate, was now distinctly visible, 360 degrees around the raft. It was now easy to see the moon, crisp and clear, shining on the face of the vast Pacific. Not knowing what was to come, we believed that this was as calm as the ocean, the atmosphere, indeed the *world* could get. How could any vast place become more calm, more still, more stopped than this? But what we did not know was that The Gyre was the calmest place on the earth; and in those early days of drifting there must have been some imperfections in the surface of the water, because more nights passed, and as they did The Gyre calmed and calmed until it settled at a state of perfection. Now it was no longer a calm ocean, nor lit brightly as if by snow, nor like a mirror. In its still-ness and in its perfection the surface of The Gyre reproduced an exact image of the moon and clouds above it. But it was something greater than a mirror image, something more incredible, more difficult to comprehend, indeed—something vastly more difficult to *believe*. Alejandro and I talked about this in passing and it was agreed among us that staring at The Gyre while on night watch was unhealthy and should be avoided. I think we both knew that it could cause the contemplation of madness because it seemed to make your mind run off into terror. Nevertheless, all of us stared at it. Each one of us stood alone at the edge of the deck during our night watch, while the other three slept, and stared. Here, standing on the hard cane poles in the brilliant glaring moonlight, with no sounds to keep you company, nothing but a silent vacuum and the sound of your own respiration, of your own wispy breath drawing in and out, you stared at thirty square miles of ocean and you saw every ridge and every contour and every shaded area of every puffy cumulus cloud above, and every scar and every mountain and every detail of every sin-gle crater on the moon's surface. And when you searched for imperfections in the water, for ripples, you became even more hypnotized by the precise image before you, a precise image that started at your feet and stretched out to every horizon. In the surface of the water you saw a frozen thing, still, *captured,* a thing that did not move and did not ripple. You stared at the ocean and yet you saw no sign of it. You stood in silence for moment after ticking moment, looking out over what was once an ocean and you saw instead the black-and-white image of a night sky superimposed on the water like a still photograph—an immense, glossy photograph of a tropical night—sharp, complete, and perfectly focused.

And whereas the darkness had been the enemy up to this time, these moonlit nights were a relief. While the other three slept peacefully in their beds, I strolled around on the deck, watching for ships on the glassy horizon, talking to myself sometimes, and sometimes thinking about my former life in the modern world, which was harder and harder to remember.

And finally, I had time to read a book. I read *The Conquest of New Spain,* Bernal Diaz's eyewitness account of how the conquistadors destroyed the Aztecs. Occasionally I sat at the radio table inside the hut, straining to read by the flickering flame of an oil lamp that lit up no more than two feet of space. The Inventors had fabricated the lamp out of a baking powder tin, filled it with cooking oil, and then inserted a canvas wick in a slit in the top. There were of course no sounds in The Gyre and so many times it was impossible to tell that I was on the water—I may very well have been in the jungle headquarters of a Latin American revolutionary group, surrounded on all sides by bamboo and a bushy thatch. Around the radio table lay the equipment of a group that was undoubtedly cut off from the world: machetes, axes, knives, tools, spear guns, compasses, batteries of every size, maps, charts, structural drawings of the raft, and a bicycle-driven generator. As the light of the oil lantern flickered, and as bright gray moonlight shot into the hut, I read of the conquistador's bloody attack on the Aztec capital, the assassination of King Montezuma, and the human sacrifice methods of the Aztecs. The author, Diaz, a conquistador himself, described the interior of the Aztecs's human sacrifice death chamber like this:

> . . . they were burning the hearts of three Indians whom they had sacrificed that day; and all the walls of that shrine were so splashed and caked with blood that they and the floor were black too. Indeed, the whole place stank abominably. . . . the floor was so bathed (in blood) that the stench was worse than that of any slaughter house of Spain.
>
> . . . the stench was so that we could hardly wait to get out. They kept a large drum there, and when they beat it the sound was dismal, like some music from the infernal regions (hell) . . . and it could be heard six miles away. The drum was said to be covered with the skins of huge serpents. In that small platform were many diabolical objects, trumpets great and small, knives, and many hearts that had been burnt . . . we could scarcely stay in the place.

And on one such calm evening in The Gyre, Alejandro went out on watch, and while making the rounds, stepped on a sea snake. Miraculously, it didn't strike him, but it was now clear to us that the snakes would be coming on board at night. It was no surprise; The Gyre was infested with them.

Sea snakes are exceedingly poisonous. Their venom is a neurotoxin, stronger than that of the king cobra, which paralyzes the victim that has been bitten so that, slowly, respiration becomes impossible. There is only one company in the world that makes an antivenom, and it is in Australia. Thankfully, they are not usually aggressive. Most human deaths come from fishermen accidentally running across them in fishing nets. Occasionally, however, there are sightings of "thousands" swarming in one area.

Bright green and yellow, the sea snakes around *Manteño II* averaged about three feet in length, were very slender, and had a flattened tail, like a rudder, perfectly developed for swimming in the ocean. They usually swam on the surface of the water, slithering along in the same motion as a snake would move across the land, wiggling in a serpentine fashion to propel themselves; but when startled, they could kick with their tails and shoot through the water like a spear.

A few days before Alejandro's encounter, I had sent Martin over the side to reset the starboard stays on the foremast. He went through the usual, arduous, surfacing and diving, pulling and fighting, and then a sea snake suddenly shot forward from the stern. It stopped and hovered on the surface above Martin, who was below and about to come up. In a split second I envisioned Martin surfacing right under the snake, it hanging off Martin's head like moss, Martin convulsing in fear, and the snake reacting by striking him. With nothing else to do, I grabbed my boot off the top of a water barrel and threw it, and instead of scaring the snake, the boot hit it. For a moment the creature was stunned, but then it came to and so I threw the other boot and it took off, swimming away from the raft right at the same time Martin's head broke the surface. "Martin!" I screamed, "Dive! Dive down! Go back under!" It took him a second to realize what was going on, then he pushed off the logs in a sudden panic and dove back under the surface. By that time the snake was ten feet away and the danger was gone, but Martin seemed to cling to this incident, and convinced himself that I had "saved his life."

"I just threw a boot."

"Were those your last shoes?"

"Well, yeah."

"I'll buy you another pair of shoes, if we ever get to land."

I was now barefoot. Soon, my feet began to bruise and swell painfully from walking on the bamboo deck, just as they had during the voyage of the *Illa-Tiki*.

We began wearing our rubber jungle boots or other foot gear on watch at night. Nevertheless, using the bathroom off the back logs was especially unnerving, because it usually required taking the boots or shoes off: In the darkness, if the sea was up, you felt masses of warm seawater flood up to your hips as waves came in, then the sudden sucking of the water receding away, like a beach surf. After the water was gone you stood there in the darkness, motionless, waiting to detect the clammy slither of a sea snake across your ankles.

Each day, during this time, Cesar maintained a sharp lookout for sea snakes. He yearned, always, to catch one. As one of The Inventors, he had fabricated a personal snake tender: a stick, about three feet long, with a loop of string at one end that could be tightened around the snake's head. Once the tender had been made, Martin wanted to get Cesar on film, catching a sea snake, and it didn't take long to spot one. At 3:30 one afternoon a snake came along the port beam, glanced off the logs, and then started swimming away from the raft. Launching the inflatable dinghy, we paddled out after it. Cesar sat up on the bow while Martin and I paddled. We pursued the snake for a hundred yards, seeing it and losing it several times. After losing it for the last time, we turned back, and when we did we were amazed by what we saw. The sky had changed since we had left the raft, fifteen minutes ago. A vast rain shower was coming over the horizon, and we were taken aback by its beauty. The sun, which was on the opposite horizon, gleamed a brilliant silver reflection on the wall of falling water in the eastern sky. It was the greatest demonstration of the color silver that I have ever seen. It was a gleaming waterfall of nature, twenty miles wide, reaching from the sky down to the surface of the ocean, curving over us like an enormous band shell. It seemed to emanate light—to *produce* light—rather than to reflect it. We could see its entire size and shape because it was so far from us, but we could also see the tiny, individual drops, floating down to earth. It was twenty square miles of cool, trickling, silver leaf, but alive, and moving. It was the most beautiful vista of my life.

"What does it mean?" Martin asked.

It was not a question, but something he pondered. What *did* it mean? If the ancients saw this as a sign, then I must sympathize. I am a man of reason, but this moment shook me. This immense beauty, this silver utopian vision, had no reason. Only a meteorological phenomenon? Perhaps. If a logical explanation can be found for *how* it occurs, which it can, then I am still forced to ask, as Martin did, What does it mean? Why would such beauty exist? I assign no religious implications to this moment, but I do ask, Why?

.   .   .

During these days of waiting it was intensely hot. The hut offered some protection, but working in the heat was oppressive. Nevertheless, the calm was a
welcomed respite because it gave us time to make repairs on the raft and to reinforce the areas that were weakening. Slowly, the raft began to list. The
Teredo navalis had started, and the individual logs were losing their buoyancy
at an uneven rate. We righted the depressing list by moving the small balsa log
pontoons from port to starboard, but after a couple of days the raft began to
tilt back the other way, which began a pattern. Every forty-eight hours we had
to shift the pontoons to compensate for a new list. We were also back to the
hellish tourniquet work. The bamboo deck was in bad shape too, and in some
cases, detaching completely from the raft. We repaired it by using a hodgepodge of spare bamboo and string made from our reserve rope supply.

We were, in fact, getting desperate for rope. Each day we unlayed another
major line. If a rope was made of three strands, we unwound it and made it
into three, smaller lines. Then, soon, this smaller line was unlayed too. Every
day our lines shrank in size and strength. In some places whole structures
were held together with the remnants of a single manila rope that we had broken down to strands, then yarns, then fibers.

The foremast was righted and reinforced through the backbreaking work of
untying and tightening the long heavy manila stays. The rear *guaras,* all eighteen of them, had become a tangled mess that took a Herculean effort to untangle. We spent eight hours under the raft, holding our bursting lungs so that
we could stay down just a few more seconds each time, pulling and jerking
and wrestling with the ten-foot *guaras* until our limbs ached intensely from
oxygen starvation and the ocean sucked all of the heat out of our bodies.

Still, things remained depressingly disheveled. Every day, something else
more urgent or more important than cleaning and arranging was on the agenda.

As we drifted on the glassy surface, we constantly saw debris floating in the
sea. Frequently the heart of the debris was a giant log that had once been a
tree on some distant shore and now had become a floating microcity of life at
sea. Here you had the entire food chain: Barnacles, sea weed, and *Teredo
navalis,* all clinging to the sides of the log. These smaller life forms were eaten
by crabs scurrying back and forth on the log, and by tiny fish, picking at the
log's sides. The tiny fish were eaten by small and medium fish, measuring from
six to eighteen inches in length, swarming around the colony. These medium-
sized fish were eaten by large dorados and sharks, who orbited elliptically
around the colony, swinging out fifty feet or so and then coming in swiftly to

attack. Perched on top of the colony were white-and-gray sea birds, taking off and landing like airplanes on a tiny aircraft carrier. They went up to about fifty feet, collapsed their wings, put their heads down, and then shot straight into the water, catching the small and medium fish. The area around this microcity was as busy as a downtown street. I wondered, privately, how long each little city had been trapped, circling endlessly in The Gyre, destined to sink there.

On January 26, we received news of a massive earthquake in Alejandro's hometown of Pereira. A ham radio operator in Bogotá came on the frequency to deliver the bad news. "The destruction is massive," he said. "We have thousands of casualties. The center of the quake was in Pereira."

At the news, Alejandro withered. He sank back on his sleeping bag and put his hands over his face. Sitting just feet away from him at the table, I asked the radio operator to find out if my friend's family was alive. Alejandro had once told me, during one of our many philosophical conversations, "I love my parents very, very much. They are the most beautiful people I know."

The wait was dreadful. The vision of having to tell my newfound friend that his beloved mother and father were gone was unbearable.

On the twenty-seventh and twenty-eighth we discovered more *Teredo navalis* in our balsa logs. It was such a dark subject inside my mind that it was hard to accept that we were, once again, going to sink. Many options lay before us, of which the most attractive was the construction of a new raft, while on the high sea. Thankfully, we received news that day that Alejandro's parents were indeed alive, which diverted my terrible feelings of sinking in The Gyre.

By January 30, we had drifted four hundred nautical miles from Montuosa Island, our last sighting of land. As we went farther out to high sea, the size and abundance of marine life increased. We sighted more sharks, although they were still skittish.

At 2:00 a.m. on the morning of February 2, we were hit by our first *chubasco*. A *chubasco* is an exceedingly concentrated rainstorm, indigenous to Costa Rican waters. Water poured into the hole in the roof where the mizzenmast jutted through, and in a three-hour period we collected eighty gallons of freshwater. I made a note in my diary that every one on board was calm during the intense downpour. On the next day, I wrote in my diary:

3 *February 1999*
I find colonies of Teredo navalis. (I) am plagued by dark fears again. Can't tell if the raft is sinking (quickly) or not.
 The course is starting to change for the worse—more north than west.

Martin is a fanatic about fishing. My admiration for Alejandro and Cesar continues to grow.

4 February 1999
Moving east now—(trapped in The) Gyre.

We were rounding our third orbit of The Gyre. The mast stays were beginning to chafe and wear. They would have to be changed and reworked. Also, about this time, large sharks appeared around the raft.

Shark attacks on the fish we caught were a frequent occurrence now. Martin would go into the water and spear a fish, only to have the sharks swoop down and bite it in half. The smell of blood and the frantic flapping of fins at the end of the spear were like setting off an alarm. The sharks sensed that the killing was easier near the raft and homed in. The moment the harpoon would penetrate a fish the sharks would bolt through the water like bullets, sometimes two or three at a time, and gobble it up so fast that it seemed as though it had disintegrated. It chilled Martin. "Man!" he said one day, after clambering aboard the raft for safety, "They attack the second the harpoon goes in! You should see them!"

The sharks were becoming an issue, and we could no longer ignore them. We worked under the raft everyday, setting and resetting the pontoons, reworking the tourniquets, and tightening and resetting the mast stays. The sharks liked to examine us while we worked by passing close to our faces: You'd be working underneath the raft with your hands over your head, holding your breath, struggling to untie a knot, focusing all of your attention on a small area, when a gray shark—its mouth open and its eyes twisted in an evil and uncoordinated fashion—would cruise by just inches from your mask. It startled you, like turning on the light in a dark closet and discovering an intruder staring at you with a knife in his hand. Just this problem alone was a serious hindrance because it broke down our ability to concentrate on repairing the raft, but we faced a more serious problem than just our natural human fear of sharks.

The problem that we faced was not the size of the individual animals but the *number* of animals. We rarely saw any sharks that were larger than eight feet and never any that were over a hundred pounds, so we didn't fear an outright killing, where a large animal would come in and make such a horrific attack that one of us died quickly from massive tissue loss and trauma. That scenario was highly unlikely. What we feared was their behavior as a group. When there is blood in the water, combined with the flapping sounds of wounded fish, sharks tend to be far more aggressive than is normally the case. If these two conditions, blood and sounds, occur where sharks are schooling in great numbers, their behavior becomes highly reckless, and hundreds upon hundreds of sharks now orbited the raft, singly and in packs, randomly attacking anything they could.

We separated into two camps, the Shark Police and the Worker Bees. Alejandro and Martin, both of whom were quite understandably nervous about sharks, would work on whatever was needed, while Cesar and I, who couldn't help but be fascinated by the sharks, would police the waters by patrolling with spear guns and hand harpoons. Typically, when there was a lot of work to do, Cesar and I went in first, to clear the area. Upon entering the water we'd immediately make a quick scan of the water, spinning our bodies around, squinting through our masks at the community of sharks. Invariably, several groups of five or six cruised together, slowly swimming circuitous routes around the raft. Whenever a pack was nearby we could see every detail of their muscular gray bodies and triangular tails waving lazily in the clear water. Occasionally there would be a large one, swimming alone and waiting for its chance. Then there would be the packs several hundred feet away, cruising at the far periphery of our underwater vision like languid phantoms in a blue, opaque fog.

We developed a method for chasing sharks away from the raft that was crude but effective. Cesar and I would speed toward the nearest school, motoring through the water on our fins. We'd hold our harpoons in one hand, pressurize our ears with the other hand, and then dive. We'd come in fast, fins flailing, our masks compressing around our faces, and then, at the last second, we'd widen our mouths, push on our diaphragm, and scream psychotically while jabbing a shark sharply with the harpoon. Even though we rarely pierced their tough skin, they always went scurrying away. Occasionally they'd turn and snap at the harpoon, but that was clearly out of panic, not because they wished to fight with us. After a while we learned to attack the sharks when they were in their most vulnerable positions. We'd come in from above and behind them and jab them sharply in the back, an area that they could not easily defend. This was highly useful because the sharks seemed to possess a somewhat communal nature about them: Generally speaking, each individual shark kept an eye on everything that was going on in the community. Whenever we made an attack on one of them, most of the others seemed to take notice—they would jump as though startled, or would suddenly begin swimming much faster than normal. This made dispersal much easier because most of the other sharks nearby would clearly register the fact that something had attacked one of their own, and would begin to clear out, leaving for better grounds. They were "dumb animals," and we were, essentially, *bluffing* them—making them believe that we were in charge of this area and that they had to leave. They seemed to have a short memory though. A pack would scurry away after an attack, disappear into the ocean, then slowly reemerge a few minutes later, materializing out of the infinite blue, looking for new opportunities to eat. It frequently took repeated attacks on one particular school to drive it away permanently.

Meanwhile, Alejandro and Martin would work on the raft. Now, with all four of us in the water, all of the action would be going on under the surface. If you'd have come upon *Manteño II* during this time you'd have thought the raft abandoned. But underneath, looking through the glass of my mask, I'd see two men, working underneath the raft, their arms and hands over their heads, struggling and pulling on the thick manila lines, holding their breath and treading water with their legs. Their black flippers would stab at the water in slow motion and the black, rectangular shape of *Manteño II* would hover motionless above them while sharks circled all around in the rich blue infinity. Cesar, muscular and compact, would be off to one side, scanning the water, working his arms furiously, spinning his body around and around, watching for sharks. We'd hand signal each other and then suddenly surface into the air and the clattering, splashing noises. He'd spit out his snorkel and yell, "How are we doing John?"

"I . . . I think we're OK. What happened to that big one in the back?"

"I got him. He left."

"OK. Let's go around front."

Then we'd be back under, breathing through our snorkels, sucking down little drops of brackish saltwater, scanning the silent world for streamlined gray forms cruising smoothly in the blue. I'd sight one coming in too close, signal Cesar, surface, blurt out instructions for attacking it over the splashing noises, and then we'd go to work. What irony. Cesar and I liked the sharks, yet we were assigned the unfortunate task of attacking them. In all the time we fought the sharks, neither Cesar nor I were ever convinced that they were mean, predatory villains; they impressed us more as dim-witted scavengers. Nevertheless, we maintained a healthy respect for them. We had seen them bite clean through the same fish that it had taken us a full minute to cut through with a sharp machete. If a shark bit one of our crew in this way it would probably sever a major artery in one of our limbs. We stood almost no chance of saving a man with that kind of wound.

Increasingly, the raft was going down in the water. Our feet and ankles were wet all the time now. Saltwater sores boiled up on our legs. They burned and ached twenty-four hours a day. We had on board some tubes of strong, steroid-based cream left over from the beginning of The Expedition, when we had been well supplied. It worked well, but we used up the entire supply within a few days. Between the eight exposed legs there were at least forty open sores festering at any one time. I had to all but order the Colombians to use their share of the cream. "Yours are worse than mine," they'd each insist, "you use it."

We were all physically declining. Alejandro had fallen down on the deck a few days before, and when he did he came up trembling, holding his hand. I said to him, "Let me look at it."

"No," he said, and turned away, huddling over the injured hand. Right before he turned I noticed that one of his fingers was grotesquely bent. It appeared to me to be a dislocation.

"Alejo," I said, "just let me look at it for a minute, OK?"

"No, I—I'm OK," he said, and then reached up with his good hand, grabbing the finger, his face quivering: "Urrgghh!" *Crick!*—he reset it in the joint.

"What the hell are you doing!?"

"I—I'm OK," he grunted, then shuffled off down the catwalk like an animal that wanted to lick its wounds in peace. Cesar signaled me to leave him alone for a moment, so I backed off. A week later he went down again and tore the nail out of the same finger.

On February 7, we held an informal meeting in the hut. "I feel we can make it another twenty days with the raft in the state it's in," I said. "After that, everything's got to go over the side to lighten the load. In twenty days we're going to have water up to our ankles all of the time. We'll have to throw all nonessential material overboard."

"You're sure we're sinking," Martin said in a confirming tone.

"I'm sure. We will throw overboard everything we can: Excess drinking water, the bicycle-generator, the center crossbeam, extra books, extra clothes, the storage boxes—even the hut. I figure we can get rid of something like three thousand pounds. We're going to strip down to the bare bones, that'll buy us another twenty days. We're still going to need twenty days or more after that to make land—Hawaii—and we're just going to have to figure out how to stay afloat."

That's the way I estimated it on February 7. Our quest for the Manteño Trading Route was ruined. We'd never make it back to Central America; and even if we did, the raft had deteriorated too much to navigate the intricacies of a coastline. If we got into a tight maneuvering situation now, we'd be helpless. The most *Manteño II* could possibly do was run in a straight line, across the open ocean, with the wind and current at her back. That meant that the only land we'd ever be able to make was possibly Hawaii, four thousand nautical miles away. But that goal was only possible if we escaped The Gyre. If we could escape and then make fifty-five miles a day across the open sea, that put us seventy-five days away from Hawaii. Technically, we could make it—if we didn't sit becalmed for days on end, if my rudimentary calculations about the raft's rate of sink were accurate, and if there were no propulsion disasters, like a broken mast, or six broken yardarms, or a wind-demolished sail. If we could escape The Gyre, we still had a chance to limp into port at Hawaii.

The dismal idea of a high-sea rescue was so awful for me that I couldn't think about it. Not only would The Expedition "fail," but more importantly we'd have to call for help from the middle of the ocean, inconveniencing the professional mariners like a bunch of helpless amateurs. The Expedition that we had worked so hard to see through, and the knowledge of raft navigation that was so hard won, would appear like some sort of idiotic publicity stunt.

It was incredibly hot in The Gyre that day, February 7, and the four of us had headaches before noon. The sun had broiled the tops of our skulls, and so we lay on our sleeping bags in the afternoon and just talked. I asked the Colombians if they knew of the story of Joaquin Cuellar. Cesar didn't know, so I told him a little of what Joaquin had told me one night back in Bahia Solano, but I will relate the entire story here, as it was told to me:

During the humid nights of December 1998, Joaquin and I talked often, sitting at his wooden dinner table in a small, cement-floored room, and on one such night I casually asked him to tell me about an incident that his brother, Mario, had mentioned. The second the request came out of my mouth, his face widened and turned pale. He said nothing for a long moment. A lightbulb hung down on a chord above us and bugs buzzed noisily around it, causing little shadows to ricochet on the walls. I could see from his face that I had been far too nonchalant about something that was deeply disturbing to him. "Uh— your brother told me about it," I said. "I, uh, I mean—if you feel up to it. I just wanted to hear your story, that's all."

In spite of mixed feelings, he felt compelled to explain himself. He began in a quiet, grave tone. "I came to the coast when I was nineteen. I went up and down the coast, to the fishing camps, to buy fresh fish (to sell to hotels and restaurants). I didn't know the sea. I spent one month here, going out on short trips. I liked it. Being out on the high sea brings me great pleasure; it enchants me.

"The day it happened was March 9, 1980. I was with two other guys, one was the captain and the other was just a sailor. The captain was a small Indian, just eighteen years old. The sailor was twenty. They didn't like me and I didn't like either one of them; they were *mala gente* ("bad people"). We went out in a wooden boat, eighteen feet long, with one motor and two paddles. I tied the motor to the boat even though they said I was stupid—you know—just a land-lubber from the big city.

"We left at 8:00 at night. The night was clear, but the wind was really strong. We had a compass, but the Indian didn't know how to use it. (Joaquin had told me before that a lot of people in that area didn't know how to use a compass.) He (the Indian) knew the coast really well; but it was night and he was having trouble. There was an argument between him and the sailor. The sailor wanted him to steer by the compass. They started fighting a little—pushing each other and grabbing each other's shirts. The sailor tried to get the tiller from the captain; they were fighting; the motor came off the back, and sank." Joaquin suddenly became very animated, "From now on," he exclaimed, "I tie the motor onto several parts of the boat!"

"So it fell into the sea during the fight. We pulled it back up. We tried to start it, but we didn't have flashlights, so we couldn't figure out what was wrong. The wind was really strong now." He then acted out a scene of three men in a small boat being thrown around by rough seas, frantically trying to get an outboard motor to run; the wind is blowing, it is night, they cannot make out anything, and they are starting to panic.

"At sunrise, we could no longer see the coast. The coast"—his eyes sank and he waved his hand out in front of him—"was gone." He was quiet for half a minute, then said loudly, angrily: "They blamed it on me!" He poked himself hard on his chest. *Thump, thump, thump.* "They blamed me! They said it was all my fault! If I hadn't had to go get fish, this would have never happened to them. They said I made them sail. They were *muy brava* ("very hostile") with me.

"We had no food and no water. Our worry kept rising. We thought that someone would look for us, but no one came. Three o'clock in the afternoon that day—still no luck with the motor. At about five in the afternoon, I started the motor, finally.

"The sailor knew what to do because he knew how to use the compass. We ran well for two hours. We were making about twelve knots. We sighted land, probably twenty miles away. The sailor gunned the motor. The Indian was encouraging him, but I told them to take it easy. 'No!' they yelled at me." He shook his head. "The motor died within sight of land." He threw up his hands and shook his head at their stupidity. "I had an ear infection, and I had brought some ear drops with me. I was so thirsty by then that I drank the ear drops; they were incredibly bitter, but I didn't care.

"On the second day, at sunrise, the land was out of sight again. We hadn't seen any boats so far. We went another two days and nights—three days now—no food or water. We were sick with fear and worry. We just sat there, thinking and hoping. They kept blaming me.

"The nights were cold." He acted like a shivering man. "For five days straight it blew hard. We had water coming on board. We bailed all the time. We had a hard hat onboard, and we bailed until we were very tired. We were scared at night of collision. We had no sleep. We were getting more and more tired. The seas were very rough the whole time. We thought the boat would crack open, especially on the fourth day. The seas were pounding us . . . pounding."

At this point, Joaquin's wife came in the room and sat down quietly. Her face showed that this was something that had disturbed her husband for a very long time. Her black eyes glared at me and her face said, "Why did you bring this up? Why? This is not a game for your fascination."

I scribbled notes as fast as I could. Joaquin saw that I was recording his story.

"The sharks came. I couldn't sleep—I was very nervous. The seas were very bad—pounding.

"On the fifth day, it was calm—totally flat! I saw a piece of bamboo, floating. I thought maybe there might be fresh water in it, so I swam out to it. It was far from the boat, and I was terrified of the sharks. I had a nylon fishing line attached to me, running back to the boat. I broke the bamboo open. It smelled like wine; I couldn't drink it.

"I wanted to live. The guys said, 'We are going to die.' I maintained the will to live. They gave up, but I continued to bail. We drifted for a long time in the calm. Later that day, we bumped into a sea turtle. I took a fishing hook and snagged its leg. We had a screwdriver—no knife—and an empty sausage can, which I rubbed on a rock to sharpen it. I cut open the turtle at the neck and let it bleed into the hard hat. My God, there was so much blood. I offered it to the guys, but they wouldn't drink it. I drank it—I was so relieved in that moment. It was so sweet. That blood was tremendous. It was sweet." He began to tear up. "Compared to thirst, hunger is *nothing*, John. Nothing! That night I dreamed the most beautiful dream of my life. I dreamed that I had a river flowing into in my mouth." His voice broke. "It was so realistic, it made me fly."

It was at this time that I noticed that the volume had been turned down on the television in the next room, and that everything and everyone in Joaquin's house had gone eerily silent.

"That night was good. It took the entire sixth day to break open the turtle's shell with the screwdriver. I squeezed every drop of blood out of the meat. The men still wouldn't drink it, or eat the meat. The men were losing faith, but that turtle gave me energy." He then reached inside his shirt and pulled out a chain with a medallion on it. The small gold coin had the Madonna and Child on one side, and his name on the other. "Do you know what this is?"

"Yes. Yes—I now what that is."

"This means a lot to me, John. It represents everything beautiful in the world. At one point, I felt like I didn't owe the other two anything else. They had no spirit; they were going to die. I wanted to live. I had seen the movie *Alive*. I was scared I might go crazy. I used a fish hook to fasten this medallion to the hard hat. I wanted people to know who I was—when they found us."

Up to that point, that sixth day, the wind had been blowing Joaquin's boat away from land, but then it changed direction.

"I made a mast out of the paddles. I made a sail out of a small piece of plastic. It worked well, too."

This of course was critical: Wind or current that travels toward land has always been the only real hope that anyone has if they are lost at sea. In his book *Adrift,* Steven Callahan tells how he survived seventy-six days in a life raft by drifting in the ocean current, from the middle of the Atlantic to the South American shore. Each day he made a crude navigational estimate of how far it was to land, and how much longer he needed to hang on. He knew, as do most other sailors, that the ocean would eventually carry him to land. The sea moves like a conveyer belt, and if you can hold out long enough you will eventually be carried along to a welcoming shoreline.

But not in The Gyre. If you were lost, drifting in The Gyre, you'd never arrive at *any* shore. You would orbit forever in a place where the ocean does not end, the world's great continents do not exist, there is no welcoming shoreline, there is no hope of landing "eventually."

Joaquin continued his story. "On the seventh day, in the morning, we saw a ship. We said, 'We can't be too far from land!' I had a new spirit to win! We went crazy, John!" He banged on the table where we were sitting, on pots and dishes, acting like a man gone crazy with hope. "That night, we went on watches. We drifted along under my little sail. The sail was working. I said, 'We're going to land.' It electrified the men. But in the morning, on the eighth day, there was no land. We saw an airplane, but no land. We caught a dorado and ate it. The men were happy to eat that dorado raw, they didn't care. On the ninth day, there still was no land; but we saw butterflies! A sure sign of land!

"The wind came up. At two in the afternoon we saw the mountains of Panama. The sailor sat up and pointed. 'Land.' The wind got stronger, and we were scared of a bad landing in the surf. We didn't have the energy to swim. That night we had a good moon. It was bright, and we saw trees floating in the water.

"At about two in the morning, on the ninth day, we spotted Cabo Marzo. We were in exactly the spot we had wanted to go the night we were lost at sea. When we landed, we couldn't get out of the boat and walk. I rolled over the side and crawled. The others couldn't even get out."

Joaquin looked down at the table, and then up at me—he wanted me to know: "They had begun funeral preparations for the captain."

He stopped there—that was enough. He became silent. He was really upset. He told me later that it was "never far away from (his) mind." I felt bad for asking about such a horrible experience, but he wasn't angry with me; he wanted to tell his story.

Being lost at sea is slow death. You have time to lose hope, to give up, to know that your life is being stolen from you. Joaquin was hurt that his life, which he valued preciously, would have been wasted—for nothing. After a long pause of silence, he pointed to himself, his voice quivering, "I want to live!" Everything was quiet again. He stood up, turned around, then rearranged some things on the counter behind him. Facing the wall, looking down, he said, "It's horrible to see people prepare your funeral."

On the eighth, at dawn, we thought we felt a puff of wind and raised sail quickly, more out of fantasy than fact. The wind wasn't real; it had only been a puff that piqued our optimism. When the little breeze died in the oppressive heat, we just left the sails to hang. The canvas was starting to mold from sitting on the deck in the heat. This had been a serious problem on *Illa-Tiki,* and I could now clearly smell that foul odor of baking mildew in the sails of *Manteño II;* it was good to let them dry out.

Shortly after noon, on the forward deck, I smoked my last cigar. The smoke rose in a straight line, streaming up until a cloud formed above me. The air around me felt like that of a small room. As far as could be seen, from horizon to horizon, the air had become completely still. I had never experienced such calm in any other place I had been on the earth. The atmosphere hung over us like a block. For approximately four weeks there had not been enough wind to keep the sail inflated. Now, for the last ten days, there had been no wind at all.

In the afternoon I took a nap, and at around 4:00 Alejandro called to me, saying that he had spotted a snarl of debris off the port side. I was still inside the hut lying down and I could hear his voice bouncing off of the ocean's smooth surface like a shout trapped in a small tunnel. I got up immediately and came out into the brilliant sunlight and saw a tangled blue mess, half-submerged, about thirty yards out. Rope! We couldn't believe our luck! Good polypropylene rope! Looking at Alejandro, I asked, "Would you go out there and get that?"

"No problem."

He put on a mask and flippers and was in the water in one minute. But then he got about fifty feet out and called back to me, alarmed by a sudden swarm of sharks. "John! The sharks—are acting—very aggressively!"

I looked at Cesar and said, "Let's do this one in the dinghy."

"Good idea," he said, and we launched the dinghy with Martin aboard. By the time we got out to Alejandro, he had reached the floating rope. Cesar went into the water to chase off the sharks, and I examined the mass of debris. Some sort of wooden boat must have lost about two hundred feet of three-eighth's inch line. It was tangled up in five or six water-logged planks. When Cesar surfaced from fighting the sharks, he called out, *"Capitan, son grande!"* (*"they're big!"*) I went over the side and dove down. The sharks were larger than normal, but many had already been dispersed by Cesar's harpoon. When I surfaced, Martin said that he wanted to go back to the raft and get the video camera. He and I returned to *Manteño II*, leaving Alejandro and Cesar to get the snag ready for towing. We were back in ten minutes, and I returned to the sharks, this time with Martin shooting. I swam with the sharks, poking them occasionally to keep them back while Martin got several sequences, and then we surfaced to talk. The moment my head came out of the water I felt a strong intuitive alarm go off. I got into the dinghy and realized that the raft was in the wrong place. It had moved. Not far enough to measure, but far enough for me to realize, subconsciously, that a huge barge like that didn't move a foot, unless pushed. Alejandro and Cesar got into the dinghy instinctively, I think, sensing a problem by the look on my face. I told Martin to get aboard "right now," and within thirty seconds of that warning, we went from normality to terror: The raft had sailed away without us.

We frantically grabbed paddles. "We should send Alejandro swimming!" Martin said, already beginning to huff and puff from paddling. *Why not? He can probably make better time than we can, and he adds weight to the dinghy without having access to a paddle.*

"Go!" I yelled. He didn't need an explanation; he took off, kicking with his black fins.

The situation was unbelievable. We were all taken aback by the sense of nonreality. A sudden thunderstorm, small and concentrated, had developed just on the other side of the horizon. It had begun sucking in the atmosphere around it, generating a sudden, localized wind. We all knew it was life-or-death. I reached back and pulled the rope snarl to the dinghy and undid the tow line. *Forget the bloody rope!!*

Manteño II sailed away to the distant horizon. The raft's details faded; it became a small gray box with two triangles above it. We had been left behind, alone on the ocean in the dinghy.

"How can this happen?" Martin blurted out uncontrollably. He was saying what we were all thinking: There hadn't been any real wind for over thirty days; and even if there was wind, the raft couldn't sail unattended. It was too bizarre to be true. Five minutes ago all was well; now we were dead. I was immediately stunned by a wave of fear. *This is all my fault. I put these men in this position. How could I have been so stupid?*

Why didn't the raft steer itself into the wind and stop? The wind's pressure on the sails should have forced it to turn up into the wind; but the wind, being sucked into a small disturbance that was now on the horizon, was changing direction roughly as fast as the raft could turn, unattended. *Manteño II* was sailing in a wide arc, and the fast moving little storm was maintaining a perfect right angle to her sails. By freak accident, the sails stayed inflated just enough, and in just the right position, for the raft to sail on its own.

We paddled fanatically. The dinghy had been deflated 30 percent because we didn't want it to expand in the hot afternoon and explode. Now it was like trying to paddle a pile of wet laundry, and it was obvious that we'd never catch the raft. I had terrible visions: Alone in The Gyre with nothing but our swimsuits. *My God! We don't even have shirts on! We'll die of exposure in a few days!* In The Gyre, there would be no way of ever getting to land; we'd be lost, going in circles until we starved, orbiting forever in the vast wasteland. I knew immediately what was going to happen over the next few minutes and hours: We would begin to lose sight of the raft after it traveled just a few miles. Once the raft disappeared over the curvature of the earth it would be impossible to track, especially when it was running in the freakish arc of the turning wind. Sunset was only an hour away and it would be all over by then: Four men in the dark, alone on the ocean, lost, hopeless. There would be an explosion of anger by one or all of the men, and then, the horrible realization that there is nothing to do—there are no odds—it is the end of everything.

The raft gained speed. We could tell by the way it was sailing away that it had picked up momentum. Martin had fins on and went over the side to kick while Cesar and I paddled. For some unexplainable reason my adrenaline drained out of me, and I was immediately fatigued. That had never happened to me before, and I had to drive myself maniacally to paddle at my maximum. Cesar and Martin were relatively coolheaded at that point. We couldn't afford a panic and we knew it.

Martin quickly switched with Cesar. Cesar was a stronger swimmer, Martin a stronger paddler. Keeping my mind fixated on paddling, I asked, desperately, "Where's Alejandro?!"

"He's still a hundred yards back!" Martin gasped.

Looking up for a split second, I caught a glimpse of a disturbance in the water where Alejandro was swimming like a man caught in an epileptic convulsion. *There's no way he'll make it . . . he was a hundred yards back when he started . . . he's going to tire eventually.* The raft was, in fact, pulling away from us as well. We were paddling and kicking as hard as we could and it was still shrinking on the horizon. Fatigue was already starting to set in. Another vision came to me: that point when we realize that we can't go on paddling. I'd have nothing to say—nothing.

Manteño II got smaller and smaller. In my field of vision it was now only half an inch tall on the horizon. For the only time in my life, I knew what hopelessness really felt like. I prepared myself for the horrible feeling of seeing the raft disappear forever over the horizon.

But then the mizzen sail deflated. Even with my blurred vision I distinctly saw canvas luffing! I couldn't help but yell out, "YEAAAA!" The other men were silent. I think the utter heart-stopping fright of the moment had paralyzed their ability to talk. The wind had picked up in intensity and that had overturned the perfect little balance that the atmosphere had used to make the raft sail on its own, but it was still making good speed under the mainsail.

Alejandro swam to within fifteen feet of the logs and seemed to stop. We could see him out there on the open sea, swimming across The Gyre, swimming for his life, crawling, throwing arm over arm, pitching his palms overhand and drawing air out of the side of his mouth. But he wasn't closing the gap. He just seemed to hang there, suspended, right behind the raft, reaching out for the logs, minute after agonizing minute. *Oh God, he can't keep that up for very long.* He was becoming desperate. The big, powerful mainsail was still full and pulling the raft well and Alejandro just hung there behind it. We held our breath in that moment; our hopes were suspended, like Alejandro, swimming, struggling, behind the raft, and then he reached out again . . . *He made it! I don't believe it! . . . I don't believe it.*

It was unspeakable relief. He pulled himself slowly onto the back ends of the logs and lay there forever. The raft continued to pull away from us and yet he just lay there. *Why doesn't he douse the mainsail?* It half occurred to me that he was too exhausted to walk; but if he had had enough left in him to make that grab, he should have enough to get up and stop the raft. I found out later that the last reach he made was indeed probably his *last* reach.

We weren't out of trouble yet. "I'm going to paddle until we get there," Martin said, with the conviction of a man who would never again rely on hope to save his life. I was hit by a sense of thanks that I wasn't in that rubber boat with Frederick. If I had been, maybe I wouldn't be alive to tell my story.

Alejandro got up, half crawling, half stumbling. We could see that he was moving with his mind and that his body was being dragged along as an afterthought. The storm came toward us from the horizon, and quickly we had a deluge. It poured rain on us as we continued to paddle frantically. If that had happened ten minutes beforehand it would have been enough to obscure the raft from our visibility.

We continued to paddle with every ounce of strength we had. We didn't know it, but Alejandro was doing battle with the superpowerful mainsail. How do you fight a thing like that when everything in you is gone? He was beyond any exhaustion he'd ever felt before. Finally, we saw the sheet let out on the mainsail, and it luffed in the wind. We cheered! There was an ugly, disorganized sigh of relief from the three of us in the dinghy. *I can't believe it. I cannot believe it.* I laughed loudly with utter relief; I couldn't help it.

Still paddling for our lives, we closed in on the raft. Alejandro wobbled to the back of the stern, and then collapsed on the back ends of the logs. His legs had been shaking badly, and when he dropped, we could see that it was against his will. As we pulled up to the stern I could see that he was crying; not just a few tears but really sobbing. He had been as terrified as is possible for a human being, and I was overcome with sympathy and shame at the sight of him. I had caused this good man—who had just saved my life—to come within a few seconds of dying. As he gasped for air, his whole body shaking and trembling, he looked into my eyes and said, "I told myself: 'I will swim forever. I will swim forever. I will swim forever. I will swim forever . . . '" His voice trailed off and he was just looking at me, aghast with fear, mouthing his words but making no sound. I knew at that moment, from my experiences, that a lesser man would have given up.

We went aboard the raft and Martin began to shed a few tears, then broke down completely. Cesar just stood there looking at the raft in shock and bewilderment: A dead elephant had suddenly awakened and sprinted out of sight. I knew that my face must show the fright, too. I went to the forward deck to make sure everything was all right. Of course everything was, but I was overwhelmed by the instinct to *do* something.

I couldn't cry out loud—I didn't react like that. But I felt the same way as the others: We hadn't triumphed over a great challenge; we had escaped an unfair death. That was what hurt us: We cried over our lives, which had just been taken from us and then given back in the span of thirty minutes. Our lives—which we had just discovered we liked a lot—would have been wasted. We cried over the injustice. We would have died for nothing.

8 February 1999
It is one in a million that a sailor sees his boat sail away, and then lives to tell about it . . .

I remember, vividly, watching the raft sail away and being astonished that it could still sail. I talked to Cesar about this later and he had had the same feeling the moment the raft took off. We had thought the raft dead, unable to carry on. Shortly after calculating how to reach Hawaii, I had begun privately working out the details of the best way to abandon the raft. But *Manteño II* was definitely alive, and with a wind it, could still make way.

Three days later the wind started, and I noticed that the raft was sinking at an alarming rate, faster than I had expected. If the raft met disaster because of the *Teredo navalis,* it would happen this way: One side would sink more rapidly than the other, causing a list. The list would start small, but would rapidly increase until it reached a point of no return. The superheavy masts, whether carrying sails or not, would lean over and crank the raft around like tremendously powerful levers. Once that started, the raft would simply lie down and die. The time it would take for the raft to go from a small list to no return might be as little as twelve hours. It probably wouldn't be a violent action, simply a great animal that has struggled for as long as she can, and now, at the end, simply refuses to go on. The entire scenario scared me and I was constantly on guard against it. If *Manteño II* was allowed to list too far to one to side, we'd lose her for sure.

During the morning of the thirteenth, the seas increased. The ocean was now surging up through the deck. When the raft pitched down the whole deck disappeared and you had the feeling of standing on the surface of the water. When it would recover, it would just barely come back out of the water.

13 February 1999
Very heavy weather. Raft not holding up well. Logs underneath (the surface of the) water, and not coming up. Seas very violent. Port beam log has broken free—fixed it with a tourniquet. Raft listing heavily to port. We've moved much weight to starboard. Men holding up well. Water is entering the back wall of the hut like the first puddle of flood water. I miss my wife terribly. I love you Annie.

Massive amounts of water are coming onboard now. It's a pathetic scene of weary men trying to save a dying ship: We're losing items overboard. Men go into the water to retrieve *guaras* washed into the sea. We get them back and tie them down. We are scurrying around the deck under a gray, dismal sky. Another surge comes over the bow and a balsa stump slides off like it's riding a waterfall. Get it! Tie it down! Hours pass; we are tiring. We have heavy flooding in the hut. Then the binnacle, the enormous stump we have used as our table since Salango, slides across the deck, almost taking the ship's compass overboard. Cesar tackles it as it slides past him and is swept off his feet. The four of us grab it and then wrestle and heave it back to the center of the deck. A gas tank breaks loose from its lashing on the side of the hut. Grab that thing! Tie it down! Then another tank breaks loose. I look at my watch; five hours have gone by now. It's getting worse. Alejandro and Cesar despair. I tell them to collect all the tools and items that are loose and store them. "Is this normal?" Alejandro asks.
    "No," I say.
    "We're in trouble, aren't we?"
    "We'll be all right."
    I duck into the hut to change into dry clothing. Martin is rigging the camera for filming. Suddenly there comes from outside a gigantic growling noise. We look out the door and see nothing but white. A low, satanic moan thunders all around us, and the masts lean over forty-five degrees. "Is that real?" Martin asks.
    "That's the real McCoy," I say, and I rush out on deck.
    It is a tropical cyclone. Cesar and Alejandro stare at the atmosphere all around the raft. Looks of stunned fascination sprawl across their faces. Only a few seconds ago we could see the great Pacific Ocean stretching to the horizon,

a vast, open place; but now there is nothing. The ocean is gone; the feeling of open space is gone; *everything* is gone. It's like a blizzard out here—total white-out conditions. It is as though the raft is inside a large room now, as though it is inside a gymnasium or a warehouse. We are surrounded by high walls made of white mist—a white, impenetrable barrier, as thick as milk, that arches up to a roof above us. The manila lines are thrumming a deep vibration, a low, bass, *hummmmmmmm*. The wind blast is hitting us directly on the starboard beam. The masts bend over to an unnatural angle. They are like palm trees on land when hit by hurricane winds: The ground that they are planted in remains level while the trunks lay over as though they are going to touch the earth. It seems impossible that the masts can lean over that far and not break out of their stays. They're past forty-five degrees, relative to the deck. The raft heels over. I stand for a moment, crouched against the wind, drops flying from my beard, and just watch: *Are we going to capsize?* I force a smile on my face. Alejandro is slightly nervous; Cesar is ready for action. It's best to keep the men busy, rather than let them stand around with their minds wandering, so I shout to them: "Help— me—with—the—pontoons!"

The masts are prying the port side upward. It has caused the pontoons to spring out and float up. The pontoons on the starboard side have broken free too, which scares me—there's no apparent reason for that to happen. *Are the lashings starting to break? Will the raft disintegrate? Are we being pried apart by the pressure of a forty-foot crowbar?* I jump into the ocean so that I can force the pontoons back under with my feet. The work, and the fact that I am in the water, seem to reassure the Colombians, as well as Martin, who is now shooting. Everyone acts fast and performs well. The wind accelerates and I swim out from the raft to recover a piece of lumber that has gone overboard. The swimming is easy. I go out only twenty feet—any farther and I'll lose the raft in the white mist—and return. I pull myself up on the deck and shout into Alejandro's ear, "I'm going to go under to look at everything to make sure it's OK!"

I dive under the raft and cruise silently through crystal blue sea. There are no signs of life. There is nothing but a blank blue emptiness. The storm is raging just three feet above my head but down below the ocean is completely calm, vacant. The raft seems to be holding up well, better than in the minor storms near Colombia when the sea had been confused.

When I surface and climb aboard it seems as though there's nothing to do. We've been tying and retying everything down for eight hours now. Neverthe-less, I don't want the men to be idle, so I tell them that we'll tie some stays to the hut to keep it from being blown flat.

We work our way to the back of the raft. We're climbing across the port side and the wind is blasting the raft. We start and stop, moving slowly, hand over hand. Our backs are to the wind now. The wind blast sounds like a wall of radio static. The spray needles us; the drops are solid now. Whether or not it is raining, I cannot tell. There is nothing but horizontal motion. All is wind.

Cesar is smiling; he has a lot of Cameron in him—a very strong sense of "The Game." I drop over the side. He follows me with a big grin on his face. Alejandro is still alarmed, but by now I know him: He is a person who becomes nervous in a dangerous situation, but he never breaks down into panic or indecision. The wind is flattening out his face. His entire head is wavering back and forth like that of an old man.

We retie the stays of the hut. Cesar and I are in the water and Alejandro is on the deck, feeding us line. Martin is behind him, braced against the wall of the hut, trying to keep the camera rig steady. He goes back into the hut to work on the camera; he's having trouble with it. As soon as we're finished working on the port side, I come aboard and tell Alejandro and Cesar that we'll do the same to the starboard. We step down off of the deck, onto the balsa logs, and wade across the sunken stern. We are trying to reach the other side of the raft. We are methodically placing our bare feet on each log, like stepping from rock to rock in a raging river. Masses of ocean are surging in on us, swirling around our waists and trying to suck us out. The static noise of the wind is blasting in our ears. We are three bearded men, dressed in rags, clinging to the back of a little bamboo hut, awash in a white, foamy sea.

There is heavy flooding inside the hut now. Masses of deep blue seawater surge in through the bamboo walls. The seawater fouls everything. There is no way to stop the ocean; there is simply too much of it.

After three hours of growling, the wind begins to decelerate. In a thirty-minute period, it goes from storm to bluster. The fighting has exhausted us. Men stumble in and out of the hut; their faces hang. All is well for the time being. In a quiet voice, Martin says to me, "We did pretty damn good today."

When the sun came up on the fourteenth of February, it was good sailing weather. We had a light breeze and moderate seas. We surveyed the damage and found that it was minimal. The only parts of the raft that had come apart were the lashings that connected the outermost logs. The mast stays had been attached to these outer logs, and the wind's force had exerted such a vertical strain that they had almost parted from the raft. The extra reinforcement that we had put in back in Colombia had been just enough to hold them. But this foretold a greater problem: The rope rot was advancing rapidly.

We sailed throughout the day, even though we were partly submerged. The Colombians dutifully went back to work repairing the deck. As night approached, the wind and seas increased again. We still held out hope of sailing out of the top of The Gyre, and into the main current to Hawaii.

18 February 1999

Night after night we are hit by storms. Waves inside the hut so big that men are floating away. Chances are ebbing away. Raft sinking. 16th and 17th we put all floating objects under the raft. Noises inside the hut at night are incredible. All surrounded by sharks, and sharks are larger. Storms at night are destroying deck. Deck on port side is gone. We all have severe saltwater rash. We reach Lat. 5°53' North, Long. 87"46 West . . . wind dies completely—raft drifting back into Gyre. Martin weakening. Cesar and Alejandro have the "thousand mile stare." All heroic.

I will fight, but inside, I am beyond anything. My God, my poor wife.

The wind died in the afternoon of the eighteenth, and we began to drift once again. The *Manteño* Expedition had been in the field for over thirty weeks now, and the four of us had been at sea for forty-nine days. At night, in the vast blackness, we picked up an American radio station broadcasting on short-wave. In between the newscasts came a song of no importance—except that it was from our former life in the modern world. Had I been at home I would have passed over it without a second thought, but out there, lost in the vacuum, it was pure honey. Inside the hut, Martin and I sat in the dark, motionless, not saying a word, not wanting to interfere with one second of that short musical remembrance of home. It made me feel as though my body was floating. It sounded so good, like seeing someone you love come back from the dead for just a few minutes. I remember each change of key being like that of a symphony. I remember thinking of the genius of American rock and roll. When it was over, we were so let down. I know that I was, and I didn't want to look at Martin, there in the dark.

19 February 1999

Now, inside the hut it is wet all the time. It is true: I am tired and miserable; but, I have 30–40 days left in me. Why not make this my finest hours (sic).

More and more the starboard quarter is going down. We have three pontoons under it, and it is still under water.

We lived *in* the ocean, rather than above it. We worked in seawater up to our knees while small waves brought sharks on deck. There were hundreds of them, and they loved to rub their bellies on the balsa logs. It was a bizarre phenomenon. The sharks would come cruising in, their scraggly teeth sticking out of their mouths, and then turn sharply at the logs to rub the white underside of their bodies. Catching them with our bare hands was quite easy now. As they'd come by we'd lift them out of the water by the tale fin. They'd wiggle and squirm so violently in our hands that our bodies would turn to rubber, wobbling in ten directions. Then we'd throw them away from the raft. They'd scurry away for a few minutes, then come back. There were so many hundreds of them that the waters around the raft now seemed to squirm with gray bodies.

At noon on the nineteenth, Alejandro pointed to the horizon, off the starboard beam. "Cocos Island," he said, and then was silent. We couldn't actually make out any land, just the jagged silver outline of a mountain, glimmering faintly on the horizon. It was more than twenty miles away. We stood and looked out across the vast Pacific Ocean. It wouldn't have mattered if the island had been two miles away or two hundred yards away, we couldn't move so much as a hundred feet without wind. We stared blankly, hopelessly. Our mouths hung open, making us look hungry, tired, despondent. We just stood, looking at a faint outline of land, not saying a word.

20 February 1999
After 50 days of drift to the east—this day we drift to the west—away from
Isla del Coco. Drift away from Isla del Coco.

On the twentieth, shortly after breakfast, we disassembled the raft. We had to get rid of any and all excess weight, and quickly. The raft had become an airship. The only way to gain altitude in a balloon is to release ballast, and so it was with us. Every piece of nonessential gear had to be thrown overboard so that our ship would float higher.

There was no break between the ocean and the deck now, the water's surface simply continued unabated across the raft. It was as though we were going through life in a shallow pool of water. All daily actions—walking, working, cooking—could only be accomplished by an enormous amount of sloshing and splashing. It was extremely hot, and the air was still. We had worked in the saltwater for days and were never dry. The saltwater sores on our feet split open, widened, deepened, and burned. At that point the main thing was to get our legs up out of the water.

As hard as it was for me to part with it, the library had to go. Alejandro knew what was biodegradable and what was not. If it was biodegradable, then it was committed to the sea; if it wasn't, then it would be burned. Alejandro handed books to me, and I threw them out the window. *The Last Days of Socrates; We; The Navigators; The Raft Book; Cosmos; The Perfect Storm;* and fifteen to twenty others all went over. The only ones we saved were those having to do with Central America. We already knew that if we didn't make it out of The Gyre, we'd probably end up somewhere in Central America.

We stored all of the small items, like diving gear, personal belongings, and tools, in the blue barrels, and then threw the walls of the hut over the side, sometimes one bamboo cane at a time and sometimes by cutting out whole sections and hurling them into the ocean. Cutting and untying the hundreds of tiny knots that held the little bamboo hut together took most of the day. When we were finished with the walls, the roof went over. We kept the hut's frame and floor though; they were made of sturdy, whole canes, and would be needed for a new structure. Debris from the raft now rested on the surface of the sea in a milewide circle around us, making it look as though we had exploded.

The wooden storage boxes went over next. We put a message-in-a-bottle in one of them, saying that they were from the good ship *Manteño II,* and that we had been trapped in The Gyre for fifty days now. We did this because we feared that if a boat happened upon the debris, a captain might assume that a ship had broken up in the area, and set in motion all those things that accompany such a terrible event. The storage boxes drifted away from the raft, floating well, like small boats.

On the second-floor platform, where the hut had been, we set up Martin's yellow tent, which we had kept since leaving Colombia seven weeks ago, and then passed the night in total peace.

On the morning of the twenty-first, we disassembled the hut's second floor. This elevated platform, which of course had been the sleeping compartment, had been built on top of six, very small balsa logs. These were now forced under the raft so that they could work as fresh pontoons. Slowly, the raft was coming up; it was working.

On the deck, there was no longer any sign of a shelter. The raft now looked like a simple, wooden platform. The deck stretched, unbroken, for fifty feet. The feeling of wide open space was immense. We stood on the ocean and looked in all directions at a flat, mirrorlike surface. As far as the eye could see there was stillness, nothingness—no mountains in the distance, no trees, no waves, no boats, no motion of any kind whatsoever—a vacuum extending in every direction to every horizon. We were the loneliest people on earth—four, haggard, weakened men, marooned on an island measuring sixty-one feet by twenty feet; an island that had never existed on a nautical chart.

For the rest of the twenty-first and twenty-second we worked on lightening the load. At around 10:00 p.m. on the night of the twenty-second, it began to blow. By 2:00 a.m. the sea had become stirred up and waves broke over the deck until dawn.

In the morning, we searched for the diving equipment and realized that it had been swept overboard in the dark. The fins, snorkels, and most importantly, the masks, were gone. Working under the raft, where hundreds of lashings held our ship together, would now have to be done blindly. This would require diving under the raft and feeling around in a hundred different places for one small tear in one rope. This was highly impractical. Now that the masks were gone there was simply no way of knowing if our vessel was seaworthy. A main lashing could break and we wouldn't know it until the raft split in half. If that happened in the middle of the night, or in heavy weather, the giant raft would become a forty-thousand-pound vise, much like a nutcracker, opening and closing at random.

During the day of the twenty-third, we built a platform on stilts, five feet off the deck, to sleep on. It was a skeleton structure that Cesar devised and built. It stood on six bamboo legs and had only one wall. It was immediately nicknamed "The Birdhouse."

25 February 1999
Alejandro is greatly affected by the loss of the scuba eq. I am weakening. We are going back into The Gyre. All weakening. Mizzen stays break— ropes rotting. Everything wet and rotting.

The rope rot was becoming serious. Mold, which grows only in fresh water, causes rot in manila rope. During our two-month stay in Colombia, the raft's ropes had been soaked by more than 150 inches of rain. We had been on the open sea for two months now and the intense heat of The Gyre had incubated the mold until it was in full bloom. We had run out of synthetic rope to reinforce or replace the rotting manila, and the manila was the only thing holding the raft together. Now, even just small amounts of strain caused the manila rope to break.

On the twenty-third, the rope holding the main crossbeam finally gave out. I had to use a twenty-foot length of the nylon anchor line to tie it back in place. Two days later we found that the stay for the mizzenmast on the starboard quarter had rotted completely through. We checked the other three stays that held up the mizzenmast and found that they were all on the verge of breaking. That really scared me. The mizzenmast would have fallen within the next twenty-four hours, maybe sooner if we had had heavy weather. Our little skeleton of a shelter was five feet from the mast. If a nine-hundred-pound pole fell on the Birdhouse it would probably cause a fatality.

I tried not to show alarm; nevertheless, I worked frantically to splice the lines. I demonstrated splicing to Cesar, and he completed one of the stays himself. He was a natural mariner, with a good feeling for the work and the lifestyle.

On March 1, Martin and I, using the leftovers from our library, began searching our maps of Costa Rica for a place to build a new vessel. We had a couple of travel books, a motley assortment of land maps and nautical charts, and our hard-won knowledge.

1 March 1999
We are moving back into The Gyre again. Our course is 140 deg. (South west). There is no wind. I am getting along better with Martin.

For a week or so I had developed a strange rapport with Martin. He sensed my despair, about The Expedition, and about missing my former life, before I had become marooned. I had been in the field for seven months without any rest and I missed my life, missed my wife, missed literature, music, and good food. We spent several mornings just talking. He listened intently, acting as though what I had to say was interesting, although I knew it was not. I didn't care. I wanted to talk about books and my life with Annie. In this way, Martin, once again, demonstrated his complexity. He had become a childlike figure during the early days of the voyage. I had to constantly scold, prod, motivate, and care for him, like one might have to do for an irresponsible, pubescent boy. Yet, during this period, he deftly reached out to me, trying to help me emotionally. The Colombians sensed it, too. They made no effort to interfere or ask about the plans for that day.

We sat in silence sometimes, all four of us, at the edge of our open-air shelter, and just thought. We just stared, stupefied for moments at a time by a vast pool of water: The Gyre. It was not a bad place; on the contrary, The Gyre burst with beauty. But you couldn't escape. You were allowed to enter there, but you would never get out. You would eventually wither, and then disappear into it.

The Birdhouse stood between the two masts, if either one fell, the crew in the hut would take the majority or all of the blow. I was ready to take on all hardships and struggle to the end, but the idea of an accident with those colossal masts was just too much. It would mean a fatality for sure. My understanding of the problems of primitive raft building, and voyaging on the high seas aboard those vessels, had finally evolved a little. I knew what we could survive and what we could not. We had finally reached the farthest extreme of our rope supply, too. I had been worried about this problem for years. Whenever I had prepared to go to sea aboard a raft I had uniformly made all of my decisions in favor of having an ample supply of rope. Each time we went out I had always spent our last dollars on more rope—even at the expense of having adequate anchors. But now, finally, we had run out. Rope held the raft together; there were scores and scores of lines, and hundreds of knots. Now that it was all giving out, I was forced to contemplate, each morning when I awoke: *Maybe she will disintegrate under the strain today, maybe not.*

On the third, fourth, and fifth of March, I made contact on the shortwave radio with Annie, back in the United States. As usual, there was an immense surge of energy from her. She immediately appealed to the Costa Rican government on behalf of The *Manteño* Expedition, working the phones day and night to save us. Even though we were far outside their territorial waters, they agreed to evacuate us. On the fifth, in the afternoon, I began calling the Costa Rican naval base at Golfito. When I made contact, the radioman on duty told me to stand by for the *comandante*. I heard him come on the frequency, and then he asked: "What is your situation?"

"We can hold out for a while, but we are definitely sinking."

"We want to come right now," he said.

"All right. All right. OK." I hesitated for a moment. We would never escape The Gyre, and we were as close to land as we would ever be. "OK," I said. "We'll go now."

"We can make your position in fifteen hours."

"Roger that. I'll fire aerial flares to help guide you in."

I hung up the radio receiver and simply began to give orders. It was all very automated. I was being carried along, as was the group, by linear logic rather than human thought. For the next twelve hours we suspended freedom of choice and simply did the next thing in a row of obvious actions: Pack your personal gear, then pack the community gear, then disassemble the raft, and on and on . . .

We gathered together our charts and logs first and slipped them into ziplock bags. Next we stuffed our personal possessions, what little there were left, into duffel bags. It was a typical afternoon in The Gyre and we worked methodically. The sea around us was calm, and the raft, as it had for over two months now, sat quietly in a vast pool of water. I knew that we had a long night of work before us, and that as soon as we had finished packing we would have to strip the raft. Many of the ship's woods and ropes were too valuable to be lost, and we would take them with us when we left The Gyre. After the raft was picked clean of anything useful, we would partially dismantle *Manteño II*—remove everything except the last layer—the logs and the main lashings—so that in the morning when the Costa Ricans arrived we would be able to finish the raft off completely. I didn't want *Manteño II* to remain intact and be a hazard to other boats.

Out on the horizon, the sun began to set. It would take all night to be ready when they arrived at dawn, so Alejandro collected everything that could be burned and prepared a fire. He set down a large piece of tin foil on the foredeck and then stacked paper and cardboard and plastic on it. After a few tries, the pile ignited, and long, slender orange-and-yellow flames began to lick the black air. The fire cast an unreal light on everything, but it was enough to see the length of the raft—enough for us to work—enough for us "to get on with it." And so we worked like trolls in a mine, with the air around us warm and still. Hours passed and there were no sounds around us but our own labor, pulling, hauling, loading—chopping solid thumps with our blades and the raft answering with the sounds of wood fibers fracturing and splintering. Around midnight, we cut down our tall blond masts. We sliced open the ropes and stays that held them erect and they fell like beautiful trees that had been cut down in malice. We stood, watching in silence as they fell, staring blankly, our faces reflecting the orange flame, our features elongated by long black shadows. We had no audience, not even waves or wind; we floated alone in a silent pool of water. And in the flickering orange light, with each step of destruction, we stopped for a moment and looked at each other blankly, asking, without saying a word: "Should we do this? Are we really going to go through with this? Completely? This can't be happening. This raft is the only thing we have in the world."

As the destruction deepened, we became more automated. Something in us turned off. Martin said later that it was "all very disturbing." Indeed. The smoke coming off the plastic fire was so thick that you could not see through it, and more than that, it was as black as the night around it. As a cloud of it passed a person, that person would disappear, or parts of their body would disappear, leaving only a head or an arm floating weightlessly against a black backdrop. We were all hacking at the lines, our hands filled with satanic instruments of destruction: axes, hatchets, machetes. We were in an immense place, a vast ocean, and yet there was no wind, no waves, nothing but an infinite silent surface and the hollow thumps and chops of four men toiling in the darkness—*thump, thump, thump, thump.* It was the end of an ancient ship, adrift and afire on a shining plate of calm water, the final end of a singular platform, floating in dark stillness, lit by a flickering orange flame and accentuated by Alejandro Martinez, a soft-spoken man with black eyes, speaking in muffled Spanish phrases, his body lit up by an intense orange light, disappearing and then reappearing, silently suspended in space, disembodied, robotically chopping, dismembering "our mother."

11

The Ritz

I cannot possibly estimate how many of the Manteño disappeared into The Gyre. Those few who escaped it probably brought back legends of a place, just over the horizon, where slow death was eternally waiting. But we did not disappear there, thanks to the ham radio operators, Annie Biggs, and the Costa Rican coast guard, and as the dawn slowly came, we waited for the Costa Ricans—the *Ticos*.

The four of us stood on the skeleton of *Manteño II* in the gray light, wearing our orange life jackets, looking haggard but well-organized. We hadn't slept during the night and we hadn't felt like it either. We had watched the sun come up, waiting for our scheduled radio contact. As the light grew, we crowded around a blue barrel that stood in the center of the skeleton raft and waited patiently, saying little. On top of the barrel lay our radio, a car battery, and an antenna. Next to the raft, the dinghy was tied up and resting quietly on the flat water. As was always the case in The Gyre, we were surrounded by thousands of square miles of perfect, open, stillness, a vast plain where nothing moved.

About ten minutes after first light, Cesar took the wires of the radio in his hands and pressed them onto the terminals of the battery, and Martin, his electric headlamp still hanging from his forehead, stretched his arm into the air, holding the little metal antenna as high as possible. "Coast Guard of Costa Rica," I called, "Coast Guard of Costa Rica: Here is the raft *Manteño,* over-"

A distant, distorted voice yelled through the static, talking rapidly, excited at finding us and eager to make contact. It was definitely the Ticos. I told Martin to fire an aerial flare, which he did, and they said that they had seen it. Then, from over the horizon, there came a guttural roar. A small gray point, like an arrowhead, grew on the distant plain of the ocean. Its powerful diesels rumbled and it spit out a steady stream of wake water. It was a gray warship, about fifty feet long, and as it closed in on us we could make out the red, white, and blue flag of Costa Rica waving over it.

Punta Burica came up, cut power, and cruised the last one hundred feet at dead slow. It was a Vietnam-era gunboat with twin engines that growled and belched black smoke, and a crew of five sailors, who stood at the railing, staring at the remains of *Manteño II*. The gunboat stopped fifty feet away, and we launched the dinghy, the four of us sitting on the hard rubber sides and paddling across the ocean like paddling across a pond. Gliding up to the back of *Punta Burica,* I reached up to the ladder and climbed up at the stern, and then walked across the hard, unbending metal deck to shake hands with Captain Aristede Moya. "Thank you for coming so far out," I said to him.

"No problem," he said. "There's no problem at all."

Captain Moya was a curly haired man in his midforties. He wore a simple white-and-blue uniform, which made him look more like a policeman than a military man. His crew admired him and liked sailing with him. He told me once: "I was sad that I didn't see your raft under sail. Ships like that are schools. I would like to sail on one someday. They are great schools."

We transferred over to *Punta Burica* all of the equipment that still remained after ten weeks of drifting. Then Captain Moya told me to cut the lashings of the raft, so that the logs would drift apart. A singular log drifting in The Gyre would present no more of an obstacle than any other large piece of debris—of which there were many, but an entire raft could cause damage if struck by a small vessel. We had already prepared for this final destruction, but it was hard for all of us when Captain Moya gave the order.

I stood on the tarred balsa logs for the last time and chopped the main lashings. Alejandro, Cesar, and Martin, already aboard the *Punta Burica,* stood at the railing of the gunboat and stared mournfully. The logs slowly separated and drifted away, and when the last line parted, I dropped into the water and silently breaststroked to the ladder on the stern of the *Punta Burica.* Climbing aboard, I stood on the gunboat's quarterdeck with seawater pouring off of me and splashing at my feet, and signaled, with a wave of my hand, "the end" to Captain Moya. He turned to the bridge, opened the throttle, and we pulled away. The ocean was like glass, so the skipper ran his boat wide-open. *Punta Burica* cruised at eighteen knots, smoothly skimming across the open sea.

.   .   .

I lay on the quarterdeck of *Punta Burica,* exhausted from nine weeks of fighting the ocean, and slept like a dead man. Alejandro awakened me at 11:00
p.m. to tell me that we had entered a narrow gulf. It was Gulfo Dulce, a long
thin waterway, much like the tropical fjord that led to Bahia Solano, back in
Colombia. After cruising for about an hour and a half, we turned into a narrow
channel, no more than two hundred yards across. *Punta Burica* slowed down
until it was creeping along in the darkness at five miles an hour. The engines
growled for another twenty minutes and then we realized we were entering a
jungle port of some sort. Emerging from the channel, we cruised into a bay,
several miles wide, with a modern steel wharf, large enough to service big
ships.

   Punta Burica came alongside the wharf in the dark and the sailors tied up
their vessel while we stood on the foredeck, still wearing our life jackets. The
press was waiting for us and we answered questions while cameras flashed in
our faces. A stooped man in his fifties, wearing an immaculate military uniform, stood among the press, and when I climbed up to stand on the wharf,
he reached forward and shook my hand. "We have been very worried about
you," he said. "*Sí. Sí. Sí.* Very, *very* worried." This was the *comandante,* Major
Desidrio Chavez, and as soon as we finished our interviews, he took us under
his wing and led us away to be fed and to sleep for the night. In the morning
he said, "I hope you will build your new raft here—*Sí. Sí. Sí.*—in Golfito."

   The Port of Golfito lay on the Osa Penninsula at the southern end of Costa
Rica. It stood precariously at the edge of a small bay, with its back to the water and with the jungle crowding around its perimeter. The Standard Fruit
Company owned and ran the town up until the early eighties when technology, Communist revolution, and just plain necessity converged to make
the situation intolerable. Then Standard Fruit packed up and left. They had
brought the railroad here, and the hospital, and the deep-water pier, and
everything else. But they left the whole thing behind like a mob of refugee gi-
ants. Now Golfito was the abandoned playground of a colossal eight-year-old
boy: Locomotives, railroad cars, and unused track were scattered randomly
throughout the area as if thrown through the air. Some locomotives lay on their
sides, some were still on the rails ready to go, and some were off in some other
part of town where there was no sign of the railroad whatever.

   The town possessed many attributes that would make it a good work site,
but Alejandro and I scouted other parts of the country for about a week after
landing. We eventually realized that for various reasons Golfito represented the

only place to build the new raft: It was the sole place where we could get balsa logs, and easily set up a base. More than that, we were somewhat marooned, broke, desperate, and when Major Chavez offered his help, we gladly took it.

After The Gyre, my "strange dual relationship" with Heyerdahl, Alsar, and others, began to come to a close. I knew how a balsa raft worked now, and so much of the mystery of those previous voyages vanished. If the balsa logs could be dried and then coated with tar they could survive hundreds of days on the open sea. But you had to do both. The tar would slow the *Teredo navalis* down, but eventually they would begin to eat the wood. With logs of dry, corklike balsawood, they'd have to eat a tremendous amount to make the raft unseaworthy. This all sounds very elementary, even obvious, but for fifty years people had believed otherwise. Based on our research, this was the only way the Manteño could have possibly done it.

The Manteño, living in ancient Ecuador, had access to tar pits, but connecting the tar pits to the rafts was difficult. The Spanish conquistadors, writing in their chronicles, mentioned briefly that they themselves used this tar to coat their own ships, but none had ever said that the Manteño used it on their balsa logs, and of the many illustrations of ancient balsa rafts, none ever appeared with black logs. This tiny distinction, this tiny gap in the historical record, created a massive problem for researchers. In the highly disciplined world of archaeology, assuming that they *must* have used it on their logs— jumping that tiny gap without any proof—was not allowed. Some archaeologists had written that the people of the Santa Elena Peninsula were indeed using tar in ancient times, but these writings revolved around tar's domestic uses. Before anyone could claim that the Manteño used it on their logs they needed either physical evidence, or a written record. All of the great balsa rafts had disappeared, so physical evidence was nonexistent, and the ancient Manteño left behind no written language. Without any raft voyagers around in the modern era, researchers had never known that the greatest threat to the ancient Manteño was the *Teredo navalis,* and that the only solution was tar.

But without a written record or physical evidence, I cannot jump the gap or make the connection either. I can, however, present the results of my research in the hope that it might help to narrow this gap: The large, ocean-going rafts were only practical if they had tar on them. It was a one-to-one, symbiotic relationship. This bold statement must, unfortunately, be supported by its negative: If the Manteño *didn't* use tar to protect their logs, then every raft that attempted a long voyage would sink! Like Heyerdahl and Alsar—and me—those ancient mariners probably passed through an evolution in thinking, where in the end they were willing to smear anything on their logs to prevent themselves from sinking, and the most handy substance, then as now, was naturally occurring tar. One of the great ironies of our years of research into the balsa raft was that Heyerdahl and Alsar probably *did* use the most authentic methods—they just *didn't know it at the time:* They dried their logs, and painted tar on them. They didn't pollute their experiments at all, they survived their great voyages because they used the seafaring technology of a culture of commercial mariners, the ancient Manteño.

Unfortunately, I cannot shed any light on exactly what Heyerdahl knew or didn't know. But because we had been misled by Heyerdahl, we assumed that Alsar was trying to cover up the raft's vulnerability to the *Teredo navalis* as well. He wasn't. His book had definitely stated that *Pacifica* got the shipworm, but *the translation had been wrong.* Unfortunately, we discovered this only after acquiring the original text. Again, why Heyerdahl claimed that rafts never got this problem, even though Alsar had gone on record as saying they did, is a mystery. Heyerdahl had been a colossus in his time, and now, in this era, with his life drawing to a close, he may have been unwilling to be completely frank with a stranger. The question of what Thor Heyerdahl knew, and many other questions like it, died with the giant in April of 2002.

But ironically, after The Gyre, Heyerdahl and Alsar no longer mattered! This was the most important step in my education: It was clear now that we were dealing with the genuine, day-to-day problems of the ancient Manteño, not the problems of Heyerdahl's theories. During Heyerdahl's and Alsar's expeditions, their rafts had been towed out to the Humboldt Current, and then had sailed for months on the vast Pacific. *But this wasn't the original environment of the* Manteño *sailing raft!* In the Humboldt Current, and later on the open Pacific, those rafts rarely sat in calm water—the type of environment necessary for *Teredo navalis.* By the time those previous rafts developed a serious infection they were probably well on their way to crossing the ocean. Actually, the voyage across the ocean could be accomplished *without* the use of tar! But not the trading voyage up the coast of Central America. In those waters, the *Teredo Navalis* would attack the raft immediately. You could make it to Polynesia without dry logs or the use of tar, but *never* to Acapulco. The environment was completely different—it involved frequent calms and warm water. We now knew that when the raft was sailed in its home waters, it would contract the *Teredo Navalis* every time, and that it would contract it early. This was the fruit of experimental archaeology: discovering the problems that the ancients would have to cope with to survive.

For any culture to become a great maritime power in the waters off ancient South America it would have to first cope with the *Teredo navalis*. The Manteño had been ideally equipped to deal with this environment. In their land, balsa trees grew in abundance nearby, and could be easily moved to the shoreline by using the river system and the tides. Once the logs were on the beach, they could be easily cured. The climate in the area was ideal. Drying out the balsa logs would require the logs to sit on land for a long time. In the steamy interior of Ecuador, where the balsa trees grew, this would be next to impossible. These steamy conditions produce ravenous termites that would attack the logs the moment they were felled. These termites are legendary and they can reduce gigantic logs to powder in just a few weeks. But on the Santa Elena Peninsula it was hot and dry, and as we had accidentally found out during The *Illa-Tiki* Expedition, putting the logs up on supports out on the scalding beach of Salango eliminated the obstacle of termites. Once the logs were dried to a point of maximum buoyancy, the nearby tar pits would produce the protective coating necessary to enhance their resistance to the *Teredo navalis*. Nowhere else on the western coast of South America did these three factors exist in one area, and it was the *relationship* between these key elements that was so critical: This relationship, available only to the Manteño, was the key to the balsa raft's evolution as an ocean-going freighter. The Santa Elena Peninsula, home of the Manteño, was the nexus of the most ideal conditions for creating a vessel that could carry tons of freight for hundreds of miles, and yet survive the *Teredo navalis*.

We had learned many, many other things about the raft as well, and finally, I was beginning to see an ancient vessel that wasn't a mystery—not at all a thing produced by a primitive people but a product of remarkable ingenuity, of sophisticated prowess, and of necessity: It was clearly the best ship for carrying the precious *Spondylus*.

Ten days after landing, we decided to set up operations in Golfito. For housing, the University of Costa Rica allowed us to take over an abandoned building that had once acted as a makeshift dorm. Sitting at the waterfront, our new home had the looks and personality of a typical army barrack of the 1940s: wooden, green, and with screen windows and a corrugated tin roof. Upon receiving permission from the university, we carried our aging equipment, our bits of rope and what food we had left, from the Coast Guard base, down a long back road to the abandoned building, and set up our new base of operations.

The barrack was divided into four rooms. The front room served as our planning room, where we met daily to design the raft and plan the voyage. There were some men who built furniture in a warehouse nearby, and one day they showed up with a dining table and chairs for our new home, which we put in the planning room. In a short while, books, CDs, axes, machetes, gasoline barrels and blocks of tar, charts of the sea and coast, sailing magazines, and pictures of girlfriends and wives completed our planning area. We set up our cooking equipment in the next room and dubbed it "the kitchen." Elsewhere in the old building we had a shower, toilet, and closet space. The mosquito screens and window shutters were falling off the decrepit structure, and its walls and doors were filled with termites, but after the hell of Camp Hardcore it was four-star all the way, and a very special place for us, one that had a special significance: When Ernest Shackleton's ship *Endurance* had been caught in the crushing ice flows of Antarctica, he had told "the boys" that they'd just spend the winter with the ship—nothing to it—just like home. In the bowels of the ship, these marooned mariners set up a game room, a beer hall, and a kind of Vaudevillian Theater in a room that they called "The Ritz." I couldn't help but see the parallels: We were in Costa Rica, alone, bankrupt, and with a bad reputation. We had had three rafts sink out from under us, and once again we were building a primitive ship "to get home." Shackleton retreated into the hold of his ship and thrived—we built our "Ritz" in the blazing heat of southern Costa Rica, and there, somehow, we rallied.

From the front door of The Ritz it was a one-hundred-foot walk to the tiny bay of Golfito. At night, the tropical frogs, numbering in the thousands, creaked and swallowed so loudly that we had to shout to each other to be heard over the racket. Perhaps the most bizarre thing about The Ritz were the coconut attacks. Coconut trees, whose branches hung over the roof of the building, surrounded the barracks. Every few days one of the trees would shed its heavy, milk-filled fruit. On the twenty-foot drop, the coconut would pick up the necessary speed to explode violently on the roof of the barrack, scaring the hell out of everyone in the building, gringos *and* Ticos. It was a swell feature of our new home. It was the most hollow, metallic sound you have ever heard, like clubbing the side of an airplane hanger with a sledgehammer. A person would be just at the edge of falling asleep, just about to drift off into a dream in the middle of the night, and then: BOOM! We never got used to it. You'd think the Ticos would be used to it, but they weren't. When one of those blasted things would suddenly explode out of nowhere, everyone in the room would jump a foot, scaring the hell out each other as well. Later on, when some of the townspeople came to kindly visit us, we'd have a coconut explosion. They'd be standing in the front room of The Ritz and then—WHAM! It was top-notch entertainment.

Early on the morning of the second day we were there, we saw a haggard old man come by to use the outdoor faucet as a shower. The next day, when he discovered that the building was occupied, he scurried off like a frightened squirrel. After a few days he figured out that we didn't consider the building to be ours, and that we considered him harmless. After a week or so, when The Ritz opened for business, we realized that we'd have to have security, and it seemed natural to hire the old man who used the faucet. We were going to have people all over the city, province, and country, and at all hours of the day and night. Somebody would have to stay behind, and the old man seemed perfect. His name was Miguel—to guard The Ritz we hired Mike, the pirate.

He went to tears when we offered him the job. We'd give him a little money and all he had to do was sleep at The Ritz during the day. A few days later, things started disappearing. One morning after this started, Alejandro and I walked to the worksite while Cesar sat on the seawall, out of sight, and watched the master at work. Miguel would make sure the coast was clear, and then take a hammer or a shovel and put it in the bushes. He then came back at night, evidently, and removed it. When Cesar asked him about it he flew into a rage, so that afternoon, Cesar, wearing an enormous grin, explained to me that an international spy had infiltrated The *Manteño* Expedition. He saluted smartly and said, "*Capitan!* We have been infiltrated by a double agent! Miguel—Secret Agent 007—he moves like a cat!"

As soon as I could stop laughing, I said, "Come on, let's go over to his lair."

"I don't know if that will do any good," Cesar said, maintaining his ridiculous salute, "he's probably already taken off in his jet pack!"

Miguel lived in a railroad passenger car built in the twenties. It was yellow, rusted, and overgrown by the field it sat in. On the walk over, Cesar sang the theme to *Mission Impossible.* When we got to the railroad car, nobody was home, but merchandise stolen from the yards and patios of houses in the area was strewn all around the inside of the car. He was an incredibly efficient thief, and that really got us going and we laughed so hard our faces turned red. When he caught his breath, Alejandro blurted out, "We hired a rat to guard the cheese!"

Near the door of the car, five or six plastic cards, held together by a rubber band, lay on a rusted metal table. Alejandro picked up the banded pack and looked at the top card, then said: "Its Miguel's ID—oh, my God—we are so stupid. Look at this guy, he's got a face like a fist."

Cesar looked at the ID, then said, in a mixture of irony and hilarity, "What a pirate—Miguel the pirate—how ridiculous."

We took his ID over to the police, not because we wished the man any harm, but because he was such an efficient thief, and was in the process of cleaning out the entire neighborhood. The police weren't willing to take Miguel seriously and neither were we. We warned the neighbors, and that was the end of it.

At night, in The Ritz, we began to plan our new raft. Martin had gone to the United States to talk to the film company that employed him, but would soon return. Alejandro, Cesar, and I began by sitting down to have a serious discussion about the upcoming dangers. Sitting in The Ritz, I told the Colombians that we'd have to build an entirely new vessel and sail it out of Costa Rica. Storm season was coming and we'd most likely face more of what we had seen in The Gyre, and worse.

As for me, I had been in the field for nine months now without rest. It was the sixth year of The Expeditions, and my mentality had changed. I was no longer on a trip away from home, no longer "out of town," no longer "just out of the country for a while"; The Expedition was my home now. I no longer felt the effects of my way of life in modern America. That previous life came to me only in brief flashes, or memories, or daydreams. I no longer thought in English, the language I had grown up with. The Spaniards had said that the Manteño's language was like Arabic, and though I did not speak the language of the ancient Manteño, I did think in the language of their descendents, and especially in the language of the raft: How much rope, how much lumber, how much tar, how much food, how much water, how many *wancas,* how many *guaras,* how to build the hut, how to launch the completed raft, the state of the logs, the state of the men, and on and on.

First, we needed balsa logs. Balsa trees are exceedingly abundant in tropical South or Central America, and are frequently seen growing by the side of the road. They grow in bunches, or "stands," in any well-lit, open space. A single balsa tree is hard to find; where there is one there are usually ten to fifteen to as many as fifty in one place. The exporting companies grow them on huge farms, hundreds at a time, lined up in rows like corn. And they grow incredibly fast. From a seed that is only a few millimeters in size, they expand to a forty-foot, eight-thousand-pound mass in just forty-eight months. It is not uncommon for a balsa tree to grow to ninety feet in just seven years, and a three foot-thick balsa tree may be only twelve years old.

The first phone calls I had made on behalf of The Expedition, back in 1993, had been to find out about the consequences of cutting down balsa trees. I called all over the country, contacting universities and environmental groups, asking about the coming destruction of my nine balsa trees. According to them I was an idiot, and would I please never call again about such an idiotic subject. Some wouldn't even return my calls. One scientist was patient enough to tell me that: ". . . balsa isn't a rain forest species, it is not an endangered species, it is not anything. And besides that, nine trees doesn't amount to deforestation, my friend."

"Oh," I said, acting for a moment as though I felt silly, but I didn't really: it seemed like a perfectly legitimate thing to worry about. Now, six years later, it was still on my mind. I was sick to death of cutting down balsa trees. I had developed a strange sentiment toward them. They reminded me of the cottonwoods of my youth, and I must have appeared a fool to many, stopping by the side of the road to admire a "weed."

As our planning continued, Martin returned from the United States. The film company had abandoned us, he said. They didn't like me, he said. The expedition was simply too dangerous, he said. They felt like they could no longer risk it, he said. He went on in the type of grim tale that only he could tell. I couldn't determine how much of his story was truth, exaggeration, or outright lie. Regardless of what was truth or fabrication, Martin would continue, whether supported by the company or not. If he could finish the documentary, he would possess credentials that few others could claim.

A couple of weeks later, in early April, the four of us boarded a *fibra* at the pier in Golfito, and prepared to acquire the balsa needed for a new raft. We wore ragged clothing, old hats, minimal shoes, and carried with us 250 pounds of rope, various machetes, tools, *wancas,* and some small provisions. Major Chavez knew a rancher on the other side of the gulf who had a large balsa stand on his property, and we were now headed that way. Our *fibra* crossed the gulf to the town of Puerto Jiménez, about a thirty-minute trip, and when it landed we ran a mile to the road, boarded the chicken bus as it was passing, and went into the country. We moved fast, slept none, fought mosquitoes and heat exhaustion, and managed to put eleven balsa logs on a foreign shore within thirty-six hours of landing. We timed our logging operation so that the logs were dragged onto the beach at low tide. When the tide rose, they floated up. We then waded into the waist-deep water, which had no surf, being that it was basically a lagoon, and heaved and pushed and manipulated the giant logs into place. When this was done, we put in the necessary lashings with the heavy ropes, and installed tourniquets at both ends.

At this point I was beginning to see the evolution of our prowess: We were raft mariners: marooned on any shore, we built rafts out of habit. And perhaps

I had changed personally as well: Between the expeditions, back in 1996, 1997, and 1998, I had sometimes spoken publicly in front of groups to whom I was introduced as an "explorer" or "expeditioner" (the latter title I felt was more appropriate). I felt somewhat like a fraud then, having only been on one expedition, but now in these last days a calm came over me: I knew that it was not possible that I could be a fraud.

When a boat showed up the next morning, the provisional raft was taken in tow. We landed back at our base within forty-eight hours of leaving, and ran the logs aground at the sea wall near The Ritz.

Within a few days we secured permission to put the logs ashore at a marshy area, half a mile down, where mangrove bushes grew wild along the waterfront. This would be the construction site for our new raft. When the tide came up in front of The Ritz, we waded out into the muddy water and began pushing the logs down to the marsh. Cesar knew there were crocodiles in the area and he hoped we'd encounter one. Creeping along through the miniature mangrove swamp, the water up to our chins, we pushed the bound logs with our bodies and squished mud between our toes, looking for a swirling movement in the water or the tail of a large reptile. But we found nothing, and Cesar was let down.

After half an hour of pushing, we reached the new construction site. There was an abrupt shelf of earth at the site, a hard-packed earthen shore where the marsh ended and the land began. You could simply take one step up here and be out of the water. A large yellow earthmover was waiting for us there, and we intended to use it to lift the logs up and hang them over the shelf so that their ends extended out over the water. To complete this operation we had to tie a rope to each individual log, then tie the other end of the rope to the earthmover's mechanical arm, so that the straining machine could hoist the floating timbers out of the water. As we began, I told Martin to tie timber hitches on the logs to prevent accidents, but he would not. He persisted in using climbing knots, and within a few minutes a five-thousand-pound log was hoisted into the air and broke free, falling in an exploding splash right in front of Cesar's nose. Martin ignored the incident, but I could not. We had been lucky that day in Salango when a falling balsa log had crushed Manuco. Cesar, who was an exceedingly coolheaded person, continued to work, but with a fearful look of alarm on his face.

If I was the designer of the new raft, then Cesar was most certainly its *jefe*. The new raft mimicked Cesar, just as *Illa-Tiki* had mimicked Enrique. The new raft was short, bulky, stout, tough, and unassuming, just like the man. Like Enrique, strength-in-construction seemed innate in Cesar. He also manifested

Enrique's quiet persevering toil. Each morning Cesar and I walked together from The Ritz to the worksite, down a back road that ran along the very edge of the marsh. At the end of the back road was an abandoned lot, where a couple of pathways led through the tall grass to our work site. Cesar knew that there must be crocodiles living in the marsh, and each day he would take a moment to creep through the mud, looking for a big lizard. His life was a life among reptiles, and one day he emerged from the tangle of mangrove trees with an enormous grin on his face. There, floundering in the mud, was a black crocodile, about six feet in length, with red, laserlike eyes. You would have thought Cesar had discovered the fountain of youth. Each morning and each night throughout the construction of the new raft, he would always take a moment to check up on the life of his giant lizard, creeping around in the mud with a flashlight until he saw its red eyes.

We were building our new raft, essentially, behind the city. The buildings all faced away from us and we worked in isolation. Golfito was sleepy and tranquil and our hidden worksite seemed especially so. We lived alone at The Ritz and had the Ticos to help us. They were as kindhearted as the rest of the coastal peoples had been. Major Chavez came by every day, driving his truck through the tall grass to talk to us and council us on getting various permissions from the government, and whom to ask in town for various favors. The coast guard unit in Golfito, which he commanded, was very much like us: a small outpost of cheerful adventurers. They helped with everything, and many of them befriended us, treating us *como hermanos* ("like brothers"). "*Sí, sí, sí,*" Major Chavez would always say to us, puffing on his cigarette: "*Como hermanos.*"

The first step in construction of the raft, as Enrique had taught me years ago, was to put it up on supports. But we wouldn't be able to use *wancas* to raise the logs because of a manpower shortage. I frequently sent Martin out on errands, and Alejandro spent many days working out our logistical problems, which sometimes left only Cesar and me at the work site. We talked to Major Chavez about our problem, and a few days later he produced the solution: a jack. The problem we faced now was that we could hardly pick it up off of the ground. It was as big as a cabinet and had been fabricated long ago out of pure iron in some great forge in Pennsylvania: It was for jacking up railroad cars. Over a period of five sweltering days, we slowly maneuvered the iron beast around the logs by dragging it, hoisting it, dropping it, tripping over it, hammering it, beating it, cursing it, and finally thanking, with the utmost sincerity, the man who'd loaned it to us. Using just two men, we had raised the fat balsa logs a foot-and-a-half off the ground. We were unable, however, to dig out the sand underneath the raft, as we had in Salango and Camp Hardcore. The new raft, suspended eighteen inches above the earth, now formed a cave with the ground. The ground sloped up on the port side, making it impossible to get in or out on that side. Cesar and I had to enter by crawling under the starboard side, then wiggle and squirm for ten minutes to work our way back into the inner recesses of the cave, where it was dark, confined, and claustrophobic. The gas fumes from the tar overwhelmed us all the time, our throats gagging and our eyes watering, and we frequently had the feeling of being in a very small, collapsing tunnel. There would be no way to get out quickly if the supports did collapse. If we had an accident of the type we had had back in Salango with Manuco, we'd have a disaster.

Throughout March and April of 1999 we worked sixteen hours a day and sometimes more. Each day it was the same routine: In the morning we'd trudge down the back road to our isolated work site, then toil in the sweltering tropical heat, chopping, hacking, pulling, struggling, tightening, and using the *wancas*. Then, in the afternoon, the rain would come and pour down for hours. We'd head back to The Ritz for planning sessions and various work projects. Construction went well. Despite the afternoon showers there was more than enough sunlight to dry the logs and make them buoyant. After six weeks of continual work, the hull was complete. It sat at the lip of the bay, pointing toward the channel, nine black logs, forty-five feet long by eighteen-feet wide, bound together by hundreds of loops of tan-colored manila rope.

At night, in The Ritz, I slept hard. I laid down earlier each night, but it didn't seem to do any good. I was exhausted in my soul. The others, too, were becoming exhausted. These months of constant building and sailing and surviving had taken a toll. This fatigue, this exhaustion, coupled with our dislocation from modern life, was becoming a problem.

One afternoon in early May, in Panama, Alejandro Martinez boarded a bus bound for the Costa Rican border. He carried with him equipment he had bought for The Expedition. Prices were good in Panama and we frequently crossed over the border to buy rope, food, and supplies. Alejandro's bus cruised down the highway until shortly after midnight, when it hit a checkpoint. The National Police boarded the bus and began asking for passports, and when they asked for Alejandro's, they saw that it was Colombian, and promptly pulled him off the bus.

It is well known that the Panamanians and the Colombians are adversaries. Panama seceded from Colombia in a United States–backed rebellion in 1903, and the Colombians think of the Panamanians as traitors and puppets of the

Americans. The Panamanians, for their part, think of the Colombians as drug runners who use Panama as a conduit for smuggling. Now, alone in the night, neither side would find anything "human" in the other—they were strictly enemies.

The Panamanians led Alejandro off to a little command post by the side of the road and into a cement-walled interrogation room, where they stood around the frightened Colombian and sharply questioned him. First, there were problems with Alejandro's passport. It had been soaked in a rain shower a few days earlier, and it looked suspicious. Next, there was his face. Alejandro had always struggled with a singular problem throughout his entire life: He was a man of towering humanity—a sensitive and subtle intellectual—cursed with the frightening face of a killer. Over the years I saw many women fall in love with him, but only after they got to know him. He once told me, using his immense talent for understatement, "I think we both know that I do not look like a nun."

Then there was the problem of his story: He went on in a rambling, fantastic tale about a giant raft made of balsa wood, about being trapped in a giant whirlpool out in the ocean, about an ancient culture that no one had heard of, called the Manteño, and about an expedition marooned on the coast of Costa Rica. "This isn't Costa Rica," they said to him. "This is Pa-na-ma. *Strip*."

His hands trembling, Alejandro took off his clothes. He was alone, no one on earth knew where he was, and he was surrounded by a hostile police force. Adrenaline waves came over him: He knew he was taking the first step that a victim takes when he "disappears." Naked and terrified, Alejandro stood before his enemies. "Bend over," they said.

"No. Please."

"We know you're smuggling drugs. Bend over."

His genitals hanging down and vulnerable, and his knees weak from terror, he slowly bent over while the policemen yanked the cheeks of his buttocks apart. Alejandro had lowered himself to the most helpless, vulnerable, degrading position a person can assume—in a small room filled with armed, pitiless enemies.

Discovering nothing, they threw him into a cell. "You will be moved to Panama City in the morning," they said.

Despondent, Alejandro sat in his cell while his mind worked and worked. He had always dreamed of being an explorer, and he loved The *Manteño* Expedition; it had been the greatest experience of his life. Now, humiliated and alone, he descended into despair.

Shortly after 2:00 a.m., the guard was changed, and Alejandro began talking through the bars of his cell to the new man. "I spent a year in the army in Colombia," he said, "guard duty sucks."

"Yes, it does," the guard said through the bars. "Man, you are in bad trouble. They are going to put you in a prison in Panama City."

Alejandro felt a shock go through him, but managed to whisper, "Maybe you could help me."

Back in The Gyre, I remember Alejandro reading *The Last Days of Socrates*. He had been greatly moved by the story of a philosopher, unjustly accused, condemned to die in a stinking cell. The author of this famous tale points out that Socrates's friends had been ready to bribe the guards to secure the great thinker's freedom. The guards would look the other way for "not a large sum of money." Wouldn't it be a lovely fluke of history if all unjustly treated thinkers had such jailers? Shortly after 4:00 a.m., Alejandro's jailer left the door of the cell slightly open, and looked the other way for a few moments. The price? A long-distance telephone card with $49.50 left on it. With a few dollars left in his pocket, Alejandro induced a man to drive him to the border, where, just before dawn, he crept across to safety.

Alejandro wasn't himself after he returned from Panama. Though he had escaped, he carried the edge of a man who had been horribly humiliated by a despised enemy. Seeing this good man stripped of his dignity hurt me too. When the edge dissolved, he seemed to have lost part of his life force. He was now moving forward on grim determination, and the astute sense that I needed him. Not only were we becoming physically tired, but The Expedition was almost exhausted too. Our tools were worn, or broken, or broken and then repaired, or broken ten times over and then repaired in ways that masked their original identity. A little hand ax bought back in the United States, made of fine shiny steel and with a handle of black carbon fiber, now resembled an old piece of scrap iron. In three hundred days of continuous clubbing, the slowly corroding head had been beaten down to a nub. After refiling blade upon blade and bolting a crude iron handle to the head, Cesar had named it "Mad Max"—it was something only a homicidal maniac would carry. But it wasn't just the tools. The food was of lesser and lesser quality every day too. The propane gas tanks we had brought to land with us from the raft were so rusted that they bordered on the verge of rupture, but we had to use them nevertheless. We were almost out of money, and in spite of all the help from our faithful patrons, the beautiful Ticos, and our own resourcefulness, we were weakening under the burden of a six-year campaign. We had all but exhausted every dollar, every favor, and every idea that a group of driven people could produce. All four of us were nursing nagging injuries, ranging from bleeding cuts to accidental machete hits to torn muscles. Insect bites festered under our skin. We had become four tar-covered men with half beards, wearing ragged shirts and rotted short pants. We could be seen tramping down the back roads of a jungle port in poorly repaired shoes that flapped as we walked, carrying axes, machetes, shovels, picks, buckets of tar, and "Mad Max."

As May dissolved into June, the University of Costa Rica notified us that they were about to begin renovating our building, and that they could only offer us another abandoned building, farther down the marshy shore. We gathered our meager belongings together and walked down to the new place, another green barrack, slightly older and dustier than The Ritz, and moved in. The new building was just a shell, and had no electricity or water. We were happy to have it though, and relieved to have a roof over our heads to fend off the nightly rains.

That first evening in our new home we had dinner in the dark. We sat around a single candle in the vacant building, eating bologna sandwiches and trying to stay cheerful, but it was hard. After dinner I went to lie down in one of the back rooms, where I had stretched out my blue nylon sleeping bag. Outside the frogs creeked and swallowed. I lit a candle, was blinded by its intense light, then opened up the moldy pages of my notebook to write:

29 May 1999
Fatigue worse and worse. Fatigue taking over.

More days passed. Then weeks. Time became an enemy. Regardless of how hard we worked, "The Wait" dominated our state of mind. We were waiting and we knew it—waiting to go back into battle against an enemy over whom we had never triumphed. The Pacific had never even given us a glimpse of a chance. "The Wait" was a strange psychological siege waged against us by the vast Pacific. We knew that we would eventually go back out there. Storms would begin increasing in frequency in the coming months and we knew we risked the chance of being hit by a hurricane. The raft had handled the storm in The Gyre with little problem, but what if we should run into a "superstorm"— what if a superhurricane simply erased us from the earth? This question, this wait, hung over us. But at the same time, we longed for the high sea. An old cliché, one that I would have had contempt for had I not felt it, was absolutely true: The sea had a hypnotic power over us. On many days, I stood on the balsa logs of the finished hull and looked out toward the little channel that led to Golfo Dulce, where we had come in from the high sea after being evacuated. This slim opening represented our inevitable return to the ocean. Like Camp Hardcore and our entrapment in the fjord of Bahia Solano, I knew we'd need some luck to escape our confinement at Golfito. From our location we'd have to navigate for thirty miles before the land would fall away and open up to the Pacific Ocean. I spent many hours thinking about escaping this confinement, and Alejandro soon adopted my habit of looking out toward the channel, as did Cesar. Looking at the channel, our only corridor of escape, we were waiting. One day, as clouds gathered for the daily afternoon rain shower, I stood on the balsa logs of the new raft, staring out toward the channel, and said to Alejandro, "I really miss being out there. I want to go back out to the—"

"—Me too. Yes. A lot."

1 June 1999
Alejandro more and more like his old self. Cesar good as well. Martin becoming a man I can't trust.

Martin was becoming too much to cope with. He was becoming more childlike every day. I kept my temper, but was about fed up with him. Finally, after an argument, he left. I talked to him several times about coming back, but he had had enough. I was deeply relieved. He had a girlfriend who lived down on the river Terraba, about two hours from Golfito. He wandered off to her, and we saw little of him afterward. It was a relief and a tragedy. Martin was the most complicated character of my odyssey. He was a grown man, permanently cemented in boyhood. He was neither bad nor good. I never called him friend, or enemy. He was completely and utterly unheroic, and yet there were moments when I was incapacitated when he undertook my responsibilities, and did so valiantly. He had the personality of a pubescent boy, and yet I had consciously leaned on him during those final days in The Gyre. He was reliable *and* irresponsible, industrious *and* lazy, brilliant *and* disruptive. He survived Camp Hardcore and he survived The Gyre, but he could not overcome his own foolishness—hardly an uncommon fate for an adventurer.

A couple of weeks later, Cesar, Alejandro, and I dragged two railroad rails to the lip of the hard-packed land of our work site. Each rail weighed approximately 250 pounds, and was made to endure the crushing strain of a speeding locomotive. We installed them so that they formed a thirty-foot track down to the seabed in front of the work site, and in the afternoon, as the high tide flooded up to the very edge of the shelf of land, a gigantic yellow earthmover gently picked up the back of the raft and it slid down the rails and into the bay. Twenty people stood by and watched. There was no ceremony or fanfair. The raft was launched in the same way a ship would be launched from a modern shipyard. We were raft mariners now, and when one of the Ticos asked me about the launch, the raft, and the voyage, I shocked myself by saying, "We do this all the time."

La Endurancia was towed to the pier and tied up at the wharf, where we prepared once again for a voyage on the Pacific Ocean. We had been talking about the name of the new raft for weeks, and it fit so well that it simply seemed to grow on our stout little vessel in the marsh, less because of our admiration of Shackelton's famous expeditionary ship and more for our own struggle. Cesar was deeply proud of the workmanship that had gone into the *Endurancia,* as was I, and of its solidness. We knew we had built a good raft for the high sea, but it had taken a toll. Cesar was still solid, still the stumplike man who had boarded *Manteño II* back in Bahia Solano, but now his limbs seemed to hang a little longer from his body when he walked. He had lost a lot of weight; and though he remained muscular, he seemed to droop, as did Alejandro, who still carried with him his disturbing capture at the hands of the Panamanians.

That night, after we launched the *Endurancia,* we shambled and clinked down the back road to our building, carrying our various blades and buckets and *wancas.* The raft was in the water, but we were too tired to talk about it and too tired to worry about it. We passed the abandoned lot that had been our work site, and then passed the marsh. Cesar made no effort to look for his crocodile; he was too tired.

A few days later, the university informed us that they would be renovating the building we were in. They had done everything they could for us, but we were now on our own. With what little money we still had, we rented a room in the hills. We would be returning to the sea soon.

12

An Ancient Fate

The wharf at Golfito was a modern structure that could be seen from miles away, a steel-and-cement peninsula, roughly a quarter mile long, that crooked out from the land like a silver-and-gray finger. A matrix of iron girders held it suspended above the water's surface, and a high, slanted roof of gleaming corrugated steel formed a massive awning over it. Reaching out and running parallel to the main shore of the town, it created a small cove of protected water behind it by enclosing the shallows near land on three sides. At the front of the wharf, where it faced the bay, the water was more than fifty feet deep and dark blue, but behind it lay warm green tropical water like that of a lagoon, and here, tied up alongside this silver-and-gray mechanical finger, lay two vessels, one behind the other. The first was a small brown ship, an island freighter, the type of aging, oblong tub that could be found servicing hundreds of remote ports and settlements throughout tropical Latin America. The second, lying quietly behind the freighter, where the calm green water lapped at the base of the iron girders, was the *Endurancia*.

The raft floated in deep green stillness. It was a primitive vessel to be sure, but it carved a clean line nevertheless. It was a squat boat, short and wide, solid and straight. A chainsaw had cut its base logs into a perfect pattern: pointed at the bow, blunt at the stern. Freshly painted and newly built, its stark colors, a soft and uniform tan contrasted against an intense black, accentuated its sharp lines. For a vessel made for Stone Age man it seemed remarkably organized, almost linear. *Manteño* and *Manteño II* had always appeared sickly, their huts and their masts had leaned at sickly angles, but this new vessel was the taut product of our prowess. Care had been taken in designing and building *Endurancia* to give it the lowest profile possible, so that it would present little resistance to the wind. We expected to be hit by multiple tropical cyclones on the upcoming voyage, and with this in mind, the hut, even though it sat up on a second-story platform, stood less than five feet above the deck. Standing up inside this little bamboo house was impossible; it was so small in fact that it did not look at all like something that would be inhabited by people, and had you seen the raft sitting at the base of the wharf on an afternoon in early June 1999, right before we set out, you might have thought the hut on the back was just a storage shed. Though it didn't have one yet, *Endurancia* would eventually have a single mast, a bipod which would be delivered in a few weeks, and this, too, would be made to cope with high winds: Two wooden poles would slant inward to form an A frame over the centerline of the raft, like the wooden arch of the *Illa-Tiki*. We had seen the stormy winds gain hold of our vertical poles on *Manteño II* and bend them over to an alarming angle. Now, aboard *Endurancia,* the air would flow easier over this bipod, and with its two legs and four rope stays, it would be more stable in high seas. The raft's deck was made of the fattest, strongest bamboo canes that had ever been used on any of our rafts, and they now lay in parallel rows, all of them cut to an exact length and tied into place by thousands of loops of fresh, supple, manila rope.

The second vessel tied to the wharf, the iron freighter in front of the raft, was the *Phoenix,* which in a short time would be towing the *Endurancia* to the high sea. It had been built in the United States at the very end of World War II, 1945, and measured 120 feet in length. A few years before we arrived in Golfito, the Costa Rican Coast Guard had intercepted it at sea carrying thousands of pounds of contraband in its hold. They, of course, seized the ship, off-loaded the illegal cargo, and then towed the little freighter into the shallows and left it there to founder. When its pumps stopped working, the hull filled up and it sank into the mud. The boat settled on the bottom, and that's the way an enterprising *Tico* named Arturo found it a couple of years later.

Arturo was intensely intelligent. In his middle thirties, he was small and enormously energetic. Everything he did was done at a frenetic pace—I can only explain his movements as one, continuous, ricochet. Well educated and friendly, Arturo came to the raft everyday and talked to us, and typically he would pat us on the back and laugh nervously, saying something like:

"Please—come over to my mother's house—so she can talk you out of this craziness." About a year before we met him, Arturo had purchased the little freighter in the mud and had pumped the water out of it. *Phoenix* righted itself and came up. He got the bilge pumps going so the ship would stay afloat, flushed the seawater out of the diesel engines, lubed them, and then fired them up. The engines may have been old, but they were still game, and with all those old horses running at once, the *Phoenix* ran like a stampede: a thousand clattering noises, barely organized, that developed an immense amount of power.

Phoenix wasn't beautiful—a drab, red-brown hull with a square white wheelhouse on its back—but it burst with personality. You could take a complete tour of the vessel in thirty minutes: cargo hold below the foredeck, crew quarters, a head, a small galley with booth seating, and some paint-coated ladders and small passageways. Its wheelhouse was a narrow, wood-paneled room, where the helmsman stood at the old-fashioned wheel and looked through the rectangular panes of glass. I would find out later that the ship was just the right size and age for developing a traditional roll: Back and forth, back and forth, swaying over in gentle but wide arcs—an excellent ship for getting seasick in. We loved her.

Aboard *Endurancia,* we continued construction. It rained every day and frequently at night as well, with some of the heaviest rainfall coming after dark, in long, windless downpours. Usually the wharf was empty, with only a few people milling around in all that open space. The coast guardsmen worked on their vessels nearby, and continued to help us all they could. As soon as the roof was on the hut, I moved in and slept with the water lapping at the logs below me and the rain crackling on the thatch above. Once again, I was living in a bamboo houseboat. Looking back on it, I can see now that I was becoming isolated. Alejandro and Cesar were the best friends I had ever had in my life; they were side by side with me every day, but still I felt isolated. All of the original members of The Expedition who had boarded the plane to go into the field a year ago were gone. The film company that was making the television show about our voyage was holding me at arm's length, and I was no longer in touch with anyone who spoke my language, which had a very weird effect on me. One day, during a phone call to Annie, I broke into Spanish in the middle of the conversation and rambled for five minutes before she asked, "Don't you know you're speaking Spanish?" I did indeed know it at the time, but I had become strangely melded to my life on The Expedition, much more so than to my previous life in the modern world. Listening to the water below the canes was now something that made me feel at home.

On June 29, shortly before we were to leave, it turned cold in the afternoon, and dark. I stood on the wharf and watched as a thick cloud bank sagged like a bloated bag over the hills in the west. Bulging down toward the wharf, it sent the air around me into chaos, and then the entire bay gasped. A cold wind smeared my face, dropped off, and then seemed to come up from the floor of the wharf. Hair, clothes, and canvas, all stood up and were sucked back toward the cloud bank. There was a three-second pause, and then a cold wind ripped thorough the rafters of the wharf. Hard drops of rain flew all around me. The concentrated squall came into the bay and ricocheted off the hills, barely disturbing the water but making the corrugated tin roof of the wharf undulate wildly. It was the third squall I'd seen since being in Golfito. I thought little of it, and when it passed, my only feelings were that it seemed small compared to the storm we'd encountered in The Gyre.

That night, I walked across the wharf at around 11:30. I was returning from dinner in town, and as I walked out over the water I noticed that a thick tropical air mass had sat down on Golfito, holding the trees still and flattening the water. It was a bright night, with a full moon lighting up the bay. To my right, two miles out, a three-hundred-foot ship hulked in the narrow channel that connected the bay to the gulf, and I stood for a moment watching its black shape creep silently into the bay. It was some sort of tanker. Profuse snarls of pipes overflowed from the topside of the vessel as though a steel jungle was growing out of its deck. Creeping toward the wharf at less than an eighth of a mile an hour, it came ahead at dead slow, turning and moving without motion, like a cloud changing shape in the sky. In the gray light, I watched it silently maneuver until it was parallel with the wharf, and lay one hundred yards off. I couldn't help but think of what would happen if one of the squally winds broadsided the tanker while it was in this vulnerable position. The profile of the ship—all of that freeboard and superstructure—would be like an enormous square sail, generating hundreds of thousands of pounds of pulling energy. If that happened, the tanker would have to drop anchor or drive out of the bay. Its captain would need for everything to go right—engines, steering, communications, anchors, everything—to extricate himself from a sweeping collision with the wharf or a grounding in the silty mud.

The ship had its deck lights on now, lighting up the bay with the color of burnt orange. The pipe jungle was covered in coat after coat of burnt orange paint, as was the hull and even the crewmen, who wore burnt orange coveralls.

From the wharf, the Ticos launched three tiny boats. They cruised out toward the tanker and then split up, one going to the bow, one to the stern, and one amidships. At both ends of the tanker, parties of antlike men threw pilot lines down to the Ticos, who stood on the floors of the wooden boats squinting up at the iron leviathan. When the coils landed in their midst, they immediately shoved off, motoring to the wharf with thin, squiggly lines trailing from their sterns to the tanker.

As soon as the Ticos had returned, the ship's lines were tied to the wharf, and for ten long minutes, fifty people silently watched, transfixed by this moonlit spectacle of tiny exhilarated men handling a 32-million-pound ship in much the same way a vessel would have been handled two hundred years ago. Each time the lines would droop, the tanker's winches would break the silent stillness with a little *tick,* which would echo against the bay. The lines would rise up and go taut, but there'd be no perceptual movement from the tanker— no wake or disturbance of the water whatsoever. Then there would be silence for half a minute, and the only way to know the ship had moved was that the lines would begin to droop again. The ship never moved toward us on the wharf, it simply grew in size until it blocked out our view of the sea. When it arrived, it didn't collide, or bump, or even kiss; it berthed itself as though it had been tied up for a week.

The Port of Golfito did not require professional piloting for ships because the waters there were so tranquil, and of course there were no tugs for fifty miles. Any vessel entering or exiting the channel leading to Golfito would be on its own. If it ran out of fuel before it reached the wharf, it ran a very serious risk of going aground or wrecking. This important fact, which had just been so profoundly demonstrated, had far-reaching consequences for me and my vessel, consequences that I could not foresee.

The next day, in the afternoon, a mountainous Russian came to the raft. He was the chief of the tanker that I had seen berthed the previous night. The chief was larger than me, perhaps six feet, eight inches, and weighing as much as three hundred pounds. He suffered from a neurological disorder, which caused a tick, so that his head and neck flexed at quick intervals. We talked for a moment, and then he returned to his job of filling his tanker with palm oil. Later, Captain Moya, the man who had skippered the *Punta Burica* during our evacuation, asked me to go with him aboard the chief's boat and ask for a little paint for the hull of the Costa Rican gunboat. Going aboard, we found the chief in the officer's galley.

"The captain here needs a little paint for the local patrol boat," I said.

"How much?" the chief asked.

"Can you spare a couple of gallons?"

"Hey!" The chief yelled out at one of his men, "get two cans of paint!"

"Thanks," I said.

"No problem," he grunted, flexing his neck. "I like your raft."

"Thank you."

"When I was young, they used to say, 'Men who sail on steel are made of wood, but men who sail on wood are made of steel.'"

"Oh, I don't know if that's so true," I said.

"Yes, yes," he said. "I've been in the Black Sea aboard open boats made of wood. It is . . . it is . . . it is . . . very bad."

The thought of a tropical cyclone or a hurricane pressured us more and more each day. Each day that passed moved us deeper into storm season. Other things pressured us too. Everyone wanted to know why we hadn't left Golfito yet. We set a date to leave but had to cancel it because we weren't ready yet, then set another date and again had to cancel, then another, and again, another delay. Each day that passed made many feel like The Expedition would fail in Costa Rica. We *had* to "get going." This is a serious problem for all expeditions: You must show progress, always. We were still shorthanded, too. Alejandro and I talked back and forth about recruiting a guy named Javier. We were desperate for a fourth person, but Javier gave me the impression of a person who could make serious problems for us once on the high sea. Alejandro now knew what I knew, and he and I agreed that Javier was a high-risk personality. A few days after I told Javier that we were not going to take him, he started making a little trouble. Perhaps I was beginning to learn.

Major Chavez had a friend named Mailor, who had been hanging around the work site and the wharf for several weeks now, and the rumor was he would be willing to go if we asked him. He was of medium height and build, in his thirties, quiet and reserved, but a nice guy, and funny; and after talking it over for a few days, we decided to take him with us on the raft. He was happy, and working with him was easy. Even though Mailor had no experience, *Endurancia* would be manned by the most-experienced crew so far. Two of the four crew members had over 65 sea days aboard a balsa raft, and I had over 120.

The days continued to pass at the wharf, and then turned into weeks. It had been four months since The Gyre swallowed *Manteño II,* and it seemed as though the elements, especially our nemesis, the endless Pacific, grew stronger and stronger all the time. Clothing and rope and wood rotted, money ran out, patience thinned and tools broke, but the ocean never slept, never tired, never needed rest. As each day went by, we became weaker and weaker. It was now July, and as we approached our upcoming departure, time seemed to stretch out even farther. The greatest problem now, greater than any other pressure, was our state of mind. We were in a hospitable place, but that had little effect on us; on the contrary, we were in fact on the verge of being homeless. The dark effects of Alejandro's capture in Panama still hung on us. The years of passionate pursuit of the raft and the voyage, the fatigue, the time, and our suspended existence on a foreign shore which was all but barren to us now, had all combined to become oppressive. It was perhaps a cliché in popular culture to picture a desperate man, stranded, marooned, willing to undergo any perils or possible dangers to get away—to simply escape the state of being marooned—but it was nonetheless true. We were haggard and worn, but above all things we were desperate to escape, far more than had been the case in Panama during the first expedition, or at Camp Hardcore just a few months previous. We missed our former lives. I could see it in the eyes of the Colombians and I knew they could see it in mine. We still loved adventure and we still relished the idea of going to sea; but we wished to go home someday too, and the only way home was to make a long voyage, and the sooner the better. Not only that, but we knew that our vessel was a perishable ship; the moment it had hit the water, the clock had begun to tick. It was not at all like a modern vessel, which can last for thirty to forty years; we knew that the raft would sink in two hundred days. Perhaps if we had awakened to a wide-open coast—if escape to high sea was easy sailing and well within our grasp, we'd have felt differently, or perhaps if we were to leave on a modern sloop, with its good speed, ease of steering and auxiliary propulsion, the strain would have been less; but the *Phoenix* would have to tow us through the same channel the Russian's tanker had come through. And getting through the channel would be just the start. Once through, the *Phoenix* would have to turn and head for the mouth of the gulf, towing us until we were fifteen to twenty miles off-shore, and fuel was scarce. The *Phoenix* would carry just enough fuel to make the tow and then return to

Golfito. The raft was trapped, backed into a corner, and we were like a small band of soldiers deep inside a foreboding land, under siege, hiding in a fort of their own making. The long tow to safety symbolized our freedom. Each day, we awoke to the sight of a narrow corridor, and beyond that, another narrow corridor. A barrier awaited us, a line that blocked our escape to the open sea and freedom from our stranded, suspended life. It was like a massive ocean current that could not be overcome or multiple lines of killer breakers—an initial gauntlet that we would have to pass through, an enormous first step, and the largest step. The only way out was through this barrier, and in those last days, we were obsessed with escape.

The night before we left for the high sea, I worked feverishly to prepare the raft. I was running a temperature and felt achy and dizzy. Nevertheless, I stowed gear and strung rigging. I cared only of one thing: getting underway. I remembered what had happened to *Illa-Tiki* when we had landed in Panama. During that expedition we had become happy and settled in our new environment. The people had been so nice to us and we had been so devastated by the voyage of madness that leaving had been delayed until it was impossible. Now, three years later, I wanted only to leave. Shortly after 2:00 a.m., I quit working. I had to get some sleep. My fever was raging, which was causing me to lose my balance. All that remained was to add some reinforcement to the bipod mast—including putting in its crossbeam.

In the morning, on July 2, 1999, Major Chavez came to the raft and shook hands with all of us. He had helped build the raft, had organized the tow, and had become an *hermano* ("brother"). The beautiful Ticos had, in fact, given us everything: balsawood for the new raft, manpower to build it with, and a place to live. The local congresswomen had even arranged to get us two hardwood poles for a new mast. Of all the great coastal peoples that we had worked with, they were the most golden.

We did some last-minute interviews, and in the afternoon we were finally ready to cast off. *Endurancia* left the pier at 5:00 p.m., pulling away slowly behind a Boston whaler. The timing was good. We would arrive at our release site at approximately 3:00 a.m. the next morning, where, fifteen to twenty miles offshore, we'd secure lines from tow, make formal farewells with the good crew of the *Phoenix*, and establish position, current, and wind directions. All this done, the sun would soon rise, and we would have seventeen hours of light with which to work out any problems, like rerigging and getting our sea legs.

The *Phoenix* now lay in the calm bay, two hundred yards from the pier, floating effortlessly in the blue-green water. Aboard the ship were Arturo, his chief, a fat and robustly capable man in his early thirties, and a pilot, a hard, wrinkled old man who was perhaps an indigenous native. In addition to these three, there were several other men below decks, watching that fifty-four-year-old beast of an engine. When the *Endurancia* had reached the water near the *Phoenix,* the four of us boarded the Boston whaler and came alongside the big brown freighter. Arturo came to the edge of the railing, and with his scratchy, excited voice, yelled, "Come on! Come on!"

Climbing aboard the *Phoenix,* we stood on the hard metal foredeck, an open area about the size of a tennis court. The bay around us was much like an inland lake, and the still air enhanced the feeling of an immense but confined space, which gave us, standing on the deck of the ship, the feeling of being on the playing field of an enormous sports stadium. People stood on the pier and shoreline like sports fans, cheering and honking horns for the *Phoenix* and the *Endurancia.* Arturo beamed. I admired him; he seemed to me a person who had been underestimated his whole life. This would be the *Phoenix*'s maiden voyage since being raised from the seabed, and Arturo now bounced around the deck, shaking hands and popping bottles of champagne. It was a sunny afternoon, and Arturo had resurrected a dead ship—it was his big adventure, his "expedition," and we were happy for him—happy for his new ship, happy to be in Costa Rica, even if we were about to leave, and happy once again to go to sea. Standing on the deck of his ship, Arturo handed a beautiful tobacco pipe to me, and said, "I want you to have this." After Mike the pirate stole my regular pipe, some of the Ticos had fabricated a new one for me out of cocobolo wood. It was an excellent pipe and I enjoyed smoking it very much, but unfortunately cocobolo wood is toxic and whenever I puffed on it my lips swelled. I thanked Arturo for the gift, shaking his hand warmly, and then we left the *Phoenix.*

The three vessels—freighter, raft, and whaler—now maneuvered slowly and silently in the calm water of the bay like giant toy boats, each of them unique, each patiently waiting its turn, each moving into its logical position without difficulty. *Phoenix* turned toward the channel while we handed our towline to the men on the whaler, and they in turn took it to the stern of the freighter, where Arturo's men tied it to their vessel. Back at the raft we heard the ship's diesels rev up; a puff of smoke popped out of *Phoenix*'s stack, and the towline slowly straightened, lifting off the surface of the water with a bounce. *Endurancia* began to gently plow the water; the surface rippled in front of the blunt prow of the raft, then turned into a wake, then cascaded past us like a small waterfall. Just like that first night four years before, during The *Illa-Tiki* Expedition, a raft, bushy and primitive, now trailed two hundred feet behind a small iron ship, headed out to sea.

Daylight faded, quickly turning to gray. We stood on the bamboo canes, watching the *Phoenix* lumber into the channel. Alejandro hung back by the doorway of the hut, resting his elbow on the top of a water barrel, while Cesar and Mailor stood on the other side of the doorway, stone-faced. I squished around on the deck in my seawater-soaked shoes, watching the raft plow the water. The bay around us narrowed, and as we entered the channel, the shoreline was suddenly close by. Palm trees, hanging down from land, drifted past us at five miles an hour. The *Phoenix* pushed forward steadily. It had not yet begun to roll from side to side; it was, however, beginning to pitch up and down, and as it did so it bobbed its head down in a long, even motion. This porpoiselike pitching was so smooth and easy that aboard the *Endurancia,* two hundred feet back, we felt nothing—the towline remained straight and taut. Our view from the raft was of the *Phoenix*'s stern, fat and round, rising up and squatting down in a succession of long, gentle bounces.

In the twilight we saw the channel open up, widen, and then fall behind us. We were entering the gulf now. We'd have to travel eighteen miles to reach its mouth, then another fifteen to twenty miles offshore for safety. *Phoenix* turned gently to port, increased speed to six knots, then to eight. Water piled over our logs and flooded past the deck, surrounding us with the sounds of white water rapids. The ship's diesels churned loudly now and the towline shot straight back, from its stern to our bow. *Endurancia* was handling the strain perfectly and showing no difficulties.

Darkness now smothered the gulf. Off our starboard side we saw sharp white-and yellow-points of light marking the town of Puerto Lopez, falling slowly by the wayside. We were now traveling down a narrow tropical corridor, where the shorelines on either side of us paralleled our course. Once again we were on the raft at night, standing on an open platform with nothing between us and the sea. Like standing at the edge of a skyscraper that has no railing, the only thing that held you from open space was your own balance. With no walls to stop it, the night came aboard and was on the deck with us. It seemed as though you could reach out and scoop up a part of that black air with your hand.

At around 7:00 p.m., two flashes of light came from the stern of the *Phoenix,* which was our prearranged signal for radio communications between the two vessels. I ducked into the hut and twisted the volume knob of the little white radio and the speaker crunched a short burst of static. Arturo's voice, sharply defined, said, "We have something to eat for you."

Leaving the hut, I worked my way to the back of the raft, where we had the *Phoenix*'s inflatable dinghy in tow. It was a calm night in the tropics and as I felt around in the dark, moving from one handhold to the other, a soft wind passed around my body, and seawater, faintly shining, slid smoothly below my feet. Stepping down onto the back ends of the logs, I turned around and handed the dinghy's towline to Alejandro and then jumped into the little vinyl boat. The line was released, the *Endurancia* sped away, and I was alone on the water, pulling sharply on the starter cord of the outboard motor.

Within two minutes the raft was no longer visible, although I could see *Phoenix*'s light well. It took me five minutes to get the outboard motor started, but when I did, it ran strongly. Speeding past the raft, the outboard motor buzzing in the dark, I quickly closed in on the *Phoenix*. The dinghy bounced smoothly over the ocean, and I came up on the ship's starboard side, twenty feet from its steel hull, and ran on a parallel course. *Phoenix* was plunging into the waves at eight knots. It was an iron monster, an enormous living thing, pushing mindlessly forward, growling and seething and writhing in the ocean. Its headlights were like two glaring eyes, shooting shafts of white light into the night. The entire ship rolled heavily to each side: one second it would swing over at a hard angle to me, swaying over in a slow, powerful motion, coming so close that it would be as though I could reach out and grab the ship with my hand—and then in the next instant it would swing twenty feet away. This uneven surging, this wallowing, sent out a chaotic bow wave that treated my little vinyl boat like a punching bag, bouncing it around like a toy. The dinghy jumped and rolled sharply, and I had to fight to stay up with the *Phoenix*. Off to my side, amid the dim light of the freighter's wheelhouse, I could see Arturo and his chief standing at the controls of the ship; and minute after minute I rode alongside, expecting them to slow down, waiting for a sign that they might reduce speed to transfer our meal. But they seemed very satisfied with their course and speed and how the tow was progressing. Instead of slowing, they were now making their way out of the wheelhouse and to the ship's railing, preparing to throw the meal out to me.

Once in position, Arturo's chief braced his massive belly against the white railing and then started waving me over. I eased the dinghy over ten feet, and then out of the corner of my eye I saw a black object shoot through the air. I threw my hand up at the same time the fat soda bottle came by my face and knocked it down. This went on two more times and then they made a gesture, signaling that they wanted to throw the iron pot with our dinner in it. Shaking my hand back and forth, I signaled "No." Seeing this, they started waving me closer, trying to get me to come right against the hull.

Phoenix was really plowing through the water. Its diesels clattered loudly and its bow lights pushed out into the dark. Meanwhile, the dinghy flapped and teetered. We were two vessels in the night, one massive and one tiny, running on a parallel course. The massive vessel churned and clattered and my vessel buzzed alongside like an insect. I climbed over wake after wake until I was three feet away from the hull, fighting to keep steady in a constant waterfall of hissing ocean. The blunt-nosed monster was smashing the waves and I was now motoring through a world of drops—millions of drops—hanging in the air, jumping and falling, flying all around me. The chief was leaning over the railing now, and I tried several times to get right on the hull so that I could reach up and take the pot out of his hand. But I couldn't bridge the gap—I was too worried about deflating the dinghy. The ship's hull had a lot of growth on it, and I thought back to that night in Panama when I had seen an inflatable dinghy sliced and sunk. If those barnacles on the *Phoenix*'s hull deflated the dinghy now, I'd go right under the ship's propellers. If I were somehow able to avoid that, I'd have the fifteen-ton raft coming from astern to run me over. I thought it too dangerous and crept away from the hull until the dinghy was eight feet out, fighting the ship's wake. Surely they would slow down now. I glanced back and forth, from my course to Arturo, and I saw him signal me "steady." I looked at my course for a split second and then looked back and saw that Arturo was already in midflight. His body flew across the gap like a jet making a landing on an aircraft carrier. Hitting the port side of the dinghy, he bounced across just as I reached up and tangled my finger in his belt loop. He then hit the far side with his hands back-pedaling furiously and came to a stop. Realizing he wasn't going overboard, he recovered and called over his shoulder, "Come alongside *Phoenix!*"

I brought us alongside and Arturo stood up halfway, bracing a knee on top of the dinghy's bulwark, and they dropped the pot down to him. We then broke off, and went back to the *Endurancia*. We quickly ate Arturo's spaghetti on the foredeck, and in ten minutes he left to reboard the *Phoenix,* which I'm sure was an adventure in itself.

Roughly forty-five minutes after Arturo left, far away lightning flickered above the land where the hills formed a crooked horizon in the west, and the air around us changed from soft and balmy to cool and clammy. The towing steadily progressed and the four of us stood on the foredeck, staring into the western sky, watching the flickers of light reveal a dense gallery of heavy clouds. They were clearly massing. We could see multiple flashes now, like dueling artillery, illuminating the various silvers, whites, and grays of an advancing cloudbank. Below the chaotic sky, the land was starting to give way. We were finally beginning to reach the sea. We could see the black shapes of the coastal headlands beginning to fall behind us on either side and open up, and as they did, the first rumbling sounds of thunder reached us. It started to rain and the surface of the sea changed from smooth to thousands of mounds of water. Small waves now broke over the bow and smashed against our deck, but our vessel showed no strain. The *Phoenix* had maintained an excellent course up to that point—but then the wind hit.

It started as neither a breeze nor a wall; it was a confused, unimpressive wind, like the wind I had experienced on the wharf. The air around us seemed to gasp, hang for a second, and then blow chaotically, gushing toward us, whipping around, and then rushing away. Rain poured down in hard, cold drops. The shower thickened and within seconds the loud clattering of drops sizzling on the surface of the water overwhelmed the heavy dieseling sounds of Arturo's engines. Millions of drops now formed a clear barrier between the raft and the ship. We could still see the pitching stern of the freighter, but only when the lightning flashed and even then it was a blurred image, its edges soft and its form distorted as though we were seeing it through an unfocused camera lens. The wind increased, and in ten minutes it reached twenty knots. The waves were building. The fat, rounded stern of the *Phoenix* continued to rise and squat—but then the ship turned slightly to starboard and quickly straightened out. Or so it seemed. The image we saw was brief—a flicker. The towing continued and again the *Phoenix*'s stern was rising and squatting before us. Half a minute passed and then it turned slightly to the starboard again and I realized it wasn't trying to turn at all: It was being blown sideways by the wind.

Phoenix was empty, a hollow iron cylinder. The small freighter carried very little fuel, and no cargo. It was floating as high as possible and was therefore presenting a broad profile to the wind. Its flat side was now like an enormous kite on a string, oscillating in the breeze. I knew that up in the wheelhouse of the *Phoenix*, Arturo and his men must be having problems maintaining course. The little freighter rolled and pitched heavily. When it recovered from its second uncontrolled turn, it pitched down and its blunt nose dug deeply into the water, which caused its fat iron stern to rise sharply, like the back bumper of an automobile braking to a hard stop. For a moment I thought we might see the ship's propeller, but then its stern sat back down in a long, slow squat.

It was all darkness and sheeting drops now. Billions of drops hurtled out of the black and clattered on the surface all around us. We stood, transfixed, staring through the drops—drops falling through the air, dripping in front of our noses, falling from the bills of our caps and hoods. We all knew our situation: We were onboard a balsa raft being towed through a storm on the black Pacific. Conditions were still manageable, but they were rapidly deteriorating. We were two miles out to sea now and we wanted at least ten more for a margin of safety. The *Endurancia* was withstanding the wind and chop well, but then the *Phoenix*'s stern swung wildly, fishtailing to port. The freighter turned completely broadside of us and we got a panoramic view of the *Phoenix*'s starboard side—the entire profile of the ship. The raft sped up for a second and then the towline went slack. For a split second it drooped into the water. *Phoenix* swerved back to the other side, correcting its fishtail, and when it did it jerked the slack out. The towline popped up, went taut, and the raft snapped forward. Everything onboard bounced. A hollow noise thumped from deep inside *Endurancia* and our mast spars jumped as though suddenly startled. We were now playing "crack the whip" with the *Phoenix*. Back at the hut, standing near Alejandro, I yelled over the raindrops, "Did you hear that noise? Was that the mast?"

Lightening flashed and in the flicker I saw Alejandro. Hard drops were pelting and spattering the top of his head as though his hair was sizzling and he was nodding "yes, yes, yes." I took a few uneasy steps forward, and halfway up the deck I stopped, crouched, and then spent a long time peering out into the dark, trying to focus clearly on the *Phoenix,* trying to measure its performance. In the rain, visibility had dropped below 250 feet. Alejandro, holding onto a mast stay, worked his way up the starboard side of the deck, and when I noticed him out of the corner of my eye I called out, "Maybe I should call Arturo."

"Yes, I think so."

Phoenix swung wide, like an enormous door turning on a hinge. The lightening flashed and we suddenly saw the whole ship in front of us. It seemed to rotate—to pivot—turning sharply to starboard until we could see a complete profile view of the vessel, from stem to stern. Its iron side glimmered for a moment in the blue-gray light—a broad metal wall with rainwater sheeting down the side of it. The raft sped up for an instant and then stalled. The towline went slack. We drifted sideways for a split second. Then the freighter swerved back. The towline straightened out like a pole, popped up out of the water, and then "the whip" cracked hard. The raft jumped forward, shuddering horribly. It was as though its whole body had spasmed. The mast jumped in its shoes and then swayed over to the portside. The lashing at the peak of the bi-pod lost its grip and slid down the port spar, locking itself halfway down. The mast and rigging were now twisted and tangled at an unnatural angle, locked there by their own ropes, as though a noose had clamped shut around the neck of the mast.

I ducked into the hut and called the *Phoenix,* telling them that we had to stop immediately. Everything eased. We slowed down, then came to dead slow. The weather cleared a little too. Over the radio, Arturo said, "We'll wait for a few hours while you guys get some rest."

It was as though he had read our minds. "Yes. Roger that. We need to rest for a while."

Arturo seemed to sense our predicament, especially the problem of fatigue. The *Phoenix* trolled at dead slow and I went into the hut, fell on some gear in the dark, and dropped into a black sleep. I woke up almost immediately, sweating. My fever was still with me and I slept fitfully for a couple of hours while the *Phoenix* stood by.

When dawn came I got up slowly and walked out on the canes of the foredeck. It was a fine day, perfect for sailing. *Phoenix* lay in front of the raft, and *Punta Burica,* the boat that had evacuated us from The Gyre, lay off our starboard side. Behind us stood the coastline, eight miles away. In the morning light I could now see the condition of our mast. It was bent hard over to the portside, but still standing. It would take some time to straighten it out, which we could do during the rest of the tow.

Leaving the raft, I went aboard the *Phoenix* to talk to its crew about getting started. Aboard the freighter, I met Arturo in the galley and said, "Are you ready to go?"

"We can't," he said. "We're out of fuel."

"What?"

"We had to run our engines all night. I've got just enough to make it back to Golfito."

"You can't take me out another couple of miles?"

"I don't have the fuel, my friend."

When he said that to me, I felt a wave of adrenaline come over me the likes of which I had not felt since I thought we might capsize in The Gyre. I knew Arturo was powerless to help me. He had done the best he could with what he had. Fuel had been desperately scarce before we began, and more than that, Arturo had never had any experience in towing another vessel—least of all a giant raft in heavy winds. He now faced the simple fact that if he towed us for another hour, dragging the cumbersome raft behind his old freighter, he'd risk running out of fuel on his return to the Golfito channel. Like the palm oil tanker that I had seen come in a few nights before, the *Phoenix* would be on its own if the weather turned bad or if it ran out of fuel. If that happened anywhere during the last five miles of its approach to Golfito, it would run aground for sure: Arturo could not risk collision with the coast. "Go aboard the gunboat," he said. "Ask the captain to take you out just a little more. All you need is a teeny, tiny bit—maybe three more miles. Just a teeny, tiny bit."

I left the galley to walk around on the rolling foredeck of the *Phoenix*. The wind was blowing in the optimal direction for us to get underway. It was just the type of wind we wanted, all we had to do was run downwind and we'd move away from the coast at just the right angle to avoid going back into The Gyre. If we could sail north for twenty miles, our problems with The Gyre would be over and we'd have plenty of distance from the dangerous coastline. All we had to do was get under sail, and we'd make it. But there was no margin for error. As Arturo had already pointed out: we needed about three more miles' distance.

By the time I began climbing down from the *Phoenix,* Arturo's pilot was already waiting for me in the inflatable dingy. We motored over to the gunboat in less than a minute and I climbed aboard to walk across the steel deck of the *Punta Burica,* and then up to the bridge. The gunboat wasn't skippered that day by Captain Moya, the man who had helped us in The Gyre. Instead, I explained my situation to a different skipper, who immediately said no.

Stepping out of the wheelhouse of the gunboat, I stood on the hard metal deck for a moment and looked at the situation: We were eight nautical miles from the coast, but with the ability to get underway. We were fine for now, but what if conditions should change? *Not good enough.* I stepped back into the wheelhouse and appealed to the captain again and he said, simply, "Huh uh," and motioned with his hand that the wind was moving in the optimal direction. He was completely unimpressed with our situation. I didn't have any type of emergency, and he wasn't giving any free rides.

I knew immediately that we were on our own and must get underway quickly. I left the gunboat and went back to the raft. The *Phoenix* returned to Golfito, and, unbelievably, the *Punta Burica* went on patrol. Within just ten minutes, we were alone, drifting.

Aboard the *Endurancia,* we worked to get underway. The sun gleamed on the wet canes and we scrambled to heave and hoist the ropes and rigging. The Colombians went to the catwalks and began preparing the *guaras* while Mailor and I tried to figure out a way to straighten the mast. Nothing was going to be workable in the short term; we'd have to use it in its bent state until we got out to high sea, where we would be able to take the time to make it right. In the meantime, Mailor and I prepared to raise sail. Within an hour I noticed the wind had changed; it was turning toward land. The Colombians had gotten the majority of the *guaras* down when I realized that our safety margin was evaporating. We had closed to within five miles of land. Everyone else sensed it too, and the moment I said, "We'll go with the number of *guaras* we have now," the four of us headed to the base of the mast and prepared to haul on the halyard.

Eight hands reached up and swarmed the hairy rope. We squatted down as a group and the sail and yardarm slowly rose. We climbed the rope, pulled in unison, and raised the sail a foot each time. Then, at four feet off the deck, the sail stopped. We pulled the line taut and nothing happened. I left the halyard and hurried to the edge of the deck to get a better look at the rigging. Standing at the edge of the canes, I sighted up the mast pole but could see nothing that would indicate a jam. Everything looked as it should be, so I told the men to release tension. The line flowed down freely and the sail dropped—no sign of trouble. Again we pulled, the four of us working as a team at the base of the crooked mast. The sail rose four feet and stopped; it would not come through. The wind had turned directly toward land now. *Endurancia* sped toward the rocks. We needed only to raise the sail ten more feet to inflate it and pull away. *Could it be the angle of the mast?* We looked at the pulley again. It didn't seem to be jammed, so we tried pulling again. We hung on the rope, all four of us as a group, our feet suspended in the air to maximize our weight. We hung and pulled and yanked and still it wouldn't come. It wouldn't budge. The raft was making a wake through the water now, being pushed before a steady breeze. Each time I looked to my right, the land became more defined. I could see individual trees now and I could hear the breakers. To fix the jam I'd have to ascend the mast and personally examine the pulley. *I'll never make it up and back in time. We'll crash.* Again we pulled. We grunted and strained. We became desperate. The four of us hung from the line and yelled "Haaaaagh!" and yet it still would not come. We were hanging, yelling, pulling, and yanking on the line. We were helpless. We'd never make it. We were heading for shipwreck. A breaker broke off our starboard side and I yelled, "Let's go with the anchor!"

The *Endurancia* was heading for a broadside plunge into the breaker line. We scrambled over the front edge of the canes and grabbed the cold steel anchor, grunting and wrestling the heavy hook to the side, knowing that it would go over hard and knowing that if one of us became tangled in the line coiled at our side we'd have a crisis. We could feel the raft gliding across the water and we knew we had to stop it right now. Taking the flukes of the anchor in my hands, I hoisted it up and heaved it out past the points of the logs. It flew in a low arc and then splashed wildly and disappeared. The coil of line came alive, flapping and wiggling on the deck, paying out in a whir as two hundred feet of line chased the anchor to the seabed. *Endurancia* changed course. The raft's nose turned slowly and the stern swung around broadly and faced the breaker line. The anchor had bitten into the seabed and held. We had stopped.

A forty-foot balsa raft made of black logs and tan canes now lay at anchor near an empty coastline. We saw no sign of life on land and no boats on the water. The *Endurancia* faced outward, toward the open sea. A small sandy beach lay one hundred and fifty yards behind us. The surf there was moderate—a single line of six-foot breakers. To our right, the shoreline ran in a series of rock outcroppings and sandy beaches. To our left, jutting out into the surf, lay Matapalo.

When the Spaniards came through the Americas hundreds of years ago they named some of the geographical features based on their relation to coastal piloting. Many points were named Punta Mala, or "Bad Point." This was a warning. Later, when other Spanish ship captains would plan their voyages, they would be able to know the conditions of many of the obstacles by simply reading the map. They would know that rounding a place named Bad Point might present some difficulties. We now lay one hundred yards from a small peninsula of rocks that protruded from land like a dead branch from a tree. The Spaniards named this place Matapalo. Translated, this means "a branch that kills."

Waves curled in from the ocean and slammed into the black rocks of Matapalo, shattering into thousands of splinters of foam. The explosive noises crackled all around us and at times they seemed to be only a few feet away. These types of noises speak very clearly to the human subconscious. After hundreds of thousands of years on the earth, the human mind knows at a deeply instinctive level that certain sounds represent destruction. There was no need for any of us aboard the raft to know the name of this place or to know the forces at work. Deep in our brains was the certainty that anything near that horrible peeling noise would be destroyed.

We spent an hour or so assessing our situation: The breeze now blew straight in toward shore. Swells rolled in from the sea and passed under us, turning into breakers a few hundred feet behind the raft. A single nylon rope, a thin white line straining against the forces of wind and wave and hardened to the point of being like a metal cable, held us from going aground. We were backed into a semiprotected anchorage—if heavy weather came now we'd have little if any shelter. There was no longer any question of emergency. The only way out was to be towed. I would have to make contact with the Coast Guard station at Golfito and warn them of our situation. That wouldn't be easy: A four-hundred-foot bluff stood above the shore, blocking our VHF signal. Shortwave radio would be a problem too. If we tried to bounce a shortwave signal to Golfito, it would probably hit the atmosphere and overshoot the Coast Guard station. Not only that but the naval base there monitored the frequency that we had always had the most trouble transmitting on.

Sitting at the table, just inside the hut, I searched the radio frequencies by slowly turning the large black knob on the face of the unit, and listening to conversations going on all over the world. Explosions from Matapalo surrounded the raft and the ocean sloshed back and forth below my feet. Shortly after dark, I broke in on two men in North America. They were saying farewell to each other at the end of their weekly visit when I squeezed the black key of the little microphone and said, "Contact."

There was nothing but silence. The roof above me dripped from the previous night's rain. In the darkness I could hear the *"drip, drip, drip"* against the creaking and ticking noises of the raft, then the radio crackled and a man's voice said, very strongly, "Contact—Go!"

I identified myself and then explained my situation. I could hear him on the other end, dutifully writing it down. He was the typical ham: Most likely he was an ex-serviceman, dedicated, responsible, and probably a veteran of many emergencies—knowing full well that his shortwave radio was our only lifeline. He would make sure, he said, through every channel available, that the station at Golfito knew of our predicament. When I turned the radio off, I was acutely aware that we would have a very long night of waiting ahead of us. Around me, in the dark, there were three faces: Mailor, the new man, appeared relatively fresh. Alejandro and Cesar showed the beginnings of exhaustion, but were still strong. For my own part, a weariness had been clinging to me since The Gyre. We had to rest.

Mailor and Cesar took the first watch while Alejandro and I flopped down in the hut. I lay on my back in the dank, dripping room, listening to the waves curl over and thunder into Matapalo. I worked my mind through scenario after scenario, and then lost consciousness.

In the dim gray of half sleep, I heard a drum roll. It was a deep bass drum, combined with a strong surge of gravity in my body, as though I was rapidly gaining altitude. Then there was the unmistakable exploding sound of a wave colliding headon with the raft. I came out of my sleep just as a few flecks of seawater sprayed my face. The raft had just climbed up and over an incoming wave. I sat up, and Cesar stuck his head in the hut, and we looked at each other for several seconds without saying a word. The two of us held still, listening to the sounds of the sea. We were at low tide—the water level around the raft had dropped. The surf line was moving farther and farther away from the beach and closer and closer to *Endurancia*. Again a large wave curled up nearby but broke behind us. I got up immediately and came out on deck to look at the situation around us. There was lightning in several places in the sky, but none directly over us. I waited for a flash, then saw that the breaker line was less than twenty feet from the back of the raft. We were still outside the surf line, but close enough to it that some of the big waves coming in could break over us. We couldn't stay where we were; if bad weather came now, we'd be in trouble. We had to find a way to move *Endurancia*.

"Come on," I said to Cesar, "we've got to try to move the anchor farther out."

Working our way forward in the dark, we felt the raft swaying back and forth in the wave surge and the deck pushing up under us like an elevator. We could see nothing before us, and so we were forced to bend down and grasp the bamboo canes to steady ourselves. By the time we stepped down off the deck and onto the bare logs up front, we were walking with our hands and feet like gorillas.

Tied to the forward crossbeam, the anchor line, made of stark white nylon, shot straight out into the ocean like a thin metal pole. The wind and waves were like an enormous hand, pushing on our vessel until the elastic anchor line stretched out like a rubber band on the verge of snapping. Sitting on the tops of the balsa logs, Mailor, Cesar, and I tried to anchor ourselves in the sturdiest position for hauling on the line. Waves pounded all around us, and the moment we grasped the line we knew it was being stretched to its limit.

"Heave!!"

We lay back like oarsmen straining to pull on their oars. We were, in reality, trying to bring the entire weight of the raft forward. The fibers in our

forearms stretched out as though part of the anchor line. It was a losing battle. We could pull the line in a few feet when the raft was in the trough of
the waves, but it was never long enough to get it tied off. The minute a new
wave would rise up in front of us the line would shoot back, just as taut as
before. It was dangerous work in the dark. If one of us got a limb caught in
a loop of this line, it would break it. All around us the sea surged up and
soaked us again and again. After an hour of fighting, we noticed that the
waves were no longer breaking nearby. The tide was flooding in and the water was deepening around us. Conditions eased a little, and we went back to
the watches.

In the morning, dawn came slowly. It was not a typical day in the tropics.
By six o'clock it was gray and blustery. The raft lay 150 yards offshore, where
there was a sandy beach. If we broke loose from our anchorage we'd go
aground on the sand. A landing there would be messy, but the raft would
survive it. We knew that help was on the way, but the previous night
had been bad, and I think everyone aboard knew that we were just barely
hanging on.

We went to work early, arranging the raft and trying to determine how to
repair the mast. It seemed locked into its crooked position. It would require at
least two days' labor to fix. We would have to have a power boat tow us to a
safe anchorage where we could do the labor. Once the mast was repaired, we
might be able to leave the coast under our own power.

The morning wore on and we waited for assistance, working and preparing.
The sky continued gray and overcast. At high tide, we were able to pull the raft
a little closer to the anchor, sitting on the forward logs and hauling on the
white line for about twenty feet until we could pull no more.

At around 10:00 a.m., I was standing on the starboard catwalk, by the side of
the hut, working with rope and talking to Cesar, who was helping me. As usual,
he was tired and worn, but solid. He wore his blue baseball hat backwards,
with his wet and stringy long hair hanging down his back. At the bow of the raft,
where the balsa logs pointed toward the sea, a six-foot wave suddenly rolled in
from offshore, curled over, and then crashed into the raft with a loud splash. Cesar's eyes widened, and he said, sharply, "John!"

I felt an intuitive alarm and knew immediately that we weren't in the place
we were supposed to be. I could feel the raft sliding across the water. Cesar
was already rushing toward the bow, with me following closely behind him.
The white line that was once like a steel pole now lay limp and lifeless. Kneeling down on the bare balsa logs, I grabbed the soft nylon and reeled it in,

working rapidly, hand over hand. There was no resistance and I knew already that the line had parted from the anchor. Cesar crouched on one side of me and Mailor stood on the other. My hands spun faster and faster and the line snaked up to the deck until the end came up through the brown sandy water, and then emerged into the sunlight. It was nothing but a fray. The strands hung from my hand, dripping, limp and dead, probably the result of lying over a rock.

We didn't wait; the instant we saw it we stood up and walked across the balsa logs to the edge of the deck. Leaning on the elevated canes for balance, I peered around the hut to see where the raft was headed. We were moving fast—but not toward the sandy beach; instead, the *Endurancia* was traveling in a tidal current, running parallel to the shoreline and speeding on a direct course for Matapalo. The raft was now slowly spinning, turning its nose around to face the rocks. It was as though Matapalo was reeling in the raft on an underwater towline. I stepped up to walk across the canes, and, looking at the others, said, "Put your life jackets on."

The raft had now turned around for a head-on collision with Matapalo. The four of us fled the front end, scurrying down the catwalks, hurrying along the spring-loaded canes to hide behind the hut. Standing on the back ends of the logs, we held on, powerless and silent. We were riding on the back of the raft now, the four of us holding on to the hairy manila ropes and looking down the entire length of the ship. In front of us, two peaks of black rock jutted up from the surf, not fifty feet away, and *Endurancia* was now heading straight for the gap between them. We were cruising fast. We could hear the roar of the ocean exploding through the peaks. The raft set up its suicide approach, and then a ten-foot wave stood up behind the stern. The raft rose up sharply. The canes at my feet suddenly tilted down. The entire ship was surfing now, riding downhill, accelerating toward Matapalo. *Endurancia* dove straight into the gap, sliding downward and plunging headfirst to an abrupt halt. The raft quivered violently under us and we were thrown forward by the sudden stop. I fell hard, throwing my hands down on the canes in front of me. A wave came in from behind and obliterated itself on the back wall of the hut. Splinters of foam shot into the air around us. Everything was chaos. The ocean covered us in heavy masses and then washed off. Huge hunks of water and foam flew all around. It was as though we were inside a gigantic washing machine; wave after wave rose up and slammed against the back wall of the hut. The pounding was horrific. Large masses flooded in, exploded, and then showered us from head to toe. Our hair hung in our faces and seawater poured off our orange lifejackets. We couldn't stay aboard—the force of the ocean was just too much. We hurried forward on the catwalks, working hand over hand through the surging waves until we reached the foredeck, and then across the logs to jump into the tidal pool behind the rocks.

The raft was now acting as a seawall behind us, covering our escape. Standing in the knee-high water, I turned around and thought for a moment of how to extricate the raft from Matapalo—perhaps we could get a line out to one side and pull her way, but then I realized that it would be of no use: *Endurancia* was now climbing through the peaks. Wave after wave picked up the thirty-thousand-pound vessel and pushed it higher and higher, pounding the back of the raft and forcing it to climb through the gap. Masses of seawater came in and shattered against the blunt ends of the balsa logs. The raft slammed and banged though the entranceway of the rocks as though the fists of the sea were beating it through a narrow doorway. Within just a few minutes the *Endurancia* had climbed so high that it hung in the air, suspended precariously between the two black peaks. It wouldn't go through, but the sea didn't mind—there was plenty of strength for the job. The massive fists punched and pounded the raft, hammering it slowly but surely into the gap. The raft ricocheted, staccatolike, against the two peaks, vibrating and bouncing and banging. Little by little, the rising tide was permanently trapping the *Endurancia* on Matapalo.

And as it did, the mighty Pacific finished the job. It punched out the back wall of the hut first. The waves broke through like firemen breaking into a burning room with axes. Canes fractured and splintered, then blew out one by one. Whole bamboo canes flew through the air. More and more we could see through the back wall of the hut where the sea was breaching it. Seawater, waves, and foam burst through the holes and flooded in. Then the hut's main columns gave way, bending down in futile resistance, sinking over at a sicker angle with each blow of the sea. The mast poles leaned over more and more, slowly dying. Everything aboard the raft was being pounded flat.

We stood on the sand behind the rocks and stared. Tools and gear flew into the water and fanned out in all directions. Debris now lay everywhere, floating in the tidal pool or washing up on land. Seawater ruined the radios, rations, and drinking water. The sails had been thrown clear and were now spread out on the rocks, which, like thousands of razor blades, shredded the canvas into ribbons. Worst of all, the incoming waves were dragging and scraping the underside of the *Endurancia* over the same razorlike rock that had sliced the sails. Within five minutes of crashing I was plainly aware that the lines underneath the raft would have hundreds of burrs in them. If they hadn't already ruptured, they would over time. The raft could survive many things, but not the destruction of its main lines. I knew it would never be seaworthy again.

Off in the distance, we heard a guttural growl. It was the *Punta Burica*, steaming for us at full speed. We could see its white bow wave splashing to either side as the boat motored across the sea. Sailors lined the deck, peering at us through binoculars. The gray boat came alongside the breaker line, slowed down, and two young sailors dove over and swam toward the beach. We saw their heads pass through the breaker line and once into the shallows they stood up from the foamy water and slogged onto the sandy beach, their T-shirts and pants clinging to their bodies. They walked up, soaked and dripping and carrying a tether. Both of them were in their early twenties, earnest and sincere, and I knew them vaguely. They said their captain wanted to know if it was possible to pull the raft free of the rocks. I told them that it was useless, and then thanked them for braving the breakers to help my vessel. They looked at the wreckage with sympathy and one nervously bit his fingernails while I explained that The Expedition was, at last, ended. The raft was completely ashore now. The tide had risen and the fists of the Pacific had finally pounded the raft up and over the rocks. A great black hulk now lay in a large tidal pool behind the rocks of Matapalo. It was a twisted shipwreck.

It would be dark soon, so I told the Ticos that they must try to get back through the surf now, or risk being stranded with us. We shook hands all around and then they waded out into the breakers, thinly slipping through the waves.

On the rocks of Matapalo, it was like the aftermath of an explosion. The hulk of the raft lay in the center of a debris field. The superstructure had disintegrated, but the main hull of nine balsa logs remained as an enormous, solid, block. The tide was still rising and the ocean was still pounding the *Endurancia,* but it would probably take two or three days of being thrown around inside this chaotic machine before the main lines would begin to fail.

Two hundred yards offshore, *Punta Burica* waited to recover its two swimmers. From the beach we could see its crew standing at the railing of the gunboat, staring at us and our raft. They were like those men who'd stood at the railing of the *Everest* on that first night, three years before, when the *Illa-Tiki* had been released to sail alone. They just stood, together as a group, staring out across the water, emitting tragic astonishment. The balsa raft had been a freakish impossibility to them in the first place; but now, to see it crashed at Matapalo, must have seemed predictable and surreal at the same time: predictable in that they never thought we had a chance; surreal in that the main hull of the raft just seemed to stay there, fixed, being blasted and pounded, but not breaking up.

I stood now on the beach and thought for a moment. Many things went through my mind but an acute feeling of sympathy hovered all around me. I knew the consequences of a wrecked balsa raft—I knew full well what this would mean, and I felt sorry for the ancient man who had endured it. I did not see his face with my mind's eye as much as I felt a dread for this man's plight: He had come north from the Santa Elena Peninsula, sailing and working and struggling, and now he was just a man standing on a beach, like me, and he was shipwrecked so far from home, in a place that he had never known before, knowing it would take months to be ready again—if it was at all possible—and he would be filled with the horrible fear that he may never see the shores of Salango again: this was *his* fate.

Night fell quickly. In the dark, we saw the gunboat's lights turn away slowly, then drift off until they disappeared into black. There were no other boats on the water now and no sign of any inhabitance on the coast. We stood on the sand, four men, alone, dripping seawater amid the debris field of a shipwreck. We were dressed in a motley assortment of disheveled clothes. Both Alejandro and I had lost our shirts; we now wore only our orange life vests for warmth. An explosion of equipment and supplies and bamboo canes lay all around us. We knew nothing of the place in which we now found ourselves. We were on a small sandy beach somewhere in lower Costa Rica, and apparently, we were at the base of an immense jungle cliff. We knew neither the cliff's height nor if it could be climbed. We knew only that the heavily-wooded jungle shot straight up and out of sight.

The tide continued to rise, invading the beach and covering it completely. We moved to higher ground, then the tide crept up to our feet and we moved higher. We said nothing to each other except to ask basic questions and to grunt and struggle in the mud and the tangled foliage. The tide continued to rise until we had our backs to the cliff. I worried for a time that we would have to begin climbing through the jungle at night, but then Alejandro and Cesar found a muddy plateau, well above the waterline, and we spread out a plastic poncho on the ground, to lie down on. Our clothes and hair still dripped cold seawater and everything was wet. Our bathing suits were caked with salt and our mouths hung open. Sitting on the plastic, the men looked at me as if to ask, "What do we do now?"

"We'll sleep until first light," I said, "then we'll organize. We'll get out of here. Try to sleep."

I laid down and felt the plastic sheet, cold and pasty, against the clammy skin of my back. Holding my arms close to my body, I trapped as much of my heat as I could. It was a clear night at the edge of the tropical forest, and brilliant. Millions of stars filled the sky and millions of insects radiated their shrill, vibrating mix all around us, punctuated by pops and whoops. Tropical frogs croaked and swallowed. I could hear the deep, thunderous explosions of tons of water on the rocks down at the wreck site. The surf pounded as it always had, since before the Spaniards, and before the Manteño. I lay on my back, listening to the breakers and looking at the bright, tiny stars in the black sky. I was, once again, marooned.

Epilogue

The most important thing in this world is to know *who we are*, and we, *us*—we come from the forces of wind, sea, calm, and storm.

ALEJANDRO MARTINEZ, after the end
of The Manteño Expedition

I have been frequently asked if I will ever again put to sea in a balsa raft. Of course I will, but this was the end of an era for me. Never again would I go into the field so green, so naive. My colleagues and I learned a vast amount of knowledge about the great balsa raft, and perhaps only a group of naive virgins would have been willing to go to this school of truth, but the tuition was steep.

The loss of the *Endurancia* proved to me that my overall approach to solving the problem of The Manteño Trading Route was fundamentally flawed. Of the many things I came to understand, having the patience of an ancient mariner—running on their schedule—was perhaps the most important. I hurried the departure of the *Endurancia,* even so far as to leave before the mast was completely reinforced. In the past I had always held the various rafts at anchor until they were completely ready. That had allowed the shipworms to get an early start on destroying the raft, and it invariably irritated people, but it brought good results. I hurried the construction of the *Manteño* as well, trying to force a modern timetable on an ancient vessel, and that vessel suffered too. These experiences proved to me that applying modern mentalities of speed and urgency to the ancient world—where all things took time and patience—always creates more problems than it solves.

The second flaw, which was also a product of the modern mentality, was to rely on towing when leaving an anchorage. This is not so much of a problem if your vessel is making an ocean crossing, like the *Kon-Tiki*, but making a complex voyage around the coast requires that your vessel be completely self-sufficient. Expecting other captains and other vessels to care about your fate is unrealistic. You must wean yourself from the idea of being towed behind motorized vessels. This is a modern mentality, and using it as a basis for decision making in such a complex ancient voyage as The Trading Route is dubious. The only safety is to leave anchorages and arrive at them under your own power. In the end, the best policy is to do as the ancients did.

This was the story of the era when we were adventurers; afterward, all would be science. In these years of adventure we moved slowly, painfully, away from reliance on popular books for information and guidance. I still admire those who went into the field before me on balsa raft expeditions, but, truthfully, they never addressed the mechanics of the Manteño Trading Route. That statement is in no way an insult to them because they weren't *trying* to address the route, nor did they ever claim to. If we now carry our own independent view of the great balsa raft—how it must be built and what its true limitations are—we are still fully aware that we stand on "the broad Viking shoulders of Thor Heyerdahl." We had Heyerdahl to fall back on; he had no one. And though Alsar remains an intriguing mystery, we, more than anyone, know that his voyages were the greatest of their type ever made. But our tiny steps toward understanding were dreadfully expensive, and to move forward we have had to leave those cherished popular accounts behind.

The progress we made during our expeditions gave us insight, but more questions remain than answers. To our mind, the true Manteño sailing raft remains undiscovered. We do not believe that *any* balsa raft built for experimental purposes in the latter half of the twentieth century was a correct interpretation of the raft seen by the conquistadors on that first fateful day in 1526. Nor do we believe that any of those vessels, including our own, would have the performance capabilities to complete the Trading Route. But from our experiments we have been able to visualize the raft that *can* make the voyage— that vessel would be vastly more authentic and vastly more capable than any other raft built in the postwar era. And so, we start now from the beginning. Years ago, we thought the end of our journey would be a place, but it is now a journey to find the truth. It is also a journey to legitimacy: The balsa raft's real function was to move *Spondylus* up and down the coast of Central America, but because so many famous expeditions used it to cross the ocean, and because those voyages were used to support theories that the scientific community eventually disproved, the balsa raft itself was seen, many times, as dubious. We wish to eliminate this questionable reputation, to remove the balsa raft from legend, and to bring it to its rightful status among the great, ocean-going vessels of history. Specifically, we desire to produce a single, well-reasoned document that will describe the Manteño sailing raft, and the Trading Route to Central America.

Whether we accomplished a lot or accomplished little, we were as pure as could be found. What I learned from expeditions is what soldiers learn from war: It is misery, but you learn who your brothers are. Without the darkness of Frederick I could not have seen, much less understood, the importance of Cameron, Alejandro and Cesar, Dower, and perhaps even my own wife, Annie. If I had not taken that great step so many years ago—to go on expedition—perhaps nothing would have happened. I would probably have grown old, flying gliders or sailing boats, but I would have never known the love of brothers, and I would have finished my life half a man. People frequently ask me about the great challenges I have faced, they ask about the war stories, the desperate times. I have all those, but they are not what is important to me: I would forgo the adventure, but I'd never give up my brothers.

It is of course Dr. Cameron Smith who is our lead researcher. He is a dedicated scientist, passionate about finding historical truth through relentless research; but he remains an expeditioner too, and he works each day to prepare our new expeditions. The Remarkable Colombians—Alejandro and Cesar, fine expeditioners in their own right—never let me forget for a moment that our work is unfinished. Dower Medina has now vanished into mythical status, helped greatly by Ecuador's continuing resistance to outside communication. As for me, I live now with Annie by the Pacific Ocean.

But I remain disturbed by what I saw on my first expedition, and inspired by what I saw on my second. Frankly, my memories are rarely pleasant. I remember my feet, swollen and cut, and I remember that it was pure hell when I was with those I didn't care about, and it was OK, even enjoyable, when I was with those I loved. The greatest moments of the expeditions, the times I remember most fondly, were when the sails were inflated and the raft sailed well across the open sea.

Sometimes, I think about the old city, Salango, in the day of the ancient Manteño. For some reason I always picture the old men, and I wonder what they thought about. When the old men of ancient Salango stood on the beach in the morning, watching the rafts leave port, did they have the same memories that I have? I know they remembered seeing the four-hundred-foot monolith, Isla de Salango, falling away behind them as they set out for the open sea. I know they remembered that strange sloshing noise the sea made as it washed around the balsa logs. They remembered swimming under the raft, spearing fish for dinner, floating silently in the crystal clear water while looking up at the bright emerald rays of the sun, piercing through the logs like the rays of God. I know this because sometimes I too think of that strange sloshing noise—the vivid water sounds coming up through the bamboo canes, reflecting off the walls of the hut, day after day. I can remember leaving the bay and watching the island fall away behind me as I set out for a long voyage. I can remember standing on a bamboo deck in my bare feet, watching a balsa raft push its nose into the turquoise waters north of Salango—yes, I can remember those things—and in my daydreams, I can see what they saw, I can hear what they heard. Now, I know some of what they knew.

Appendix:
The Factory in Salango

On the far side of Enrique's house there is a gray wall, a barrier of cinderblocks standing ten feet-tall and capped by curls of razor wire like ugly, scraggly hair. This is *La Fabrica* (The Factory), a phrase that is always uttered by every *Salangueño* with a mixture of resignation and disgust. *La Fabrica* can be best described—from its exterior, because I myself have never seen inside its massive iron doors—as a fortress. If you stand at the base of the wall you distinctly know that you are near a large box; the massive walls disappear some 200 feet down either side and then turn sharply in hard right angles. What is strange about it is its anonymity, its ability to blend in, its ability to be there and yet not be seen. It is a large structure, but its gray nondescript walls at the far end of town can be easily missed. Not only is it largely invisible but it is largely unknown. If you ask the Salangueños who owns *La Fabrica* they will answer, depending on who you ask, variously: the Polish, the Peruvians, the Americans, or even sometimes, their own Ecuadorans. They don't even seem to be sure of what is made there. Every few days, two large fishing trawlers cruise into the Bay of Salango and dump off enormous loads of fish into two large hoppers, large open chutes floating just offshore that are connected, underwater, to The Factory. Later, the iron doors of the fortress open and trucks leave with something aboard them—the main belief is cat food, although the townspeople, whenever they say that, say it with a distinct uncertainty.

When the trawlers come the processing begins, and the gray fortress begins to billow out clouds of gray and white smoke. This smoke is foul, acrid, and it blankets the town. Shortly after the smoke, the waste comes. *La Fabrica* spews out a revolting red and gray oil into the bay, fouling the water and the beach. The composition of this oily waste is widely discussed. There is a sound argument that it is an organic substance that can be absorbed by the ocean, but those who have lived in the town their entire lives assert that the bay was a clear body of water before *La Fabrica* was built some years back, and that the sea life in it was far more abundant. A sound argument can also be brought that the people of a poor country can be helped economically by industry, that good, steady jobs can be generated by a nearby factory, but nearly all Salangueños, regardless of their poverty, refuse to work there. It has always been rumored that some of the townspeople may be working there quietly, discreetly, unwilling to admit it.

Above the perceived injury, there is the insult. The world of *La Fabrica* seems to have no regard and no sympathy for Salango. The large fishing trawlers frequently change their oil in the bay, pouring the black waste from their engines directly into the water just a few hundred feet from the beach. I have seen this personally. Some, including a number of the town's smartest people, believe that the only way they will ever be able to rid themselves of its curse will be to block the road, bodily and with trucks, and to hold their ground, forcing the government to arrest them all. Dower and two of his brothers have narrowly escaped problems with the authorities on several occasions during protests in which they have tried to do just that.

But when it isn't letting out smoke or waste, it doesn't seem to be there at all. Salango continues on as old and ageless and untechnological as it has always been. This could be the root of the problem: it sheds its waste on Salango, and then goes back to not being there. The Salango city council is trying to build a legal case, or at least a logical, factual protest that can be brought to their government to ask that, at the least, a screen or filter be put on the factory's stacks, to filter the smoke and oil before it is released on top of their town.

The Salangueños always helped my cause, and now I hope to help theirs. The Salangueños feel they are being grievously wronged. I ask, on their behalf, for a fair and open hearing on this matter—fair and open for both sides, so that Salangueños can be given an outlet for their grievances, and so that all may benefit. Recriminations, confrontations, attacks, destruction—all of these things, in my opinion, will only cause both sides to entrench even further. But greater cooperation and sensitivity must come at once. Times have changed. In the past it was perfectly acceptable for a factory in North America or Europe or Asia to cause such problems, and yet still be seen as beneficial. But that era is now ending, and the new and better era can be embraced by all. Great factories now flourish in my country, in Europe, and in Japan, that are regulated and yet profitable, so why can't this be true in the ancient town of Salango?